Sociotherapy and Psychotherapy

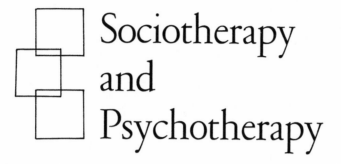

Sociotherapy and Psychotherapy

Marshall Edelson, M.D.

THE UNIVERSITY OF CHICAGO PRESS
CHICAGO AND LONDON

The Austen Riggs Center, Inc.
has chosen this book as
number 6 in the
AUSTEN RIGGS CENTER
MONOGRAPH SERIES

Standard Book Number: 226-18430-7
Library of Congress Catalog Card Number: 73-94997
The University of Chicago Press, Chicago 60637
The University of Chicago Press, Ltd., London
© 1970 by The University of Chicago. All rights reserved
Published 1970. Printed in the United States of America

For Jonathan, Rebecca, and David

☐ Contents

☐ Acknowledgments

Robert P. Knight, the late medical director, and Edgerton McC. Howard, associate medical director, of the Austen Riggs Center provided opportunities that made the writing of this book possible.

Thomas Main, medical director, Cassel Hospital, England, discovered me floundering in organizational life and encouraged me to study as well as participate in it.

A. Kenneth Rice and Pierre Turquet of the Tavistock Institute of Human Relations and Tavistock Clinic, England, helped me to increase my understanding of small group processes, intergroup relations, and organizations, and to develop greater skills than I had for participating in group life. Working with them and with the staff of the Group Relations Conference at Mount Holyoke College, which was in 1965, 1966, and 1967 sponsored by the Tavistock Institute, the Washington School of Psychiatry, and the Yale University Department of Psychiatry, was an especially valuable stimulus to my thinking.

I am grateful to Lars Borje Lofgren for his confidence in my motives, capacities, and thought, which enabled me to persist in this writing despite periods of discouragement and self-doubt.

Richard Spahn was a companion of the intellect during much of the period when I was writing this book; it would be impossible to mention each idea, enthusiastic response, or question of his that started me up again or kept me going on some always interesting but baffling inquiry. I am indebted to many colleagues and patients in places where I have been a staff member or consultant, who worked with me, talked with me, who were interested in my thinking and experiences, and who shared their own with me. Among my colleagues I want to mention especially Marvin Geller, Maurice Marcus, and Roger Shapiro.

I owe much to the intelligence and competence of Elizabeth Anderson, who typed the final draft of the manuscript; the understanding and helpfulness of Louise Bubriski, secretarial supervisor; and the cooperation of members of the secretarial staff, Austen Riggs Center, who helped at various times along the way.

The writing of most of this book occurred during or after a period when I was steeped in the writings of Sigmund Freud and Talcott Parsons. I feel that it is appropriate that their names be linked; they share the spaces of thought and willingness to be alone there. My debt to Talcott Parsons, not only for the content of many ideas but for a way of approaching conceptual problems in general and the study of social systems in particular, must be apparent from the many pages I have referred to him and his work, as well as—for those who know that work—even from those pages where to avoid repetition I have not made such reference.

My wife Zelda has labored with me in rewriting and editing, in addition to maintaining a home where I can spend hours at my desk and still be a part of the whole that nourishes me; for that, no expression of gratitude is adequate.

☐ Introduction

Problems of group life are central in our time. Our experiences include genocide; world wars; the existence
of atomic weapons with its implications for cooperation
and conflict; the efforts to establish supranational entities; emerging nations; revolutions; the pressure of
population and the competition for resources; the rise
and fall in dominance of continents; civil strife; the
struggle by minority groups for rights; the crowded city;
the development of delinquent youth subcultures; the
impact of mass media, rapidly accelerating increase in
knowledge, and technical innovation; and the prepo-
tency of organizations as means for goal-achievement in
increasingly complex, differentiated societies.

Men spend more and more time in groups, are more
and more dependent upon others for the achievement
of ends, and must perforce accept that their very survival is linked to the vicissitudes of little understood
and relatively uncontrolled social processes.

Knowledge and mastery of group life are crucial
imperatives now. Yet, the exploration of man's relation to his group may inevitably lead to the fourth great
wound to his narcissism. First, he discovered that the
earth upon which he lives is not the center of the universe. Second, he discovered that the species to which
he belongs is not a new creation but has developed from
"inferior" species. Third, he discovered that the mind of
which he is so proud includes realms unknown to him,
directing, rather than directed by, his conscious will.

Now he is in danger of discovering that at least some of what he considers his unique individuality only exists as that which is shared with others; that behavior, feelings, and thoughts he experiences as determined from within or expressions of his personal history are in fact governed by features of his immediate situation or are an aspect of his unwitting participation in some process involving interactions between himself and many others; that a part of his individuality depends both in its origins and for its maintenance upon interactions with others; that much of his individuality is in fact social. Perhaps difficulties in the development of a science of sociology are related to resistances to accepting this additional pain.

I know I would rather have a discussion with my colleagues—sophisticated men— about their relation to planets, their evolution from apes, or their unconscious sexual and hostile impulses, than about their untestable shared beliefs, their values, or the norms they take so for granted that these are rarely put into words. If one stumbles into questioning, or commenting with a neutral attitude about, a seemingly innocuous belief or procedure that has come to be invested with any degree of sacredness— even though no one has recognized that this quality is now inherent in it—then one is likely to be confronted by a sudden astonishing fervor, acerbity, and confusion. It is difficult to achieve a dispassionate examination in a group (where it is often especially relevant and necessary) of a man's participation in it, of the relation between himself and others, of his conformity or lack of it to group norms. It is difficult whether or not in individual minds there is conscious knowledge about these matters. When values, and the beliefs or norms associated with these values, are questioned or threatened, shared unthinking indignation passes quickly into moral furor and on to innumerable forms of cruelty and destructiveness. These responses are always present, even if latent, drawing upon vast reservoirs of energy, and apparently ready for instantaneous arousal.

In group life, man is committed to, and torn between, involvement and individuation. On the one hand, he wants to share, to be a part of; he fears being alone in his group, cut off from others. On the other hand, he wants to be and to become himself; he dreads having his identity annihilated by lack of response or by some response that is unrecognizable as belonging to himself. He finds himself involuntarily "joining in," swept by sudden feelings, unable to—even not wanting to— think, remember, keep facts straight. What man has not said to himself after such experience in a group: "Who was I then? Who am I really now?"

Man needs the group to be himself, to meet his needs, to actualize his values through the achievement of ends. Yet the group, which will make use of his skills and his emotional bents, has no use for him when these do not fit; the group is capable of destroying that in him which is not of it—the judgment, perception, or thought of the individual man. The desire to protect individuality is a powerful inducement to circumspection, evasion, secrecy, and sophistry, which are in varying degrees the ordinary features of a man's behavior in all groups.

At the American Psychiatric Association session on General Systems Theory, May 1966, Dr. Warren M. Brodey, demonstrating a point about driving elements in systems, asked each person in the audience to feel his own pulse and tap the flloor with his foot in time to it, while he—Dr. Brodey—banged with a gavel on the podium. The taps started out a chaotic pattern of individual rhythms, then rather rapidly came closer and closer together in a loud irresistible series of regular beats in time with the gavel. It was almost impossible to tear away from the group rhythm once it was established and return to the rate of one's own pulse.

Groups are like that. They frighten me. I imagine that is one of the reasons I'm interested, and struggle to master my experience, in them. That, and the fact that the problems of group life appear to be those to be solved in our time if we are to survive. It may be that in group life individuality is always in peril. It is also true that man's nature is in part born of his participation in that group life. In fact, ideals and values that he shares with other men are at the same time himself and the essential elements constituting the group to which he belongs. These shared ideals and values, which are the emergent characteristic of social systems, give individual action its direction and individual experience meaning.

The family is man's first group. Alert children puzzle about the riddles of family life: not simply, where babies come from, but also the fundamental sociological questions. How, given conflict of want and need, is order to be maintained and a chaos of quarrel and strife averted? How are aggression and sexual impulses to be controlled? How are the strong to be limited and the weak protected? How is competition for what is available to be regulated? How is what is desired to be distributed? How is it to be decided what shall be sacrificed for what? How is cooperation to be brought about? How is commitment to values, rules, beliefs, or goals held important by all to be created and maintained in the face of disappointment and doubt? How are people to be organized to do what and in what way in the interests of achieving shared ends?

The more malintegrated the family and the more aware the child perhaps, the more desperate and persistent the questioning. The answers the child sociologist formulates are fateful for his participation in the community of man.

I have not outgrown these childish concerns. I have read all my life—these questions are also the province of the novelist—and I have joined groups, hoping for some enlightenment about them. As a boy I thought about the Jewish people, who committed themselves to an idea—and survived. (Perhaps my identity as a Jew is in part responsible for the permanently idealistic character of my thinking and therefore my emphasis in this book upon ideas—values and value systems—as crucial variables in rendering social phenomena explicable.) As an adolescent, I was aware of concentration camps; I was a member of a Zionist youth organization, caught up in the dream that somewhere a people could gather, escape hate, and build the promised land. Now I think I know that given the nature of man and his environment that promise cannot be kept. The perfect society is not attainable, hardly even imaginable, but attempts to cope with and understand the unavoidable dilemmas of social life continue to intrigue me. In the same way I believe a therapeutic community is impossible, but I find the effort to approach it exhilarating.

I eschew simple ideals. There are no single causes in social life, no most important factors, and rarely an easy choice between bad and good. Most often, we face a choice between two or more precious values—to choose one is to lose, dilute, or spoil the other. Typically, what is most desired has in it the seeds of that which is most abhorred (the great novelist must be ironic). What we experience are complex equilibria in which multiple essential functions and aims struggle and find some often precarious balance. That was the vision of Sigmund Freud concerning the person-ality system and of Talcott Parsons concerning the social system.

The tendency in my thinking (e.g., about social phenomena) to assign a pre-potent, independent role to ideas determines also in part my attitude toward theory-building. No theory is right or true in the sense of being a single inevitable conse-quence of experience. Theory is an arbitrary creation. I do not believe that one can approach experience with an open mind and extract ideas from it. One comes to phenomena with ideas. On the basis of these one selects from the phenomena even what will be experienced. One sees phenomena with the eyes of ideas no matter how vague. An idea or theory is an invention; one invents, and then sees whether or not the invention fits some aspect of the phenomena, and if so how much. Theories are or are not useful in imposing order upon the phenomenal chaos. A theory may be useful in ordering one realm of phenomena, useless or essentially inapplicable in another.

I have noticed that many people are bored or restless in groups, particularly if the tight hold of a rigid agenda or unambiguous task is relaxed. Such people do not like meetings. I judge this to be a reaction to experiencing oneself subject to forces of which one knows very little; and perhaps above all to finding oneself experiencing too much too quickly and unable to make sense of what is going on. The complaint—by many individual psychotherapists, including those working in hospitals, for example—that groups, that meetings, are uninteresting is often associated with a relative absence of adequate conceptual tools for distinguishing the relationship between apparently unrelated contents, for responding to the emergence of themes, for detecting the vicissitudes of crisis and its resolution, for identifying the end toward which events occur and the meaning of apparently trivial happenings.

Group life has its frightening moments, but it is enormously complex; for one who has eschewed the simple ideal, the single-factor theory, the two-variable corre-lation, in favor of dialectical theory the attempt to understand it is, therefore, intellectually satisfying. I have found many ideas in this book helpful in making sense out of the jumble and the unceasing bombardment of statements, feelings, and movements in groups; I hope others will too. Using these ideas to observe and think, I find I am actively participating rather than being swept along or drowning; occa-sionally, my head above water, I feel below what I am immersed in and at the same time see a bit of what is about me.

What I hope is demonstrated by the following chapters, which have nothing to do with proof or prediction but are exercises in the development of theory, is the growing power to order complex phenomena that is conferred by a necessarily com-plicated, increasingly adequate, but still rudimentary, incomplete, conceptual model. The repeatability of the observations upon which this model has been tried for fit and the validity, range, and usefulness of the model used to order them remain to be discovered according to the canons of empirical science; this study is, in every sense, exploratory. I publish my still developing ideas in the expectation that I shall hear from others, working in different settings, even entirely different realms, whose views about these theoretical issues will transcend what in my own thinking may be rooted in particular circumstances and not have the general significance I mis-takenly give it.

The aim of this book is to provide sociotherapy as a treatment methodology with a theoretical foundation.

Toward that end, a theory of groups, which is applicable to a wide range of group phenomena, is outlined. The theory embraces alike at one degree of complexity the small unstructured face-to-face group and at another degree of complexity the large organization with its differentiated group structures and multiple specific functions. This theory of groups with its applications argues for the usefulness of the general system theory of Talcott Parsons to psychiatrists and others working in the mental health field for their work with groups and in organizations. By the exposition, emendation, extension, and application of that general system theory, its availability to this professional group will hopefully be increased.

The development of such a theory of groups contributes in particular to the integration of the psychoanalytic view of the personality system and social system theory. To psychoanalytic theory is added a "filling in" of the structure of one of its major but residually treated constructs: external reality—especially the social reality with which personality interacts and articulates. The theory of external reality presented here is especially relevant to a consideration of those aspects of personality suggested by such terms as "values," "systems of values," "internalization of values," "commitment to action," and "types of action." Ultimately the concern here is with the way in which the personality and social systems articulate with, mutually regulate, and make exchange with, each other.

As a further foundation for a methodology of sociotherapy, this book contains a system theory of organization and makes use of this theory in formulating a theoretical model for the organization of the psychiatric hospital. Included are an analysis of the functions performed within a psychiatric hospital organization and the relations between these functions; a discussion of the dilemmas of both equalitarian and hierarchical organization; and a consideration of the way in which organization must vary with changing definitions of tasks or goals and theories of the treatment process.

With this foundation it becomes possible to discuss milieu therapy or the therapeutic community in relation to functions that must be performed in a psychiatric hospital whose task it is to cope in a variety of ways with mental illness and its consequences. It becomes possible to define the therapeutic community, with theoretical and technical specificity, not only ideologically or humanistically. Sociotherapy and psychotherapy may then be differentiated as methods of treatment, and the province and techniques of sociotherapy—viewed as a necessary ally of psychotherapy in psychiatric hospitals and residential treatment centers—delineated.

The conceptual choices I have made, the assumptions and conceptual strategies I have adopted, may be judged in terms of their consequence for the consistency, coherence, or aesthetic qualities of the resulting theory. Judgment concerning the heuristic value of that theory, of course, requires in addition examination of the uses to which it is put in ordering data. Originally, it was intended that, in a series of chapters from a "sociotherapist's journal" constituting an extensive "case history" of a therapeutic community, this general conceptual framework and particular view of sociotherapy would be applied in detail to the ordering of a specific empirical realm—the group and organizational processes of a psychiatric hospital. Publishing exigencies, however, and the desire to focus upon a careful exposition of the theory and its development in this work, resulted in the decision to present that empirical data in a separate volume, which I hope can soon be made available to the reader. Meanwhile, if this book is read with the reader's own group experiences in mind to supplement those relatively few illustrative examples I have included, the relation of this theory to empirical experience may be at least adumbrated.

Sociotherapy and Psychotherapy

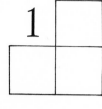

Sociotherapy and Psychotherapy in the Treatment of Schizophrenia

In this chapter an attempt in the medical tradition is made to base a method of treatment upon knowledge of a particular illness. The roles of both individual psychotherapy and the therapeutic community in the treatment of schizophrenic patients are derived from a conception of the nature of schizophrenia. The example of one illness serves to introduce a consideration in later chapters of the contributions of, and relations between, individual psychotherapy and the therapeutic community in the treatment of hospitalized psychiatric patients in general.

Psychotherapy is a method of treatment the focus of whose operations is the internal state or personality system of an individual. Sociotherapy is a method of treatment the focus of whose operations is the situation—particularly the social system (e.g., a hospital community)—in which that individual is treated.

The following propositions, which are examined in detail in later chapters, are some of those underlying the use of both sociotherapy and psychotherapy in the treatment of the schizophrenic person. There is a basic homology or correspondence in the structure of the personality system and its subsystems and the structure of external reality—especially the social system and its subsystems—which impinges upon that personality. This homology is a consequence of the fact that both systems may profitably be viewed as goal-seeking and value-oriented. The same concepts, thus, are relevant in

3

the study of them both. Both systems, for example, may be understood in terms of selection of, and strivings to attain, ends. In both systems, phenomena may be usefully subsumed under the category mobilization and mastery of means—adaptation. It is heuristic to regard such processes as goal-attainment and adaptation in both systems as governed by normative elements—that is, by norms and values. Further, the social system and the personality system in this conceptual framework are articulated by common values guiding action in both systems and are interdependent and mutually regulatory. Finally, a hypothesis: the sensitivity of the personality system's structure to influence by the social system or aspects of it, and its potentialities for change as a result of such influence, continue into adulthood.

SCHIZOPHRENIA[1]

How a physician treats a schizophrenic patient depends on his conception of the nature of the disorder, the outcome he seeks, and the attitude he takes toward the patient.

Schizophrenia is a way of life, which has been described by W. Ronald D. Fairbairn (1952), Frieda Fromm-Reichman (1950, 1959), Lewis B. Hill (1955), and Harry Stack Sullivan (1956, 1962). This way of life includes the following.

The schizophrenic person overvalues, is intensely interested in, and indeed is often uncannily aware of, inner reality. This may be manifested, for example, by intellectualization, a deep attachment to (what may seem to others) odd ideas, and an affinity for strange inner states. He is at the same time detached from, disinterested in, and even ignorant or unconscious of, many aspects of external reality.

Such a person has an attitude of indifference to, if not contempt for, the limits of time, space, personal and biological characteristics, and the facts of social response and social structure. Although most persons recognize such limits as conditions that must be taken into account by one who considers action, the schizophrenic person thinks and acts instead as if he regarded himself as omnipotent.

He tends to orient himself to another person as if the other were part of himself, or exclusively in terms of the other's use to him. His dominant techniques for relating to others are taking and incorporating on the model of the infantile relationship with the mother.

However, he has also been convinced by experience that the mother upon whom he depends is fragile beneath her brittle exterior and that she is unable to tolerate the expression of his feelings or impulses or any separation from him. With this realization, he faces the dilemma that if he grows, differentiating himself from her, she will then in some way "crack up." Compelled to save her because he feels this necessary for his own survival, he may develop in such a way that in some relationships, at least, he appears to be altruistic—sensitive to, and considerate of, another's needs and wishes. Often this means that he is sacrificing, with much inner rage, his

---

1. The material in this section, greatly condensed, and in the sections "Electroshock and Other Organic Therapies," "Chemotherapy," "Hospitalization," "The Therapeutic Community I," and "Psychotherapy I" in somewhat different form has been published previously (Edelson 1966a).

own wishes, values, independence, even sanity, as if this were essential for the protection and maintenance of the matrix in which he exists.

The use of such techniques as incorporation in relating to others, and his experience of his mother's overwhelming anxiety in relation to him, result in the guilty conviction that his own love destroys others and that any close relationship seems to spell doom to his own or another's integrity. Therefore, he avoids attachment to others by such means as passive aloofness and active hatefulness.

He is deeply anxious about, and has many defenses against a dread sense of inner emptiness, which may be exacerbated by loss of any kind, but primarily by separation from overvalued inner contents, or from others he feels to be part of himself or sources of supply. His defenses against loss and separation include repression and withholding of affect, and various other forms of retentiveness. Expressive action is, therefore, often flat and monotonous. Narcissistic insouciance, detachment, and isolation have a similar defensive purpose, as does secretiveness: a "hiding within" that may itself be concealed behind paradoxical masks of playing roles, showing off, histrionic displays, and pseudo-emotional outbursts.

The ultimate loss is loss of self through disintegration. In the attempt to avoid this catastrophe, he blots out anxiety-arousing aspects of reality, both the threatening facts of the external world and the feelings with which he cannot cope.

The schizophrenic person wants love, yet because he feels love is dangerous he is unable to permit himself to love or be loved. Instead he is compelled to hate and be hated. Barred from loving, he may even give himself up to what satisfaction he can derive from hating. However, whether he loves or hates, the result appears to be the loss of the other upon whom he depends. A profound pervasive sense of futility, the characteristic feeling of schizophrenia, supervenes.

Schizophrenia is also an ego-disorder, which is inextricably linked to the schizophrenic way of life, helping to maintain it and in turn being fostered by it.

The ego is an abstraction, referring to a certain group of functions performed within the personality system and necessary in identifying, choosing to act upon, and integrating: the needs, impulses, and feelings of inner reality; the conditions and stimuli of outer reality (physical and social); and a set of internalized moral obligations, expectations, and sanctions—termed the superego.

Ego-functions are carried out by the apparatuses of perception, memory, thinking, and control of motor expression.

Discriminative functions make possible the distinction between what is within and what is external to the person, and the differentiation of self and not-self (including other persons).

Adaptive functions make possible a constructive relationship between the expression of impulses and feelings, and conditions—especially social conditions—in external reality.

Integrative functions make possible ordered, meaningful perceptions; a relatively consistent value system; a coherent, continuous sense of self; and organized thought and behavior.

All such functions are impaired, in varying degrees, in the schizophrenic person.

Schizophrenia thus involves an impairment of a specific subsystem of the personality. The etiology of this impairment is problematical but seems to include the influence of both constitutional factors and early interpersonal relations (especially between the infant and mothering person). These kinds of influence interact with each other and appear to be of different degrees of importance in the development of the disorder in different patients.

The ego-disorder shapes the schizophrenic person's way of life; in turn, this way of life pursued over a period of time increases the severity of the ego-disorder and therefore the vulnerability of ego-functions to episodes of acute, more or less pervasive, failure.

At some point, the compromised or undeveloped ego-apparatuses are unable to function as necessary in the face of demands arising out of situational or developmental vicissitudes. They may be overwhelmed by shock, terror, or anxiety. They may be rendered ineffective by the depletion of energy, supplies, nutriment, or stimuli necessary to maintain them—as a result of physical illness or exhaustion, loss, isolation, wounds to self-esteem, or the exacerbation of unresolved conflicts.

Thus schizophrenia may first come to the attention of others as ego-failure, described, for example, by Paul Federn (1952), and manifested by the following.

Ego "boundaries" are disrupted or, in other words, the discriminative functions fail. The ability to distinguish between inner and outer reality is impaired, resulting in a loss of the characteristic feeling of self and reality; and confusion about what in experience is part of self and what belongs to external reality. States of depersonalization and estrangement are examples. The person may be overwhelmed by the invasion of images, feelings, impulses, and ideas that, since they are ordinarily excluded from consciousness, are felt to come from outside—a terrifying experience. At this stage, a person is not necessarily withdrawn; he may still be intensely interested in reality. His knowledge of reality, insofar as this depends upon cognitive reality testing, may be unimpaired at the same time that—because of the disruption of ego boundaries—his experience of reality is increasingly altered in quality. What he experiences feels in relation to his own ego remote, unfamiliar, unreal, or uncanny.

The sense of reality—the feeling of what is self and what external reality—no longer corresponds to the cognitive evidence of "reality testing." Logical thinking may be used to explain the discrepancy between reality-as-felt and reality-as-evidentially-known in a way that involves falsification of reality and shutting out aspects of reality that might disturb the anxiety-relieving explanation. Thinking is also impaired in a variety of ways by the confusion of inner and outer reality. Delusions, varying degrees of thought-disorder, and ultimately, of course, impairment of adaptive and integrative functions, are consequences.

Withdrawal from external reality, including relationships with others, and regression (a simplification of the personality system to one resembling an earlier, more helpless, dependent state) may also follow. Withdrawal from reality and regression are not primary but are secondary to the disturbance in the sense of reality occurring as a result of ego-dysfunction. Such secondary pathology represents at least in part attempts to escape from the kinds of experiences associated with the failure of discriminative, adaptive, and integrative ego-functions. Federn (1952) says of the primary psychosis, it is not a defense but a defeat of the ego.

Different resolutions of ego-failure, or, in other words, of the so-called acute schizophrenic episode may be described in order of increasing degree of malignancy or relative difficulty of reversing the process:

1. There may be reconstitution to a previous level of functioning, usually as the result of appropriate treatment; frequently such treatment results in reestablishment of neurotic (phobic, hysterical, obsessive-compulsive) defenses. The possibility of subsequent modification of the ego-disorder and schizophrenic way of life through further treatment is optimal.
2. There may be increasing constriction of experience and functioning. The patient accepts and submits to a chronic, empty, limited "burned-out" form of the schizophrenic way of life.
3. There may be a crystallization and maintenance of a more or less pervasive paranoid explanation of the world, which was initially developed to account for, and ward off, the terrible, uncanny experiences of ego-failure.
4. There may be, finally, an increasingly profound withdrawal and regression, preoccupation with simple bodily functions and pleasures, and progressive deterioration of ego-functioning.

Treatment must be concerned first, if ego-failure exists, with the reconstitution of ego-functioning. Special attention must be given to the discriminative functions and to the feeling and thinking disorders associated with their failure. The attempt at reconstitution should occur in a way that mitigates tendencies toward the development of the second, third, and fourth outcomes just described.

Second, an attempt may be made—and must be made, if there is to be a decrease in the subsequent level of vulnerability to ego-failure—to alter the schizophrenic way of life and the underlying ego-disorder.

Such an attempt may have as its goal mere adjustment or, ambitiously, a more satisfactory, even creative, relatedness to the conditions, especially social conditions, of external reality. The emphasis is on improvement of adaptive functions.

Treatment may also have as a further goal building more viable structures, and relationships among structures, within the personality system. Then there must be an additional emphasis on the improvement of integrative functions.

It may be noted here that such conceptual distinctions and categories are introduced for the sake of clarity and orderly thinking; they are, of course, not reflected in a sharp separation of such functions and operations in reality, where these tend to be intermingled and interdependent.

As a result of summarizing a complex treatment process in abstract terms, a joint human enterprise of infinite subtlety—carried on interpersonally and interdependently by the physician and patient acting together as allies and striving in their interactions to be in empathic touch with each other—may end up sounding as if what is involved instead is the physical or psychological manipulation of a passive, malfunctioning organ-like subsystem of the personality by a competent physician.

Such an impression may not be completely avoidable, given the limitations of communication within the scope of such a presentation as this. It perhaps may be partly offset by anticipating the discussion of treatment with the insistence that it is to the former, not the latter, kind of enterprise that the attitude of the physician is oriented in the treatment of the schizophrenic person.

Such treatment is founded, first and foremost, upon the physician's decency, kindness, and wisdom as a human being; his identity as a scientist; his self-knowledge; his disinterestedness—all of which help to guarantee that he will not exploit the patient for the satisfaction of his own material, physical, or emotional needs; and his respect for the patient as a necessary, helpful partner in the work of treatment rather than as an object upon which to exercise his skill and influence.

The existence and mobilization of the human resources in each with which to build such an alliance is both a crucial condition for, and principal part of, treatment. Without this attitude, all efforts to describe the "repair of ego-functions" or the "alteration of a way of life" become merely the writing of notes, correct, interpretable, but not music.

A different kind of interpersonal experience than the schizophrenic person has ever known is necessary as the condition for the learning to take place that will modify an ego-disorder and a way of life. This experience is most likely to occur through individual psychotherapy, founded on psychoanalytic understanding of personality and therapy, especially as such therapy is carried out in an environment, usually in a hospital, having the characteristics of a so-called therapeutic milieu, or therapeutic community.

Description of this treatment approach will constitute the main effort of the remainder of this chapter.

ELECTROSHOCK AND OTHER ORGANIC THERAPIES

As a preliminary, it is perhaps necessary to state that, in general, the use of electroshock and other organic therapies should be eschewed in the treatment of the schizophrenic person. This will be understood to follow from the conception of schizophrenia as a way of life, which is not unlearned as the result of such therapies, and from the attitude toward the schizophrenic person as an ally in the treatment process rather than an object of it.

Such operations done *to*, or performed *upon*, the patient may tend to strengthen his conviction that he is a worthless, bad, impersonally regarded object, whose feelings and impulses are intolerable to others. They may lead to his withdrawal from an active, feeling participation in interpersonal interactions. They may exacerbate his tendency, especially in the face of anxiety, to cope by shutting out external reality. They may re-enforce his passive reliance upon magical powers, events, or supplies, to relieve his suffering. They tend to justify his perception of his illness as an inexplicable, inexorable event inflicted upon him by a cruel fate, rather than a way of life which he has learned, which may be no longer necessary or appropriate but to the perpetuation of which he continues to contribute, and which (especially with skillful help) he himself has the resources to understand and alter.

Such therapies have the great danger, especially when used in the treatment of acute ego-failure, of contributing to the resolution of such an episode by the development of further constriction of experience and functioning, loss of the potentiality for creativity, and the quiescent acceptance of a chronic schizophrenic way of life. The withdrawal of interest in making any further effort to change, especially when the discomfort that must inevitably be associated with such an effort is compared by the patient to the relatively anxiety-free withdrawn or regressed state, makes him much less available to psychotherapeutic methods, should these be subsequently sought and attempted.

CHEMOTHERAPY

Chemotherapy, especially when used as the sole treatment or in a way that precludes meaningful interpersonal experience because of effects upon the patient's consciousness, may have the same results as those therapies just described.

However, it is possible to use chemotherapy meaningfully as an adjunct to psychotherapy with specific patients and in specific circumstances:

Temporarily, usually in a hospital over a period of days or weeks, after a trial of adequate interpersonal means has not proved sufficient in time, relatively high doses of chemotherapeutic agents may be used as a constraint on assaultive, suicidal, or hypomanic behavior that is an immediate threat to the safety of the patient or others, or that may permanently alienate him from those whose help he needs.

Temporarily, usually in a hospital over a period of days or weeks, when alleviation has not proved possible by interpersonal means, chemotherapeutic agents may be used to reduce the terror, anxiety, or inner excitement resulting in acute disorganization of ego-functioning, so that such functioning may improve to a level where meaningful interpersonal contact becomes possible.

Relatively low doses of chemotherapeutic agents may be used over an indefinite period of time, for example, in the following two kinds of circumstances: (1) When there is not much hope for any great modification in the patient's way of life and the goal is to sustain him at his present level of functioning by offering him indefinitely, either periodically or upon request, the counsel of a reliable, interested, understanding advisor, at the same time perhaps reducing chemotherapeutically the level of anxiety in his responses to stress (thereby the effects of such anxiety upon ego-functioning). (2) When the patient in psychotherapy is so little able to master even small amounts of anxiety that simply attempting to maintain a relationship with the therapist (despite the latter's skill and tact) is enough to result in ego-disorganization.

The use of chemotherapeutic agents, and alterations in such a regime, should be informed by the recognition that the patient's response is determined in large part by such factors as the magical, nonrational, and symbolic character of his dependence upon these medications, which come to have many interpersonal meanings to him. Such meanings include, for example, "part of the therapist," "a tie to the therapist," "the therapist's interest or care," "potent supplies," or "independence from the therapist or indeed from any human agents." Likewise, ordering such medication may be interpreted, for example, as a lack of confidence in the patient's resources, and discontinuing such medication as sadistic deprivation or punishment.

Frequent changes of dosage and from one chemotherapeutic agent to another, especially done haphazardly in an effort to keep up with the patient's symptomatology, do not inspire confidence. Giving on occasion a single dose of a chemotherapeutic agent, ostensibly because the patient is upset (often actually to relieve the distress of someone coming in contact with, or attempting to care for, the patient by doing something *to* the patient) is not useful. If a single dose is effective, recourse to the patient's own resources and to helpful interpersonal experiences is likely to be just as effective and is certainly preferable in terms of the long-range strategy of therapy.

Rational indications for the initiation or cessation of such a regime, or for changes in dosages or specific agents, should be discussed with the patient; should be linked, preferably, to his own behavior and explicit or implicit communications; and should involve, when possible, the patient's own initiative, agreement, observations of events before and after, and evaluation of any observed effects. These comments illustrate one of many kinds of transaction that should not be unilaterally controlled overtly or covertly by either the physician or patient member of such an alliance. Each learns to take the observations, feelings, experience, and recommendations of the other into consideration, although the final decisions that emerge from consultation are now in the hands of one, now in the hands of the other, depending on the nature of the issue.

HOSPITALIZATION

Perhaps, in a period such as ours when the emphasis has almost all been on the side of "keeping the patient out of the hospital," or "getting the patient out of the hospital as *rapidly* as possible," a word might be written here to refocus on the psychiatric hospital milieu as potentially at least a specific and frequently necessary instrumentality for the treatment of an ego-disorder like schizophrenia.

If the therapeutic community of the psychiatric hospital or unit is in actuality therapeutic, it should be available to the patient as long as necessary, however long that might be—with the provision, of course, that appropriate steps must be taken to mitigate the undesirable side effects of this (as of any) treatment modality. That is, a therapeutic hospital community must not only make a specific contribution to the therapy of each patient but provide as well for the prevention and mitigation of general undesirable side effects that tend to arise not alone from the nature of the illness but from the nature of the psychotherapy and hospitalization used in its treatment.

Such side effects include the following. A hospitalized patient-group may reinforce illness as a way of life for its members, with an associated lessening of the influence of heretofore relatively potent values upon behavior. Skills and productive social behavior may deteriorate through disuse in the absence of the stimuli and expectations of family, job, school, and extended community setting. Withdrawal and regression may tend to occur as untoward by-products of the necessarily fostered dependency upon professional personnel, emphasis in therapy upon introspection, and some degree of isolation from the outside world.

The patient, however, may need hospitalization to protect him or members of society from physical danger or to prevent him from doing serious harm to his own or others' social interests. His hospitalization may be necessary to maintain the functioning of others in his family, whose own emotional balance may be otherwise seriously compromised by enforced interactions with an emotionally ill person who must be continuously cared for. Most important, perhaps, from a treatment point of view, hospitalization removes him from stimuli and encounters that tend to provoke, exacerbate, and perpetuate—rather than alleviate—his difficulties and way of life.

To treat such a person, whose entire life and personality are disrupted, by one, two, three, even four sessions a week in a physician's office courts many disasters, not the least of which is the continued outrunning of therapeutic effort by burgeoning psychopathology.

On the other hand, some hospitals can be more than a necessary way station for the relatively rapid patching-up of acutely ruptured ego-functioning. The hospital or residential treatment center can be as well a school for living, in which the immediate life situation in the therapeutic community is exploited to provide corrective experiences and new learning. The patient's way of life then begins to change, and his potentialities for growth and development begin to be realized.

Experience in such a school for living can provide an enrichment in the life of a young schizophrenic patient, opening up doors for his future, comparable to that provided to his more normal counterpart in college. Certainly such experience is preferable to rapid return to the world outside the hospital, and the maintenance of a constricted, zombie-like, marginal existence there as a chronic chemotherapeutically tranquillized, schizophrenic person.

The goal, then, is not to keep the patient from or out of the hospital, but to change the psychiatric hospital to create a therapeutic community within it that contributes to the patient's treatment as long as he requires it. The length of stay will depend on what is required to achieve a specific goal of treatment for a particular patient. Both the therapeutic community of the hospital and individual psychotherapy have specific contributions to make to achieving the goal of reconstituting ego-functioning in the treatment of acute ego-failure, and also to achieving such further goals as the subsequent modification of the schizophrenic way of life through the improvement of adaptive and integrative ego-functions. The choice of goal depends on such factors as the history and progress of the illness, the assets (skills, capacities, resources, and healthy areas of functioning) the patient brings to the work of treatment, and the limiting conditions of his age and social-economic and family situation.

THE THERAPEUTIC COMMUNITY I

In the treatment of acute ego-failure both the therapeutic community and the psychotherapist attempt to mitigate the influence of those factors that have imposed an excessive demand on, overwhelmed, or depleted the patient's ego; to temporarily and in part provide what the patient cannot provide because of his impaired ego-functioning; and to help the patient restore such functioning.

With regard to mitigating demands upon the patient's ego, the therapeutic community provides a moratorium from those demands that have proved too much for a vulnerable ego: for example, increased demands to function adequately in a new school, job, or family situation arising from either environmental change or entrance into a new social-biological developmental phase.

Shock, terror, and anxiety are reduced by removing the patient from the complex situation or individuals perceived by him as catastrophic or inimical and placing him in a simpler situation, in which he is treated consistently, reliably, gently, honestly, and respectfully.

Energy reserves are replenished by treating any physical illness, and creating the conditions—not only chemical but social—that will make it possible for the patient to rest and sleep. The effects of loss, isolation, and loneliness are reduced through reassuring transactions with others. Wounds to self-esteem are avoided through protection from further insult and failure. The patient is offered realistic opportunities for possible achievement in programs of work and recreation that are appropriate developmentally, socially, culturally, and in the level and complexity of performance required.

With regard to performing an auxiliary ego function, the therapeutic community offers external controls to patients whose inner controls over behavior are imperfectly developed or have lapsed: i.e., order in the external world to the patient whose inner world has collapsed into chaos.

A locked door is the traditional way to provide an external control over the patient's impulsive, disorganized, or self-destructive behavior. Another way is to create a situation including appropriate social responses to the patient from those, both staff members and other patients, who are important to him because at this point he depends on them for (and sees them as powerful enough, and inclined, to provide) care, help, and satisfaction.

The therapeutic community should be organized so that the relationship of any patient to staff and other patients is such as to make for this perception and expectation of them. Their response is experienced ideally as dependably forthcoming and in a direction leading to control, not undisciplined or lawless expression, of impulses.

Staff members are crucial members of the group involved, because they are able to represent the desired directions that group influence should take and to some extent to thwart undesirable directions it might take if they were absent. Patients are also crucial members of the group. They have the power to influence each other by virtue of the cohesiveness created by their shared peer status. They sometimes have great understanding of how to reach each other. Their continuous propinquity makes for opportunities to frustrate or satisfy each other in a thousand ways while living together. Such considerations provide one way to understand the usefulness in the therapeutic community of a daily meeting of both patients and staff.

The rules and regulations, and the regular, planned daily routines of eating and sleeping, work and recreation, discussion and action—routines which patients participate in designing—are an effective, impersonal framework for action. Patterns of cause and effect and the conditions limiting action should be as clear and simple as possible. Ideally, consequences follow action, privileges and penalties are related to manifestations of responsibility and irresponsibility, and the delegation of responsibility (in elections, for example) is related to evidence of ability, in a predictable rational way.

Joint participation by staff and patients on committees or in groups that supervise or coordinate work and activities programs, or act as policy-making or judicial bodies making decisions about rules and regulations, privileges and penalties, and the delegation of responsibility, is necessary to bring about such a framework for action.

As the patient adapts to this orderly world and finds his way within it, he is increasingly able to cope with the disorder and confusion within himself. It is as if thought itself derives its structure from the structure of the experience of external reality.[2]

With regard to restoring the patient's ego-functioning, the therapeutic community helps to free him from bondage to alien feelings, impulses, and ideas within, which have invaded his consciousness. As he participates in the discussion at daily patient-staff meetings of the problems arising in living and working with others, though his participation be at first a listening one, he learns to understand the links in the chain leading to a particular outcome. Fantasies and misconceptions about events, people, and relationships (often fostered in informal groups) can be corrected in a setting where the effort is to make the information about all aspects of the environment, especially the social environment, readily available and freely—nondefensively—given. Rumor has an antidote. The contagion of emotion, sweeping through a group far ahead of the cognitive understanding of its origins and often leading to epidemics of impulsive behavior, can be to some extent checked.

The shaping and domination of thought and perception by feelings, fantasies, and primitive ideas within, are mitigated. The patient's confusion lessens as he is increasingly able to take into consideration the nature of reality outside himself in his thinking and behavior.

The tendency to withdraw from external reality and to regression is at the same time thwarted by the encouragement and pressures to participate with others in the varied life of the therapeutic community, and to take some responsibility for almost all aspects of group living—activities and work programs, relations between staff and patients, rules and regulations, social problems, and the policies and organization of the hospital itself.

The sense of belonging to a worthwhile and satisfying group—the therapeutic

---

2. Patients may experience the environment as an extension of the self and act accordingly. Weiss (1964), who considers agoraphobia primarily an ego-disorder, describes how what the agoraphobic patient feels as part of his ego extends over a portion of the environment lying beyond his motoric powers. According to Weiss, such a patient feels helpless, apparently in part because he can no longer trust his ability to predict the effects of intended movements.

Such patients also act as if the experience of ego and the experience of external reality are structurally homologous. The absence of an external confinement in agoraphobia is experienced as the absence of an internal barrier against drive tension. The external restricting situation in claustrophobia is experienced as an internal blockage of a needed outlet for drive tension. Change in the environment, similarly, is reacted to as if it were a theatened internal change.

The dependence of ego-functioning and ego-structures upon external stimuli and cultural nutriment has been discussed by Rapaport (1954, 1958) in his writings on relative ego autonomy. Weiss adds clinical evidence for the ego-supportive role of the environment in accounts of patients who cling to home, a familiar place, or a reliable person as a way of clinging to a threatened identity, or who wear particular clothing to ward off intruding, repressed ego states. Aspects of external reality are used to replace or augment a missing or deficient aspect of ego-functioning (Edelson 1965).

community—and the feelings of solidarity with its members develop if all goes well and come to be increasingly important to the patient. The values of this therapeutic community emphasize the ends of learning about and changing oneself, and the obligation not only to seek competent professional help but also to make an effort oneself to achieve these goals. Such values then begin to have a potent effect upon the patient, counteracting the anxiety-spurred wish to give up and settle for a life of incapacity and chronic illness.

PSYCHOTHERAPY I

A similar process develops in the relationship between patient and psychotherapist, the two of whom might be viewed as constituting a specialized dyadic group that is part of the therapeutic community.

The psychotherapist begins by establishing a solidary relationship with the patient. He does this in part by serving as an auxiliary ego for the patient—observing, caring, acting, controlling action, in the patient's interest, only so long as the patient is incapacitated, and always in part as a model for, and teacher of, more adequate ego-functioning. It is, of course, cruel to leave crucial decisions up to a patient who is a slave to whim and confusion; but it is also necessary, even as advice or firm direction is given, to arouse in the patient an active interest in his own physical and psychological survival.

To notice that a preoccupied, disorganized patient is thirsty; to bring the dryness of his lips to his attention; to offer him water; to prevent such a patient from behaving in ways he will later be ashamed to remember; to see that the excited patient sleeps; to direct him to eat when he ignores the necessity to do so; to explain in simple language to a confused patient what is the nature of the place in which he now lives, who are the people with whom he comes in contact, what is the meaning of the events which perplex him—these are the interpretations that matter.

The psychotherapist should not join in the patient's bizarre, disordered world, but invite the patient to enter his world. He should not use the private language and thought processes of the patient, but invite the patient to understand and use *his* language and thought processes. It is better for the therapist to say to the patient, "I don't understand you," sometimes adding, "thank Heaven!"—and insist on their working out together what was meant until it is actually intelligible by usual standards or both realize that there was no meaning but only manifestations of stereotypy and chaos—than for the therapist empathically to intuit meanings, reinforcing the patient's isolation in his special inner world and his conviction that he is magically understood there by one other special person. When the therapist does understand, he should make explicit to the patient by what steps, including empathy, observation, and inference, he arrived at understanding, and preferably offer such understanding as a hypothesis to be further investigated together. Oneness with the patient should occur on a rational ego-level and as a result of common devotion to the psychotherapeutic task—not on a level of impulse, fantasy, or shared grandiosity. The psychotherapist seeks to reach and help the patient maintain the islands of healthy ego-functioning buffeted by fierce seas, rather than immerse himself in—or be distracted by his or the patient's fascination with—the archaic and pathological;

as a result, the patient becomes in his ego-functioning more and more like the psychotherapist.

As this relationship develops, it may be used as a bridge for the patient to relationships with others. By learning to tolerate increasing quantities of feeling and anxiety in this relationship, the patient is supported in his efforts to face situations that are more anxiety-arousing and complicated than the more easily controlled transactions with the psychotherapist. In the relationship with his therapist, the patient may be helped to understand the world in which he lives—the meeting he has just attended or the activity in which he has taken part and his response to them. Above all—this is a necessary foundation for any further therapeutic work— the patient, in the relationship with his therapist, comes to feel a realistic concern for his own welfare, to care, to care about, and to take care of, himself.

The therapist, in face-to-face encounters in which the patient may be continually aware of him and what he is like, then helps the patient understand his conflicts with, and his responses to injuries from, external reality, showing him how these led to his acute ego-failure and how they are reproduced in his life in the hospital and, even more vividly, in interactions with the therapist.

Turning the patient's attention to the miniscule details of the way his ego operates in itself improves ego-functioning. The specific impairments that lead to unpleasant, uncanny experiences, the mechanisms by which the patient deals with conflicts with the real world, and the consequences of the use of these mechanisms, should be exhaustively examined.

Delusions and hallucinations when present should be interpreted, for example, as manifestations of ego-disorder, as evidence of breakdown in perceptual-thinking apparatuses responsible for discriminative functions, leading to confusion about what is within and what without, rather than interpreted as symbolizations of internal conflict. The psychotherapist should avoid the tendency to romanticize psychotic pathology by attributing meaning and motivation to what are often non-individual, stereotyped manifestations of disorganization and the ultimate failure of any psychological system. This kind of romance sometimes leads to the unfortunate notion that the catastrophic experience of the psychosis itself—regression to a state of disorganization—is necessary for a new beginning, in some way leads to more profound healing, and should be encouraged.

The therapist should not focus on historical determinants of the conflicts with reality, the memory of which is likely to arouse feelings of shame, guilt, anxiety, and worthlessness, with which the patient cannot cope. Since the patient defends himself against all feelings because any feeling is likely to strain the capacities of his impaired ego-functioning, the psychotherapist should not analyze the patient's neurotic defenses against specific impulses or feelings, which may be a necessary line of defense against being overwhelmed from within, but rather focus on supporting the patient's efforts to master feelings of any kind.

In the treatment of ego-failure, it is not resistances to the uncovering of conflicts between the subsystems of the personality that should be the focus of psychotherapeutic attention, but rather the resistances that interfere with the recovery of ego-functioning: denial or falsification of reality; attitudes of omnipotence; apathy, aloofness, withdrawal; regression.

The patient's difficulty is not that he cannot remember the past nor that he is unconscious of his impulses; it is that he cannot forget these, his consciousness is flooded by them, and he cannot screen, select, pay attention to the claims of the reality outside himself. The dictum, to make conscious what is unconscious, must be interpreted to mean to help the schizophrenic person become aware of reality and his response to it. The therapeutic community and individual psychotherapy work in concert to make this possible.

THE THERAPEUTIC COMMUNITY II

An analysis of the contribution of the therapeutic community and individual psychotherapy to the improvement of adaptive and integrative ego-functions depends on distinguishing four types of problems arising in any social system or in any sub-system of a social system (Parsons 1951; Parsons and Shils 1951; Parsons, Shils, and Bales 1953), and therefore in the therapeutic community and in such sub-systems of it as the daily patient-staff meeting and the individual psychotherapy dyadic group.

In any daily patient-staff meeting, for example, the following may occur:

1. The group, given an accepted desired end, may be concerned with orientation to the environment or situation in which the end is sought; with determination of the conditions limiting action; with mobilization of available resources; and with choice of means to the goal. Decisions are usually governed by cognitive standards, involving efficiency and rational verifiable hypotheses about means-ends relations. Conflicts are the result of error and ignorance. Seeking or sharing information, and seeking or offering orientation, education, and interpretation are typical activities.

2. The group may be concerned with goal-consummation. One form of such activity is decision-making about the relative priority of a number of competing ends. Conflicting values (appreciative or expressive, cognitive, moral) are usually at issue. Suggesting action or appealing to prepotent norms or values—or rejecting these—are typical activities.

3. The group may be concerned with integrating its units—individuals or sub-groups—following the strains created by motion toward a particular end. Often, this involves an attempt to increase the actual influence or control of a value or norm shared by members of the group over the conduct of a deviant member. Expression of positive and negative sanctions, and the utilization of mechanisms of social control are typical activities. Mechanisms of social control include permitting the deviant member to express himself and be heard; attempting to draw him into a solidary relationship with other members of the group; refusing to reciprocate his unacceptable wishes, expectations, or provocations; and rewarding him for desired behavior (Parsons 1951). The ultimate desideratum is to achieve socialization (the internalization of shared values and norms) since penalties and coercion are, by comparison, notoriously inefficient mechanisms of social control.

4. The group may be concerned with improving or restoring the internal condition of its members, so that each member may contribute maximally to problem-solving efforts. Typical is the release of individual tensions which have built up as a result of problem-solving activities moving toward a desired end, or as a result of

inconsistencies in the system of norms, values, and expectations to which a member of the group has been exposed. The consequence of such tension-release is that individual tensions are not otherwise discharged in deviant behavior. Also typical in a group working on this kind of problem is the maintenance of patterns of expectations, value-priorities, and performance through culture transmission and ritual-symbolic activity. In addition, cultural innovations may be created that transcend and transmute apparent inconsistencies and conflicts, leading to the internalization of new patterns.

If the individual psychotherapy dyad is regarded as a social system in microcosm, any individual psychotherapy session, like any other group meeting in the hospital, may be concerned with any one or a combination of these system problems.

Typically, in most parts of the hospital program, however, movement tends to be from system problems concerned with means to those concerned with goal-consummation to those concerned with integration to those concerned with tension-management and pattern-maintenance. That is, there is movement from concern with the nature of external reality and achieving ends in it—the raison d'être of the patient-staff meeting and its constituent community action groups—to concern with the repair of any strains that have resulted between or within individual members (or subgroups) of the total group as a result, particularly, of collective strivings toward shared goals.

Typically, movement in individual psychotherapy tends to be in the reverse order, from concern with the inner state of the individual—the raison d'être of individual psychotherapy—outward eventually to interest in his orientation and adaptation to the environment in which he lives. So, in individual psychotherapy, there is, first, permission for the patient to express and release feelings and tension and to describe and investigate his inner state—and thus, the creation of solidarity between patient and psychotherapist. These developments ordinarily precede attempts by the psychotherapist to deal with the patient's efforts to achieve gratification, especially in the relationship with the psychotherapist. The psychotherapist seeks to avoid reciprocation of the patient's pathological expectations and wishes, but to reinforce new learning by the patient about himself and the world in which he lives and desired modifications of his behavior.

Both in the patient-staff meeting and in individual psychotherapy, the effort must be made to integrate the patient with other members of the group (in one case, patients and staff, in the other, the individual psychotherapist) if the job is to be done (in one case, problem-resolution in the everyday life of the hospital, in the other, alteration in the individual patient's way of life and alleviation of his ego-disorder). Integration involves the creation of solidarity among members of a group on the basis of the values they share, the responsibilities to which they consequently commit themselves, and the legitimized expectations of each other that they predictably and mutually fulfill.

A particular schizophrenic person's pathological behavior in relation to such values, responsibilities, and expectations may be found to be deviant in any one of the four ways described by Talcott Parsons (1951) in his discussion of types of deviance. First and foremost perhaps, his deviation may involve passive alienation from values and norms shared by others in the social systems in which he participates; such alienation is expressed in evasion and withdrawal. Second, his passive conformity to such values and norms may be expressed in a ritualistic compliance "to the letter not the spirit." Third, although perhaps not as frequently, his active conformity to values and norms may be expressed in driven, compulsive, joyless performance and demands for similar performance from others. Fourth, he may express his active alienation in aggressive flouting and challenge of such values, responsibilities, and expectations.

The latter is usually associated with antisocial acting out; a person who deviates in this way is especially difficult to integrate into the collectivity of a hospital community or that of individual psychotherapy, the damage he does being relatively intolerable to a social structure, if the structure is to survive. So the schizophrenic person who has committed himself to aggressive hatefulness to keep others away from him poses an especially difficult treatment problem, and is indeed often not seen as ill at all but as wicked and criminal.

In any event, it might be noted that any one of these four types of deviant behavior, no matter how "quietly" it is carried out, ultimately wreaks havoc on efforts to carry out the work of the therapeutic community as a whole or the work of any subsystem of it—such as a work program, an activities program, the patient-staff meeting, or the individual psychotherapy collectivity. When this is recognized, powerful pressures on the patient may develop in the therapeutic community in the direction of socialization—not a mere acquiescence to the values of his society, but an active, understanding, even creative implementation of them, as well as a collaboration with others in the effort to integrate and modify them.

The schizophrenic way of life conflicts with the imperative prerequisites for task-achievement and problem-resolution in the therapeutic community. The solution of any of the four types of system problem in the patient-staff meeting, for example, requires that the way of life of schizophrenic persons in the group change.

If the first type of problem (having to do with the mobilization of resources, the recognition of conditions limiting action, and the choice of means) is to be solved, the schizophrenic person must be lured from his preoccupation with inner reality to pay attention to the interesting, complicated, even exciting events in external reality. In this connection, it may be noted that the patient-staff meeting should not be an obsessive, dull, business meeting with a prearranged agenda. Life in the therapeutic community should have some of the characteristics of a good drama: suspense, surprise, revelation, tragedy, sudden humor, some moments of tenderness.

If means are actually to lead to a desired end, then orientation to the environment, information, education, and interpretation must be used to change the schizophrenic patient's indifference to the conditions that limit action to a recognition of such limits. His secretiveness must change to openness, so information may be available. His ignorance must change to knowledge, and his autistic ideas and fantasies about events in reality to rational verifiable hypotheses about means-ends relations.

If the second type of problem (having to do with the selection of ends to be striven after, and the attainment of such ends) is to be solved, then encouragement, suggestions, example-setting, offering gratification through achievement, and appeal to prepotent values of the therapeutic community (especially by such figures as the physician who represents and embodies the cultural tradition of health values) must be used to change the schizophrenic patient's lethargy to energy and his indifference to caring. Indecision and ambivalence must change to commitment and choice. Withdrawal and passivity must change to taking action; in other words, the marked preference for autoplastic adaptation (changing oneself) must change to some effort, when appropriate, at alloplastic adaptation (doing something about the environment).

If the third type of problem (having to do with integration) is to be solved, then the previously discussed mechanisms of social control (permissiveness, creation of solidarity, refusal to reciprocate certain expectations, and the reward of others) must be used to change the schizophrenic patient's preference for taking and incorporating to more sophisticated transactions with others. Compulsive altruism must change to a mature differentiation from others and ability to collaborate with them as separate human beings. Repression of feelings, insouciance, and hiding within must change to a capacity for giving response to, and being sensitive to the response of, others. Regression must change to responsibility.

If the fourth type of problem (having to do with tension-management and pattern-maintenance) is to be solved, then provision of opportunity for, and acceptance of, appropriate tension-release, and the transmission of normal cultural patterns (including attitudes and skills) must be used to change the schizophrenic patient's apathy and incapacity to willingness and skill, so that these necessary resources are available to be mobilized as performances required for the achievement of goals. Passive surrender to tension, through either driven discharge or suppression, must change into active mastery of tension, through ego-controlled discharge or restraint under the influence of recognition of consequences and the suitability of time, place, and circumstance. A disintegrated ambivalence toward life experience must change into attempts to understand and integrate the values to which the patient has been exposed in his family, peer-group, school, job, and in the hospital. (Individual psychotherapy is the subsystem that has perhaps the heaviest, though not the exclusive, responsibility for the solution of this kind of problem in the therapeutic community.)

If these four problems of any social system are not solved in the therapeutic community, then there is failure, which affects the daily life of the patient and those other patients and staff with whom he works and lives, and with whom he shares the goals and values of treatment. Cumulative encounters with such failure and the explicit, didactic connection of it in the therapeutic community to characteristics of the schizophrenic way of life may provide a powerful incentive to the schizophrenic person to change that way of life. Such an outcome assumes the following. The patient is identified with the therapeutic community (its members, values, and goals). He has access to resources, such as psychotherapy, to help him change, should he become motivated through his experiences to change, his way of life. The therapeutic community provides opportunities for him to experiment in action with new ways of living. Members of the community work to become aware of, and to eschew any, vested interest in the schizophrenic way of life of any one of them. Members of the community work to accept individual growth, by seeking to become aware of and to accept the social strains that are inevitable concomitants of continuous change in the individual members of a social system. Finally, with social institutions involving information-sharing and examination of social processes, the therapeutic community opposes any individual patient's attempts to escape awareness of the consequences of his schizophrenic way of life for himself and others in the group of which he is a member. These statements comprise a condensed formulation of what is meant by a therapeutic community, and of the aims of sociotherapy as a treatment methodology.

It is clear that an enormous variety of kinds of participation and skills are required by staff in the therapeutic community, because a variety of processes, part of any sequence of action, reflecting intrinsic imperatives of all social systems, occur in such a community. Not only understanding of the mechanisms of social control, which is also part of the equipment of the individual psychotherapist, is involved. Also necessary are the skills of the educator, interpreter, scientist, man of action, exemplary model, moral leader, dramatist, artist, and teacher of specific social and technical skills, as well as the ability to recognize the relevance or irrelevance of a particular kind of contribution to the particular type of problem with which the system or subsystem of it is at any particular time concerned. Not only the direct utilization, but the teaching, distribution among staff persons and groups, coordination, and appropriate deployment in particular situations, of such skills in the therapeutic community defines in part the practice of sociotherapy. Sociotherapy, as the art of maintaining a social system in which the treatment of an individual patient can best occur, like psychotherapy, is a necessary part of the treatment of the schizophrenic person.

The existence of experiences in the therapeutic community, which interpenetrate with the work of psychotherapy, mitigates the tendency of the schizophrenic person to turn the office of the psychotherapist into an extension of his hidden, inner world.

Sociotherapy in the therapeutic community relieves the strain on the psychotherapy collectivity, which could not bear the entire burden of the heavy task of the socialization of the schizophrenic person.

It is especially difficult for the psychotherapist early in the work alone in the office, as he attempts to communicate acceptance to the patient and to form an alliance with him, not to reciprocate the patient's regressive expectations, provocations, or demands for gratification. The response of the group, the members of whom can back each other up and no one of whom is related so crucially to the patient, offers another line of support to the treatment effort, hopefully, for example, holding steady the expectations for responsible behavior, while neither harshly rejecting the patient as a result of his deviant behavior and ousting him from the group in one way or another so that he is inaccessible to influence, nor falling into the trap of expecting too little and permitting, rewarding, and reinforcing behavior that is part of his illness.

Under certain conditions, the patient may be able to accept being confronted in the group by frank responses to his behavior, when a similar confrontation by the psychotherapist upon whom he is coming to depend and who at that time means too much might be perceived as sadistic or punishing.

Solidary relationships in the therapeutic community maintain integration of the patient and treatment situation when his relationship with the psychotherapist is seriously strained by psychotic distortions, or exacerbations of anxiety or hostility. Similarly, of course, the psychotherapist may offer a base of solidarity when strain exists between the patient and the group.

Although, presumably, psychotherapy and sociotherapy, while different, are ideally mutually reinforcing enterprises and do not undercut each other, it may be that it is most advantageous to have them somewhat out of phase with each other. If both in the hospital community and the psychotherapy session, the patient's expectations are not being reciprocated and his way of life is being interrupted—in the community because otherwise some task cannot be accomplished, and in psychotherapy because otherwise the work of psychotherapy cannot be done—severe strain and a crisis in treatment, with flight or destructive acting out, may result. It might be best that when one collectivity is in a problem-solving, moving-toward-a-goal phase with all its concomitant strain, the other be in a social-emotional phase with emphasis on solidarity and the opportunity for tension-reduction. How to achieve this—and whether or not it occurs automatically under certain conditions—is problematical.

PSYCHOTHERAPY II

The psychotherapist interprets the nature of the patient's ego-operations as revealed by his behavior and reported inner experience in the here and now: in his everyday life in the hospital, and especially in his transactions with the psychotherapist. Memories of the past should be utilized when relevant to illuminate present experience, not explored *in vacuo*.

It becomes apparent that the patient uses mechanisms for coping with inner reality that are similar to those used for coping with external reality (Anna Freud 1942). Such ego-operations should be interpreted as constituting the schizophrenic way of life, which gradually—as its nature is clarified and its consequences exposed—becomes alien and unacceptable to the patient.

However, the psychotherapist should be careful to recognize with the patient and with him to safeguard positive, adaptive functions served by various defense mechanisms, usually, but not exclusively, those related to the neurotic mechanisms of defense: obsessive, compulsive, phobic and counterphobic, and hysterical character-formations. He should also be careful not to support rationalizations of pathological formations: for example, that regressive loss of control over feelings and behavior is somehow related to the attainment of greater freedom and is therefore therapeutic; that regressive loss of control over thought, and passive succumbing to disordered, autistic experience, is somehow related to creativity and is therefore to be sought; and that irresponsible acting out in the service of undisciplined gratification is somehow related to spontaneity and growth and is therefore a desired outcome of treatment.

The patient's ego-functioning is modified through his relationship with the psychotherapist. Unreliable primitive mechanisms such as introjection should be interpreted, and give way to imitation of, and eventually to mature identification with, the psychotherapist. The latter, to make this possible, should avoid concealing himself behind a bland, passive neutrality; he should be an active participant and feelingly present. When appropriate, he should share his way of thinking and responding to reality with the patient. Magical and distorted perceptions of the psychotherapist should be meticulously interpreted and counteracted as soon as they are recognized.

The patient's interpretations of, responses to, and attempts to master experiences of separation and loss should be a continuous theme in psychotherapy and investigated even in their tiniest manifestations, for example, around momentary interruptions during the session, the beginning and end of the session, weekend breaks, holidays, vacations. Mastery of the experience of the termination of treatment and achievement of a mature differentiation from the psychotherapist provide the test of these labors (Edelson 1963).

The psychotherapist, at first felt to be part of the patient, later becomes, if all goes well, a valued but separate ally, relatively dependable but with an existence of his own, a consultant whose opinions or views lose magical, determinative, absolute status and come to be considered as simply part of the facts of external reality to be taken into account.

The goal of psychotherapy should not be the ability of the patient to fulfill some particular set of conventional social expectations, whatever these might be, but to become able to grow again. It is the bringing of this process into existence, and the creation of the conditions that nourish it, that are the principal concerns of psychotherapy.

As the patient is able to care for and control himself, and manage his daily life without continual chaos, crisis, catastrophe, and self-destructiveness; as he increasingly learns to observe himself and his responses to inner and outer reality, and to report his observations openly to the psychotherapist; as he is able to tolerate increasing quantities of anxiety and so to acquire the psychological space to investigate with curiosity what he is like and how he came to be that way—then, and not until then, psychotherapy should become more and more an inquiry into the nature of his past experience: an integrative exploration of what has gone before that he is now ready to make part of who he is.

In the final period, the patient begins to have the experience of himself as one person, partly as he is able to put together various aspects of himself and feel they belong to him, and partly as he is able to integrate his different experiences of the psychotherapist: psychotherapist in office, psychotherapist in meeting, psychotherapist on street, psychotherapist with family. These become one man, an entire—not partial—human being.

It is as if coherence within is to some extent dependent upon experience with a coherent, integrated social environment. Such an environment is experienced as free of ambiguity about what is expected, inconsistencies of response, and covert splits among (and confusion, denial, defensiveness, and intolerance in) significant figures. Coherence within seems to be also dependent upon coherent relationships with at least some people in that environment who manifest warm, steady feeling and care.

SOCIOTHERAPY AND PSYCHOTHERAPY

Individual psychotherapy and the therapeutic community are both specifically directed, albeit in different ways, to the alteration of the same ego-impairments in a particular illness. They are integrated in the treatment of schizophrenia by the common requirement of both to focus on the patient's relation to external reality. The dynamics of treatment arise out of the conflicts between the imperatives of individual psychotherapy and of the therapeutic community—the requirements of external reality—and the schizophrenic way of life.

Since both the therapeutic community and individual psychotherapy focus on the patient's relation to external reality, the boundaries between these two enterprises in the treatment of schizophrenia should be easily permeable in both directions, with a ready exchange of information concerning the patient's experiences in different settings. Individual psychotherapy, then, may be viewed as essentially a dyadic collectivity among other collectivities within the therapeutic community, having a specialized task in relation to the internal state of the individual patient.

However, individual psychotherapy and sociotherapy are differentiated. The prepotent concern of the former is, ultimately, with the individual personality system and in particular with its internal integration. The prepotent concern of the latter is with the patient's situation: the therapeutic community as social system. The boundaries between the two enterprises need not necessarily in all treatment situations be highly permeable, with staff and information freely passing from one to the other. In fact, it might be useful in working with certain problems, with certain patients, or in certain settings, or in attempting to analyze problems arising out of the interaction between these two technical operations, to regard the individual psychotherapy enterprise as outside the therapeutic community, that is, as part of its situation, and conversely the therapeutic community as part of the situation of the individual psychotherapy enterprise. Each enterprise, that is, may be regarded as establishing conditions, providing resources, or supporting norms and values that determine decisions, or limit or enhance particular kinds of achievement, in the other.

Individual psychotherapy—perhaps especially as it begins to focus more and more upon the internal integration of the personality—and the therapeutic community are not necessarily or even ideally acting in concert, but may be in phase or out of phase with each other. Some out of phaseness between the two enterprises, in fact, as has been pointed out, might be optimal, one providing a base of solidarity at a time the other is pressing forward. How is this to be achieved?

In any event, the relationship of these two enterprises—whether or not they will in particular situations facilitate or interfere with each other—is certainly more problematical than the utopian one usually imagined. The very difference of the foci of psychotherapy and sociotherapy means that in the same situation one is likely to give priority to consequences for a particular individual personality system and the other to consequences for the social system involving the interactions and welfare of many individuals; the difference in the hierarchy of priorities of the two enterprises can be a source of strain between persons representing them. In addition, if both enterprises press at the same time for the achievement of their own particular aims—insight, for example, in individual psychotherapy and task-accomplishment or the solution of social problems in the therapeutic community—strains develop within the patient in both areas because of the interference with his schizophrenic way of life. Each enterprise may then (often covertly encouraged by the patient) blame the other for upset and disruption in treatment.

Further clarification of such problems as these depends upon providing in subsequent chapters a theory of groups and a theory of organization as a foundation for sociotherapy.

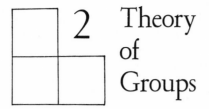

2 Theory of Groups

Sociotherapy focuses upon and operates with a social system rather than a personality system; the life of a group—a group is constituted by what individuals share—rather than the life of a single individual; the situation or external reality in which a person acts rather than his inner world. As a foundation, sociotherapy requires a theory of the social system, and of the articulation of social system and personality system.

With regard to the latter problem, psychoanalysis has much to offer. Sigmund Freud (1921, 1923) developed the concept of a superego formed by identification with social objects; this process involves the internalization of the values and norms of society such that these, in fact, become constitutive elements of the personality system and the basis of its articulation with the social system. As Parsons has pointed out, Freud's view of the ego as a precipitate of abandoned or renounced object-cathexes (Freud 1923) implies a generalization of this process of internalization by which the superego is formed. Patterns other than moral values and norms—for example, patterns of instrumental beliefs about reality or patterns of expressive symbolizations such as may be involved in the development and expression of feelings—may also be internalized as a result of social interaction and identification with social objects and as such constitute other aspects of the ego than the superego (Parsons 1964).

Other lines of psychoanalytic thought contribute to

the understanding of the articulation of personality and social system. Anna Freud showed that the ego utilizes measures in dealing with external reality that are parallel to defenses against aspects of inner reality (Anna Freud 1942). Reich discussed the ego's defensive operations as these are manifested not only in ego-alien symptoms and resistances to free association but in action, in an ego-syntonic way of life (Reich 1949). Hartmann described the ego as an organ of adaptation to a complex psychosocial reality, as well as an organ of defense; even its defensive operations may have adaptive value. The ego must be viewed in terms of achievement as well as conflict; in Hartmann's work, psychoanalysis explicitly extends its interest to action as well as intrapsychic events (Hartmann 1958, 1964). Erikson concerned himself with the particular psychosocial reality in which the ego develops and functions —the relation between society, the family, and the individual being one of interdependence and mutual regulation. He emphasized the importance of object-relations and techniques for dealing with them in development and the significance of the integration of membership in various collectivities for giving meaning to experience (Erikson 1950). Fairbairn based his theory of development upon the vicissitudes of the ego's early object-relations: the internalization not only of dichotomized representations of the object but of relations with objects, such that these come to form the structure of the ego (Fairbairn 1952).

However, despite these contributions, in much psychonanalytic writing and certainly in the popular misconceptions of psychoanalytic theory, external reality is synonymous with and totally comprised by conditions or obstacles which frustrate the aims of the individual personality. In this oversimplified view, such aims are determined by physiologically derived id-strivings, impulses, and wishes—rather than shaped primarily by values and beliefs learned in a social milieu and drawing upon sources of libidinal, aggressive, or neutral energy in the physiological organism. External reality is conceived to be merely a constraint upon, and at war with, the id.

Parsons, of course, on the contrary, and congruent with psychonanalytic contributions previously cited, emphasizes the significance of the internalization (within individuals) of value patterns shared by individuals (i.e., institutionalized in groups), and, therefore, of membership in collectivities and identification with social objects, for the development and structure of personality. In his case, this view of personality has its point of departure in a complex, systematic theory of the social system itself.

Parsons' seminal work, *The Structure of Social Action* (1937), is a closely reasoned, intricate argument seven hundred and seventy-five pages long. This volume is surely one of the most brilliant, significant, and perhaps relatively neglected integrations of theoretical-historical developments in the social sciences. It is interesting that apparently some, at least, of Parsons' critics (Black 1961) are unfamiliar with or do not refer to this early work of his. In it Parsons emphasizes the importance of understanding a man's theoretical formulations in terms of historically persistent issues, the controversies that claimed his attention, and the positions to which his own is a reaction. Similarly, the development of Parsons' own thought throughout the next three decades can hardly be understood without referring to his own analysis at the beginning of this period of the issues and theories, divergencies and convergencies, to which his own thinking is related. What comes later is in many ways an unfolding of what was immanent in first one, then another aspect of this early work.

Woodrow Wilson is reported to have said shortly before his death, "The world is run by ideals. Only the fool thinks otherwise."[1] That in somewhat overstated form is the gist of Parsons' *Structure of Social Action:* that normative elements or values constitute an indispensable, independent conceptual element in any theory attempting to explain social processes. A voluntaristic theory of action, including necessarily the subjective intentions of actors (whether these be persons or collectivities), is contrasted with positivistic and idealistic theories of action. In the positivistic theory of action the only orientation to the situation is through scientifically valid empirical knowledge, and the end and normative elements tend to be excluded or assimilated into the situation. The significant subjective element in determining action becomes valid empirical knowledge; or the significant subjective elements in determining action become unscientific, that is, error or ignorance. If normative elements are admitted, they are assumed to be random. In the idealistic theory of action nonsubjective elements (means and conditions) tend to disappear, and action becomes an emanation or expression of normative elements; rationality is irrelevant as a subjective element; phenomena are symbolic modes of expression or embodiments of meaning; and the schema *meaning-expression* replaces the schema *means-end.* In the voluntaristic theory of action, the normative elements that guide goal-seeking processes do not however determine absolutely their course (as Wilson's statement might suggest) but rather interact and are interdependent with nonnormative elements such as the means and conditions constituting the actor's situation. In opposition to positivistic theory scientific valid knowledge does not exhaust the significant subjective aspects of action; when subjective elements do not fit this category, it is not explicable only in terms of ignorance and error or of the dependence of such subjective elements upon nonsubjective elements. Within actors there is obligation or commitment—the action of which is independent of external sanctions—to expend effort to overcome obstacles to realize ideals or actualize values: thus, the term voluntaristic. The emergent property constitutive of a society is the existence of a common, more or less integrated, system of ends or values shared by its members.

The theory of action has been developed by Parsons and his colleagues in a series of works over a number of years.[2] The following ideas are of central importance: the conception of a system of action; the view of the system of action as boundary or

---

1. *The New York Times Book Review*, November 13, 1966, p. 7.

2. The theory of action is discussed in the following works: The historical emergence of this theory from the work of such men as Pareto, Durkheim, and Weber, and its relation to other theories is described in Parsons (1937).

The theory itself is developed in the following works: Parsons 1951; Parsons *et al.* 1951; Parsons and Shils 1951; Parsons 1953; Parsons, Shils, and Bales 1953; Parsons and Bales 1955; Parsons and Smelser 1956; Parsons 1959; Parsons 1961a; Parsons 1961b; Parsons 1964. A concise statement of a late form of the theory of action is to be found in Parsons 1960b.

Applications of the theory in diverse empirical realms are described in the following, as well as in some of the preceding works: Parsons 1954, 1957; Parsons and Fox 1958; Parsons 1960a.

equilibrium maintaining; the differentiation of four subsystems of any system of action—that is, adaptation, goal-attainment, integration, and latency (pattern-maintenance and tension-management).

These four subsystems essentially derive from the four conceptual elements that define action as a frame of reference: the situation (means and conditions); the actor's goals or ends; integrative elements, such as norms; motivational commitments of energy or effort to actualize patterns of values or value-orientation through the attainment of ends. Each subsystem has a different function or aim essential to meeting a particular requirement of the system. That is, each subsystem is concerned with solving system-problems having to do with a particular aspect of action: definition of, adaptation to, or mastery of a particular situation; attainment of object-relations that are ends in themselves; integration of relations between parts of the system; maintenance of patterns, and commitments to these, within parts of the system. Structures in a system of action may be understood in these terms; also, phases in the process of action.

Each subsystem of a system of action may itself be differentiated into four further sub-subsystems. The aim or function of each of these sub-subsystems, however, is defined in reference to the aim, function, or goal of the subsystem itself rather than in terms of the requirements of the entire system.

The four fundamental subsystems are theoretically distinguishable but not necessarily, with reference to particular empirical phenomena, coordinate to particular concrete entities. The subsystems are conceived to be interdependent, with varying outputs and inputs from and to each other. Such subsystems, also, compete for resources and commitment; their ends or values conflict in seeking priority. The relationship between these four subsystems, in other words, determines complex equilibria-states of the system, in the same way that the relationship between subsystems of the personality do (as formulated by psychoanalytic theory). The "existence" of these four subsystems as structures or processes in particular empirical phenomena (of course, they do not exist in the phenomena but are only conceptual inventions useful in ordering them) is guaranteed insofar as the assumption that a particular empirical system can indeed be heuristically viewed in the frame of reference of action as defined is confirmed.

THE NATURE OF THEORY

All theory is an expression of the passion to join the many into one. Some thousands of years ago, such yearning achieved monotheism. In art it is responsible for the subordination of content to form, the search for resemblance, and the ubiquity of metaphor. In politics it results in order and the triumph of union over civil strife. In the human being it produces a coherent sense of identity. In science the desire for integration is manifest in the attempt to comprehend the most diverse phenomena within one general system of concepts.

No set of concepts includes all the phenomena. A theory is distinguished as much by what it excludes as it is by what it includes. Any set of concepts helps to explain some aspects of the variegated, ever changing, complex, many-sided, concrete, empirical reality, but not all aspects. This is true even of one so useful as the conceptual framework involving particles of mass in space-time, which is able to encompass much of experience but not all. A conceptual framework is never the same as, nor should it be confused with, the concrete reality for some aspects of which only it is designed to account.

Theory is not necessarily induced only from observation of the particulars of empirical phenomena. Man is free to create ideas, and systems of relationships between ideas, without concern for their applicability to empirical reality, just as he delights in creating sounds before these are linked with determinate meanings.

In fact, a theoretical system, insofar as it consists merely of formal concepts (those not coordinated with aspects of empirical reality) and the propositions stating relationships between such concepts, may develop or exist independently of interest in empirical reality. Pure mathematical systems are examples.

Ultimately such a formal theoretical system may be discovered to fit (by a process of coordinating formal concepts to concepts representing aspects of empirical reality) an empirical system consisting of interrelated aspects of empirical reality. If the fit is good, the formal theoretical system and empirical system are structurally homologous. The fit of non-Euclidean geometry to empirical reality is an example.

To paraphrase Einstein: the relation of theory to sense experience is like a wardrobe number to an overcoat, not like soup to beef (Einstein 1950, p. 64).

Einstein has also stated the epistemological position relevant to such a view of theory.

> [The scientist] accepts gratefully the epistemological conceptual analysis; but the external conditions, which are set for him by the facts of experience, do not permit him to let himself be too much restricted in the construction of his conceptual world by the adherence to an epistemological system. He therefore must appear to the systematic epistemologist as a type of unscrupulous opportunist; he appears as *realist* insofar as he seeks to describe a world independent of the acts of perception; an *idealist* insofar as he looks upon the concepts and theories as the free invention of the human spirit (not logically derivable from what is empirically given); as *positivist* insofar as he considers his concepts and theories justified *only* to the extent to which they furnish a logical representation of relations among sensory experiences. He may even appear as *Platonist* or *Pythagorean* insofar as he considers the viewpoint of logical simplicity as an indispensable and effective tool of his research (Einstein 1949, p. 684).

Parsons' theory of action is a general system theory. As we have seen, systems of action (personality systems and social systems) are characterized by intentionality or goal-seeking. The essential process, governed by normative or value elements, is the attainment of goals by an individual or collective actor through the use of means, and adaptation to conditions, existing in the situation of the actor. In this process the actor is oriented to future states (which as ends have value) involving the relationship of the acting system to objects in its situation. The frame of reference is comprised by the conceptual elements situation (means and conditions), ends, norms (integrative arrangements), and values.

Parsons makes this theoretical model explicit, deriving its concepts from a definition of the properties of any system of action. Then, throughout his many empirical and theoretical works, he seeks to apply the consequences of logical operations with the conceptual elements of the model to empirical systems assumed to have homologous properties: that is, personality systems and social systems.

A more detailed formulation on theory, general system theory, and formal models is presented in appendix A.

Group versus Individual

It is true that "group" is an abstraction, but so also is "individual" (as opposed to "social"). No concrete human being is empirically observable as a social human being apart from individual aspects of himself. Nor is any concrete human being ever empirically observable as an individual apart from the precipitates of his membership in groups. Psychological and social systems are not only logically homologous theoretical entities but are also inseparably interpenetrating aspects of any concrete social or individual entity.

A VARIETY OF GROUPS

A bewildering variety of groups waits to be encompassed by one conceptual framework. A group getting together every Friday night to bowl; actors on stage performing a play; an orchestra and string quartet; a choir; a street-corner gang; a political party rally; a technical staff meeting in a factory; a professional or administrative staff meeting in a hospital; a court deciding guilt or innocence; legislators debating laws; a small unstructured training group at a group relations conference; a cabinet meeting; a therapy group in a prison listening to a member's dream; students in a classroom learning mathematics or history; a congregation worshipping; members of a family, going off to work and school, at supper, in the garden, in their beds: is there one conceptual framework to explain all these?

At present a variety of concepts, by no means members of one conceptual system, are used to describe and analyze group phenomena: formal-informal, power structure, prestige, status, role, communication network, information flow, sociometric choice, authority, organization, community, face-to-face group, culture, tradition, norms, in-group, out-group, clique, consensus, decision-making, leadership, laissez-faire, democratic, authoritarian, basic assumptions, fight-flight, pairing, dependency, work group, projective identification, introjected objects, psychotic anxiety, common group tension, required and avoided relationship, competition, cooperation, collaboration, sibling rivalry, resistance, transference, wishes, fears, cohesiveness, goal, valence, barrier. Some concepts appear especially useful for describing one kind of group or group process; other concepts another kind. What concepts might be most widely applicable?

Much group theory is derived from experience in, or is applicable to, one but not all of the following: small face-to-face groups with relatively simple structure and ambiguous goals; more highly structured groups with definite tasks; or organizations with extremely complex structures and a hierachy of specific goals.

The following theory of groups is intended in its complexity to be applicable to empirical systems of widely disparate size and character in which many different kinds of structures and processes are involved (if in no other way than in their relative absence). In other words, in these empirical systems basic concepts of the theory and the relationships between these concepts have applicability but different values.

The following examples, which will be analyzed after the presentation of the theory, are not meant to validate these ambitious hopes for the theory—only to illustrate the possibility of their actualization. The validation or invalidation of claims for the theory depend not only upon further work by this writer but by many other investigators as well.

Example One: The People of Israel

Upon Mount Sinai, the Lord gave Moses the two stone tables of the law. The people of Israel, meanwhile, bade Aaron to make them a god, for they did not know what had become of Moses, who had brought them out of Egypt. Aaron collected their rings and made a golden calf; the people worshipped the calf as the god that had brought them out of Egypt. Feeling merry, they planned a feast.

The Lord, waxing wrathful, told Moses to go down to his corrupt, stiffnecked people, who had turned away so quickly from the path commanded them. Moses defended the people, but upon returning down Mount Sinai with the tables of the law, he heard noises not of war but of song and revelry. Then, seeing the calf and the dancing, he became angry, broke the tablets, took the calf, smashed it, ground it up, mixed it with water, and made the people drink the mixture.

"Whoever is on the Lord's side," he called, "stand with me." These he commanded to slay the rest. Then he prayed the Lord to forgive the people.

The Lord said, "Now go, lead the people to the place of which I have spoken to you, the land flowing with milk and honey." The Lord again hewed the two tables of law and made a covenant with the people of Israel.

Example Two: A Patient-Staff Meeting

Members of a patient-staff meeting in a small psychiatric hospital discussed the fact that no one wanted to volunteer to work in a patient-staffed nursery school. Some people wanted to be paid, especially since they had experience in this field and felt the demands upon them were those of work. Hints appeared that conflicts over who was to be boss were somewhere in the background not yet to be discussed.

An additional theme in the meeting involved two patients about to be discharged. They were gloomy, bereft, as if the hospital were callously turning them out-of-doors, and hopeless about the future. Their friends were upset and angry at the hospital.

It had been decided the previous day not to have the usual good-bye party for them because everyone was so tense that the party would likely end up a drunken, morbid, vomit-splashed brawl. One patient said she was worried about the two who were leaving and felt badly that there would be no party; it seemed to her that the place was falling apart.

The two patients talked about the feelings that had led them to present themselves to others as victims of a cruel institution and about their concerns for the future.

Facts that seemed reassuring to the members of the group emerged: the two had an apartment they planned to share and had already paid the rent. One said she had been looking forward all year to a party.

Memories of other patients who had left and done well came up. One patient who had left the hospital but was visiting the meeting spoke of the fun she had cooking for herself; she requested people to come and help her paint her new apartment.

Gradually, the sense that being discharged from the hospital was the climax of much effort and the achievement toward which all in the hospital had worked entered the discussion; now, warm laughter and expressions of good will and wishes for good luck intermingled with sadness and farewell.

The members of the group decided to have a good-bye party; a number of patients who had been rehearsing a new rock-and-roll band volunteered they were "ready to go!"

Example Three: A Ship at Sea

Joseph Conrad, in his tales of the sea, luminously depicts group life. In his Preface to *The Nigger of the Narcissus* (Conrad 1947*a*) he writes about the artist: "He speaks . . . to the latent feeling of fellowship with all creation—to the subtle but invincible conviction of solidarity that knits together the loneliness of innumerable hearts, to the solidarity in dreams, in joy, in sorrow, in aspirations, in illusions, in hope, in fear, which binds men to each other, which binds together all humanity— the dead to the living and the living to the unborn" (Conrad 1947*a*, p. 706).

The vicissitudes of solidarity, "the solidarity in mysterious origin, in toil, in joy, in hope, in uncertain fate, which binds men to each other and all mankind to the visible world" (Conrad 1947*a*, p. 708), form the theme of this story.[3]

New crew members board the ship *Narcissus* under the critical but friendly glances of the old hands. The scene in the crowded forecastle where bunks are assigned, bottles and tobacco are shared, dire tales are told of the ship to disturb the uninitiated, meaningless curses are exchanged as men push and reel against one another, and the two groups become one, is a masterpiece of cinematography, the consummation of Conrad's avowed aim: "by the power of the written word, to make you hear, to make you feel—it is, before all, to make you *see*" (Conrad 1947*a*, p. 708).

Among the many men described are Old Singleton, the savage patriarch, Charley, a puzzled youngster, and Donkin, whom they all knew—"the man that cannot steer, that cannot splice, that dodges the work on dark nights; that, aloft, holds on franti-cally with both arms and legs, and swears at the wind, the sleet, the darkness; the man who curses the sea while the others work . . . [who] knows all about his rights, but knows nothing of courage, of endurance, and of the unexpressed faith, of the unspoken loyalty that knits together a ship's company." Last to arrive is the Negro, James Wait.

It soon becomes apparent that Wait is ill, perhaps dying. The presence of death,

---

3. Quotations in this section are from the story *The Nigger of the Narcissus* (Conrad 1947*b*), unless otherwise indicated.

an enemy within, disturbs the group. Song is dampened. Men feel vaguely guilty. A pie is stolen from Wait; suspicions spread. A sense that wickedness flourishes aboard ship shakes the confidence of men in each other and of master in crew. Nothing anyone does for the tyrannical, contemptuous Wait pleases him.

Donkin, envious of everyone's possessions, is left alone. Insolent, he is tamed one night by the mate with "decency and decorum, and with little noise." The men are silent about the loss of one of his front teeth: "The etiquette of the forecastle commanded us to be blind and dumb in such a case, and we cherished the decencies of our life more than ordinary landsmen respect theirs." Charley, disregarding the mores of the group, jokes about the tooth, receives a box on the ear by one of his friends, and is grieved by this rebuke. "We were sorry for him, but youth requires even more discipline than age."

The men continue to try to be decent to Wait, who sometimes works, other times not, and receives their offerings ungratefully. They oscillate "between the desire of virtue and the fear of ridicule"; they wish to save themselves "from the pain of remorse," but do not want "to be made the contemptible dupes of [their] sentiment."

Old Singleton asks Wait, "Are you dying?" Then, mildly: "Well, get on with your dying, don't raise a blamed fuss with us over that job. We can't help you." The men cannot decide whether Wait is dying or malingering; they cannot decide how to interpret the meaning of what they see. They alternate between skepticism and compassion. Once, the watch refuses an order to wash out the forecastle because "Jimmy objected to a wet floor." The mate reports to the captain that James Wait is "disturbing the peace of the ship."

Then the ship is struck by a gale. Confronted by danger from without, the men give hardly a thought to Wait. There is no leisure "for idle probing of hearts." The storm rages savagely, pitilessly; the ship's survival is in doubt. The mate refuses to go below: "I must see it out—I must see it out." Hour after hour, Old Singleton sticks to the wheel. "He wouldn't let go . . . He steered with care." When the men complain about the captain's risk-filled efforts to save the ship—"much he cares for us"—the mate retorts angrily, "Why should he care for you? . . . We are here to take care of the ship." Donkin grumbles rebelliously; the men shut him up. With the ship pitching, tossing, and threatening to founder, the cook struggles to provide coffee for the exhausted men: "As long as she swims I will cook! I will get you coffee."

However, as soon as the storm is over, trouble breaks out between the men and officers. The men are exhausted, burning and shivering, torn by the longing to be done with it and the wish to do things well, and confronted by wreckage and the destruction of their belongings. Each one faces also what has been disclosed of himself: Charley, his youth, his insignificance; Old Singleton, his age, his mortality; the cook, his heroism. Now Donkin becomes a leader of the men, playing on feelings of injustice and being unappreciated. Wait, the "fit emblem" of the men's aspirations, becomes the focus of their grievances. The men are kept from refusing duty only by the thought: "If we all went sick what would become of the ship?"

The cook, righteously zealous, divested of his humanity, attempts to save Wait from damnation by arousing him to an admission that he is dying. Wait in rebuttal insists on working. When the captain refuses to let Wait work apparently as punishment for malingering—compassionately not exposing his denial that he is dying—the men are close to mutiny; an iron belaying pin is hurled at the captain, who seemingly will not let a sick chap get well.

The mutiny is aborted by the captain who calmly identifies Donkin as the man who had thrown the belaying pin and speaks to the men "like a Dutch uncle" and by Old Singleton, who says: "I have seen rows aboard ship before some of you were born . . . for something or nothing; but never for such a thing . . . You can't help him; die he must."

Despite this confrontation by the truth, the falsehood that Wait will not die continues to poison the "moral tone of our world." Old Singleton's idea that as soon as the ship reaches land Wait will die is too painful, too unsettling, to be accepted.

Donkin, with a "desire to assert his importance, to break, to crush; to be even with everybody for everything; to tear the veil, unmask, expose, leave no refuge—a perfidious desire of truthfulness," determines to destroy the delusion that has bound the men and Wait together. Malevolently, he reveals to Wait his doom. Land is sighted; Wait dies. His "death, like the death of an old belief, shook the foundations of our society. A common bond was gone; the strong, effective and respectable bond of a sentimental lie."

The voyage ends. The ship arrives at her destination; the crew disperses.

PROBLEMS TO BE SOLVED BY A THEORY OF GROUPS

A theory of groups should account for the orderliness of group life. In social setting after social setting, the predictability of human behavior is obvious; as social scientists we take it for granted, focusing instead upon those relatively infrequent freak events that we did not anticipate and that seem too complexly determined to explain. Instead of pondering, for example, upon the remarkable fact that everyone behaves as expected, sitting around a conference table hour after hour, no one taking off his clothes or lying under the table, we are impressed rather with the idiosyncratic daydream of this one or itch of that one.

Furthermore, the patterns of interaction in the same group remain on the whole clearly the same through changes in membership and despite the bewildering variety of individual motivation within the members of the group. Various individuals are able to, and do, perform the same act or carry out the same group function, although each one may achieve thereby a quite different kind of personal gratification; the particular nature of this gratification does not seem an essential consideration in attempting to explain group life.

Criteria for the identification of group versus individual aspects of phenomena are not easily formulated. There is no "skin" or concrete boundary around the group as there is around an individual organism. *Group* is an abstraction, though it refers to empirical phenomena, in a way that *organism* is not. *Individual* is also such an abstraction, if one means the individual aspects of an organism divorced from all social aspects.

Perhaps, that which is idiosyncratic, unpredictable, and random in a social setting should not be considered an aspect of group but of individual phenomena. The emergent characteristic—the sine qua non—of group life may be in fact the existence of shared values that order patterns of action. What is shared by group members may include object-representations or definitions of the situation, expressive symbolization of goals, norms, or particular kinds of object-relations. To some degree, the nature of these will depend on the ideals, values, or patterns of value-orientation shared by members of the group.

The nature of such values helps to explain the form of group structures as well as characteristics of processes of collective action. Change in the values responsible for a particular order is an additional phenomenon to be explained by a theory of groups.

The individual personality system and the social system are two different systems. The phenomena of each is explained by a distinct set of concepts and laws. The boundary between them is marked by the necessity to pass from one such set to the other in accounting for phenomena. A personality theory or theory of groups might include, however, suggestions for a third set of concepts and laws linking these two systems, identifying the points of articulation between them: the specific ways in which they are interdependent and influence each other.

What is a Group?

A group is a system of interaction, the parts of which are interdependent. This interdependence is the effect of a system of values shared by individual members of the group. The internalization of, and commitment to, such a system of shared values is what distinguishes the social aspects of a person from his individual aspects.

Persons are members, or parts, of a group in their social aspects only; their individual aspects are part of the situation of the group and, therefore, do not enter into the constitution of it as a system. To regard a group (abstraction) as made up of persons (concrete entities) in both their individual and social aspects (abstractions) is likely to lead to conceptual confusion, making it difficult, for example, to distinguish what is part of, or within, the group as a system and what lies outside of it as part of the situation to which it adapts.

A group may be said to act when the following are true. The members of a group act together (or some member whom they have chosen to represent them acts) to expend effort (using means, adapting to conditions, and overcoming obstacles) to achieve ends. The allocation and direction of effort, the relation of the efforts of individual members to each other, the choice of means, and the choice of ends are shaped both by a system of values shared by the members of the group and by aspects of the object-situation in which the action occurs.

A Theory of Object-Relations

The present theory of groups is a theory of object-relations.[4] The simplest unit is two objects and the relation between them.

An object may be social, symbolic, or physical. A person, a group, a society are examples of social objects. Social objects as subjects or actors may "act." Action is a process, involving the expenditure of effort in an object-situation to achieve ends;

4. The general theory of action is essentially a theory of object-relations. See, for example, Parsons (1960b).

this process is guided by values or normative elements. A word, a painting, a value are examples of symbolic objects, which have arbitrary (as opposed to intrinsic) meanings for social objects. A chair, a desk, an automobile are examples of physical objects, which are parts of the object-situation that have intrinsic meanings for social objects. Systems of symbolic objects are not systems of action; neither are systems of physical objects. A concrete entity (person) may be in one of its aspects a social object, in another a symbolic object, and in still another a physical object.

"Loves," "runs from," "destroys," "possesses," "perceives," "next to," "represents" are examples of relations. A relation is that connection or association between objects defining them as temporary or permanent members of the same class or set. That is, the relation states the criterion by which certain objects are to be included in the defined class or set and other objects are to be excluded. The relation—not the objects—constitutes a particular class or set. The objects may change in every respect but the relation between them without dissolving a particular class or set.

Interaction

The parts of a system are interdependent: a change in one part of a system is followed by a change in another part of the system, that change followed by one in another part of the system, and that change in turn causing a change in the initially changed part of the system.

Interaction is action within a system of interdependent social objects. The action of each social object as subject or actor includes a relation with the other social object(s) in the system of interaction as a means or end. The action of one social object is contingent upon the expectations and expected responses of the other social object(s). These expectations and expected responses are derived from norms—injunctions obligating an actor to act in a certain way in a particular situation—shared by members of the system of interaction. Such norms are derived from a system of values. Action, therefore, in a system of interaction is ultimately guided by the system of values shared by the interacting social objects.

Values

A value is a proposition that an object-relation is desirable as an end in itself, without reference to its status as a means to any other object-relation, and that furthermore it is *more* desirable as an end than an explicit or implicit alternative object-relation. The notion of value is meaningless except in so far as it includes the existence of alternatives between which an actor has a choice; a value guides a choice by designating which alternative is preferable. An indication of preference between alternatives is an essential ingredient of the meaning of value.

A hierarchy of priorities and a degree of internal consistency characterize relations between values in a system of values. One value may have greater potency or priority than another. On another scale, one value is to one degree or another consistent or compatible with another value.

A value is ultimately derived from feelings or vague sentiments, from a system of propositions of existential meanings (beliefs about or interpretations of reality that are empirically unverifiable), or both.

Commitment to Values

Commitment by a person to a value may be said to exist when the value is associated with a sense of obligation to actualize it or bring it about in reality through action; the value, thus, guides the expenditure of effort in action. The amount of effort expended to overcome obstacles in order to bring the valued relation into being or to maintain it against efforts to change it is a measure of the intensity of commitment.

Internalization and Institutionalization of Values

Internalization of a value in a person has occurred when commitment to it exists and does not depend for maintenance upon external sanctions: pain or pleasure brought to bear by other social objects in the interest of creating and maintaining such commitment. Institutionalization of a value in a group has occurred to the extent that the value has been internalized by the members of the group. As has been discussed, a system of institutionalized values is the essential characteristic of a group, as opposed to an individual, entity.

Ends

An end is a state of affairs, a particular kind of object-relation, toward the attainment or maintenance of which action is directed. The end may be "ideal," that is, conceivable but not concretely existent. It may be "transcendent," that is, conceivable but never empirically observable. It may be an existent desired state of affairs that will change unless energy is expended to maintain it.

The Object-Situation

An object-situation consists of those objects outside an acting system constituting means, conditions, or obstacles to the achievement of an end. A means is a cultural, physical, or social object that can be used, changed, or transferred from one social object to another, to bring about a desired end. That is, a certain kind of relation to such an object is a precondition to the realization of the end. A condition is a cultural, physical, or social object that cannot be used or changed to bring about a desired end; it is a constraint upon the acting system, limiting from outside the latter the application of effort to achieve an end. An obstacle is any object in the object-situation constraining the use of a particular means so as to prevent the attainment of an end. If the obstacle is alterable, a relation to it (destroy it, influence it) may become a means to the end; if it is not alterable, it is a condition to which the acting system must adapt by abandoning the end or by circumventing the obstacle through the adoption of some other means to the end.

The Acting System

The acting system is an abstraction; it is only that aspect of a concrete organism or group that makes an effort, normatively guided, to use means to bring about a desired end. Other aspects of a concrete organism (e.g., capacities, the body) or of a group (e.g., characteristics of members in their aspects as individuals) may be means or conditions. A value (a cultural object in a cultural system of such objects) may be, if internalized or institutionalized, part of the acting system; if it is not internalized or institutionalized, it may be part of the object-situation, existing for the acting system as a means, condition, or obstacle to the attainment of an end.

Effort

Effort is the expenditure of energy by an acting system to bring about a desired end. A measure of total effort is the amount of energy expended through a period of time. The intensity of effort is the amount of energy expended per unit of time. In another of its aspects, effort has direction; that is, it is normatively guided, involving the expenditure of a quantity of energy to bring about an increment of the change in the object-situation or in the acting system—ultimately, in the relation between the acting system and its object-situation—necessary to achieve or maintain a desired end. In this sense, effort is analogous to a vector such as force: the amount of expended energy per unit of change in the direction of the end sought.

Boundaries of the Group

The group as a social object or social system has, as parts of its situation, or is bounded by, the cultural system, the personality system, and the behavioral organism. The cultural system is an organization of cultural objects. The personality system is an organization of subsystems of cognitive, cathectic, evaluative, and motivational dispositions. The behavioral organism is an organization of physiological processes, energy sources, and capacities for learning and behavioral response. The behavioral organism responds or behaves in the concrete physical environment. The physical environment (as is true also of other groups or social systems) does not directly bound the social system but only stands in relation to it through the "region" of (or through mediation by) the behavioral organism.

THE DIMENSIONS OF BOUNDARY AND TIME

There are two crucial dimensions in the preceding conceptual frame of reference. The first is implied by the distinction between the social object and its situation: in other words, the boundary between the acting system and its object-situation. The second is implied by the notion of action as a process of actualization, realization, or attainment in time.

Autonomy-Heteronomy

The distinction between the acting system and its object-situation gives rise to a variable or coordinate describing an alternative concerning the location or the "arena" of a process of action in an analogically "spatial" sense. This is the coordinate then designating the alternative, inner-outer, or as I shall call it to sharpen its value implications, autonomy-heteronomy. Action processes may occur entirely within the acting system (autonomy) or involve interchange across the boundary between the system and its object-situation (heteronomy).

In a hierarchy of preferences, priority may be given to the characteristics of the system itself as determinants of the course of action, and to the consequences to the acting system itself in the evaluation of a possible course of action (autonomy); or priority may be given to characteristics of the situation as determinants of the course of action, and to the consequences to the integration of the acting system and its object-situation—or to consequences to a larger acting system including the smaller acting system as part of itself (heteronomy). Preference may also be given to attributing causation either to characteristics of the object-situation or to characteristics of the system. On still another level of analysis, in deciding upon a definition of a state of affairs, priority may be given by the acting system to its own representation of itself as object or priority may be given to the representation of it by another system.

The Hierarchy of Control

A choice between these alternatives decides whether the acting system will constrain, cause, or control one or more of its bounding systems, or whether one or more of these bounding systems will constrain, cause, or control the acting system of which they constitute the situation. This leaves the question open concerning the hierarchy of control between cultural system, social system, personality system, and behavioral organism—ordinarily perhaps proceeding from first to last in the order stated, each one controlling or being the condition for processes in the next one. The actual hierarchy in a given circumstance might vary; this possibility needs to be left open, if problems of changes in the structure of a system (in addition to equilibrium processes involving balances of input and output in the exchanges across boundaries between systems) are to be studied.[5]

Potentiality-Actuality

The time aspect of action is represented by a variable or coordinate describing an alternative concerning when in a sequence of events a process of action occurs. This is the coordinate then designating the alternative, future-present, or as I shall call it, potentiality-actuality.

Action may be governed by reference to the future or it may be governed only by reference to an immediate state of affairs. Acquiring a means, for example, is significant because it may be used in the future to achieve an end. A goal attained, however, is the consummation in the present of a process of action; it is an actual end of action and has no necessary future reference.

Activities oriented to the future may be deemed preferable to consummatory ones. Building structures (reservoirs of potentiality) may be deemed preferable to partici-

---

5. Parsons takes a somewhat different position; he apparently assumes that the order of control—cultural system controlling social system controlling personality system controlling behavioral organism—is always the same (Parsons 1961b).

pating in actual processes that such structures make possible. The discussion indicates that the dichotomies means-end, structure-process, potential energy-kinetic energy, bound energy-mobile energy, as well as future-present and potentiality-actuality, are all aspects of the meaning of this coordinate.

A SPACE-TIME LOCATING FOUR FUNCTIONS

These two coordinates together give a space-time with four regions: a space in the abstract mathematical sense. These regions locate four types of functions, performed in any social system, in fact, in any system of action, including therefore personality systems, groups, and societies. Such a paradigm makes it possible to analyze both personality and social systems with the same concepts and therefore to compare events in the two systems and to describe their points of articulation.

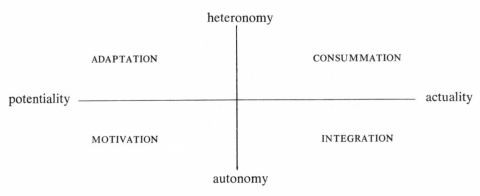

Fig. 1. The four functions of a system of action.

Function means a type of action leading to a particular kind of goal. The achievement of these particular four functions is a precondition of, or required for, the system's survival. "System-requirement" may be used as a synonym for "function" when these four functions are discussed. As indicated in figure 1, the four types of functions given by the two coordinates, autonomy-heteronomy and potentiality-actuality, are adaptation, consummation, integration, and motivation.

Such a functional analysis of a system of action, social system or personality system, is theoretically similar to the analysis of the personality system in psychoanalytic theory according to types of functions: the so-called structural theory involving the concepts ego, superego, and id, representing the classes ego-functions, superego-functions, and id-functions.

The Heteronomous and Autonomous Functions

Adaptation and consummation together comprise the task regions in which means are acquired and mastered to achieve ends. These are the heteronomous functions, a crucial aim of which is the integration of the system with its object-situation, with the systems bounding it, or with a larger system including it as a subsystem. Motivation and integration together comprise the regions in which the system itself is maintained as a distinctive configuration. These are the autonomous functions, a crucial aim of which is the integration of units of the system with each other and the maintenance of these individual units in some optimal condition.

THEORY AND THE TYPE OF GROUP STUDIED

Many differences in conceptual schemes concerning group processes seem to have to do with the type of group studied. If a so-called training group is formed, which has no task outside the group-maintenance regions, or if (as is also often the case with a therapy group) it is unstructured or its goals are ambiguous, then adaptation and consummation functions are likely to be neglected in the resulting theoretical formulations about its processes.

In these circumstances, the emotional and interactional aspects of group life are put under a microscope, as it were, and this is the advantage of such conditions for studying certain group processes; but by "focusing down" aspects of reality are overlooked. The application of propositions about groups derived in this way to the operation, for example, of a complex organization, in which task functions are highly differentiated and predominate, is likely to be inadequate and misleading. Similar difficulties also result, of course, when formal organizations are studied without considering the impact of informal groups and their processes within such organizations.

Similarly, rich data and important theoretical propositions were gained from the study of id-psychology in the early days of psychoanalysis, when what was investigated were the productions of a personality system whose ego-functions had been deliberately minimized through use of the reclining position, the reduction of external stimuli, and the ambiguity of the figure of the analyst, or through sleep as in the study of dreams. Later, an ego-psychology was developed, redressing the imbalance and leading to a more complete understanding of the total personality system as it usually functions especially in relation to external reality.

A Hierarchy of Priorities

Since the types of functions are defined by alternatives (potentiality-actuality, heteronomy-autonomy), which may also be value-alternatives, then in any group priorities may be established between these four functions. Where heteronomy and potentiality are valued most highly, adaptation functions will be given highest priority. Where heteronomy and actuality are valued most highly, consummation functions will be given highest priority. Where autonomy and actuality are valued most highly, integration functions will be given highest priority. Where autonomy and potentiality are valued most highly, motivation functions will be given highest priority.

Since all types of functions must be performed, however, if the system is to survive, a rigid imbalance in their performance will lead to great difficulties if not dissolution of the system. If, for example, truth (adaptation) is always preferred to harmony and the exclusion of incompatible elements (integration), or if truth is always sacrificed in the interest of harmony, then the system may not survive.

Group Dynamics

The dynamics of a group may be understood in terms of the conflicts between these four requirements or functions and how such conflicts are resolved. These conflicts arise when, to survive, the group must respond to changes within and without by the exercise of one or another of these four functions: the achievement of one or another of four types of ends. But the effective exercise of one function may (or seem to) be incompatible with or conflict (or seem to conflict) with the effective exercise of another.

In the theoretical model being described here, an ideal optimally functioning system, meeting all exigencies and performing all necessary functions, would include all value-alternatives somewhere within the system; these opposites would be integrated by relating each value-alternative to an appropriate function and situation.

TYPES OF OBJECT-RELATIONS

To define the four types of functions (adaptation, consummation, integration, and motivation), we must first detour to define types of object-relations. Since a type of function is the achievement of a particular kind of end, and ends in this theory are defined in terms of object-relations, we must have a way of classifying types of object-relations. The alternatives possible are in the type of relation between acting system and object, and in the way in which the object itself is regarded or defined by the acting system.

We may refer again to our two basic sets of system-alternatives, potentiality-actuality and heteronomy-autonomy. The first describes a dimension of which time is a crucial aspect; the second describes a dimension of which extent or boundary is a crucial aspect. Alternatives concerning types of relation may be subdivided into one set involving time or implying a process in time, the other set involving extent or boundary. Likewise, alternatives concerning how the object itself is to be defined may be subdivided into one set involving time or implying a process in time, the other involving extent or boundary. The alternatives concerning the type of relation are inhibition-discharge (time) and restriction-expansion (boundary). The alternatives concerning the way in which the object itself is to be defined are being-doing (boundary) and personal-impersonal (time).

To compare discussion of these alternatives with Parsons' discussion of pattern variables, and to prepare for subsequent references in this chapter to types of action, standards, and interests, the reader may want to review definitions paraphrased from Parsons' works on the theory of action in appendix B.[6]

---

6. I have changed the terminology used by Parsons (1960*b*). Autonomy-heteronomy is roughly equivalent to his internal-external; potentiality-actuality to his instrumental-consummatory; inhibition-discharge to his affective neutrality-affectivity; restriction-expansion to his specificity-diffuseness; being-doing to his quality-performance; personal-impersonal to his particularism-universalism. The reasons for such changes have to do with the following:

In my attempt to clarify the relation of these alternatives to, and derive them from, such axiomatic concepts of the conceptual framework as time and boundary, I tried to choose words that would suggest that derivation. Parsons' early derivation was from types of motivational orientation (cognitive, cathectic, evaluative) and types of value orientation (cognitive stan-

Inhibition-Discharge

An acting system may inhibit consummation of a relationship with a goal object in the interest, for example, of evaluating consequences (inhibition) or may consummate such a relationship immediately, for example, and without evaluation (discharge). At one point in time, an acting system may do one or the other; it cannot do both in relation to a particular object. Discipline, delay, evaluation (inhibition) or expression (discharge), the containment of energy in relation to an object (inhibition) or the release of energy in relation to an object (discharge), maintaining affective neutrality (inhibition) or expressing affect toward an object (discharge), may be given priority.

Restriction-Expansion

An acting system may relate to an object within the scope of specified boundaries, limits, or restrictions (restriction); or without regard to specified limits, by transcending limits, or in realms and ways beyond the scope of specific limits (expansion). The acting system may prefer to have a specific interest in an object (restriction) or many, diffuse interests in an object (expansion). Likewise, it may prefer to relate either to a specific aspect or part of an object (restriction) or to many aspects of an object (expansion). In the former case, the part not the object is important and the same part in any object would do; in the latter case, the whole object, not any specific part, is what is important. Similarly, an acting system may prefer either a contractual relation with an object specifying mutual obligations and rights (restriction) or a general attachment to an object with commitment to a plurality of unspecified, even unforeseen responsibilities, rights, and ties (expansion).

Being-Doing

An acting system may classify or define an object in terms of the object's immanent or inner qualities, those attributes the object does nothing to attain (being); for

---

dards, appreciative standards, moral standards). The alternatives were essentially choices between these. I do not believe that his alternatives for classifying objects were derived strictly from axiomatic concepts of the theory of action. See Parsons and Shils (1951, fig. 2, p. 248).

It was not until later that he saw that the set of alternatives self-orientation and collectivity-orientation as the axis internal-external was superordinate to the four other sets of alternatives. At this time he added another superordinate axis, instrumental-consummatory (Parsons 1960b).

He did not, however, revise his original derivation of the pattern variables, which as I have indicated in this chapter are derivable from the two superordinate axes; these in turn are related to the two fundamental aspects of action—that it is a process of actualization in time and that it involves a basic distinction between an acting system and its object-situation. Relations between the acting system and its object-situation are focused either upon the type of relation sought by the acting system, one set of alternatives now having to do with time and one having to do with boundary, or upon the definition of the object-situation, again one set of alternatives now having to do with time and one having to do with boundary.

It has also been my experience that people have great difficulty remembering Parsons' terms and making them their own; I wanted to choose words that would more directly indicate their meanings. In addition, I wished to find words that would be somewhat more natural and easier to use than Parsons' in explaining particular empirical phenomena in which I am interested.

example, sex, age, family membership, given statuses. In other words, the object regarded is categorized in terms of being, not doing, in terms of what it is, not what it does; or an acting system may classify or define an object in terms of the object's performances or achievements, past, present, or potential (doing)—its behavior in relation to what is outside itself. The object is categorized in terms of doing, not being, in terms of what it does, has done, or can do, not what it is. As value-alternatives, one or another of these alternatives is preferred or given priority by the acting system.

The alternatives activity-passivity, at least insofar as one gives priority, in regarding oneself, to what one achieves or to what one is, to being or doing, provide an aspect of the meaning of this set of alternatives. However, activity-passivity, as commonly used, have many meanings (besides, of course, the phenomenal one of action-inaction): whether what is at issue is action, the aim of which is to realize the ideals and values of a personality system, or behavior, which is determined solely by the situation or the physiological organism; whether causation springs from, or is attributed to elements, within or outside the system (autonomy-heteronomy); whether or not assertion of the intentions of the acting system takes priority over the integration of such intentions with those of other systems or simple submission to the intentions of other systems (autonomy-heteronomy); whether or not evaluation of consequences occurs in the sequence of events leading to consummation (inhibition-discharge); whether energy sources are adequate or deficient; whether motivational commitment is adequate or deficient. Probably, activity-passivity, in the latter two meanings, are best applied to the problem of balance-imbalance in the ratio of input and output, to problems of interchange, between subsystems. Determining the relation between the performance of one function (one subsystem) and the performance of another function (another subsystem) is the theoretical problem.[7]

Perhaps no other concepts are currently used in such confusion by psycho-analytically oriented psychotherapists staffing psychiatric hospitals. These concepts, especially since they are often used to evaluate the participation of patients in the social milieu of the hospital, require more than most the perspective of a sociological as well as a clinical frame of reference.

Rapaport wrote about activity and passivity metapsychologically not phenomenally; that is, he was describing the ego's functioning in relation to id-tension, discharge processes, and external stimulation (Rapaport 1958). The metapsychological meaning of activity and passivity tends to get confused with the meaning active or passive behavior or the classification of patients in terms of degree of health or illness, that is, of deviance. A person who is behaviorally passive may be in an internal state of ego-activity, and a person who is behaviorally active may be in an internal state of ego-passivity. Furthermore, deviant behavior may be either active or passive: compulsive performance (dominating others, compulsive enforcement of norms) and alienation (rebelliousness, aggressiveness towards social objects, incorrigibility) on the active side, and compulsive acquiescence (submission to others and perfectionistic ritualistic observance) and passive alienation or withdrawal (compulsive independence, evasion) on the passive side (Parsons 1951).

---

7. Parsons (1951) uses the concepts activity-passivity in formulating types of deviance. However, he does not relate this set of alternatives to axiomatic concepts of the theory of action nor does he derive it from other sets of alternatives—the pattern variables.

When activity or passivity is used to discuss a patient's participation in the social milieu of a psychiatric hospital, what is often involved is a value-orientation toward persons as social objects. A value-choice may be made in each specific interaction between orientation to a person in terms of his qualities and attributes or in terms of his performance or achievement—between being and doing. The expectation in the latter case is that the person is committed to the achievement of goals and expressive performances; and, therefore, orientation to him is in terms of his effectiveness or success in such achievement.

To orient to individuals in terms of doing rather than being is a dominant characteristic of American culture. Clinicians tend usually to speak within the framework of this value-orientation rather than metapsychologically. The usual concept of mental health and illness is culturally relativistic; mental health tends to be equated with capacity for achievement or performance: this, in fact, appears to be the basic social meaning of any kind of illness, physical or mental, in our culture.

Activity also has a significance in the discussions of hospital staffs other than either interest in ego-activity or an orientation to actual performance or achievement. It is, in addition, a symbol of success; to this extent, there may be relative indifference to the instrumental relation of a particular activity to the attainment of specific goals. In a hospital whose goals have to do with treatment and where many of the evidences of progress in psychotherapy (both process and result) are hidden from view, it is difficult for many members of the hospital community to judge the patient's achievement and, therefore, whether or not the hospital is accomplishing its goals. Such judgments are especially important to those who live and work in a hospital milieu, in order for them to be able to respond with appropriate approval or disapproval in the presence or absence of such achievement, to derive a sense of satisfaction in their own part in contributing to the achievement of the hospital's goals, and to maintain hope for the possibilities in their own future. A nurse might state, for example: "If patients are not active (participating in the activities of the hospital program, working, taking on responsibilities), I lose an important index that patients are actually getting well in the hospital and, therefore, a most important source of my own job satisfaction."

The difficulty with activity as a symbol of achievement (as the possession of money might represent success in the extended culture) derives from the imperfect relationship between behavioral activity and achievement in psychotherapy. If there is a good match, things go smoothly as far as social interaction in the hospital community and the evaluation of the patient's participation there are concerned. If there is an imperfect match, strain results. An additional difficulty for the hospital community derives from the fact that the possession of activity as a symbol of success threatens to cause scarcity of therapeutic attention, which is actually what patients who have come to a hospital to get well are likely to regard as the prepotent significant possession; therefore, such activity may be eschewed.

Impersonal-Personal

An acting system may classify or define an object in terms of its intrinsic properties, irrespective of any relationship in time with the acting system (impersonal); or in terms of its immediate relationship with the acting system (personal). For example, "a mother" is an impersonally regarded object, "my mother" a personally regarded one. The acting system may choose to view the object abstractly, timelessly, as a member of a general or universal class (impersonal); or as a member of a particular, perhaps unique, or special class defining an actual relationship in time between object and acting system (personal). Priority may be given to a consideration of characteristics of the object having no dependence upon, or relation to, the attitudes or existence of the acting system—what exists independently and separately, what is differentiated and individuated (impersonal); or to a consideration of characteristics of the object depending upon the object's belonging with the actor to a particular common inclusive system—what is presently shared, fused, or incorporated (personal). Involvement requires a personal value-orientation, individuation the possibility of an impersonal value-orientation.

FOUR GROUP-FUNCTIONS

If we place each alternative determining a type of relation or definition of an object in the paradigm of figure 1, according to a position on a time dimension (horizontal) or a boundary dimension (vertical), then certain alternatives are associated with each one of the four types of functions, as in figure 2.

Each sector of the paradigm in figure 2 may be considered to represent the shared values of a group, of a specialist subgroup of a larger group that is divided into concrete subgroups with differentiated functions, or of an abstract subsystem of an undifferentiated group that is conceived to move from one subsystem to another. These values specify for each function the type of relation between acting system and object to be sought and the way in which the object is to be regarded or defined by the acting system. For example, we may have a group whose members are most deeply committed to adaptation values (work group), a subgroup that performs adaptation functions for a larger inclusive group (fact-finding committee), or a group that at a particular moment in time performs adaptation functions (any group currently preoccupied with mastering means or adapting to conditions necessary to achieve a given end). For convenience in the following discussion we shall use the terms "adaptation group" or "adaptation group-function" to refer to any of these three cases.

Each group (adaptation group, consummation group, motivation group, integration group) has at least four components, related to the four basic components of action effort, norms, object-situation, and ends. These four components, which are derived from the shared value system of the group, are (1) shared motivational commitments; (2) shared integrative norms or standards; (3) shared adaptive definitions of the situation or shared object-representations; and (4) shared meanings or significances of goal-objects.[8]

---

8. The term Consummation Group or consummation group-function roughly corresponds to Parsons' term goal-attainment. I wished to differentiate a certain kind of goal-attainment, that is, consummatory, from other kinds of goal-attainment involving relationships with the goal-objects characteristic of Motivation, Adaptation, and Integration Groups.

The term Motivation Group or motivation group-function roughly corresponds to Parsons' terms pattern-maintenance and latency. Latency is a confusing term, suggesting as it does a

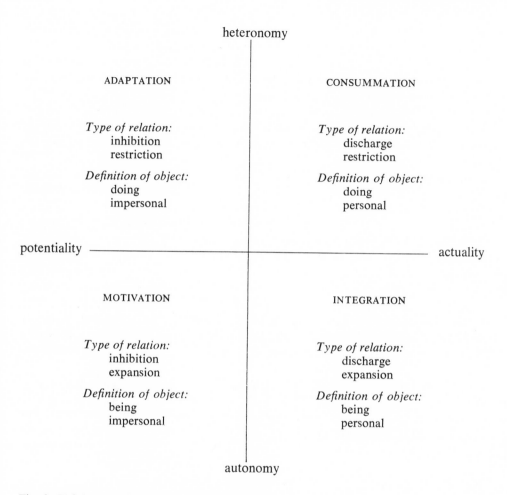

Fig. 2. Values associated with the four functions of a system of action.

The Motivation Group

The Motivation Group is in the region autonomy-potentiality. The primary inter-est is in the condition of units and structures constituting the group itself. Here, values at the most general level are institutionalized: values that are neither situation-specific nor function-specific but from which situation-specific, function-

---

process occurring outside group life. Although what goes on in the Motivation Group is focused on the individual unit as a system in itself (thus, on intrapersonal conditions such as states of conflict, tension, or value-internalization), nevertheless, active observable group processes are clearly involved in the creation, maintenance, restoration, or alteration of these conditions.

The term motivation suggests more directly than the term pattern-maintenance that the creation, maintenance, or restoration of patterns in a group has especially to do with the crea-tion, maintenance, and restoration of motivational dispositions: ways of orienting to an object-situation or, in other words, ways of thinking, enjoying, and evaluating that are linked to sources of energy and intention. See Parsons (1960b, 1961b).

specific norms are derived. The institutionalization of values in a group depends on the degree and extent of their internalization by individual members. The Motivation Group generates such internalization and copes with states or exigencies that might prevent or undo such internalization and lead to behavior deviating from the major values of the group. Such states and exigencies include inconsistency in the culture or value system itself, leading to strain within personality systems; states of dissatisfaction and conflict in personality systems; and states in the physiological or behavioral organism, such as illness and fatigue, that cut down energy resources available for the actualization of values in action.

Motivational commitments in the Motivation Group are dispositions to "believe" —to be committed to the actualization of internalized general values. Such dispositions include dispositions to "have faith in" values, or objects symbolizing these values: ultimate values cannot be justified by empirical-scientific demonstration.

In the establishment of such motivational commitments, energy resources are linked to values. Values are not simply perceived as facts in the external world but become constituents of personality systems. Such values are then associated with the sense of obligation to actualize them by expending effort, overcoming obstacles, using means, to achieve ends.

The members of the group are motivationally committed to relationships with objects that represent or symbolize the values of the group and therefore command respect and allegiance. Such objects include the group itself; social institutions and organizations; sacred, religious, cultural objects; charismatic leaders.

Inhibition is valued as a way of relating to objects. Discharge and gratification are subordinate to a disciplined consideration of the implications of, and consequences for, the group—its institutionalized values—of any course of action. Emotional intimacy is subordinate to awe and reverence; there is a sense of distance from the object.

Expansion is also valued as a way of relating to objects. The individual member's respect and allegiance, his faith in—and fidelity to—the institutionalized value system, are not limited or restricted, but rather have an all-or-none wholehearted quality. When values are internalized, the individual can be depended upon to follow wherever they lead and to accept their implications in any one of a multitude of unspecified concrete situations.

This does not exclude the possibility that for the individual personality system in relation to the group, the value institutionalized may be autonomy rather than heteronomy. That is, the individual may be expected by the group to give priority, in considering courses of action, to consequences for the personality system over consequences for the group, in other than a limited realm of action. Such a group regulates the bounds beyond which the individual cannot go, but within these bounds he is free to—is indeed expected to—consider his own interests primary. However, although the emphasis may be on individuality, freedom, autonomy, these values are themselves institutionalized and carry with them a sense of obligation to actualize them. To be individualistic in such a group clearly does not mean to be "against" the group, rather the reverse. In the same way, on the other hand, the value of heteronomy rather than autonomy may be institutionalized for the individual personality system; consequences for the group rather than for the personality system are to be given priority in considering courses of action.

If autonomy rather than heteronomy is institutionalized for the group as a system, consequences for motivation or integration group-functions or both are given priority over adaptation or consummation group-functions or both in considering collective courses of action. If heteronomy rather than autonomy is institutionalized for the group as a system, then the reverse is true. It is essential in an analysis of institutionalized values to distinguish for what system they are institutionalized.

Value-alternatives autonomy-heteronomy are linked to beliefs emphasizing, on the one hand, the opposition of group life to what is unique and individual in man—his needs and wishes—or, on the other hand, the indispensability of group life as a condition for the development and expression of human wishes and needs. The value of the Motivation Group—with the group not the personality system as the system of reference—is ultimately autonomy. The values of the group may be viewed as causative and are expected to be determinative, constraining the personality system and other systems bounding it and taking priority over the requirements of such systems.

Norms in the Motivation Group regulate the behavior of members of the group, especially the expression or manifestation of belief. Such norms are chosen in terms of relevance for maintaining the institutionalization of values, especially by integrating such values with beliefs concerning the meaning of existence and the nature of the universe. The ultimate standard is the good or the ideal. The expression or manifestation of beliefs is justified or normatively approved if it is linked with, derived from, or supports institutionalized values. In this group it is not people primarily that are the objects of integrative concern but rather cultural objects—values and beliefs or ideas concerning man, nature, and society—and the integration or harmonization of these with each other.

Members are bound not by feelings toward one another, but by their disciplined commitment to shared values and the beliefs linked with these. Their respect for one another on this basis is supposed not to fluctuate with ups and downs in personal feelings or as a function of specific rewards and punishments. Not what a man has done, does, or will do—rather his enduring beliefs are what is important about him. A high philosophical seriousness or religious fervor is the tone of the interactions between members of the group, as well as a sense of timelessness or of investment in some future state of affairs when ideals will be actualized.[9]

Generalized esteem and belonging, rather than specific approval, is the integrating response to him who is committed to the group's beliefs and values: he is "one of us." Generalized loss of esteem, rather than disapproval of specific "doings," is the response to him holding deviant beliefs and values. The persence of "evil," rather than criminal behavior, constitutes the integrative crisis of the group. If an indi-

---

9. Some of the phenomena from which Bion (1961) infers the Pairing Group (for example, messianic hope for a future utopia) might be in the present conceptual system characteristic of the Motivation Group.

Bion's conceptual system is not, I believe, adequate for the following reasons.

There is in it the bias of rational, utilitarian positivism: that man's behavior is understandable in terms of a model of action guided by "scientific" standards of rationality or departing from such standards of rationality due to ignorance and error. Ignorance and error in his system are due to unconscious processes.

His formulations tend to suggest that phenomena included under Pairing, Fight-Flight, and Dependency Groups (which in the conceptual system described in this chapter might be

vidual cannot be won over or redeemed from his state of alienation, then a casting into the shadows (elimination or isolation of the evil one) is a frequent response to such an integrative crisis.

Adaptation exigencies faced by the Motivation Group are events difficult to make sense of in terms of the institutionalized values of the group; the cognitive beliefs resulting from such experiences seem incompatible with, or imply values that seem to contradict, institutionalized values. An allocation of rewards and punishments, gratifications and deprivations, that does not seem to correspond with expectations derived from institutionalized values (a situation that is, to some degree, inevitable in any group) is an example of such an adaptive exigency. Why do some, who deserve, not get, while others, undeserving, get? Why me, not him? Why him, not me? The adaptive exigency is represented by the question: "What is the meaning of this?" Another adaptive exigency arises from inconsistent behavior by objects symbolizing institutionalized values, for example, by leaders or representatives of an organization. Such behavior may have its roots in inconsistencies in the value system itself.

These adaptive exigencies are represented in the group by existential interpretations of experience in terms of institutionalized values. Such interpretations require an impersonal, expansive view of experience.

Strains caused by adaptive exigencies may be resolved by a variety of means: the reconciliation of experience and values, or of inconsistencies in the value system, by rationalization, segregation, or other accommodative mechanism; attempts to change the situation so that it conforms to a greater extent with institutionalized values; more infrequently, the alteration of the institutionalized value system in the direction demanded by adaptive requirements, or by the elimination of inconsistent or incompatible elements.

Goal-objects symbolizing institutionalized values (the group itself, its charismatic leader, a social institution or organization, a sacred object) are defined in terms of their enduring immanent qualities as beings not doers, whose significance transcends any immediate personal relation. The leader of a Motivation Group cares nothing for the world or situation in which the group exists; he cares nothing for the per-

---

characteristic of Motivation, Consummation, and Integration Groups, respectively) are irrational rather than non-rational, pathological or dysfunctional rather than functional, and significant primarily in their opposition to the Work Group. In other words, work or rational instrumental action (in the present conceptual system the Adaptation Group or adaptation group-function) is the model by which all action is judged and the embodiment of cognitive standards to which or from which action either conforms or deviates.

In the theory of groups described in this chapter, all four group-functions are seen to be indispensable requirements of a social system. All four goals (albeit, each one may be given a different priority) must be achieved to some extent, at least, if a system is to survive.

Since Bion does not formulate his Groups, other than the Work Group, as functional, it is difficult in his framework to understand the relation of such groups to each other (except that three of them are opposed in their aims to the Work Group). It is also difficult to understand the process by which passage occurs from one group to another group phase. Later, in this chapter, attention is given to this problem in terms of the input into, or the output from, each group-function from, or to, other group-functions.

However, Bion was an excellent observer, and it is noteworthy that an attempt, such as the one described in this chapter, to develop a systematic theory of groups from an axiomatic conceptual framework should result in four categories that, to some extent, seem to include the phenomena subsumed by his own four categories.

formance of tasks dictated by the necessities of that situation; he cares only that the group fulfill an ideal or actualize the values he represents.

The outcome of a process of action in a Motivation Group, responding to adaptive and integrative exigencies, is a change in the meaning of such a goal-object, in the degree of respect and allegiance commanded by it, from what would have been had there been no action. One gains or loses "faith in" or "respect for" it. This outcome is indicated in part by the ratio of commitment and alienation in the group at the end of a process of action compared to what it was at the beginning.

Figure 3 is a paradigm representing the Motivation Group.

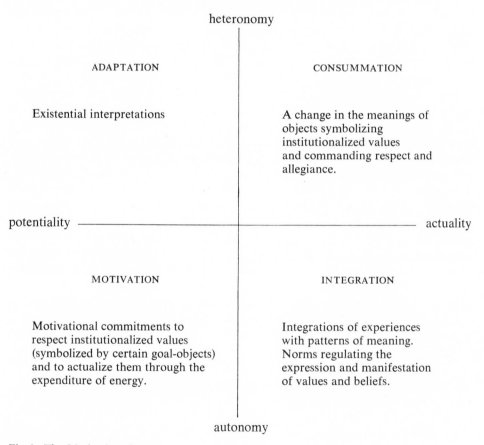

Fig. 3. The Motivation Group

The Integration Group

The Integration Group is in the region autonomy-actuality. The primary interest is in the present relations between members of the group and in the norms regulating such relations. In considering a course of action, such norms take priority over the requirements of, or integration with, bounding systems. The dominant attitude is that "we must be who we are, as represented by the characteristic pattern of relationships between us, in the face of any outer or inner threats to these internal arrangements."

Norms are situation-specific, function-specific derivatives of general values. They are injunctions concerning ways in which members of the group are to behave in relation to one another in specific situations and in achieving specific ends to which members of the group are committed. The Integration Group is primarily concerned with the generation and maintenance of such norms and the extent of their influence over actual conduct. It copes with exigencies undermining the integration of the group. Such exigencies comprise deviant behavior within the group in relation to norms or to one or more members of the group, the leader of the group, or the group itself. These exigencies may arise from the physiological behavioral organism (inability to learn or respond), from the personality system (states of deprivation and disaffection), and from the cultural system (changes in the state of knowledge requiring alterations in internal arrangements).

Motivational commitments in this group are dispositions to identify with objects representing the requirement to behave responsibly and morally. Commitment is to moral or responsible action, which is characterized by primacy of moral standards and evaluative interests. Evaluative interests include the cathexis of systems of values and norms, as well as of such activities as integrating, resolving conflict, and evaluating consequences.

Members of an Integration Group act responsibly; that is, they are governed in the choices they make by institutionalized norms. Identification involves the internalization of relationships with objects—that is, the internalization of patterns of interaction that are models of mutual (reciprocal and complementary) expectations and actions—together with the norms regulating these. Similarly, there are dispositions to love: in the sense of attachment to a social object affectively (discharge) and unrestrictedly (expansion) in a context of varied interests and sought satisfactions as well as a multitude of specified and unspecified rights and obligations. ("Love" in this sense does not include merely seeking and giving a specific gratification.) These are essentially dispositions to participate interdependently with others in seeking to achieve common ends or to actualize shared values. Members of an Integration Group want to be together and do things together, harmoniously, according to established patterns characterizing the group. Individual members value and internalize ways of relating embodied in actual relationships in the group.

Above all, the group seeks to maintain a state of solidarity, in which members feel that expectations are met in the group, that predictability and order are characteristic of experience in the group, that therefore goals are possible to achieve, that leaders are concerned with one's needs, and that one can rely on one's associates for support. The state of affairs dreaded and avoided is anomie or normlessness. Members feel others are indifferent rather than concerned. Apathy rather than hopefulness reigns, since norms have lost their power to influence conduct and therefore nothing is dependable, predictable, or orderly (Merton 1957).

According to the norms of the Integration Group, members ought to regard each other personally. A member of the group is important to others not because of any abstract, general attributes, but precisely because he belongs to the group; it is on this way of regarding a member of the group that expectations are based. Members ought not regard each other as, for example, merely useful for some specific contribution, but rather should be able to count on each other in many ways and in many contexts for help, support, and response.

Choices between alternatives for action in this group are made according to evaluative standards, specifying criteria of right and wrong. What is right and what is wrong, according to what evaluative criterion (e.g., consequences to an individual, consequences to the group), and under what circumstances, must be agreed upon; essentially, such agreements constitute the integrative norms of the group.

An atmosphere of moral judgment prevails. Approval and disapproval of specific behaviors in the here-and-now are the integrating, regulating responses to actions conforming to, or deviating from, group norms. A person deviating from such norms is likely to be regarded as criminal or mentally ill, in part depending on the decision that he may or may not be held responsible for his behavior, that he voluntarily chose to deviate or that his deviation resulted from conditions beyond his control. How to decide this kind of question always poses a serious dilemma for this group. Behavior deviating from group norms constitutes the integrative crises of the Integration Group. Control of such deviant behavior through various mechanisms is the specific task of the Integration Group.

Each type of group engenders its own kind of deviance. Motivation groups, failing to establish motivational commitments or to win respect and allegiance, may produce individuals who are excessively autonomous and alienated, who evade normative requirements and are hyper-independent in relation to social objects. The social object is regarded by the deviant individual impersonally, as outside any system to which he belongs and merely a part of his situation. The deviant individual himself "is" rather than "does," and tends to be passive or withdrawn. In a way, the deviant individual is a caricature of the distant sacred object that is supposed to command respect.

Integration groups, failing to establish solidarity or identifications, may produce anomic individuals, who observe norms ritualistically without any sense of their meaning, without any hope that such observance will lead to achievement, and who passively submit to, rather than identify with, social objects. The social object and deviant individual are seemingly part of one inclusive system. The deviant individual "is" rather than "does" and tends to be only passively compliant. In a way, the deviant individual is a caricature of the model, morally right object of identification.

Consummation groups, failing to establish gratifying relations, may produce deprived individuals who, unable to count on gratification, attempt to dominate social objects, righteously demanding compliance with norms, in order to wrest and secure the gratification that may not otherwise be forthcoming. The social object and deviant individual are part of one inclusive system. The deviant individual "does" rather than "is." By his behavior the deviant individual in a way mocks the gratifying object, who is supposed to perform gratifyingly in relation to him. "If you do not give to me, I will make you."

Adaptation groups, failing to provide impersonal doing means-objects which can be used to achieve ends, may produce a frustrated individual, who aggressively attacks social objects and incorrigibly flouts norms. The social object is regarded by the deviant individual impersonally, as outside any system to which he belongs and merely a part of his situation. The deviant individual "does" rather than "is." In a way, the deviant individual says of a social object which is supposed to be impersonally regarded in terms of its degree of usefulness: "I regard it impersonally as 'no use to me' and destroy it, without concern for moral or appreciative values, with regard only for standards of efficiency."

Individual deviance in this paradigm has been considered primarily from the point of view of the failure of social or group functions rather than personality system functions. Furthermore, the form of individual deviance is considered likely to be significantly determined by the dominant values of the very group function that has failed.

Deviance is not a matter of phenomenal conformity or alienation, but should be defined functionally, as behavior leading to a decrease in the extent to which values and norms are institutionalized in a group, or to some degree preventing such institutionalization. The effect of such behavior on others in the group, then, and on the degree to which values and norms are and remain internalized in the personality systems of others in the group, is what is crucial in a consideration of deviance.[10]

Mechanisms of control of deviant behavior also require the participation of each type of group. In the Motivation Group, the deviant or potentially deviant individual's tensions, dissatisfactions, and disaffections are accepted within limits in order to permit some expression of them, again within limits, in order to reduce their intensity and thus the likelihood that such intrapersonal conditions will lead to deviant behavior.[11] In the Integration Group, solidarity and support are offered. Desired behavior leads to approval and other positive sanctions, deviant behavior to disapproval and other negative sanctions. In the Consummation Group desired behavior leads to gratification and deviant behavior to deprivation. In the Adaptation Group desired behavior leads to access to desired means-objects and deviant behavior to their nonavailability.[12] The converse of these processes, of course, enter into those failures of each group which result in deviance, previously described.

Accommodations to deviant behavior include finding and providing an area for activity in which deviant behavior has some usefulness for the group and insulation

---

10. Parsons (1951) similarly describes four kinds of deviance (overconformity, ritualistic compliance, rebellion, withdrawal) categorized according to combinations of the alternatives activity-passivity and conformance-alienation rather than according to combinations of the pattern variables. Merton (1957) also describes four kinds of deviance (innovation, ritualism, retreatism, rebellion) comprising somewhat similar phenomena. He categorizes these kinds in terms of combinations of the alternatives acceptance or rejection of culture goals and acceptance or rejection of institutionalized means. The present chapter categorizes types of deviance in terms of the two sets of alternatives for regarding or classifying an object (personal-impersonal and being-doing) and relates the types of deviance to the four group-functions. Deviance in this framework has especially to do with problems in object-relations.

11. This is the tension-management function of Parsons' latency or pattern-maintenance subsystem (Parsons 1961b).

12. The view here is that Motivation, Consummation, and Adaptation Groups contribute outputs to the Integration Group that are crucial to the achievement of the latter's aims. Parsons, however, describes four mechanisms of social control (permissiveness, solidarity, refusal to reciprocate unacceptable demands for gratification, and manipulation of rewards) all of which he sees as belonging to the integration subsystem (Parsons 1951; Parsons, Shils, and Bales 1953; Parsons, Bales, et al. 1955).

of other members from influence by the deviant individual; for example, through education of them or by isolating him so that effects of his behavior are limited in scope.

Coercion and extrusion are extreme responses to deviant behavior. The first is costly and inefficient by comparison with internalization of shared values; the individual will continue to behave deviantly whenever it is expedient to do so; that is, whenever he can evade enforcement. The second results in a failure of integration and the loss of a member of the group.

Adaptation in an Integration Group requires the representation of the moral situation of the group; that is, moral evaluation of the current situation in terms of a system of norms. Members of the group, in defining the moral situation, attempt to answer the following questions. What are the norms represented in the moral universe of the group? What are the rules, regulations, expectations? What norms apply in this situation? To what extent do these norms govern or influence behavior? How are people behaving in the here and now, with reference to a set of expectations? What are the implications for the norms of the group, for example, of the diffusion of new knowledge into the group? What norms (which now must be taken into account) have become part of the present situation of the group as a result, for example, of the behavior of new or deviant group members, of innovations by new group leaders, or of contact with other groups?

The discovery that group norms influence behavior and that such normatively guided behavior leads to the achievement of shared goals tends to confirm the sense of the rightness of the norms shared by group members. Similarly, present group norms are challenged and a sense of their rightness undermined, when undeserved deprivation or failure to attain gratification despite behaving according to group norms, deviation from group norms, or the existence of other norms holding out promise for, or actually leading to, goal-achievement, occur. This process of moral validation or invalidation of a cultural system of norms leads to a certain level of confidence, or possibly to change, in such a system.

Adaptive efforts to evaluate the moral situation of the group may be frustrated, for example, by idealization, projection, rationalization, or secrecy.

Group members, in order to bolster a waning sense of solidarity, or to ward off a threat to that solidarity (e.g., from splits in the group), may idealize the moral situation of the group. This results in a precarious state of pesudo-integration or pseudo-solidarity. "We are a wonderful group. All is well here." The group ignores or dismisses trouble spots, preferring to dwell on all that is reassuring and going well.

Group members, similarly, may act as if a threat from within was from outside the group. "The enemy is out there."

Members interested in change and innovation often rationalize deviations from the norms of the group, by relating, with various degrees of sophistry, such deviation to accepted group values such as "freedom," while concealing more unacceptable implications.

Aspects of a present situation may be kept secret to protect deviant members from sanctions. This also prevents, of course, mechanisms of social control, which conceivably could result in altering deviant behavior and bringing a deviant member "back into the group," from being applied. Also, secrecy may be supported by some who, ambivalent about norms, participate vicariously in others' deviance, while apparently supporting group norms. And deviant behavior is often tolerated and protected by secrecy because of its function in making possible release of tensions mobilized by strains in the group; for example, underprivileged or discontented members are thereby permitted a way to "let off steam."

Apparently deviant behavior (some acting out or apparently impulsive behavior, for example) may be an outcome of, or maintained by, institutionalized values; such values, for example, may encourage selfish or inconsiderate behavior by prescribing individualism, giving priority to the interests and wishes of the individual, and insisting upon individual responsibility for making a wide range of choices. In other situations inconsistencies in the system of norms or in the previous application of sanctions, or a relative lack of solidarity, may make confrontation of, and debate with, a challenger to the group's norms inadvisable and, therefore, encourage "sweeping things under the rug." In addition, the exposure of deviant behavior might force the application of sanctions, leading to resentment, increased tension, retaliation and counterattack, and even greater deviance.

For all these and other reasons, leaders of the group often connive at secrecy, feeling sometimes that knowledge of deviant behavior presents even greater difficulties than ignorance of what flourishes in hiding.

Goal-objects in the Integration Group are objects of identification. Through processes of action, members become affectively attached to each other and to a shared leader. They come to have many interests in each other, participate interdependently to achieve common goals, and grant and accept a multitude of specified and unspecified rights and obligations. The leader of the group is a model for mutual (reciprocal and complementary) expectations and actions. Relationship with him involves identification: the internalization of patterns of interaction with him and the norms regulating such interaction.

The outcome of a process of action in an Integration Group, responding to adaptive and integrative exigencies, is a change in the meaning of an object of identification—that is, in the degree of identification (or in the degree of internalization of patterns of interaction) with such a model—from what would have been had there been no action. Members of the group change their behavior, or maintain it against pressures to change, as a result of a process of action in the group. Members of the group to a greater or lesser degree identify with each other or the leader of the group. This outcome is indicated in part by the ratio of solidarity and anomie in the group at the end of a process of action compared to what it was at the beginning.

Figure 4 is a paradigm representing the Integration Group.

The Consummation Group

The Consummation Group is a group driven by wishes and fears, drawn together by passions of love and hate, caught up in expressions of satisfaction, enjoyment, erotically or aggressively tinged humor, panic, grumbling complaint, frustration, or fierce denunciation. This group is the opposite of the Motivation Group in every way: mood, value-alternatives chosen, goals sought. There is, typically, raucous

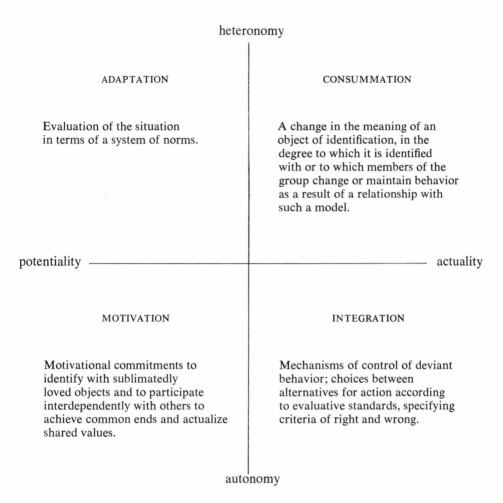

heteronomy

ADAPTATION

Evaluation of the situation
in terms of a system of norms.

CONSUMMATION

A change in the meaning of an
object of identification, in the
degree to which it is identified
with or to which members of the
group change or maintain behavior
as a result of a relationship with
such a model.

potentiality ———————————————————— actuality

MOTIVATION

Motivational commitments to
identify with sublimatedly
loved objects and to participate
interdependently with others to
achieve common ends and actualize
shared values.

INTEGRATION

Mechanisms of control of deviant
behavior; choices between
alternatives for action according
to evaluative standards, specifying
criteria of right and wrong.

autonomy

Fig. 4. The Integration Group

joking, a hectic libidinal flush, excitement, and intense emotion instead of high seriousness and austere fervor; preoccupation with the here-and-now rather than timeless verities; wanting and getting instead of commitment and belief; discharge instead of the inhibition of specific impulses and their subordination to the fusion of many interests and commitments. There are goal-objects of attraction and avoidance, which *do*, which gratify or deprive, in an immediate personal relation, rather than goal-objects of respect and allegiance, which *are*, which are defined in terms of enduring immanent qualities transcending any immediate personal relation.

The Consummation Group is in the region heteronomy-actuality. The primary interest is in integration of the group with its situation, such that wants depending upon relations with objects in that situation are satisfied.

The group and its situation is not equal to a plurality of individual organisms and their environment, although it is true that in this region members of the group are more dependent on the conditions of the outside world for the achievement of goals than is the case in autonomous regions. The group is constituted by values and norms, beliefs and mutual expectations. These are one kind of entities, obeying one kind of laws. As one passes from the realm of such entities into the situation of the group—consisting, for example, not simply of other groups (other systems of values and norms) but of personality systems and physical objects (including physiological organisms)—other entities obeying other kinds of laws are met. The integration of the group and its situation is partly a matter of establishing relations between entities obeying different kinds of laws.

Motivational commitments in the Consummation Group are dispositions to wish, to want things, to enjoy, to seek gratification and avoid deprivation, to love objects of gratification and to hate objects of deprivation. Commitment to consummation involves a determinate interest in an object, a restricted release of energy, or expression of a specific emotional state, in a present relation with an object. The immediate relationship with a goal-object, defined in terms of its performance in personal relation to the acting system, is gratifying: desirable in and of itself without regard to its status as a means to any other goal. Commitment to the establishment of relations with such objects is commitment to expressive action, which is characterized by primacy of appreciative or aesthetic standards and cathectic interests. Cathectic interests include the cathexis of systems of expressive symbols, as well as of such activities as feeling and enjoying.

Norms in this group regulate choice among wants or ends as well as, for example, the expression of feeling, according to appreciative or aesthetic standards of appropriateness and taste. "Votes" for competing ends are regulated by such considerations. Just as an ultimate standard in the Motivation Group is "the good," and in the Integration Group is "right and wrong," so in the Consummation Group the ultimate standard is "beauty" (appropriateness, form, unity) or some variant thereof. What end among these ends should come first? What end among these ends would be most gratifying? What is the hierarchy of ends shared by members of the group? What will a particular choice of ends cost in the sacrifice of other possibilities of gratification? Who will be disappointed? Whose wants will be gratified? What kind of gratification is appropriate to seek and have?

Members of a Consummation Group do not identify with each other or with a leader; they enjoy or fight with, are drawn to or fear, satisfy or frustrate, a leader, each other, or members of other groups. "What fun he is!" "What can he (or that group) do to harm me—to keep me from getting what I want?" "I will give him what he wants." "I won't please him."

Integration crises may be caused by a distribution of gratifications and deprivations, of satisfactions and burdens, that is unacceptable to one or more group members. The group seeks to maintain a state of optimal gratification for the maximum number of members of the group, and to avoid a state in which deprivation outweighs gratification.

Deviance is inappropriate, ugly, or distasteful behavior rather than evil, illness, or criminality.

Adaptation in a Consummation Group is a process of symbolizing a situation expressively, rather than cognitively; of appropriately representing euphoric or dysphoric states; of defining or reacting to the situation through appropriate expressive symbolizations of it as actually or potentially depriving or gratifying. Adaptive processes in the Consummation Group contribute a body of expressive symbolizations, which are felt to be appropriate, aesthetically satisfying, or tasteful, to the cultural system of the group; and result, to the extent these are internalized, in shared ways of responding to and representing a situation's gratifying and depriving aspects.

Confusion comes about, for example, through an inadequate appreciation of the relative possibilities for gratification and deprivation in relationship with a particular object: when wishes hold sway without attention to dangers or painful consequences in reality, or fears of fantasied danger result in the inhibition of wishes even when their fulfillment holds in reality little possibility of pain.

Threats of deprivation constitute adaptive exigencies or crises. An adequate recognition of the existence of such threats is, of course, essential for mastering or adapting to them.

Cathectic goal-objects are defined in terms of their inclusion with the acting system in an immediate personal relation, in which performance leading to gratification or deprivation is of primary importance. The outcome of a process of action in a Consummation Group, responding to adaptive and integrative exigencies, is a change in the meaning of such a goal-object: addition to, or subtraction from, the shared cathectic significance, value, or meaning (in terms of a continuum of gratification and deprivation possibilities) of a goal-object for the members of a group from what would have been had there been no action. One gains or loses "desire" or "wanting it"; one loves, hates, or fears more or less. One discovers what reality has to offer in the way of enjoyment and pain, how things taste, what things are good or bad for gratifying wishes. This outcome is indicated in part by the ratio of gratification and deprivation in the group at the end of a process of action compared to what it was at the beginning.

Figure 5 is a paradigm representing the Consummation Group.

The Adaptation Group

The Adaptation Group is in the region heteronomy-potentiality. It is characterized by the inhibition of consummatory gratifying relations with immediately available goal-objects and the restriction of interest in an object to its capacity to serve as a means to the achievement of a goal or goals in the future. A means-object is significant in terms of what it does or can do and its intrinsic properties and potentialities.

On the lowest level of generality, adaptation involves the acquisition of a particular means-object, which is consumed in the achievement of a particular goal. On the highest level of generality, adaptation involves the acquisition of the most generally useful means-objects. These can be used in the achievement of many, even-as-yet undefined goals, and they are symbolic, never consumed but only exchanged or transmitted in the process of achieving a particular goal. Knowledge, money, and power are such means-objects. These determine the extent to which consumable particular means-objects may be acquired.

Knowledge of an object-situation may be regarded as a precondition to the acquisition of any other means. Adaptation, then, may be primarily, at one level, the

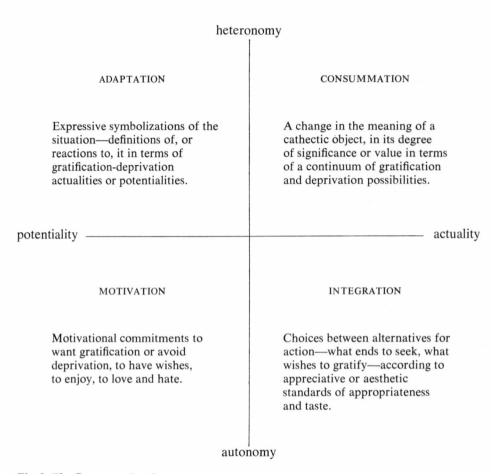

Fig. 5. The Consummation Group

generation, acquisition, or transmission of an adequate cognitive "map" (cognitive representations) of the object-situation. Adaptation thus involves first and most generally as a precondition of mastery or possession of means-objects (or accommodation to objects as conditions of action) the generation, acquisition, and transmission of representations of reality or object-representations.

In an Adaptation Group, the type of relation is cognition of or generation, acquisition, and transmission of. Objects are symbolic objects belonging to a cultural system: object-representations, empirically verifiable existential beliefs, propositions about means-end relations, cognitive definitions of the situation. As we have seen, symbolic object-representations are part of any group-function, actually an aspect of adaptation processes within any group: in the Motivation Group, shared interpretations of events in terms of some general system of nonempirical beliefs and values; in the Integration Group, shared moral evaluations of reality in terms of a system of norms; in the Consummation Group, shared expressive symbolizations of reality on a dimension of gratification and deprivation; finally, in the Adaptation Group, shared, empirically verifiable, existential beliefs, shared cognitive knowledge of means-end relations (what we know or have learned through common or transmitted experience works), and shared cognitive definitions of an existing situation.

In order to have cognitive knowledge, consummatory gratifications must be postponed or inhibited, interest in an object must be focused upon determinate specific aspects of it, and the object must be defined in terms of its intrinsic properties, irrespective of any immediate relation with the acting system, and in terms of its past, present, and potential behavior or performances in relation to other objects.

The Adaptation Group is the opposite of the Integration Group in every way: in its mood, type of relationships, and primary values. It is a disciplined work group. Its members regard the world and each other dispassionately and with restricted interest in those aspects that are specific means to given ends. Efficiency and expediency regulate action in relation to each other and to other groups. A leader is valued not for who he is, or as a model for identification, or as an object of gratification, but because he makes things possible, because he knows and shows how to do things, because he knows what means will lead to a given end—what works.[13]

Motivational commitments in the Adaptation Group are dispositions to know, to understand, to apply knowledge, to be competent and skilled, and to acquire and make use of facilities, resources, opportunities, and media, as means to a given end or to a wide variety of possible ends. These dispositions to generate, possess, use, exchange, or transmit all kinds of, but especially the most general, means-objects constitute commitments to instrumental action. Instrumental action is characterized by primacy of cognitive standards of validity (or empirically verifiable truth) and cognitive interests. Cognitive interests include the cathexis of systems of empirically verifiable beliefs, as well as of such activities as knowing and investigating.

Norms regulate choices among courses of action or different means to a given end according to cognitive standards of validity and efficiency. What means will achieve the given end most effectively, efficiently, and expediently? The ultimate standard is truth, according to the canons of empirical science.

Relationships with a leader, with others in the group, or with members of other groups, are sought to the extent they are useful or serve as means to a given end.

Deviance is incompetent behavior, based on ignorance (verifiable means-ends relations are not known), error (verifiable means-ends relations are misinterpreted or distorted by misinformation), or lack of skill. Education and interpretation correct ignorance and error. Integrative response to desired behavior is to reward it by making access to means-objects available, to deviant behavior is to punish it by cutting off access to means-objects.

Integrative crises occur when, for example, there is a distribution or allocation of means-objects that is felt to be unfair by one or more members of the group.

Adaptation in this group is a process of formulating and validating cognitive representations of reality, of acquiring information or facts about the empirical situation. Inadequate representations of empirical reality may result when accurate

---

13. Fritz Redl (1942) has defined types of central persons around whom groups form. These include those central persons with whom group members identify; those central persons who are the objects of love or hate and aggression; and those central persons who provide means for drive satisfaction; and parallel, to some extent, types of leaders described here of Integration, Consummation, and Adaptation Groups.

representations threaten existing internal arrangements, in other words, threaten the Integration Group. The conflict between truth and harmony, between integrative and adaptive exigencies, between the Integration Group and the Adaptation Group, is an important dynamic in many groups.

In a particular process of action, what is the balance between the unfolding of immanent potentialities (analogous to the growth of an organism arising out of its particular internal arrangements or integration) and the reaction to, and dependence upon, external exigencies? One can imagine a concrete group the history of which seems determined by the inexorable unfolding of its immanent possibilities, and internal arrangements even seem to select the particular external events to which the group will respond (relative domination by the Integration Group or integration group-function). On the other hand, one can imagine a concrete group the history of which seems determined by a series of reactions and changes consequent to external events (relative domination by the Adaptation Group or adaptation group-function).

In the Adaptation Group, adaptive crises may occur when needed or valued means, resources, or facilities are unavailable or lost.

Goal-objects are defined in terms of intrinsic, abstract, general, timeless characteristics, and their past, present, and potential performances in relation to other objects. The outcome of a process of action in an Adaptation Group is a change in the meaning of such a goal-object, in the degree to which its utility or power to serve as a means to desired ends is valued, from what would have been had there been no action. One comes to conclusions like the following—or their converse, to one degree or another: "He is useful." "That is really true about the world we live in." "That works." "That is valuable as a means to a lot of things we want." "Now we know better how to do it or get it." Knowledge is thereby validated, and the knowledge of what works or has utility becomes part of the shared resources of the group. This outcome is indicated in part by the ratio of knowledge and ignorance or error, skill and incompetence, availability or posseession of means-objects and their nonavailability, in the group at the end of a process of action compared to what it was at the beginning.

Figure 6 is a paradigm representing the Adaptation Group.

RELATIONSHIP BETWEEN THE FOUR GROUP-FUNCTIONS

The dynamics of any concrete group may be understood, in part, in terms of the consequences of the relationships between these four group-functions: The Motivation Group, the Integration Group, the Consummation Group, the Adaptation Group. Similarly, intergroup phenomena, or the interactions between concrete groups (each of which represents one or another of these four group-functions in a particular process of action, or each of which has given to one or another of these functions a more or less enduring priority) may be understood in terms of the consequences of the relationship between such group-functions. It is postulated that no more than one group-function in a particular system can be maximized during a unit of time in a process of action. This limitation results from limitations in the amount of effort available in any system; and from differences in the types of re-

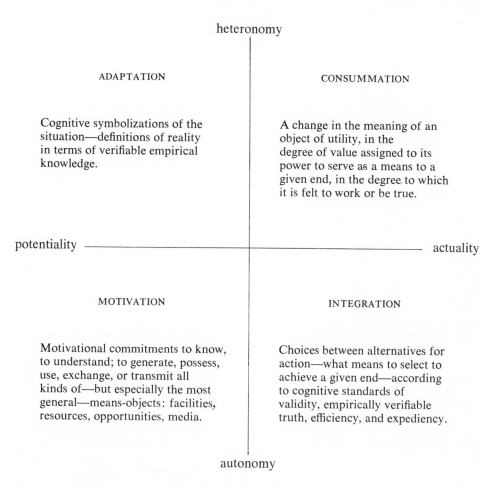

heteronomy

ADAPTATION

Cognitive symbolizations of the situation—definitions of reality in terms of verifiable empirical knowledge.

CONSUMMATION

A change in the meaning of an object of utility, in the degree of value assigned to its power to serve as a means to a given end, in the degree to which it is felt to work or be true.

potentiality ———————————————— actuality

MOTIVATION

Motivational commitments to know, to understand; to generate, possess, use, exchange, or transmit all kinds of—but especially the most general—means-objects: facilities, resources, opportunities, media.

INTEGRATION

Choices between alternatives for action—what means to select to achieve a given end—according to cognitive standards of validity, empirically verifiable truth, efficiency, and expediency.

autonomy

Fig. 6. The Adaptation Group

lations sought and the ways in which objects are defined or regarded that are required by different group-functions. The relationship between group-functions may be described in terms of conflict (between what, for example, may be or appear to be incompatible goals or functions or requirements in a given situation during a particular process of action). This relationship may also be described in terms of competition (e.g., for the commitment of members to actualization of different sets of values, which, in a given situation during a particular process of action, represent incompatible alternatives or dilemmas).

The relationship between the four group-functions may also be described in terms of the degree of approximation to an optimal balance of inputs and outputs. The relative force or weight of a particular group-function, in its conflict or competition with other group-functions, depends upon both input from behavioral physiological organisms, personality systems, and cultural systems, and output to behavioral physiological organisms, personality systems, and cultural systems. The stability and history of a system, composed of a concrete group carrying out all four group-functions or a set of concrete subgroups each of which is differentiated to perform a particular group-function, depend upon relationships between the inputs and outputs of each group-function.

The Cultural System

The cultural system consists of systems of values and existential non-empirical beliefs, moral and ethical norms, expressive symbols, and empirical scientific knowledge, as well as the concrete objects serving as vehicles of, and transmitting, these.

The Personality System

As we have seen, Freud's structural and dynamic theories correspond roughly to Parsons' view of a system of action. A system of action has four interdependent subsystems, each meeting fundamental requirements of the system, each dependent upon the others' functioning to fulfill its own aims. Yet all four necessarily compete and conflict, the outcomes of such processes being represented by complex equilibria-states of the system. Both the social system and the personality system are such systems of action.

To the extent that Freud turned from his attempts to explain psychological phenomena neurophysiologically, he escaped falling into the fallacy of misplaced concreteness, that is, believing that all phenomena *are* the movements of masses in space and time. He saw the need to develop a conceptual framework applicable to psychological systems. As he developed this framework, he placed less emphasis on understanding psychological phenomena in terms of processes of automatic causation (through the movements, for example, of quantities) pushing the system from without. He placed more emphasis rather on understanding psychological phenomena in terms of the purposes of the individual pulling the system from within, that is, in terms of the ends or goals toward the attainment of which psychological processes were oriented. To understand the meaning of a psychological phenomenon is to understand the goal-strivings (and their relation to each other) underlying it.

The economic theory of Freud has both emphases. At times, it reflects the effort to explain psychological phenomena neurophysiologically. At other times, it appears to have the status of Parsons' postulate that effort, energy, or cathexis are allocated among values or ends. If this were not so, then to speak of a choice between ends would be meaningless. Then, of course, effort, energy, or cathexis are allocated among different goal-objects, and, it follows, also among the four subsystems of a system of action.

To the extent, of course, that the goals or ends are determined solely by the claims of the physiological organism (the id or instincts) upon the psychological system, then psychoanalytic theory becomes what Parsons calls a radical anti-intellectualistic positivistic theory of action. Since the physiological organism is part of the situation of the psychological system, goals or ends have no independent conceptual status but are reduced to conditions.

However, psychoanalytic theory cannot be reduced either to biological theory or behaviorism. Freud was committed to a conflict theory of personality, so that outcomes are a resultant of the conflicting aims represented by different conceptual elements. He moved toward and continuously developed the structural theory in which the ego and superego are not simply extensions of the id but independent internalized-representations of external reality and of society. The autonomy of the claims of external reality and society are guaranteed by what Hartmann called the conflict-free ego-apparatuses (such as perception) as well as by the internalization of social values and norms out of social experience (values and norms that, once internalized, no longer depend upon social experience to act as shapers of ends) (Freud 1921, 1923; Hartmann 1958, 1964).

The personality system might be viewed as constituted by four subsystems: the id, representing the claims of the physiological organism in the psychological system; the superego, representing the claims of society insofar as these involve specific prescriptions for behavior in interaction with others and expectations of their contingent behavior (norms); the adaptive ego, representing the claims of the situation or external reality; and the ego-ideal (for which it is somewhat difficult to find a consistent conceptual status in psychoanalytic theory), representing the claims of internalized ultimate values and ideals.

The superego and ego-ideal, then, following Parsons' discussions of the superego (1964), become the particular subsystems of personality where personality system and social system articulate, the internalized values and norms within the personality system articulating with the shared or common systems of values and norms of the society.

However, the superego and ego-ideal, once norms and values are internalized, may function independently of social experience; the adaptive ego and id do not function independently of current experience with external reality, on the one hand, or the current claims of the physiological organism, on the other. In other words, two of the subsystems are on the boundary between the personality system and its situation and two function within the system.

The physiological organism, on the one hand, and external reality (including society), on the other, are actually both outside the boundary of the personality system, part of the situation of the personality system rather than constitutive of it. It is less precise to speak of the claims of the body and society and more precise to speak of the aims of subsystems of the personality system in a conceptual formulation of the personality system comprised of a cognitive or adaptive ego; a libidinal, expressive, or executive ego; a superego; and an ego-ideal.[14]

The adaptive ego functions to represent, and achieve adaptation to or mastery over, the situation. The situation includes the claims of the physiological organism and of society. To the extent that norms and values represent claims of external reality (society), these norms and values are part of the means and conditions mastered and adapted to by the adaptive ego in the service of the goal-strivings of the personality system. To the extent physical processes or impulses represent claims of external reality (a reality that is analytically external through phenomenally experi-

---

14. Compare with Fairbairn's view (1952) that personality consists of ego-structures and the objects to which these are related and that the ego consists of a central (observing or preconscious) ego, a libidinal ego (identified with, and attached to, an internalized exciting object), and an internal saboteur (identified with, and attached to, an internalized rejecting object).

enced as inside), these impulses represent means and conditions to be used or adapted to by the adaptive ego in the service of the goal-strivings of the personality system. The adaptive ego corresponds to the adaptation subsystem of a system of action.

The adaptive ego is a subsystem of dispositions to form cognitive representations of objects and relations between objects, in the service of possessing, using, or mastering such objects. Cognitive processes of reality testing, including perception, discrimination, and generalization, are regulated by euphoric and dysphoric states of understanding and confidence, on one hand, and confusion and uncertainty, on the other.

The executive ego functions to organize behavior to achieve goals or consummate relations with goal-objects. The personality system does not achieve such goals or relations itself but, through processes of cathexis-allocation and control over the motor apparatus, through its effect upon or outputs to the physiological behavioral organism. The adaptive ego limits the executive ego by determining what goals are possible to achieve; the executive ego controls the adaptive ego by determining what means will be selected; that is, those means actually leading to achievement of an end chosen by the executive ego to be consummated. The executive ego corresponds to the consummation (goal-attainment) subsystem of a system of action.

The executive ego may be called the libidinal or expressive ego to stress its cathexis-allocation function. In other words, it is a subsystem of dispositions to allocate (distribute) cathexis, including consummatory value and attention, to different objects. Such allocations are regulated by euphoric and dysphoric states of gratification and deprivation, and of pleasure and unpleasure or signal-anxiety.

The superego functions to maintain the influence of internalized norms or role-expectations over conduct; such norms or role-expectations integrate interactions with others and provide standards according to which choices are made. The superego also functions to integrate these norms or role-expectations with the internalized values of the ego-ideal. On the basis of such integrations, choices faced by the executive ego concerning goals as well as other kinds of alternatives are evaluated and thereby controlled. What integrative standards are relevant is limited by the cathexes of various goals by the executive ego; in fact, that integrative standards are brought to bear at all depends upon the cathexis of goals by the executive ego. The superego corresponds to the integration subsystem of a system of action.

The superego is a subsystem of dispositions to actualize or objectify in action mutual (reciprocal and complementary) expectations and patterns of interaction. These dispositions are maintained and reinforced by dysphoric and euphoric states (guilt and virtue), serving as negative and positive sanctions or internal responses to failure and success in acting in accordance with such expectations.

The ego-ideal functions to commit energy resources (input from the physiological organism) to the actualization of internalized values. At this level consequences of physiological or instinctual processes become constitutive of the personality system. The ego-ideal controls thereby the superego-commitment to role-expectations, but is also limited as to what values may be actualized, and in what way, by the particular role-expectations internalized and the extent to which role-expectations are internalized. The ego-ideal corresponds to the motivation (latency or pattern-maintenance) subsystem of a system of action.

The ego-ideal is a subsystem of dispositions to actualize or objectify in action representations of ideals. Euphoric and dysphoric states (self-esteem and shame) signal the degree to which action approximates ideals. Such a subsystem is more or less internally consistent, and more or less compatible with other subsystems of the personality.

The synthetic functions of the ego are encompassed by the hierarchy of control indicated in the previous discussion. The extent to which the ego-ideal, first of all, and the superego integrate the entire personality system by determining the values to be actualized in the achievement of ends, the very patterns of orientation to be adopted in approaching experience, and the norms according to which goal-setting is to proceed has been insufficiently appreciated perhaps in psychoanalytic theory. That the adaptive ego's malfunctioning, for example, is often secondary to malfunctioning of the ego-ideal—nothing is worth striving for and, therefore, there is nothing worth mastering the environment to attain—is suggested frequently by experiences with patients who have some degree of ego-impairment or character-disorder. That values and patterns of value orientation have their origin and receive their commitment in early social experiences and in the relation to the body does not necessarily argue against their later secondary autonomy.

The synthetic functions of the ego is, also, another way of talking about the fact that adaptive ego, executive ego, superego, and ego-ideal are subsystems of a total system. Each must function and in relation to the others if all requirements of the system are to be met to one degree or another, so that the system survives as a particular constellation of intrasystemic relationships, the boundary between itself and its environment (including society and the physiological organism) is maintained, and its necessary relationships with social, physical, and cultural objects are established and maintained. The hierarchy of control and the maintenance of boundary and equilibrium states (therefore, many synthetic functions) are characteristics of the entire personality system as a system of action rather than characteristics of any one subsystem.

Every subsystem of the personality is in part a consequence of identification: in part the result of the internalization of patterns (expressive, instrumental, or moral) and the internalization of kinds of object-relations experienced in groups. The ego-ideal is a precipitate of object-relations in the Motivation Group. The superego is a precipitate of object-relations in the Integration Group. The executive ego is a precipitate of object-relations in the Consummation Group. The adaptive ego is a precipitate of object-relations in the Adaptation Group.

Inputs and Outputs

Inputs to the Motivation Group are energy resources (from the behavioral physiological organism); systems of values and nonempirical existential beliefs, and the concrete entities objectifying and transmitting these (from the cultural system); ego-ideal functions or dispositions (from the personality system). Outputs from the Motivation Group are restoration of depleted stores, or mobilization and arousal, of energy (to the behavioral physiological organism); confirmation of systems of values and nonempirical existential beliefs, or changes in these, in the concrete entities objectifying and transmitting them, or in both (to the cultural system); the generation, maintenance, and restoration of internalized values and nonempirical beliefs—that is, the formation, alteration, and maintenance of the ego-ideal (to the personality system).

Inputs to the Integration Group are innate thresholds of sensitivity to others' approval and disapproval, and innate capacities to learn purposeful patterns of interaction (from the behavioral physiological organism); systems of moral and ethical norms, laws, rules and regulations, and the concrete entities objectifying and transmitting these (from the cultural system); superego functions (from the personality system). Outputs from the Integration Group are learned patterns of responsible action (to the behavioral physiological organism); validation of systems of norms, or changes in these, in the concrete entities objectifying and transmitting these, or in both (to the cultural system); the generation, maintenance, and restoration of internalized norms—that is, the formation, alteration, and maintenance of the superego (to the personality system).

Inputs to the Consummation Group are innate thresholds for the toleration of deprivation and anxiety (from the behavioral physiological organism); systems of expressive patterns or symbolizations, and the concrete entities objectifying and transmitting these (from the cultural system); executive ego functions (from the personality system). Outputs from the Consummation Group are learned patterns of expressive action (to the behavioral physiological organism); validation of systems of expressive symbolization, or changes in these (to the cultural system); the generation, maintenance, and restoration of patterns of cathectic allocation—that is, the formation, alteration, and maintenance of the executive ego (to the personality system).

Inputs to the Adaptation Group are given apparatuses of memory, perception, and cognition (from the behavioral physiological organism); systems of empirical scientific knowledge, and the concrete entities objectifying and transmitting such knowledge (from the cultural system); adaptive ego functions (from the personality system). Outputs from the Adaptation Group are learned patterns of instrumental action (to the behavioral physiological organism); verification of empirical knowledge and confirmation of standards of competence (to the cultural system); the generation, maintenance, and restoration of patterns of reality testing and mastery—that is, the formation, alteration, and maintenance of the adaptive ego (to the personality system).

Interdependence of the Inputs and Outputs of the Group-Functions

The inputs and outputs of the four group-functions to and from each other are interdependent, the extent of one depending upon the extent of another.

Outputs from the Adaptation Group to other group-functions are means-objects, to make possible gratification of wants or avoidance of deprivation (to the Consummation Group); knowledge of the situation or the task, to guide the formation of effective patterns of collaborative action (to the Integration Group); knowledge of what works, to reinforce commitment to cognitive standards and to beliefs and values from which patterns of instrumental action are ultimately derived (to the Motivation Group).

Outputs from the Consummation Group to other group-functions are goal-objects, motivating the instrumental action necessary for their attainment (to the Adaptation Group); expressive symbolization of the situation, to mobilize and guide collaborative action in choosing and pursuing common ends (to the Integration Group); experience of what gratifies, to reinforce commitment to appreciative standards and to beliefs and values from which patterns of expressive action are ultimately derived (to the Motivation Group).

Outputs from the Integration Group to other group-functions are objects of identification, motivating the collaborative responsible action, according to shared norms, necessary to choose between alternative means and to achieve shared knowledge and mastery of, or adaptation to, a situation (to the Adaptation Group); moral evaluations of the situation, legitimizing the choice to pursue in concert a shared end (to the Consummation Group); experiences of solidarity, to reinforce commitment to shared values and nonempirical beliefs from which norms governing interaction are ultimately derived (to the Motivation Group).

Outputs from the Motivation Group to other group-functions are commitments to remembered patterns, traditions, knowledge of what works (to the Adaptation Group); of what gratifies (to the Consummation Group); of what leads to solidarity (to the Intergration Group). The degree of these commitments depends upon the compatibility of a particular pattern with the system of institutionalized values and beliefs characterizing the group.

The Study of Two Kinds of Group Process

In studying a process of action in a concrete group over a relatively short period of time, we may assume a given maintained system of values and beliefs. Then we may study in such a group what consummatory goals are pursued, what responses are made to adaptive and integrative exigencies, and what is the relation of such goals and responses to each other and to the given system of values and beliefs.

In studying a concrete group over a relatively long period of time, we may investigate changes in the system of values and beliefs characterizing the group and the consequences of these changes. Then, the output of the Motivation Group to other group-functions consists of changes in the meaning and acceptability of patterns that are more or less consistent with a changed or changing system of values and beliefs.

Changes in the system of values and beliefs occur as a result of developments inherent in any such system: the logical and psychological consequences of inconsistencies within it, or of strains between it and situational requirements, for example. Changes may also occur as a result of contact with another group and the diffusion of beliefs and values from one group to another.

In summary, we may study what an entity does, given what it is, or how the entity itself changes.

Imbalance in Input-Output between Group-Functions and Personality System

If the output from the Adaptation Group to the personality system is excessive in relation to the outputs from the three other group-functions, then phenomena related to the hypertrophy of the adaptive ego result. These phenomena may be classified according to the combination inhibition-restriction; that is, dispositions of the personality system to form these types of relations with objects. Examples of such phenomena are rigid overcontrol of impulses and feelings; constrictedness and inhibition; preoccupation with the consequences of action, leading to procrastination, hesitation, and doubt; and tendencies to direct only definite specific interests to objects, to separate oneself from objects, and to compartmentalize objects within rigid boundaries, as in intellectualization and obsessiveness.

If the output from the Consummation Group to the personality system is excessive in relation to the outputs from the three other group-functions, then phenomena related to the hypertrophy of the executive ego result. These phenomena may be classified according to the combination restriction-discharge; that is, dispositions of the personality system to form these types of object-relations. Tendencies to have only definite specified interests in an object, which is to be exploited for gratification or to be avoided, a part only of such an object being important (the same part in any object would do), may be combined with undisciplined impulsivity and emotionality. Acting out, open aggression, flight, primarily pleasure-oriented behavior, are examples of such phenomena.

If the output from the Integration Group to the personality system is excessive in relation to the outputs from the three other group-functions, then phenomena related to the hypertrophy of the superego result. These phenomena may be classified according to the combination discharge-expansion; that is, dispositions of the personality system to form these types of object-relations. Intense feelings of guilt or self-righteousness, emotional demands for others to behave in certain ways toward one, and for union with others, tendencies to direct a wide variety of needs and wishes toward objects without regard to any limits in the relationship and ignoring or attempting to transcend any boundaries between the self and another, are examples of such phenomena.

If the output from the Motivation Group to the personality system is excessive in relation to the outputs from the three other group-functions, then phenomena related to the hypertrophy of the ego-ideal result. These phenomena may be classified according to the combination expansion-inhibition; that is, dispositions of the personality system to form these types of object-relations. Overcontrol of impulses and feelings, attempts to transcend boundaries and limits, straining toward ideal states, excessive pride and hypersensitivity to slights and humiliation, asceticism, mysticism, and grandiose delusional systems, are examples of such phenomena.

Likewise, excessive inputs of adaptive ego, executive ego, superego, or ego-ideal functions, to any group from personality systems bounding it may lead to the dominance, respectively, of the Adaptation Group, the Consummation Group, the Integration Group, or the Motivation Group in relation to other group-functions.

DISCUSSION OF EXAMPLES

Discussion of Example One: The People of Israel

The group at Mount Sinai, then, was primarily a Motivation Group. The values of this group were undergoing change, for example, from a belief in a plurality of gods, associated with valuing the achievement of consummatory goals in the here and now, to a monotheistic belief in a transcendental Being, associated with valuing mastery of a hostile environment in the service of His Law. Adherence to the latter belief, as yet poorly institutionalized, readily gave way in the face of a change in the situation (the absence of the leader representing that belief) to a return to practices derived from old beliefs.

This group may also be considered from the point of view of the mechanisms by which a value system comes to be regarded as sacred and its actualization comes to be established as a moral obligation or responsibility accepted by all group members. A leader develops who is an object of awe and respect, commanding allegiance because he symbolizes sacred ultimate values; this, then, is the outcome of Moses' mysterious disappearance upon, and return from, Mount Sinai where he communicated with God and received His Law. The stone Tables of the Law similarly become objects of awe and respect. The charismatic leader then helps to rid the group of old values through ritual symbolic actions (making the people drink the ground calf), the extrusion of recalcitrant dissidents (slaying those who do not stand on the Lord's side), interceding on behalf of those who wish to be forgiven their transient trespasses (praying the Lord to forgive the people), and by the imposition of trials, the survival of which holds promise of great reward, as well as by allowing time to pass and an older generation to die out (wandering for forty years until a new generation has arisen, untainted by the values of the days of slavery, and worthy to enter the land flowing with milk and honey). The covenant between the group and God represents the institutionalization of a system of values and beliefs, which each member of the group then requires himself to actualize and objectify through many different kinds of actions in the specific situations in which he finds himself. Order in the group depends upon adherence to the covenant.

In response to a change or conditions in the outside world (slavery, challenges offered by the beliefs of other tribes), any group may change itself (accept new values and beliefs) or change the source of the disturbance (flight, destroy the enemy hosts). In response to an integrative threat (the deviance of nonbelievers or the moral relapse of the weak), a group may extrude or isolate the source of the inner disturbance (murder or confinement), or change this source (contrition, expiation, forgiveness, reintegration).

An external threat may be internalized, as when the difficulties wrought by outside challenge or natural forces, such as alien cultures or desert hardships, are attributed to inner threats (the unbelievers in our midst); or when external exigencies are represented in the shape of internal states—that is, individuals or groups within take on the appearance of what is actually an outside menace. Likewise, an internal threat may be externalized, as when difficulties arising from inadequate institutionalization of values are attributed to outside forces, the enemy without; or when internal exigencies are represented in the shape of a relationship with what is external—that is, conflict within the group is ignored and its manifestations attributed to conflict between the group and an external force.

These sets of alternatives are described by the dichotomy autonomy-heteronomy.

Discussion of Example Two: A Patient-Staff Meeting

In the patient-staff meeting previously described, the output of a Consummation Group in the direction of deprivation rather than gratification resulted in disturbances in integration-functions and adaptation-functions. The shared perception that two patients about to be discharged were being forsaken by the hospital was associated with upsets, frustration, anger, and a rising degree of anomie: refusal to participate in work activities associated with the sense that things could not be counted upon to happen as usual and that the place was falling apart.

An exploration by an Adaptation Group into the actual facts, and an interpretation by a Motivation Group of the meaning of these events in terms of the ultimate values of the hospital community, led to a new expressive symbolization of the situation. Previous feelings were now deemed inappropriate and feelings of gratification over the achievement of goals began to develop. This process concluded with a change in the meaning of the goal state (discharge from the hospital), that is, a change in its degree of value in terms of gratification possibilities for the members of the group.

The output of the Consummation Group to the personality systems of the patients was an alteration in the allocation of cathexis by the executive ego.

Discussion of Example Three: A Ship at Sea

Conrad's tale depicts a group torn between adaptive and integrative imperatives—on the one hand, the storm without, on the other, death within. At first the energy of the group is given over to the integration of new hands, their initiation into the etiquette of the forecastle. Donkin represents the man who does not share in any solidarity with others, who cannot be counted upon to fulfill any of his shipmates' expectations of him that he contribute to the work of the group. He can be counted upon to try to destroy anything that binds other men together, their values, their duty, their illusions. About him, there is little ambiguity, and he is soon disciplined, emerging only briefly later as a leader of the group when its members are disaffected and rebellious. Conrad offers here an example of how leadership shifts from one person to another, depending on the goal of the group and on which group-function has primacy. Wait, the dying man, represents the threat from within that will tear loose the fabric binding the group together. He is ambiguous. It is difficult to judge his behavior so that a position in relation to it that is consistent with group norms may be taken. He conceals the truth about himself from others, perhaps unable to bear such knowledge himself. He throws out misleading clues. In attempts to deal with his deviant behavior (he does not work on a ship where work is prepotently valued), men begin to behave deviantly themselves. A pie is stolen. Suspicion develops; mutual confidence diminishes. The decision concerning whether he is malingering or dying cannot be made. The view that he malingers arouses guilt; the view that he is dying, fear. The men waver between skepticism and compassion, between the fear of remorse, the fear of ridicule, and the fear of death itself. These tensions and inconsistencies interfere with a wholehearted and disciplined commitment to the work of the ship.

Then the storm strikes, threatening the survival of the ship. It is the magnitude of the threat that determines the primary of work demands and that drives out thoughts of Wait. The ship becomes more important than any individual on board; the solidarity of the group is based on this shared concern for the ship and confidence that each member will perform what is expected of him. Donkin's grumbling is not tolerated. The cook rises to heroism. This immense effort at goal-achievement in relation to the situation, however, as is usually so with movements toward goal-achievement, leaves exhaustion and strains in its wake. It is as if solidarity around a shared goal is drawn upon and depleted as the goal is achieved. The men are ill, torn by the desire to do well and the longing to rest, and confronted by personal losses and self-revelations. Donkin becomes a leader, playing on feelings of discontent and unfair treatment. Still, the supreme shared value, concern with the welfare of the ship, keeps men from betraying their duty. Increasingly, however, Wait and the captain's behavior toward him become the focus of grievances; mutiny threatens.

Conrad then shows the consequences for a group, the vulnerability of its solidarity, when it is unable to tolerate change in its internal arrangements, when its solidarity is based on a lie or illusion about reality. As there develops an increasingly great strain or incompatibility between the values and beliefs of a group and the knowledge of empirical reality in which the group pursues and achieves its goals, then the group as an entity finds it increasingly difficult to survive. The men refuse to face that Wait is dying, and that *he* cannot be saved; this denial continues to lead to deviant behavior and poisons the moral tone of the ship's community. It is Donkin, the destroyer, who destroys the delusion that Wait will survive. Wait dies; his death disrupts the society constituted by the belief that he will not. As if to represent the dissolution of that society, the voyage ends and the men scatter.

CONCLUSION

The theory of groups developed in this chapter is founded upon the basic distinction between an acting system and its situation, upon the view of action as a process of actualization or goal-achievement in time guided by values and the norms derived from these, and upon concepts of object-relations: dichotomous alternatives for classifying objects and ways of relating to them. Such a conceptual framework has made possible the description of four group-functions: the Motivation Group, the Integration Group, the Consummation Group, and the Adaptation Group. It is in terms of the nature of these, and the relation between them, that group structures and processes may be understood. It would seem that this theory of groups might have a wide range of applicability, bringing together and making sense of a universe of apparently disparate, large and small, far-flung phenomena.

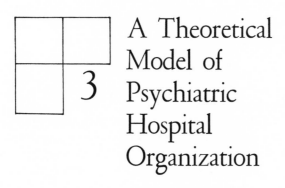

A Theoretical Model of Psychiatric Hospital Organization

3

The psychiatric hospital is a social system; therefore, a system of action. Concretely, it is a collectivity composed of subcollectivities; in some of its aspects an organization, in some a community.

Definitions

For greater ease in following the discussion of psychiatric hospital organization, the reader may wish to review the following definitions, which are paraphrased from Parsons' works on the theory of action.

A social system is an interactive system of a plurality of persons oriented to one another. It is a collective actor in the sense that members interact with each other in the interest of attaining shared collective goals. A collective goal may be prescribed by legitimate authority and be the goal toward which the need-dispositions (not necessarily the same) of more than one member of a social system are directed; or it may be the goal toward which the same need-dispositions of a number of members of a social system are directed. A need-disposition describes a consistent enduring tendency or disposition to orient and act in certain ways in relation to one or more objects: essentially, to orient and act to attain relationships with goal-objects. A need-disposition is acquired through a process of action; that is, learned,

75

rather than innate. A shared collective goal is a collective goal pursued simultaneously by a plurality of individual members of the same social system. A collectivity is a social system with shared collective goals; with a pattern of value orientations that, when threatened, members will act in concert to defend; and with a boundary defined by the roles constituting the social system and thus including members and excluding nonmembers having no roles in the system.

An organization is a collectivity, in which instrumental action has primacy; the activities and contributions of members, organized in a system of cooperative relations, are directed to the achievement of a specific goal: usually a certain state of exchange or relationship with its environment, or a product, which is characteristic of the particular organization. A community is a collectivity whose members share a common territory as a base for daily living.

A role controls mutual orientations and actions aimed at obtaining a certain relationship between actor and a social object or objects. In other words, it defines an actor's participation in an interactive process and includes a set of complementary expectations concerning his own actions and those of others, as well as specific functional content and location in a system. Role-expectation describes an expectation that an actor will orient and act in certain ways in relation to one or more social objects. A role-expectation may be part of the actor's situation; or it may be internalized—that is, part of his own internal system. In this latter case, it is a special kind of need-disposition, since the expectations are integrated with a disposition to act in conformity with them. An internalized role-expectation mediates relations between the individual actor and a social system. A role, then, is a normatively regulated orientation by an individual actor to a collectivity as an object; it includes the actor's role-expectations of himself and his expectations of others' concerted contingent reaction to what he might do. Role-expectations (or the roles of which these are one constituent) are the allocative foci of social systems, each one assuring that some requirement of the social system will be met, in the same way that need-dispositions are allocative foci of personality systems, each need-disposition assuring that some requirement of the personality system will be met. (Allocative foci are the parts of a system among which functions, means or resources, time, attention, occasions, or cathexis are allocated.)

A value orientation is internalized when it is integrated with or part of a need-disposition to orient and act toward objects, to establish relationships with goal-objects, in accordance with particular values. A value orientation is institutionalized (this, like internalization, being a matter of degree) when it is part of a role-expectation internalized by a number of members of a social system, and therefore no longer dependent upon external sanctions for maintenance. In other words, a role is institutionalized when the complementary role-expectations and the sanctions reinforcing action in conformity with these are integrated with patterns of value orientation common to members of a social system. The solidarity of the members of a collectivity is manifested by the institutionalization of shared value orientations, resulting in commitment to orient and act in certain ways in roles. The stability of the collectivity as a system (the maintenance of its boundary and equilibrium state) is dependent upon such institutionalization.

A System View of the Psychiatric Hospital

As a system of action, the units of a psychiatric hospital as social system are sub-collectivities interacting with each other or with individual actors (in their roles as members of the hospital or of a subcollectivity of the hospital); individual actors interacting in their roles as members of the hospital; or subcollectivities, or individual actors in their roles as members of the hospital or of a subcollectivity of the hospital, interacting with collectivities or members of collectivities in the situation of the hospital.

The boundaries of the psychiatric hospital organization are defined by its primary goal and the internal arrangements for attaining that goal. The theoretical subsystems of the organization (motivation, integration, consummation, adaptation) are defined by subgoals into which the primary, more general goal may be analytically differentiated. Theoretical subsystems of these (sub-subsystems of the organization) are in turn defined by further differentiation of each subgoal into even more discrete, specific aims, functions, or tasks, each of which is part of what is necessary to achieve the subgoal.

A concrete collectivity within a hospital may be part of one subsystem or several subsystems or all subsystems. The extent to which concrete collectivities in a hospital each are differentiated to perform the functions of one subsystem is an index of the degree of differentiation of its organization. An organization is segmented rather than differentiated to the extent that collectivities tend to perform the same functions at different levels of authority in a hierarchy, in different geographical areas of the hospital, or with respect to different populations in the hospital.

Each subsystem of the hospital may be characterized in terms of functions contributing to the solution of particular problems that must be met by the entire hospital as system. Each such system-problem requires certain value orientations (preferred attitudes toward, and ways of classifying, objects) for its solution. The collectivities of a psychiatric hospital organization, pursuing their particular aims, and in so doing interacting with each other and adapting to their common situation, may be studied in terms of such a theoretical model. Departures from expectations aroused by the model (e.g., the pursuit of a covert, rather than a system-required or collectively avowed, aim is inferred by the observer) must inevitably occur, given among other factors situational exigencies and integrative strains. The model is heuristic in stimulating the formation of hypotheses to account for such departures.

THE PRIMARY FUNCTIONS OF THE PSYCHIATRIC HOSPITAL

Motivation and integration group-functions have primacy for the psychiatric hospital with respect to society, of which the hospital is a subcollectivity. The hospital is concerned with the internal states (and their alteration) of individual members of society, who are designated patients, and the integration of these patients and others (individuals and collectivities) in society. Insofar as the malintegration of the patient and others in society with whom he may be in conflict is the criterion for admission to the hospital, the hospital is conceived as serving an integration group-function for society. Insofar as malintegration of the personality system with concomitant internal dysphoric states or maldevelopment of the personality system (resulting in insufficient resources) or both, especially as these result in incapacities to function in society, are the criteria for admission to the hospital, the hospital is conceived as serving a motivation group-function for society.

Tensions within the individual, resulting from malintegration of the personality system, interfere with his motivation to fulfill role-expectations in society. Tension-management is a part of the motivation group-function of the hospital. Its short-term aspect includes providing opportunities to express or release tension within certain limits, which, however, are wider than those limits imposed outside the hospital. Its long-term aspect includes efforts to alter malintegration of the personality system through learning processes.

Pattern-maintenance, the creation and reinforcement of patterns of orientation and action required for participation in society, is also a part of the motivation group-function of the hospital. The reinforcement of such patterns existing within the individual is its minimal aspect; it includes the provision of opportunities for the implementation of these patterns through participation as members of intra-hospital collectivities in processes of action leading to relations with objects involving states of commitment (in the Motivation Group), solidarity (in the Integration Group), gratification (in the Consummation Group), and confidence (in the Adaptation Group). These relations and states are the intrinsic consequences of such processes of action and the responses of others to participation in them. Such responses include esteem by others of the patient as a whole insofar as he participates in actualizing shared values or meets shared standards (in the Motivation Group); approval by others of his specific performances, and affective manifestations of his solidarity with them (in the Integration Group); the making possible by others of gratification of various of the patient's specific wishes (in the Consummation Group); and the granting by others of such rewards to him as access to desired means (in the Adaptation Group).

Socialization, the creation of new patterns within the individual, is the maximal aspect of pattern-maintenance. It involves the process of learning: generalized need-dispositions to fulfill, rather than thwart, role-expectations; actions (including general skills) and orientations required for the fulfillment of broad categories of roles in society; and specific skills and orientations required for the fulfillment of specialized roles in society (this kind of learning perhaps being of less importance than the two other kinds for a hospital). Mechanisms of social control (Parsons 1951) include permissiveness to express existing tensions within limits; establishment of a solidary relationship; refusal to reciprocate or fulfill deviant expectations; allocation of rewards for approved performance. These mechanisms of social control are more immediate processes for coping with (preventing further development of, or reversing) tendencies or need-dispositions within the individual to act deviantly in relation to role-expectations. It is deviance for its own sake, rather than deviance as a result of a rational evaluation of the gains to be derived from it, that is usually characteristic of the psychiatric patient. Such need-dispositions, resulting in strain in any collectivity in which the individual participates, arise, when well-established, from failures or insufficiency in socialization; when transient, from strains or conflicts in the present situation. The psychiatric hospital, to achieve its aims, must cope with both well-established and transient tendencies to deviance by processes of socialization and social control.

Insofar as the hospital is part of the motivation subsystem of society, its output is an alteration within the patient's personality system; there is, theoretically, no output to its external environment. Evaluation of this kind of achievement is difficult. Insofar as the hospital is part of the integration subsystem of society, its function will be evaluated by society in terms of alterations in the degree of integration of some collectivity of which the patient is a member outside the hospital.

THE FOUR SUBSYSTEMS OF THE HOSPITAL

The organization of a psychiatric hospital may be analyzed in terms of the four group-functions adaptation, consummation, integration, and motivation. Various programs, committees, or other groups in the hospital may be viewed as differentiated to carry out one or more of these functions necessary to the attainment of the hospital's primary, most general goal: coping in a variety of ways with mental illness or psychiatric disorder.

The four subsystems of the hospital, then, analytically speaking, are adaptation, consummation, integration, and motivation. Again, it should be emphasized that concrete collectivities within the hospital and subsystems of the hospital do not necessarily coincide. A subsystem is a theoretically differentiated set of elements and processes. A collectivity may make a contribution in one, but also in more than one, of the subsystems of the total social system—the hospital. On a different level of analysis, any examination of the processes and structures of a concrete collectivity as a social system itself must include the four subsystems adaptation, consummation, integration, and motivation, interpreted in terms of the particular aims or functions of the collectivity in relation to its situation or other systems of action. Like any system of action, any collectivity within the hospital—like the hospital itself—is confronted by all four system-problems. A particular collectivity within the hospital, then, may be compared with other collectivities within the hospital in two ways: in terms of the system-problem or system-problems of the hospital as social system to which it makes its primary contribution or in terms of the proportion of time and effort it allocates among the four system-problems it faces as a system of action itself.

The adaptation subsystem of the hospital includes the following tasks:

1. in the adaptation component or phase—cognitively understanding the situation the hospital is in, and responding to changes in that situation;
2. in the consummation component or phase—obtaining or generating facilities, such as personnel (patients and staff), physical objects (equipment and supplies), necessary media of exchange and resources (money, information, knowledge), and occasions or opportunities to achieve desired states;
3. in the integration component or phase—weighing the consequences of choice between means (facilities) in relation to a given purpose or goal;

4. in the motivation component or phase—maintaining physical facilities and capacities for performance.

The consummation subsystem of the hospital includes the following tasks:

1. in the adaptation component or phase—becoming aware of, and clarifying, the aims of, or ends sought by, individual and collective members of the hospital, and their various wishes; determining what exists in the way of appropriate opportunities or occasions for, or barriers to, gratifying such wishes, fulfilling such aims, or attaining such ends;
2. in the consummation component or phase—deciding a wish will be gratified or an end pursued; allocating a means (facility, occasion, media of exchange) for use in attaining a goal in preference to some other goal-attainment; allocation of tasks and functions among individuals and groups; allocating rewards (money, recognition, which are considered to be rewards insofar as they are desirable as ends in themselves, irrespective of any uses they may have);
3. in the integration component or phase—uniting individual and collective members of the hospital to bring about gratification of wishes or the achievement of goals; settling conflicts arising over competing wishes or aims through a process of evaluating and assessing the consequences of their respective gratification or fulfillment; dealing with the consequences for relationships in the hospital between individuals, groups, or enterprises of the gratification of one wish or the achievement of one goal at the expense of others or of the allocation of facilities to one individual or group at the expense of another;
4. in the motivation component or phase—maintaining the motivation of members of the hospital to want and actively seek desired ends; dealing with the consequences for an individual member or particular group of a given allocation of facilities, or of the gratification of a wish or the achievement of a goal at the expense of other wishes or goals that he or it may have.

The integration subsystem of the hospital includes the following tasks:

1. in the adaptation component or phase—evaluating individual and collective members of the hospital, in terms of whether or not they are conforming to shared norms; evaluating which members of the group, in their orientations and actions, represent norms to be institutionalized or internalized by others; determining what norms are available, and what norms are needed, to be institutionalized;
2. in the consummation component or phase—deciding upon or gaining agreement that members of the hospital will conform to (feel obligated to implement in action) shared norms, or prescriptions for specific orientation and action in specific situations; deciding upon the sanctions necessary to achieve conformity to norms; achieving institutionalization of norms; bringing about identification with someone embodying an institutionalized norm;
3. in the integration component or phase—when any kind of a choice (between means, ends, norms, or values) is to be made, assessing the value standards or

norms that might be applied in a specific situation; dealing with consequences to relationships in the hospital between individuals, groups, and enterprises of the decision to adopt a norm and thereby bind members to its observance;

4. in the motivation component or phase—maintaining the motivation of members to affiliate with others in a moral community of shared values and norms; dealing with the consequences for an individual member or particular group of the adoption of a norm, that is, dealing with his or the group's inability to accept the norm or (accepting it) to live up to it.

The motivation subsystem of the hospital includes the following tasks:

1. in the adaptation component or phase—interpreting the meaning of events in the hospital, especially in terms of some general framework concerning ultimate values and related beliefs and normative sentiments about health and treatment;
2. in the consummation component or phase—achievement of an attitude of respect and esteem for the hospital, or for a decision or action of the hospital or a collectivity representing the hospital, on the part of individual and collective members of the hospital;
3. in the integration component or phase—when there is a choice or disagreement, assessing and weighing alternative interpretations of the meaning of events in terms of some general framework concerning beliefs and normative sentiments about health and treatment; finding a basis for a selection among such interpretations of one around which individual or collective members may unite;
4. in the motivation component or phase—maintaining the motivation on the part of an individual or collective member of the hospital to be committed to the hospital, that is, to the ultimate values and related beliefs and normative sentiments about health and treatment it represents; dealing with the difficulties an individual or collective member of the hospital has in being or becoming so committed.

VALUE SYSTEMS OF PSYCHIATRIC HOSPITALS

The common value system shared by the individual and collective members of a psychiatric hospital includes values, beliefs, and normative sentiments concerning health and therapy, and the less general norms derived from these, prescribing specific attitudes and actions in specific situations. Such a value system includes ideas about the nature of health and disease and the status and expectations of ill persons. Examples of such ideas follow. Illness should be viewed as a state resulting from other factors than the person's own qualities alone and as not changeable simply by the person's own inner resources (an effort of will). Ill persons should be exempt from certain expectations; such exemptions should be contingent on their recognizing they are ill (insight), their refraining from giving positive value to or rationalizing as desirable such a state or attempting to recruit others to adopt it, their seeking competent help to change it, and their making an active effort to collaborate with the agents of such help.

A particular hospital may be characterized by the particular system of values, normative sentiments, beliefs, and norms it has concerning health, disease, and treatment. Types of value patterns determining ways of defining or classifying healthy and ill persons may be formulated by combining preferences for regarding social objects impersonally or personally, as doers or beings. Such combinations are impersonal-doing, impersonal-being, personal-doing, and personal-being.

Impersonal-doing defines the way in which objects are regarded in an Adaptation Group. Health is viewed as the disposition and capacity to achieve, according to impersonal standards, any number and category of goals, and to regard objects impersonally in their relation to tasks to be performed. The patient tends to be evaluated primarily in terms of the functioning of the adaptive ego. Instrumental action, initiative, efficiency, tend to be prepotently valued. A hospital in which this view predominates is likely to emphasize the goal of improving capabilities and developing resources such as self-knowledge. Individual psychotherapy focused on insight, and learning skills through training and education, might be preferred treatment modalities.

Impersonal-being defines the way in which objects are regarded in a Motivation Group. Health is considered an ideal state of affairs, depending upon the existence of a set of qualities; illness, a departure from that state. What the patient is (what qualities he possesses) is more important than what he does in distinguishing health from illness. Therefore, for example, an ill person tends to be considered bad or possessed by evil, or, if the impersonally regarded qualities belong to the physiological organism, organically damaged. Health is commitment to and manifestation of an ideal; illness involves the patient's lack of disposition or incapacity to live in terms of respect for values or objects representing values. The patient, insofar as his personality system is an object of interest, tends to be evaluated primarily in terms of the functioning of the ego-ideal. A hospital in which this view predominates is likely to regard its chief tasks as custodial care of the ill and the protection of others from them. Manipulation of the physiological organism might be a preferred treatment modality.

Personal-doing defines the way in which objects are regarded in a Consummation Group. Health is the disposition and capacity to form and maintain personal relationships with objects through gratifying performance. The patient tends to be evaluated primarily in terms of the functioning of the executive or libidinal ego. Is he able to enjoy and express himself? How does he allocate cathexes? Expressive action, appropriateness, aesthetically pleasurable behavior, tend to be prepotently valued. Maintaining enjoyable relations with members of a family, for example, through appropriate gratifying performances in relation to them, is considered more valuable and healthier than individualistic achievement at the expense of such relationships. A hospital in which this view predominates is likely to emphasize the enhancement of expressive capacities for gratifying relations with others as the goal. Family therapy, group therapy, an individual psychotherapy focused on relationship and the expression of feelings, might be preferred treatment modalities.

Personal-being defines the way in which objects are regarded in an Integration Group. Health is the disposition and capacity to affiliate and identify with others valued as members of the same group. The patient tends to be evaluated primarily in terms of the functioning of the superego. Responsible action, moral rightness, fitting harmoniously into a network of relationships, tend to be prepotently valued.

Illness is sometimes considered a form of criminal deviance or a manifestation of social irresponsibility. A hospital in which this view predominates is likely to emphasize as a goal the adjustment of the patient to the expectations of others and to the work and social conditions existing in the society to which he is to return. An attempt to duplicate such expectations and conditions in the hospital, the patient's exposure to them through participation in various hospital programs and groups, and individual psychotherapy focused on directive management or interventions by the psychotherapist concerning what is the right thing to do, might be among preferred treatment modalities.

Because there is a tendency to consistency of values in a social system, the hypothesis may be formed that the value patterns governing views about what makes a "good hospital organization" and a "good staff member" will tend to coincide with the value patterns governing views about health, illness, and treatment. To the extent they do not coincide, manifestations of strain and instability should be found attributable to the discrepancy.

For example, in the first type of hospital, on this hypothesis, there may be a general emphasis on individualism. Authority is distrusted, because it might interfere with individual achievement. There are no absolute goals; emphasis is on the process of achieving a plurality of ever-changing goals; therefore, traditionalism has no foothold. The important facts about any member of the hospital (staff or patient) are likely to have to do with his capacities for performance and the extent to which he can be counted upon to refrain from interfering with others' performances and strivings. Problematical for such a hospital are the achievement of any sense of collective responsibility; the place or opportunity for personal relationships; and the response to inadequacy, or to interference by one member with the achievement of another. In this type of hospital, adaptive processes, and instrumental standards and action, will tend to have primacy with reference to the organization and maintenance of the hospital itself. The hospital is likely to be individualistic-bureaucratic, in the sense that authority exists primarily to see that people are provided with the conditions to do their jobs and protected from interference in carrying them out. Roles are differentiated in terms of the technical requirements of a task and assigned in terms of an individual's capabilities. The individualistic-bureaucratic hospital prides itself, and is primarily seen by patients and staff, as an object of utility. What it is good for, how it can be useful to its members, are its significant characteristics.

In the second type of hospital, the status of people (who they are, not what they can do) counts for everything. These statuses are defined impersonally, so that, for example, a physician is an object of respect irrespective of his performances. The organization of the hospital may be considered an ideal state of affairs; people, then, are classified as either for it or against it. Priority, therefore, is given to considerations of the consequences of any act for the hospital rather than for the individual: does it promote and maintain, or interfere, with the ideal state of affairs? People in authority are expected to see it is the promotion and maintenance of an ideal state of affairs that occurs. The important facts about any member of the hospital are his worthiness of esteem and respect; his disposition to respect the hospital as a source of right and authority; his status determining how he should be treated by others; his disposition to treat other people as their status indicates they should be treated.

Problematical for such a hospital are the place of or opportunity for individual achievement or personal relationships; and the response to someone who does not know or does not accept his place, someone who demands inappropriate treatment, or someone whose worthiness is not commensurate with his position. In this type of hospital, pattern-maintenance processes will tend to predominate. It is likely to be authoritarian-bureaucratic, in the sense that the hierarchy of roles and relationships will be determined by people's qualities; members of the organization may occupy positions by virtue of the prestige attached to some characteristic, for example, rather than ability. The authoritarian-bureaucratic hospital is an object of authority and respect, caring for its members and doing to them what it deems their condition requires.

In the third type of hospital, individual activity is valued, but in relationship with others in the hospital: in the formation, maintenance, and in the defense (when threatened), of such relationships. The set of interactions in the hospital is a primary source of gratification to its members. An individual's way of relating is judged by appreciative standards, not in terms of instrumental or moral values. Matters of good taste and aesthetic considerations are crucial. Anything that disturbs gratifying relationships (including individual achievement) is deprecated. The appeal is to tradition (how things have been and are and should continue to be, because "we like it that way") in the face of such disruption. Authority enforces tradition. The important facts about any member of the hospital are the extent to which he "fits in"; his disposition to relate in a way gratifying to others and to reciprocate appropriately. Problematical for such a hospital are the regulation and channeling of individual actions (including instrumental actions) so these do not interfere with a gratifying state of affairs; and the response to people who are not able to express themselves appropriately or respond or relate well to others. In this type of hospital, cathectic processes, appreciative standards, and expressive action will tend to have primacy. Such a hospital, for example, may be quite small, and perhaps isolated, so that staff members may have and depend upon many informal social contacts with each other outside the hospital. Under these conditions, equalitarian organization may be defended as an order necessary for protecting gratifying relationships among members of the organization. The "oasis" hospital is an object of cathexis, a source of satisfying experiences, and may be especially valued as a respite, retreat, or pleasurable sanctuary from the demands of the external world.

In the fourth type of hospital, the set of relationships in the hospital as given qualities have a moral rather than a gratificatory aspect. It is expected that every individual will adjust to the existing state of affairs, fit into it, behave harmoniously with others. Therefore, authority tends to be considered unnecessary; the good will of responsible members will maintain order. However, authority is welcomed as a source of stability when necessary, if it is used to support not interfere with the given order. Work is a necessary evil; achievement tends to disrupt the valued pattern. Moral obligation (the obligation to consider the welfare of and consequences for the hospital as primary, to accept existing standards and arrangements) is reinforced by appeals to tradition, which guards the stability of a moral order and incidentally therefore maintains vested interests. The important facts about any member of the hospital are whether he can be considered the right sort of person, and in tune with others; his disposition to believe in and act according to the norms others accept; his disposition to conform or step out of line. Problematical for such a hospital are keeping order, when faith in the good will of individuals turns out to be unjustified; the regulation of individual actions, so these fit in harmoniously with the existing order, which members have a moral obligation to maintain; and the response to people who don't fit in, who do not believe in the standards and order others value and feel a moral obligation to maintain, who are disturbing elements. In this type of hospital, integrative processes, moral standards, and responsible action will tend to have primacy. Such a hospital may regard itself as an example of what is right for other hospitals to follow. Its leadership is seen especially as possessing moral integrity. The "moral exemplar" hospital is an object of identification, a source of the "right way of life."

Of course, these are ideal types; all concrete hospitals are mixtures in varying proportions of these ingredients. The four value systems described are based upon four ways of defining social objects, each one of which is essential to the aims of one of the four subsystems of any social system. Each of the four value systems, then, must be manifested in some form in some concrete collectivity, process of action, or program within any hospital, inasmuch as different collectivities, processes of action, or programs are differentiated to fulfill the aims, and therefore actualize the value orientations, of each one of the four subsystems of the hospital as a social system, and represent thereby the allocation of some effort to the solution of each one of the hospital's four system-problems. The differences between these value elements, inevitably represented somewhere and to some degree in every hospital, is one source of strain and conflict within any hospital organization.

Because there is a tendency to consistency of values in a social system, although of course no society is in this sense perfectly integrated, another hypothesis may be formed: that a particular view of health and treatment and a particular type of hospital organization are likely to be found with greater frequency in a society in which the dominant value patterns coincide with those underlying such views and organization. To the extent they do not coincide, manifestations of strain and instability should be found attributable to the discrepancy.

Strains in the Psychiatric Hospital[1]

Hospitals are chaotic, enigmatic places in which to work. A. K. Rice once referred to hospital organizations as examples of "motivated disorganization." And, indeed, it is not uncommon to hear psychiatric hospital administrators say somewhat ruefully, but with an unmistakeable note of pleasure, how unorganized their hospitals are. Organization is associated by them with "head," with intellectualism, detachment, cold expediency, or authoritarianism; disorganization invariably with "heart," warmth, and a high valuation of "human relations." The havoc wreaked upon human relations as well as task achievement by some kinds of carelessness about organization, while well documented, often goes conveniently unnoticed.

---

1. Some material in this and following sections first appeared in somewhat different form (Edelson 1967).

Such disorganization may result from difficulties in thinking about organization. The following examples are intended to be typical of certain trends in thinking about organizational problems in psychiatric hospitals; as such, of course, they are somewhat oversimplified.

One, I shall call the case of the interfering situation. Dr. Smith regards the interaction between psychotherapist and patient as *the* process of treatment. All factors impinging upon that process from outside it are conceived to be obstacles interfering with it. For his patient, and usually for himself as well, Dr. Smith wants maximum freedom from the conventional requirements of the situation, or from the demands and expectations of collective life in the hospital; these are apt to be seen as, at the least, imperfectly adapted to the particular needs of the individual patient or staff member and as interfering, therefore, with treatment. This point of view, when extended, tends to conceive any demands made upon either staff or patient—for example, definitions of roles and role-boundaries—as constraints rather than as enabling task-performance. The typical maneuver, here, is to attempt to insulate the treatment operation from its situation, which usually means ignoring the impact of the situation upon the treatment process and, therefore, misunderstanding many of the vicissitudes of the latter.

Two, I shall call the case of the vanishing situation, which is a close relative of the previous example. Dr. Jones is devoted to the ideal of individualized treatment. Every patient should receive the treatment exactly appropriate to his need. The choice or application of treatment is not to be affected by the types of patients in the hospital, neither by their capacities nor by the social situation their interactions with each other and with staff create. Treatment is not to be determined by the nature of hospital buildings or other physical facilities; available staff skills; or geographic setting. Since every treatment operation is, of course, affected by these factors, maneuvers may include attempts to dilute their impact, even at the cost of effective treatment, as well as to ignore it. A focus on the inner world of the patient or his interactions with the therapist as of primary importance in the treatment process helps to accomplish such maneuvers, as do efforts to prevent group formation, minimize formal group activities, and reduce the commitment of the patient to any collectivity other than the therapist-patient dyad, for example, by proscribing planned group activities or breaking down living units often with emphasis on the needs of privacy. When the functioning of the hospital community requires commitment to formal group enterprises, and when group life, whether formal or informal, has an impact upon the ability of the hospital to achieve its goals, such efforts tend to obscure rather than clarify these processes.

Three, I shall call the case of the unlimited resources. Dr. Brown believes deeply that nothing should interfere with therapy. He dislikes, as do many advocates of the importance of "good human relations," saying "no." He tolerates poorly the disagreeable conflicts that come when the realities of limited resources and competing operations are faced. His response to a request for personnel is to stretch personnel without regard to the effects of multiple, sometimes conflicting assignments upon task-performance. His response to a request for money for some enterprise in the hospital, for example, a group project in the therapeutic community, is, "if it helps patients get well, there is no worry about money, we'll get the money." The logical outcome of such a policy is bankruptcy. However, the more frequent outcome is that reasons of varying degrees of sophistry are adduced to show that the proposed project is not therapeutic but is rather related to undesirable patient pathology, for example, infantile greed, passive sloth, or what have you. The decision, in other words, is made in a way that, instead of increasing patients' respect for the limitations of reality, rather decreases their self-esteem. Secrecy is another maneuver useful here; no patient or staff member or group is to know what another has requested and received, lest bad feelings be exacerbated. The consequence is that competing operations cannot present their claims in open discussion; it is, therefore, difficult to assess the merit of such claims in terms of the situation and the organization's hierarchy of priorities or to win wide consent for decisions about such claims. Often, the left hand does not know what the right hand is doing, and suspicion of unfairness flourishes, to the detriment of the total organization.

Four, I shall call the case of the exploited threat. Dr. Green has set priorities on the basis of his conviction that one rather than another kind of technical operation will most likely lead to the achievement of the hospital's goals. Instead of presenting this decision as either a technical decision (one means is more effective than the other to achieve a particular goal) or as a value preference (one technical operation is preferred over another on the basis of values other than effectiveness), he tries to persuade the members of the organization that the situation makes the decision inevitable. For example, there is not enough money to support individual psychotherapy, on the one hand, or the financial situation of the hospital requires greater investment of staff time in seeing patients individually than in participating in group activities. Dr. Green hopes that a particular pattern of staff assignments can thereby be justified by the threat from without—not enough money. That the decision is ideological rather than technical is often apparent from the lack of analysis of the consequences—and what accommodations to these will be needed—following from the decision to rely primarily on psychotherapy or on the therapeutic milieu. That the availability of resources is not the actual issue can sometimes be seen rather easily, because the question is so often clearly not how to mobilize resources but how to allocate what resources the hospital does have. What is often not clear is that an apparent decision about means is actually a decision about ends—what goals are to be preferred and sought over other goals. Staff members in a large mental health center, for example, may speak as though they were primarily concerned with mitigating the patient's intrapersonal conflicts, while their actual operations involve mitigating strains between the patient and groups in his environment.

The following examples have to do with potentially fatal disparities. One is that between the valued integration of individual and group members of the hospital organization, on the one hand, and the requirements imposed by a changing situation, on the other. Two is that between the goal of the hospital organization, on the one hand, and the actual motivational commitments and skills of its members, on the other.

One, I shall call the case of the strain between integration and adaptation. The members of a hospital organization are likely to regard a certain kind of integration —democracy or equalitarianism, for example, or certain rules or procedures, or certain kinds of committees or groups—as an end in itself, irrespective of its relevance to the achievement of the hospital's goals or to changes in the situation requiring new forms of integration. Such changes may include the introduction of new, and perhaps crucially different patients; the entry of new staff possessing skills heretofore absent; the loss of staff and crucial skills; the discovery and transmission of new knowledge making new ways of achieving goals and even new goals possible; and changes in society's needs and expectations of the hospital or in what other groups will support as legitimate, perhaps necessitating the adoption of new goals and new ways for members of the hospital to work together to achieve these.

A particular kind of interaction between groups and individuals may be valued for reasons other than effectiveness in the achievement of work goals. The importance of equalitarianism and permissiveness, for example, may be rationalized as important for successful treatment. That the investment in such an ideology is not related solely to the achievement of treatment goals is clear when the ideology is held applicable to work with patients whose illness is exacerbated by such a way of working, or when the failure to delegate responsibilities and authority to carry them out interferes with task-performance.

Two, I shall call the case of the strain between goal or task and commitment or skill. The goals of a particular hospital organization are usually determined by its relation to its situation: what other groups in the situation outside the hospital expect and hold to be legitimate, as indicated by the support (in terms of finances and personnel) available for particular efforts; the image other groups have of the hospital and the often changing needs of these groups, as indicated by the type of patients referred to the hospital. The ideological commitments and particular skills of a staff group may or may not be relevant to such goals.

Commitment to permissiveness, for example, in an organization whose young patients are increasingly characterized by acting out, drug addiction, and other forms of sociopathy, may result in great strain. It may appear that to the extent such commitment is maintained, the goals of the hospital are not achievable: permissiveness may increase the anxiety of patients who feel at the mercy of their impulses and consequently the extent and intensity of their acting out such impulses; alienation and aimlessness may be exacerbated by what looks like a neutral noncommittal attitude on the part of staff in relation to various types of socially disruptive behavior.

The presence of different kinds of patients may change the definition of what effective treatment is; no staff group is likely to be able to change its skills and the personal investments these involve as rapidly as the patient population may change at times.

The staff members of a mental health center may be mobilized to accomplish the rapid return of patients to the extra-hospital community; they employ the skills relevant to, and judge the success of their efforts by, this outcome. If the mental health center is responsible for the patients in a particular geographical area, inevitably the inpatient population will consist increasingly of patients with chronic rather than acute illness. The motivational commitments of the staff are not to value attitudes and types of action relevant to the treatment of this new population; morale under these circumstances may sag, or the staff will seek to evade the actual task by a variety of maneuvers that affect adversely the hospital's relation to outside groups upon which it depends.

The commitment of a staff may be to intensive individual psychotherapy. The staff may have some difficulty accommodating to the kind of psychotherapy that is actually possible, given the limitations of skills of inexperienced trainees, who have often not had prior intensive psychotherapy themselves, and who are often unable to cope effectively with the experiences inevitable in seeing patients three or four times a week. The effort to develop a theory of psychotherapy which will make such psychotherapy "good psychotherapy," which will set goals achievable by psychotherapists with such skill-limitations, or which will account for observed effects (e.g., the disruption apparently induced in a borderline or psychotic patient by what is taken for granted as an adequate interpretation is accounted for by the supposed effects of interpretation itself as a form of intervention), often involves a lot of staff time and some sophistry.

It is extremely painful to face that one's skills or personal qualities are irrelevant or inadequate to a particular task. Various rationalizations must be employed to make it possible for an organization to imagine that its task has remained unchanged when it is changing, or to make it possible to retain the services of particular individuals whose skills, beliefs, or preferences are no longer relevant to the achievement of the hospital's goals.

As a professional person lives on, he is increasingly likely to try to alter the task of the organization or the view of that task rather than to change the professional identity it has taken a lifetime to build to conform to the requirements of a new task. In any kind of organization, if such a person has a position of leadership, from which for one reason or another he cannot be ousted, he may lead the organization to its doom. Many ideological fights in psychiatric hospital organizations are not motivated simply by desires for power; the fights ultimately are over whose skills will find opportunities for exercise; whose personal qualities will matter; whose professional identity will survive in the organization.

Difficulties in another direction have to do with a facile, opportunistic alteration in the hospital's goals to meet what may be a temporary shift in its circumstances—new sources of support, treatment fads, reactions to current societal stresses. Such a hospital organization may have little commitment to anything except unsystematic eclecticism or a hodge-podge of technical operations. Such rapid shifts and eclecticism may undermine that confidence in the organization necessary to command the allegiance of patients or staff to its work. There is in such an organization no lasting devotion to any point of view or method—a devotion characteristic (rather than as is commonly misunderstood uncharacteristic) of the scientific enterprise; therefore, there is little possibility of developing the skills to test the limits or effectiveness of that point of view or method.

Demoralization and alienation are evidences of disparity between goal or task and commitment or skill. The response to such symptoms of organizational strain is often a yearning for charismatic leadership. Such leadership may be embodied in a tradition, in a past golden age of the hospital, in historical figures, in documents and formulae apparently offering solutions of timeless validity. Such leadership may be embodied in a man the force of whose personal qualities seems sufficient to still doubts and awaken hope. Such leadership is not technical; it does not derive its authority from "what works," from an examination of particular situations and the identification and application of knowledge and technical skills specifically relevant to current problems. The cost of such leadership may be measured by persistent problems that cannot be spirited away through the comfort afforded by personal magnetism, ritual, or the reaffirmation of untested or untestable beliefs. The strained organization will sometimes complain that its leadership does not have enough charisma, when it is relevant technical mastery, some resolution of the disparity between task and skill, that is wanted. It sometimes escapes notice that a leader may be potently charismatic and the organization still fail.

As some of the above examples suggest, motivated disorganization may have functional as well as dysfunctional aspects, reflecting as it often does not simply poor thinking about organization but accommodation to inevitable strains. Such strains arise from conflict and competition between the necessary enterprises, functions, or aims, and their intrinsic values, encompassed by any hospital organization. Strains also arise from the fact that the systems within which change is sought by psychiatric hospitals are never simply passive objects of change but are persons with value-preferences and intentions of their own. Therefore, their participation as integrated members of the hospital, while problematical, is required to bring about the desired changes. In addition, strains arise from the fact that the hospital is both a community (where people live together and therefore must cope with the variegated, far-ranging, frequently unanticipated problems, and achieve ends impossible to specify in advance, that are generated by a group sharing a common territory) and an organization (whose members are devoted to cooperative, instrumental effort to achieve a predetermined, specific end).

Emphasis on the community—characterized as a therapeutic community—aspect of the hospital is often associated with a view of organization and organizational problems almost naively assuming as pre-eminent likeness, concord, and a communality of interests among all the members and parts of the organization. Problems are thought to arise because members do not understand their interests are the same. Through free and open discussion, for example, such problems, essentially related to misunderstandings, should disappear. The important question, according to this view, is how can people communicate with each other and so join together in realization of their common interest?

But even a casual look at any psychiatric hospital exposes an astonishing variety of groups, points of view, jobs to be done, and value positions—many apparently incompatible or interfering with each other. The hospital is a veritable cauldron of conflicts, tensions, and apparent and concealed purposes. The questions actually crucial for problem-solving are, what are the differences, for example, in ends sought and value positions, and in what ways can individuals and groups representing essential functions battle out their differences?[2]

---

2. Etzioni describes two approaches to conflict in industry, one emphasizing faulty human relations as the source of such conflict, the other attributing objective significance and a positive function to such conflict. The former frame of reference has been applied to mental hospitals, with the result that conflict tends to be attributed to misunderstanding brought about by lack of communication and its mitigation sought in increase of communication. That real differences in interest and opinion may be involved, that communication may only result in the drawing of clearer lines between individuals and groups and in an increase in tension, and that the

Organization implies complexity, organic structure, and interdependent parts; each part has a special separate function, but also the relation of each part to any other is to a large extent governed by its relation to the whole. Organization is, in one sense, a way of defining the pathways and procedures by which different functions are coordinated and carried out, and differences are at least faced and in some way resolved. The organization of a hospital determines the norms, rules, or patterns guiding the choices that must be made as its goal is pursued.

A discussion of the psychiatric hospital as community often implies a view of it as a closed, self-sufficient system, and is often used to emphasize the importance of focusing upon internal relations. The hospital, however, is an open system. Its organization is determined by, and concerned with, not only autonomous functions relating the parts of it to each other and maintaining these parts in optimal condition for participating in the organization, but also heteronomous functions relating the hospital to its situation: the extended society of which it is a part. Such functions are ordinarily the responsibility of an administrative system within the organization.

Heteronomous functions of the administrative system include the legitimation of the hospital (e.g., through conformity to legal requirements, public relations activities, and appeals for support) so that it may operate in the community; relations with such recipients of the hospital's services as referring physicians, community agencies, and the patients and their families—including admission and discharge procedures, and determination of the need for service and the requirement of payment for it; the acquisition of facilities, including financial resources, personnel, and physical facilities; and the integration of the hospital into the larger community. This integration may be accomplished through such mechanisms as the institution of contract with professional personnel that maintains standards of competency and training; the exercise of responsible authority (e.g., in commitment procedures and medical decisions) that takes into account the membership of the patient in groups outside the hospital; and the acceptance of universal standards of good practice and conformity with general social standards of acceptable conduct (Parsons 1957).

Autonomous functions of the administrative system include the socialization of members of the organization or the implementation of the value systems of the organization; the integration of the organization by enlisting the loyalty of personnel and, therefore, by considering and seeking the belief of personnel in the rightness of decisions; the maintenance and improvement of adequate facilities providing a base for professional performance; and the allocation of authority and responsibility in

---

resolution of differences depends on such organizational factors as the distribution of authority and power, tend to be overlooked (Etzioni 1960). Whyte makes a similar point when he questions the assumption in the ideology of the modern corporation or of group dynamics as a social movement that the interests of the individual and the group are always in harmony and that an individual may find the fulfillment of all his significant needs by being a "good" group member (Whyte 1956).

Conflict among administrative and professional groups and between the instrumental goals of the hospital and the requirements for the maintenance of the hospital, and the competition between the needs of different functions within the hospital or the competition between groups to perform high prestige functions, are discussed, for example, by Smith and Levinson (1957). These and other sources of strain in the psychiatric hospital are also discussed by Loeb and Smith (1957).

such a way as to ensure the opportunity for personnel to operate effectively (Parsons 1957).

The purpose of the psychiatric hospital organization, its primary collective goal, is to cope in a variety of ways with the consequences of emotional illness for the individual patient, for the patients as a social group, and (to some extent) for society. The hospital discharges this responsibility through the technical operations of a professional system within the organization.[3]

The relation between groups representing different functions within the administrative system or the professional system is associated with a variety of intragroup and intergroup strains in the psychiatric hospital.

For example, professional personnel, including physicians, psychologists, and nurses, are responsible not only to the hospital but to the professional group to which each belongs. Professional personnel must perform according to standards set by groups outside the hospital; it is always conceivable that these might conflict with expectations within the hospital. Any role definition at marked variance to that of the professional group to which a person belongs may be literally felt to unfit him for functioning in any other setting and is strongly resisted. It is a fact also that promotion in a psychiatric hospital is usually limited to promotion within one's own professional group and that one can only go so far as one's group goes in the organization. Naturally, then, each group looks to its own superiors for supervision and direction. These conditions result in professional groups, each of the members of which is strongly oriented to the values, activities, and ways of looking at things of his own group, and not always especially familiar with those of other professional groups. Strains between professional groups under these circumstances are inevitable. The hospital organization should be designed to allow for, and cope with, such strains.

The administrative system and the professional system are, of course, both necessary. The professional person is required for the performance of technical operations and for the evaluation of such operations: the evaluation of the competency of those who perform them and the adequacy of the conditions under which they are performed. The administrative system is required to provide and safeguard the conditions that make possible an adequate performance of professional functions. Yet, the relation between these two systems, too, is associated with a variety of intragroup and intergroup strains in the psychiatric hospital.

Housekeeping and dietary activities are examples of areas that are a source of conflict between administrative and professional groups in the hospital, since the way in which housing and eating are arranged has significance for the effectiveness with which treatment goals are achieved.

---

3. Parsons' formulation of the functions of the professional system in terms of services provided by the hospital may be paraphrased as follows. One service is custodial, the physical care of patients within the hospital. Another is protection, the safeguarding of patients and others from the harm, physical or social, that patients might do to themselves or others. Still another is socialization, the education of patients in the direction of understanding and accepting social expectations, within the hospital and outside of it. A final service is therapy, the treatment of patients with the aim of recovery from emotional illness (Parsons 1957). Any particular hospital may be characterized by the priorities it assigns these services. A different formulation of the functions of the professional system was begun by Edelson (1967) and is developed in a later section of this chapter, "A Theoretical Model of Psychiatric Hospital Organization."

The administrative system must mediate effectively between the sources of financial supplies and professional parts of the organization. In order to justify the trust of society, the sources of financial resources, whether legislative bodies or private donors, must have some controls over the uses to which money is put. This alone, if nothing else, would introduce a line of authority and responsibility in any psychiatric hospital organization, no matter how equalitarian it sought to be. In addition, the exercise of authority inevitably arises from the fact that the organization must, in order to carry out its functions, have some degree of control over the situation in which it performs them. However, members of the professional system tend to be suspicious of authority. They are deeply concerned with their own autonomy and wary of any control over their activities by administrative personnel. At the same time they insist that the administrative system provide them with favorable opportunities for the exercise of their special professional skills.

Administrative and professional needs, requirements, responsibilities, and activities not only have to be coordinated, but when they are incompatible, there must be some way to assign priority to one over the other. Organization determines how the conflicts and strains between these two systems are to be resolved.

It is generally accepted that recognition must be given to the special skills of professional personnel, to the protection of their integrity and autonomy, and to their ultimate responsibility for the policy decisions involved in the carrying out of professional activities. Such recognition may be attempted by sharpening the distinction between administrative and professional questions to ensure that professional personnel are consulted in cases involving the latter. It may also be attempted by blurring the distinction between administrative and professional parts of the organization and involving at least some members of the professional staff in the process of making administrative decisions.

The allocation of authority and responsibility can be a positive enabling function of administration (not often associated with authority by those who fear authoritarianism). Any part of the organization may be protected in this way from undue interference from other parts in the performance of its function; that is, its relative autonomy safeguarded. For example, a decision necessary to carry out a responsibility may be protected by the allocation of authority and responsibility from overt or covert veto by individuals or groups not bearing the consequences of, or accountable for, the decision.

Ultimately, the confidence of professional personnel in administration and their support of administrative decisions depend upon their knowledge that administration is facilitating successful achievement. Such confidence is related to awareness that administrative decisions occur in such a way that they take into account the varying consequences of any decision for different parts of the organization and the relative burdens and rewards accruing to these different parts as a result of such decisions. This confidence is also related to the administration's recognition of, and deference to, the professional staff in their capacity as responsible and expert members of their professional group, irrespective of their particular position in the hospital organization. Recognition and deference unrelated to position in an organizational hierarchy are hard to indicate on the typical organizational chart, and manifestations of them in the daily life of the hospital contribute to the impression that the hospital is an example of motivated disorganization.

Other sources of strain (manifested in tension within individuals, conflict or disagreement between individuals or groups, or difficulties between a group and its object-situation, that is, difficulties in carrying out heteronomous functions) may be listed as follows. There may be inconsistencies or inadequacies within a value system itself. That is, internalized or institutionalized values may form an incoherent system, or may not meet the requirements of particular system-problems. There may be discongruity between the requirements of different collectivities, sharing common members, or between the requirements of the same collectivity in different situations or at different times. There may be discongruity between the requirements of the personality systems of members of the collectivity and characteristics of the collectivity, or between the requirements of the collectivity and characteristics of the personality systems of its members.

In studying a particular collectivity, it is important to consider the mechanisms employed to avoid or resolve strains arising from various sources, or to accommodate to them when they cannot be avoided or resolved, as well as to observe the changes in the structures and processes of the collectivity itself born of such strains.

Any strains may result in value patterns necessary to meet the requirements of a particular system-problem being insufficiently internalized or institutionalized. For example, dissensus among staff members and inconsistency in the same staff person mean that expectations of and responses to patients by the same person in different, but apparently similar, situations or by different people in the same situation, may differ. Then, the patient tends to regard the values and norms of the hospital expediently, as part of his situation rather than himself, and he may use an apparent commitment to some value or conformity to some norm in that situation to rationalize disregard of or deviation from another.

However, a negative value is not necessarily to be placed on strain. Strains may result in useful changes in a social system as well as produce dysfunctional effects. The presence of strains is not a satisfactory criterion of social pathology. It is indeed difficult to conceptualize—from the stance of the observer frame of reference for which the normative elements in the situation and system under study do not have any necessary normative implications—what would constitute a pathological social system. One might judge pathology from the point of view of one's own value orientations; from the point of view of the discrepancy between what is actual from what is sought by the social system under study (although such a discrepancy itself might have some functional effects for the system); or from the point of view of the degree of integration of the parts of the social system (although malintegration over a period of time may result in change in the social system, not necessarily just its dissolution). When change results from strain, it may be difficult to decide whether the social system that has changed has nevertheless retained its identity or the system has actually been dissolved and replaced by what is essentially a new system.

Examples of Strains Resulting from Inconsistencies within the
Value System of the Hospital

ADAPTATION VERSUS INTEGRATION VALUES. The psychiatric hospital in the United States exists in an achievement-dominated culture. Its predominant value patterns are those appropriate to instrumental action, requiring discipline, inhibition of interest in immediate discharge, and a restricted orientation in relation to objects, which are categorized impersonally and in terms of what they have done, do, or will do. Congruently, the organization of the hospital, insofar as it is an organization that is part of the occupational adaptation subsystem of society, selects its members, patients and staff, according to impersonal-doing criteria. The relevant criterion is the universal class of individuals to which a member belongs: the class defined in terms of complexes of performances, for example, incapacitated ill person, physician, nurse, administrator. A staff person is selected, and tasks or functions are assigned to him, in terms of instrumental capacities, involving disciplined inhibition of affective or discharge propensities and specialized differentiated skills. On the other hand, restricted aspects of a person also qualify him for membership as a patient. That is, a person is brought to the attention of the organization only in those aspects involving his illness and will be admitted to the hospital only insofar as he is ill.

Similarly, means to accomplish goals are selected by classifying objects impersonally and according to restricted interests in them: is this an effective method of treatment? In solving problems, situations are symbolized cognitively, requiring a disciplined neutral attitude to objects classified in terms of their potential or actual performances in relation to the collectivity and its goals. What does the science of human behavior tell us about this behavior? To what is it related? What is its cause? What will be its effects?

However, the hospital is also part of the integration subsystem of society (as are collectivities concerned with legislative and judicial functions). Its concern, therefore, is with processes requiring value patterns different from those of the adaptation subsystem, prescribing, for example, an affective orientation to patients and expansive interests in them, if they are to be integrated into a solidary collectivity (whether this be the psychotherapy collectivity, the hospital itself, or the society to which patients will return) or if *any* aspect of the patient and his actions is to be followed up in the interest of the integration of the personality system. Patients, then, must be seen in terms of being rather than doing—who they are in some enduring sense, what they are as persons, rather than simply what they are doing now or did yesterday—and personally, as members belonging to a solidary collectivity: "my patient, our patient." Thus, a patient, once he is a member of the hospital or one of its collectivities, must be regarded in a different way than any patient or ill person. Weighing the consequences of action for individuals and collectivities, insofar as such a process is to result in integration of the person or collectivity, involves an orientation to the patient in his belongingness to a collectivity, or in the belongingness of some part of his personality system to him, and therefore an interest in a multiplicity of aspects and relationships. Evaluation of a patient's behavior depends on consideration of norms and the systems of values to which these belong, and on affective attitudes toward, or caring about, whether or not a patient conforms to certain norms, for example, to those expectations making it possible to treat him or possible for him to participate in society. In the hospital emphasis is on the network of expanded interests and obligations with which discharge tendencies are integrated, rather than merely on propensities or capacities to gratify specific need-dispositions or to be similarly gratified.

Another aspect of this dilemma between adaptation and integration values involves the attitude to the hospital and its collectivities or individual members. Response to the hospital, or to any collectivity or individual member of it, as an object of utility is in terms of what it has done, is doing, or may do for the patient, evaluated according to impersonal criteria: how efficient is it in curing patients? Response to the hospital, or to any collectivity or individual member of it, as an object of identification, however, is in terms of relatively enduring qualities, not dependent upon the vicissitudes of immediate performance, and the inclusion of the patient in a solidary collectivity.

Conflict and disagreement about the relation of the nature of the hospital's organization (e.g., bureaucratic versus democratic) to the effectiveness with which the hospital accomplishes its treatment goals are similar to dissonance between values associated with the spiritual aims of the church and those values associated with the mundane imperatives of organization (e.g., to obtain and allocate means—such as money—necessary for the achievement of such aims).

Attempts in a psychiatric hospital to reduce strains arising from inconsistencies in a value system include the segregation of administrative (analogous to "mundane") and treatment (analogous to "spiritual") functions; or the performance of both kinds of functions by the same person. The former attempt may give rise, however, to conflicts and disagreements between collectivities or individuals responsible for different functions. Concentrations of power in an individual or collectivity may result in the sacrifice of one kind of function in favor of another. The latter attempt may cause strains to develop within an individual or collectivity at the same time responsible for different functions. Limitations in the capacities or resources of an individual or collectivity may result in the abrogation of one kind of function in favor of another.

In a hospital where the organization is suited to efficient adaptation and achievement, there may also be insufficient institutionalization and reinforcement of values necessary for integrative processes. Integrative attitudes and actions may be thwarted or unavailable. On the other hand, integrative processes may be prepotent in a hospital in which there is also insufficient institutionalization and reinforcement of values necessary for efficient adaptation and achievement. Instrumental attitudes and actions may be thwarted or unavailable.

SCIENTIST VERSUS THERAPIST. Is it possible to be a scientist and a therapist? Are the values of one compatible with the values of the other? The cognitive standards of science are values in a medical organization; but the relative degrees of achievement of motivation and integration goals are difficult to evaluate by cognitive standards. Ideologies, or systems of unverifiable beliefs, arise to rationalize what the hospital or its individual or collective members are doing in cognitive terms, especially in areas where knowledge is still unavailable or incomplete. Authority or tradition function to win and reinforce acceptance of such beliefs, because these cannot be justified by cognitive standards, and people cannot be persuaded to commit themselves to unverifiable beliefs and values by logical processes. The use of mechanisms such as authority or tradition, rather than standards of validity, in a culture in which science and scientific method are valued, itself gives rise to strains within or between members of the hospital.

Arguments between members of a hospital staff about organization or treatment may, for example, be about the respective merits of a therapeutic community approach, psychotherapy, or uses of medication; different ways of proceeding in the therapeutic community program or psychotherapy; the respective merits of equalitarian and bureaucratic organization. Since such arguments have roots in ideological beliefs or value preferences rather than empirically verifiable propositions, they are replete with sophistic derivations, rationalization, and bitterness, quite incongruous with the claim opponents make to scientific attitudes and validity.

Because it is difficult to evaluate scientifically—that is, according to cognitive standards of validity or empirical verifiability—whether a hospital or one of its collectivities is achieving its goals, consensus among members that the values and beliefs of the hospital or collectivity as to its methods and achievements are right and correct is crucial in maintaining confidence in the hospital or collectivity. The degree of such confidence and the associated degree of hope that goals will be attained determine the extent to which members will be motivated to fulfill expectations and thus the stability and even survival of the hospital or collectivity. Fierce (apparently scientific) ideological arguments among staff shake the confidence of members in the rightness of the hospital and therefore disrupt its solidarity or integration.

In a situation of minimal solidarity, an apparent deterioration in the behavior of one patient in treatment, the discharge of a patient who is not doing well or does not believe in the hospital or in treatment, the resignation of a dissatisfied staff member, are all causes of integrative crisis, and may result in a contagion of such incidents. In this sense, unverifiable ideological beliefs—in the presence of inadequate, incomplete knowledge or in areas where empirical knowledge will never be available—are a necessary integrative mechanism for a hospital. Skeptical scientific attitudes toward them may be destructive to the solidarity of the group that is necessary for its functioning or for taking any collaborative action.

New scientific discoveries may be disruptive in the same way. In relation to these, however, the institutionalization of a positive valuation of change through empirical discovery and improvement of technology may mitigate, but cannot completely resolve, such strains.

BUREAUCRACY VERSUS PSYCHOTHERAPY. Are the values underlying participation in a bureaucratic organization—for example, the valuation of disciplined, specialized performances—compatible with those underlying participation in a psychotherapeutic interaction? In any society there is some differentiation of functions and therefore recognition of different competencies. The differentiation of competencies tends to result in different degrees of responsibility being allocated for the affairs of the collectivity. The greater the degree of responsibility, the greater the concentration of facilities and, therefore, also rewards. To the extent different prestige comes to be attached to different functions, such prestige differences may be thought to prevent open communication and solidarity among staff members. Such lack of open communication and solidarity may in turn affect adversely the treatment enterprise. By the same reasoning, differences of prestige and status between patients and staff may be deplored, on the basis that such differences interfere with the development of solidarity between the two groups required for treatment.

In a small group, the function of which does not require complex task differentiation for effective goal-achievement, the attempt may be made to ignore differences in competency and to distribute responsibilities, and therefore facilities and rewards, among all members of the staff equally. Such an attempt is likely to result in strains, arising in part from the discomfort of those who are unable to accept the required degree of responsibility and from the discontent of those who do not feel adequately rewarded for individual achievement or that their special competency is given adequate scope or opportunity. This discontent may be exacerbated by the discrepancy between the degree of recognition within an equalitarian organization and the prestige available to various of its members in groups outside of the organization. Individuals who have much less or much greater competence than others on the staff may tend to leave the organization. A permanent group of persons with relatively the same degree of competence may then exist, in which tradition understandably supports vested interests or existing arrangements. For members of such a group reward is not likely to derive from the efficiency of its achievement, toward which end it is not especially well organized, but from a sense of solidarity with others. This sense of solidarity is continuously vulnerable to strains arising from lack of capability, discontent, or from the organization's failures in adaptation or achievement.

PERSON VERSUS DOCTOR. Is it possible to be a whole, fully human person interacting meaningfully with another person, if one is a doctor interacting with a patient? The requirements for a relatively uninhibited, affective, and expansive interest in the patient in psychotherapeutic interactions may be felt to conflict with traditional medical values of disciplined neutrality and a restricted interest in the patient: the physician has only the right to be concerned with the illness. The affectivity of the psychotherapist, however, is still disciplined and inhibited, compared to the relationship in which immediate gratification is permitted and expected; the relatively expansive interest of the psychotherapist is still restricted, compared to the relationship in which every claim—rather than only specific defined obligations—must be granted that do not conflict with a greater claim. The dilemma, however, is unavoidable. If the attitude toward the patient is too restricted, he may be confirmed in an identity built upon the patient role. If the attitude toward the patient is too expansive, deviant wishes and expectations may be unprofessionally reciprocated.

VALUES AND PRESCRIPTIONS FOR ACTION. While there may be agreement about general beliefs and values, for example, in the area of health and treatment, specific prescriptions for action derived from these and specific expectations of staff members or patients cannot be unambiguous and clear-cut; such derivations are usually characterized by some degree of sophistry and rationalization. These second-order norms—what should be done in psychotherapy, in the hospital community—although derived from institutionalized beliefs and values, may have a wide divergence. So, for example, there may be arguments in a specific situation about the degree to which a patient's behavior should be interfered with, if the result is to be therapeutic. The same degree of interference may be considered, on the one hand, conducive to submissive conformity at the cost of a developing capacity for healthy autonomy and independence; on the other hand, conducive to the development of healthy inner controls through identification.

Reasonable self-interest (considering consequences of action for the integration of the personality system) is valued as an aspect of health. A sense of responsibility (considering the consequences of action for the integration of the collectivity to which an individual belongs, whether it be the psychotherapy collectivity, the hospital, the family, or the extended community) is also valued as an aspect of health. In a specific situation, however, there may be considerable disagreement about which of these should be given priority. For example, to what extent is a patient's right to privacy compatible with the collectivity's right to examine and interfere with his actions in the interest of its welfare and the achievement of shared treatment goals?

Uneasy, but never final and unambiguous, agreements shared by patients and staff about the areas in which a patient may act without concern for obligations to the collectivity (only the limits of his action are regulated by the collectivity) and the areas in which a patient is expected to meet specific expectations of the collectivity, may mitigate, but do not completely resolve, strains arising over such questions. In different hospitals, such questions may be resolved differently. In one hospital, for example, so long as the patient meets specific obligations to the collectivities of the hospital in which he participates, he may—in fact, be expected to—otherwise give priority to considerations of self-interest. In another hospital, any action of the patient with any members of the hospital may be subject to scrutiny in terms of its consequences for the collectivity and the achievement of shared treatment goals. If the action has an impact on others that is relevant as contribution to or interference with the achievement of such goals, consideration of such consequences are expected to be given priority. In the patient's informal interactions with other patients, for example, he may be expected to give priority in any particular interaction to consequences for the other patient's health and to the integration of the other patient in the hospital over consequences for his own gratification. Is the other person's illness exacerbated or reinforced by the interaction? Is his motivation to collaborate in a treatment effort lessened? Are the health values of the hospital undermined?

Similar questions arise over the confidentiality of communications in psychotherapy with respect to other groups in the hospital. When does giving priority to the solidarity and integration of the psychotherapy collectivity, by segregating it as a sanctuary in which confessions of deviant behavior are privileged communications, prevent the patient (by keeping his actions secret) from learning from the responses of others, and therefore help to maintain his deviance as well as contribute to deterioration in the solidarity of the hospital through the effects of such secret deviant actions upon the internalization and institutionalization of its values?

Strains Arising from Conflicting Requirements

Following are some examples of strains resulting from discongruity between the requirements of different collectivities, sharing common members, or between the requirements of the same collectivity in different situations or at different times.

HOME VERSUS HOSPITAL. The informal community of patients, who live together, tend to adopt value patterns appropriate to intimate family life. These may conflict with those instrumental value patterns of collectivities in the hospital organization devoted to adaptation processes. Patients are likely to regard each other in terms of possibilities for the gratification of specific need-dispositions. In the interest of achieving shared treatment goals, the organization may expect patients to orient to each other within a context of expanded obligations and the consideration of consequences for multiple relationships and enterprises. Patients are likely to regard each other affectively, personally, and in terms of being: "he's one of us, he doesn't belong, I like him, I hate him." This clashes with the organization's neutral attitude and impersonal concern-with-doing criteria for the selection of patients for admission or discharge: "He has an illness we are able to treat here; he will be able to perform in a way that will result in his benefiting from treatment here."

Patients may, on the other hand, assume and resent that the organization is making decisions on the basis of affective personal attitudes, or concern with a patient's status or possessions rather than his acts: "He's being discharged prematurely because they don't like him, because he doesn't have enough money." That the organization selects patients for admission or discharge also on the basis of qualities (the possession of money) rather than solely on the basis of performance (motivation to collaborate in an effort to get well) contributes to such strains. Likewise, such strains are exacerbated, when admission or discharge is based upon integration values rather than upon the patient's fitting the criteria of being ill and needing treatment: "The kind of hospital we value, characterized by harmonious collaboration, does not permit the admission or retention of a patient incorrigibly aggressive in flouting norms."

INSTRUMENTAL VERSUS MORAL VALUE-ATTITUDES. Value patterns prescribing collective orientations to patients appropriate for the moral evaluation of their behavior in terms of its consequences to groups in the hospital may impinge upon value patterns prescribing instrumental orientations to patients appropriate for making assignments, for example, in a work program in terms of skills or instrumental interests. If the same collectivity orients to patients in both ways (a patient-staff work committee, for example, not only assigns patients to work areas but is responsible for judicial processes when patients do not fulfill obligations to the hospital community), patients may feel angrily in a specific situation that one value pattern is prepotent when the other should more appropriately apply. There are similarly conflicts between collectivities whose primary responsibility is to get the job done and those whose primary responsibility is to deal with deviant behavior in such a way as to increase solidarity and integration, each collectivity feeling that the other is undermining its efforts.

PRIORITY OF INTEGRATION IMPERATIVES. The fact that the hospital is continuously receiving new patients, whose selection guarantees at least some deviant behavior, and continuously losing old patients, who have internalized shared norms and expectations, means that a degree of disequilibrium and instability is always present. (The degree of instability to which the group must accommodate depends on the rate of change of its patient and staff members, and the effectiveness of its integrative mechanisms.) The inevitability of such instability means also that time and effort for adaptation and achievement must necessarily be sacrificed to a greater extent than in more stable organizations to integration imperatives. It is clear that mechanisms for integration are likely to be of central importance in a psychiatric hospital; the contribution of the staff members participating with patients in the hospital's collectivities is more importantly in the direction of the representation and support of values than in the direction of the demonstration of specific skills or the formulation of specific plans. Yet, the psychotherapist, imbued with the empirical-cognitive values of science, may feel uncomfortable or embarrassed in psychotherapy or in the hospital community when affective attitudes toward norms are required as part of a process of integration. Such embarrassment may spread over all discussions in any hospital collectivity, no matter what its function, when moral questions or matters of value preference are involved. Responses to performance (positive and negative sanctions, particularly in the form of the manifestation of positively or negatively cathected attitudes, such as approval or disapproval, esteem or dis-esteem) may be necessary for maintaining motivation to fulfill expectations and therefore for preventing and altering tendencies to deviate from expectations. Such responses may not be forthcoming, however, because of the influence of attitudes expected of the psychotherapist: that he be disciplined and reflective in his response, especially in order to avoid unknowingly gratifying or reciprocating wishes considered deviant or part of the patient's illness (e.g., praising performance that actually represents compulsive acquiescence in reaction to underlying rebellion, or responding negatively to behavior in response to the patient's provocations in a way that supports his pathological formations).

AUTONOMY VERSUS HETERONOMY. The emphasis in psychotherapy on the priority of ego-integration or autonomy with respect to the patient's personality system may clash with the emphasis in other collectivities in the hospital on the priority necessarily given to collectivity-integration or heteronomy, to questions of obligations to, and the consideration of the rights of, others. Conflicts between nurses and administrators, on the one hand, and psychotherapists, on the other, arise here.

EXPRESSIVE VERSUS INSTRUMENTAL AND RESPONSIBLE ACTION PRIORITIES. The psychotherapy collectivity highly values expressive action, the symbolic expression of feeling in appropriate verbal patterns. In collectivities where output is supposed to be instrumental or responsible action, seizing opportunities for expressive action as an end in itself, and preoccupation with what is the best way, according to appreciate standards, to express feelings, may supersede interest in instrumental and responsible action, evaluated according to cognitive and evaluative standards.

PROBLEMS IN TENSION-MANAGEMENT. If the psychotherapy collectivity is to receive tensions for analysis, it may be dysfunctional for other collectivities to dissipate such tensions, for example, by rituals or prescribed conventions. The psychotherapist in the hospital community may deprecate guilt-assuagement through rituals around work, confession, and expiation (punishment), and the dissipation of anxiety and grief through rituals in response to separation or intrusion (committing oneself to membership in the group by announcing plans in a patient-staff community meeting to remain for treatment, discussing with the group plans for and following discharge, good-bye parties). The psychotherapist may prefer that such tensions be tolerated until they can be discussed in psychotherapy. At some point, however, the piling-up of such tensions in the community may result in disruptive acting out or exacerbations of deviant, destructive behavior. Collectivities in the hospital rely upon such rituals—symbolic expressions of the shared values of the group reinforcing the internalization of such values—to mitigate tension, avert or decrease deviance or destructiveness, and (especially when shared experiences are involved) increase solidarity and integration. A hospital showing excessive disregard for community rituals will accept patients acting out tension by not fulfilling expectations; a precarious degree of instability in the hospital community may result. A hospital going too far in the other direction may have "quiet" patients, who are difficult to treat with insight psychotherapy.

It is clear then in a hospital including an individual psychotherapy collectivity, with its particular imperatives, that other collectivities must function within certain limits. For example, the use of physical coercion, preference for repression rather than expression, the imposition of negative sanctions for self-expression or self-exploration, all conflict with conditions required for psychotherapy. The toleration of tension, even the mobilization of tension, within patients may be necessary in a hospital in which psychotherapy utilizes such tensions for analysis and change of personality systems. Such tension mobilization may occur, for example, through alteration of the object situation in the direction of maintaining definite expectations irrespective of the conflict of these with the wishes or dispositions of indvidual personality systems and holding to or preventing escape from consequences accruing for nonfulfillment of such expectations. The existence of such tensions means, of course, that the achievement of the adaptation and integration goals of hospital collectivities other than psychotherapy may be compromised to some extent.

Personality versus Social System

Following is a discussion of strains resulting from discongruity between the requirements of the personality systems of members of the collectivity and characteristics of the collectivity, or between the requirements of the collectivity and characteristics of the personality systems of its members.

Parsons and Shils (1951) have described how a social system categorizes an individual in certain ways for certain purposes; such categorization may conflict with the way an individual sees and values, and needs to see and value, himself. A social system decides who shall occupy a role, what he shall do, how his role relates to other roles. Such decisions may conflict with an individual's needs to withdraw from, evade, or rebel against expectations, or may be thwarted by the individual's lack of skills or failure to internalize through identification value orientation patterns required for a role. A social system allocates rewards and sanctions, the effect of which depends upon an individual's orienting to others as objects of gratification, generalized attachment, and identification. A social system has integrative structures, such as bodies of laws, law-makers, and law-enforcers, the effectiveness of which depends upon an individual's ability to accept and internalize the priority of collective over personal interests within limits and on appropriate occasions. If the individual is not able to do so, strain results.

Personality systems are organized to attain gratification of need-dispositions.

To some extent the hospital functions to refrain from gratifying all need-dispositions in the interest of making it possible for patients to learn need-dispositions that are not deviant or pathological; to accept the necessity of discipline, preceding gratification by evaluation; and to establish new hierarchies of priority of need-dispositions. Patients prefer staff to have as expansive an interest in them, and to gratify as many wishes, as possible; staff members incline to restricted attitudes.

Each collectivity in a hospital may have expectations of a patient he feels unable or disinclined to fulfill; require resources, capabilities, and discipline a patient may not have; take attitudes toward and categorize the patient in ways he cannot accept or tolerate: differing markedly from his own cognition and cathexis of himself and his need to see and feel about himself in this way. Even the requirements that a patient accept his illness as such and collaborate actively with others in its treatment conflict with his passivity, alienative need-dispositions, and wish to protect himself from pain through denial and rationalization.

A patient's requirements for gratification may be such that to require inhibition of the desire for immediate discharge of him, a prerequisite for effective instrumental action, may be intolerable to him. His needs for response may be greater than can be satisfied given the allocative conditions and expectations for performance in a particular collectivity. His view of his own adequacy may differ from others' views. His own expectations as to what he deserves may be disappointed by a particular distribution of rewards or negative and positive sanctions.

He may insist upon being regarded in terms of his being a member of the group (no matter how he acts) when doing is considered relevant in the collectivity (what he does or does not contribute to the performance of tasks or achievement of goals). He may desire special treatment on the basis of personal considerations—"I'm your friend, your patient"—when impersonal criteria are relevant in the collectivity: such-and-such applies to anyone in a given category.

A patient's need to alienate himself from others or from norms and expectations will conflict with the requirement of any collectivity that expectations be fulfilled if a degree of integration is to be maintained sufficient to achieve shared goals. What a patient sees as essential for his own integration (a certain degree of privacy or noninterference as he pursues his own goals) may be considered by the collectivity incompatible with its integration or the achievement of its goals. For example, a patient who seeks personal educational or occupational goals outside the hospital may, in order to pursue such goals, wish exemption from sharing the chores of the hospital community required to maintain it and to achieve its goals.

That patients have idiosyncratic attitudes toward authority (extreme ambivalence, for example) may make special mechanisms for manipulating rewards and deprivations necessary. A large degree of participation by patients in decision-making may be required to mitigate a situation in which authority's normally integrative prescriptions for group life are not consistently considered legitimate or acceptable. The consequent wary use of authority by staff, when prompt firm action by leadership is required to meet integrative crises, is of course an additional source of instability. In addition, the delays and frustrations imposed by the process of group decision-making or the reluctance by those in authority to grant positive or impose negative sanctions are in themselves sources of strain.

THE EQUALITARIAN ORGANIZATION

One attempt to resolve the strains existing in psychiatric hospitals is represented by the so-called equalitarian organization, which tends to approximate in its value patterns and emphasis on integration the previously described moral exemplar type of hospital. The equalitarian organization is characterized by attempts to "blur" status differentiations; flatten hierarchical structure; create maximum communication between all members of the organization; and create maximum participation in decision and policy making about all problems (administrative or professional) by all members of the organization (Jones 1953; Robert Rapoport 1956; Robert and Rhona Rapoport 1959).

There have been some qualifications, warnings, and uneasiness even by thoughtful advocates of the equalitarian organization. For example, Hamburg, in advocating the facilitation of communication between all groups and a broader participation in the decision-making process by patients and staff, has written:

> This is not to say that everyone should communicate with everyone else about everything that goes on, or that everyone participates in *all* decisions; the relevance of a given person to a particular decision must be considered in deciding whether he should participate in making it. This viewpoint does not mean that people with administrative responsibility "pass the buck" to those who are in no position to make the decision, nor does it mean an endless series of conferences in which there is much communication but no effective action (Hamburg 1957b).

Robert Rapoport, in commenting on the inevitability of status differences even in an equalitarian organization, admits that despite the effort at "blurring" such differences what at best is achieved is a "quasi-equalitarian" organization:

> The fact that these differences exist formally as inherent in the hospital system of which the Unit is a part is a precondition that the Unit cannot remove in its present circumstances, but that its staff tend to blur as much as possible in order to achieve a quasi-equalitarian mode of functioning (Rapoport 1956).

However, the equalitarian organization is felt to be more therapeutic. In an equalitarian organization the patient is confronted by his peers (rather than an authority figure) who remind him of his effect on others; such confrontation is thought to present a new reality to him to which he will not respond in old ways. The patient's participation in communicating widely with others and in decision and policy making is thought to provide him with the opportunity to learn or enhance social roles other than that of the "sick person," to improve his capacities for reality-testing, and to reduce his noninvolvement.

A rigidly hierarchical formal structure, on the other hand, is described as creating an impersonal experience for the patient, since all responses and expectations are related to his status within the structure and not to his individuality. Concepts of patient needs are generalized and reflect the opinions of upper echelon personnel who control communication and are impervious to individual whims, preferences, and eccentricities. Behavior is acceptable only to the extent that it conforms to the hospital's value systems and tends to become increasingly automatized; there is little chance for spontaneity, and enthusiasm wanes as a proposal or request goes through channels. In general, such a structure augments what is automatic, ritualistic, and formal at the expense of flexibility, individualization, and innovation. Treatment under these circumstances must become de-individualized and relations between members of the organization distant, noninvolved, and fragmented (Kahne 1959).

Nevertheless, there are certain possible consequences of the characteristics of the so-called equalitarian organization that must also give pause (Caudill and Stainbrook 1954; Caudill 1957, 1958; John and Elaine Cumming et al. 1957; Etzioni 1960; Hamburg 1957a, 1957b; Henry 1954, 1957; Jones 1953, 1957; Kahne 1959; Perry and Shea 1957; Robert Rapoport 1956; Robert and Rhona Rapoport 1959).

Some Definitions

Before going on to consider these consequences of a particular social structure or organization for human behavior within that organization, the reader may wish to review the definitions of such concepts as role, responsibility, authority, and consultation so that such words may be used non-pejoratively and without prejudice in the discussion.[4]

The role of an individual in an organization is his position or job in it and is ordinarily defined by the function or functions he is expected to perform. If a particular position or role is defined by a number of functions, some of which do not belong to, but one or more of which do enter into the definition of, a different position or role, the two roles are said to overlap. A person may have more than one role, or multiple roles, in an organization. A role may be divided between, or co-delegated to, two or more persons. It is because an individual is assigned a role that he becomes a member of an organization, the structure of which determines the nature of the formal relations between roles. The structure thus determines which relationships must be established between what individuals occupying particular positions; such relationships occur not because of the wishes of the individuals involved but because of the task demands of the organization.

To each role belong particular responsibility, and, ideally, commensurate authority to carry out the responsibility. The relationship between superior and subordinate is defined by the direction of the delegation of responsibility and authority. Responsibility is always for something—activities, persons, materials—and implies duties and obligations with respect to these. The holder of responsibility must bear the consequences of his decisions in relation to, and his behavior toward, these activities, persons, and materials. That is, a subordinate is accountable to his superior for the consequences of the way in which he discharges his responsibilities. (It should be noted that the superior, in turn, is responsible for his subordinate.) Authority defines what a person occupying a given role may do with respect to the activities, persons, and materials for which he is responsible: to whom he may issue directives, to what use he may put the materials for which he is responsible, what he may authorize someone else to do. The formal structure determines the direction in which, and the persons upon whom, an individual is permitted to exert influence.

Power is the actual influence an individual (or group) exerts, and may or may not

---

4. These definitions paraphrase, for the most part, those given by Thomas Main in personal communications and Jaques (1952).

be the same as the authority he (or the group) possesses because of his (or its) role. Power is determined by personal (or group) qualities, capacities, skills, knowledge, and strength. If the responsibility attached to a role is greater than the authority possessed to carry it out, the responsibility is experienced as a burden. Likewise, there are problems for the organization when the power of an individual or group, and the authority attached to the position occupied by the individual or group, are disparate.

The value attached to a role is its status. The value attached to a person is his prestige. A person's prestige may be affected by the status of the position he occupies; the status of a position may be changed by the prestige of the person occupying it.

The attachment of authority to a role, and the use of that authority by a particular individual occupying that role, are permitted by delegation and approval from a superior, cooperation of colleagues, support of subordinates, and the individual's own capacity to accept the responsibility and authority. Such authority ultimately derives from those outside the organization—for example, its sources of financial resources, the customers for its services, the arbiters of its community standing, and to some extent the professional groups to which professional personnel belong— the withdrawal of whose support would seriously jeopardize the organization's existence. The individual(s)—or group(s)—for example, the Medical Director, who is directly responsible to, and whose authority is supported by, these sources of authority outside the organization carries correspondingly great authority within the organization.

Professional personnel also possess authority irrespective of their position in the organization by virtue of their membership in their professional group. Such personnel also are granted authority within the organization because of the self-evident demands of a technical job requiring specialized skills. If such task-demands are ignored (e.g., by ignoring the instructions of professional personnel arising out of the requirements of the task) production of services falters or fails.

An additional source of authority in a democratic organization resides in the consultation mechanisms which result in the support of subordinates as well as superiors for those occupying positions calling for the exercise of authority. Through consultation mechanisms, those who will be affected by a decision or policy or who will play some part in its implementation participate in the process of making it. Consultation mechanisms make it possible for subordinates to express their dissatisfaction with the exercise of authority, to demand a change in policy or a better implementation of it, to give and receive relevant information. Such mechanisms, of course, impose to some extent a check on those carrying authority; but in the long run are thought to be justified because they permit a more complete, because more extensively supported, authority.

Consequences of Equalitarian Organization

A principal goal of the equalitarian organization is the distribution of responsibility and authority equally throughout the group. This usually results in effect in the multiple subordination of each member of the organization to all other members;

blurring of roles, so that it is unclear who is responsible for what; maximum over-lapping of roles, so that many individuals are responsible for the performance of the same function; the holding of multiple roles by each individual, so that everyone is responsible for many jobs; and determination of the distribution of information by personal rather than organizational criteria.

In the equalitarian organization hierarchy, by definition, is shunned. As a result, charts of organization, anything approaching line organization, with clarification of authority, responsibility, and role relationships, tend to be anathema. Such designations tend to be regarded as imprisoning the individual in his role and frustrating the realization of his full potentialities as a human being, rather than as establishing enabling boundaries that permit him to work effectively and autonomously. Of course, simply issuing an order or passively complying with one does not solve problems. But in the equalitarian organization, even when giving orders or receiving orders are task-oriented transactions necessary to implement principles agreed upon after consultation, they tend to be regarded as unpleasant, intrusive, insulting or humiliating behaviors, the willing performance of which is probably expressive of personal psychopathology.

An autocrat, or authoritarian paranoid person, exercises power and authority far beyond the limits of his responsibility, for the sake of gratification not task-accomplishment, without concern for the consent of those he commands. It is not necessary in these times to justify the importance of safeguards, however cumbersome, whatever the price in inefficiency, against undue concentration of power and authority in such an individual. Nor should it be necessary to decry again, as those who have attempted change in many state hospitals have had to, the tradition-bound, inflexible, impersonal, automatic, ritualistic bias of the authoritarian person. This bias, of course, finds its easiest expression in a rigidly hierarchical organization and, holding sway there, prevents any change: intrapersonal, interpersonal, intergroup, or in the structure or organization itself. However, authoritarianism (unsupported autocracy) and authority (delegated and consented to) are not synonymous; nevertheless, they tend to be considered so in an equalitarian organization.

In the equalitarian organization, there is a minimum delegation of authority and responsibility, which are ideally supposed to be distributed as equally as possible throughout the group. The group (not individuals) is supposed to make decisions; all decisions require the sanction of the entire membership. Every worker is, as a result, essentially responsible to everyone else in the organization for his performance. This may be recognized as an extreme example of what has been termed multiple subordination; every worker receives directions not from one superior, not from several superiors, but from every member of the group—and is accountable to every member of the group.[5]

---

5. Henry (1954) has discussed in some detail the effects upon an organization of multiple subordination. His discussion is summarized by the formulation that system stress is directly proportional to the power possessed by organizational units and the functional overlap of such units and is inversely proportional to the consensus among them; and stress in task performance is directly proportional to the number of commands and the number of persons a worker must respond to and inversely proportional to the consistency of the commands he receives and the interrelatedness of the operations for which he is responsible. In response to stress, workers

The equalitarian organization tries to avoid differences in prestige being dependent solely upon the status of different roles, and typically tries to accomplish this by blurring roles. Any role may be occupied by all members of the group; any individual may occupy all positions. For example, any psychotherapist feels authorized to function also as an expert administrator, nurse, sociotherapist, activities therapist, and, with patients, as "just another member of the group." Similarly, any nurse may function also as a psychotherapist, an administrator, a sociotherapist, an activities therapist, and just another member of the patient group.

In the equalitarian organization, as a result, the holding of multiple roles by any individual, and the holding of overlapping roles (and therefore the performance of the same functions) by many individuals, are at a maximum. There is a minimum delegation of responsibility; no one is accountable to any one superior; there is no sharp definition of what is expected of any particular position in the organization. Therefore, task-performance, choice of role-relationships, and choice of communication channels are likely to proceed on a completely voluntary basis. The assumption made is that given a large number of conscientious, varied, talented individuals, whose store of good will is dependable and inexhaustible, the required work will be done.

There is in such an organization no criteria by which any individual or group may determine the need to know or distinguish relevant from irrelevant information; everyone could presumably have equal interest in all information. Any individual may decide for himself to what information he should or wishes to have access, as well as what information he wishes to make available and to whom.

What are some consequences of an organization with such characteristics and tendencies?

The multiple subordination of each member of the organization to all other members exposes everyone to a variety of directives, opinions, points of view, and theoretical positions. The effect may not be simply the enrichment of everyone's thinking, but rather uncertainty and confusion about the job and what is expected; indecision; and hesitation to act independently, especially in front of others. No matter who might be pleased, there is always someone else who just as surely will be displeased. There is no protection of the kind that resides in having a benevolent superior who is able to guarantee his subordinate the autonomy to discharge his responsibilities within the limits of his authority as his judgment dictates. Anyone may question and interfere with anyone else's decisions; overt and covert vetos (often rationalized as "honest disagreement" or the right to express one's own point of view) by members of the group of each other's actions are the rule not the exception.

A great deal of time and energy may be spent by every individual to gain and maintain the goodwill of his peers (including those who are, for the most part, only remotely affected by a particular action of his) since everyone is dependent on the consent of everyone else to do anything. Alliances must be forged, bargains made,

---

may become excessively dependent upon the supervisor; avoid the supervisor; seek or create an all-powerful savior; become apathetic; seek now one person, now another, with whom to discuss troubles and of whom to seek advice; and develop covert social structures.

and new ideas or proposals that will jeopardize or antagonize anyone avoided. This is especially so when an individual's behavior may be discussed and held against him by his entire peer group; the consequences of his behavior thus may affect many areas of his life.[6]

The group may be counted upon not to "vote in" anything too disagreeable or anxiety-provoking, even when the decision is required by the task to be accomplished. Unpleasant issues are referred to committees for consideration, a process which often takes months, sometimes until the circumstances of the original referral are largely forgotten or have been already resolved in some way, probably unsatisfactorily. In the event that the final decision does displease someone, no one has to take the responsibility for it; the decision is now a "group product." Relatively innocuous ideas gain the widest acceptance; conformity pays off in amicable relations; excellence threatens to disrupt the equilibrium of an equalitarian distribution of status and power. Therefore, mediocre rather than disturbing intellectual performance subtly comes to be most valued. Compromise rather than boldness or consistency in policy and decision making, as well as a pastiche of points of view, become the typical products of the group process.[7]

Because of the blurring of roles, it is often impossible to tell who is responsible for what; so many are involved in everything that goes on. While it is true that role-blurring may diminish dependency upon authority and the exertion of undue influence by status-bearers and thus raise the general level of responsibility felt by everyone for everything, it is nevertheless also true that role-blurring may be used to conceal who in particular should be held accountable for a specific situation.

There are so many individuals who must be consulted, so many groups who must participate, so much hesitation by any individual or group to make a decision unless everyone has been in on it, that even small proposals and requests may be some time before coming to decision. Just as in the rigidly hierarchical organization, ironically enough, spontaneity and enthusiasm tend to diminish in the process, and apathy ensues. Such apathy may alternate with outbursts of anger and suspicion. Since decision-making is often so slow, frustration builds. Because it is so difficult to tell where power resides in the organization and who is exerting it upon whom, suspicion grows that someone or other is preventing decisions or manipulating things behind the scenes. If any individual or group tries to break through the lethargy and make or push for a decision, there is an outburst of hostility centering around the feeling that everyone's right to participate in making all decisions is being threatened.

Another source of anger, especially in patients when they are told that in a therapeutic community they will have an equal voice, is the perception that various members of the hospital staff are hypocritical and secretive. This perception arises from evidence of, and some recognition of the necessity for, the exercise of authority in such an organization, even when its location is hidden and the boundaries of

---

6. Frightening ubiquity of consequences is not uniquely characteristic of authoritarian, rigidly hierarchical, "total institutions," but may be a feature of equalitarian or apparently peer group governed organizations as well (Goffman 1957; Whyte 1956; Friedenberg 1959).

7. For one discussion of the effect on creativity of the emphasis on group process, see Whyte (1956).

its possession blurred. The young patient must discover his identity partly through conflict with authority. He is baffled because he cannot discover who is making the decisions that affect him. But he knows that somehow authority is there, among all those equalitarian staff members, each of whom keeps stating, "I'm not an authority figure. I'm your buddy, your friend, a human being like you, just another member of the group." The patient begins to recognize that democratic constitution-making (in place of an ongoing resolution of current problems) and appeals to tradition and precedents, rules, and policies, established by the group, may be used as much as naked autocratic power to thwart change. Authority may simply be choosing to use such tools in an equalitarian organization to manage him. Confused, still distrustful and resentful, the patient turns to erratic, rebellious, senseless, often guilt-ridden and self-destructive delinquency or to a premature, essentially fearful, "good citizen," passive compliance with group standards, expectations, and values.[8] The heroic opposition to, the protests about the unjustness of, the chivalrous struggle with, a clearly visible rational holder of authority and responsibility is, one would suppose, the heart of a democratic process and necessary for problem-solving and change. But such a fight in an equalitarian organization may be drowned in a sea of pseudo-goodwill, apathy, and a defensive idealization of the relations between individuals and groups.[9]

Since no staff member knows what his position really is, each individual is anxious about his prestige and status, and engaged in a constant endeavor to find out his actual value to others. Under these circumstances, jealousy, rivalry, and competitiveness are intense. Furthermore, such strivings are given free reign to be expressed, in the absence of any of the constraints, afforded, for example, by definitions of roles and role-relationships in an organization. Individuals improvise their roles, not only as part of the expression of such strivings, but because there is no other guide as to who is responsible for what or has the authority to do what. Of course, each one's conception of the scope and boundaries of his own responsibility and authority may differ from another's view of his role or may overlap a province another has chosen for himself. Covert and overt struggles develop, often disguised as ideological or "theoretical" in nature. Irrespective of individual psychopathology, individuals working under such conditions tend to regard other individuals as presumptuous power-seekers, on the one hand, or devious, irresponsible saboteurs undermining legitimate effort, on the other. Since the group is the final arbiter, various kinds of appeal to it and pressures upon individuals to take sides occur. Conflicting loyalties split the organization. Decision-making becomes paralyzed as members of the group, all dependent upon the goodwill of others to win consent for their activities, sense that with each issue, there is "more here than meets the eye."[10]

---

8. For a discussion of these phenomena in the modern business organization and in the high school see Whyte (1956) and Friedenberg (1959).

9. For discussions of the importance of conflict and opposition to the growth of the adolescent and to creative problem-solving processes in a therapeutic hospital community, compare Friedenberg (1959) and Sivadon (1957a, 1957b).

10. For a discussion of the effects of role improvisation by a new member of an organization, whose functions are vaguely defined, see Henry (1954). Such effects include the development in members of the organization of feelings of reference, hostility, betrayal, and tendencies to secrecy.

The maximum overlapping of roles, with many individuals responsible for the performance of the same function, may not lead to a desired expansion of the range of competencies of various individuals. It may lead instead to much duplication of effort, as well as to loss of an individual's pride in a unique, autonomous achievement for which he has specialized training and skills. Individuals whose prestige derives partly from their membership in a profession with high status, such as medicine, or who exercise a highly valued function such as the psychotherapeutic function, may do all right, since their power to influence, already great, is simply augmented by the notion that they are also capable of making significant contributions to every decision concerning administration, nursing, activities programs. However, an individual with less prestige (e.g., the nurse or activities staff member) finds his self-esteem dwindling as he loses the sense that his function or contribution is unique. Its performance does not seem to depend on his special skills. He does not feel the pleasure of occupying a particular realm of responsibility that he alone carries the authority to discharge with all the talent, creativity, and imagination at his command. Since anyone can do his job and he has no special responsibility for it, and no particular authority upon which to act, he may become resentful of or excessively, defensively awed by others (the doctors or psychotherapists). He may become somewhat apathetic ("someone else will do it or has already done it"). He may depreciate himself and become preoccupied with what others think of him or how others respond to his work ("the psychotherapist really doesn't care what I am doing with the patient; no one thinks my work is as important to the patient's treatment as the psychotherapist's is"). Or he may seek ways to insulate himself (e.g., through nonparticipation in conferences of the extended group, lack of understanding of the work or position of others, and intense identification with members of his own professional group).

In a hospital where individual psychotherapy does not exist and where the therapeutic milieu is the primary treatment modality, the psychiatrist may find he is the captive of his team, the members of which are determined he shall not be an authoritarian leader and are quick to impose sanctions if he exercises individual responsibility on his own. The psychiatrist, who has been trained to bear responsibility and to exercise the authority necessary to discharge it, may find himself increasingly anxious about the care of patients for whom he feels responsible even though he is unable to take the steps he feels necessary to implement such responsibility. He may ultimately find himself apathetic, harried, or dissatisfied, and decide to leave the hospital for private practice; it rarely occurs to him to attribute his malaise to the equalitarian milieu in which he has worked.

The holding of multiple roles by each individual (everyone is responsible for many jobs) may provide an opportunity for an individual to escape imprisonment in meaningless, unsatisfying piece work. It may also create conditions in which an individual may use one job to escape from another when the possession of responsibility for the latter becomes awkward, arouses anxiety, or involves unpleasantness. In addition, an individual trying to perform multiple roles may find that one position requires attitudes, points of view, actions or the protection of interests that do not necessarily coincide, and that may conflict, with what is required by the other position. In such an event, inaction, a muddled presentation, an inconsistent stance, or abrogation of one role for the sake of the other, may occur. As a consequence, the decision-making process suffers, since the clear presentation of a point of view, the representation of a crucial interest, or the performance of a timely action, are for these reasons too often missing when a problem is tackled.[11]

Disparity between responsibility and authority and between authority and power are rife in an equalitarian organization. A nurse, for example, may find that she has a vast amount of responsibility for the welfare of patients under her care simply by virtue of her training, her physical location, and her on-the-spot contact with the patients, but relatively little authority to discharge it, since action is usually considered best initiated in and approved by the entire group or its committees. On the other hand, an individual with relatively little responsibility for nursing may have authority over equipment or people upon which or whom the nurse depends. Thus, such an individual is in a position to interfere considerably with the nurse's ability to carry out her responsibilities. An individual (a physician, an administrator, or member of the activities staff) may in a group discussion, for example, have the power to influence others in such a way that a decision is brought about for which the nurse, and not he, must bear the consequences.[12]

In the equalitarian organization, everyone is interested in everything. There is no way of determining the relevance of any information for any individual's work. An enormous amount of time is spent talking, writing, and meeting to reach the ideal that everyone know everything. Conferences become bull sessions with opinions expressed and influence exerted by those who do not have to bear directly the consequences of a particular decision. Decisions are often interminably stalled by such irresponsible interventions. There is no adaptive screening of information, because the group defends continuously against the possibility that somehow information in one place and not in another will signal the absence of or result in upsetting a truly equalitarian distribution of authority and power. Information is distributed according to idiosyncratic wishes and fears rather than task-requirements. One might suppose that the defensive blocking of information (as opposed to adaptive screening), which has so often been described to occur in a hierarchical organization, would be less prone to occur in the equalitarian organization. Not at all. Since lines of responsibility and authority are not clearly defined, any person is free to ignore the demands of the task for which everyone (therefore no one in particular) is responsible, and to respond only to his own anxiety or obey only the dictates of his own wishes in determining whom he will tell what (Etzioni 1960; Henry 1954; Jaques 1952).

Motives Supporting Equalitarian Organization

The sociologist and anthropologist can teach us about the consequences of a particular social structure for human relations and behavior. The psychoanalytically

---

11. See Jaques (1952) for a discussion of organizational phenomena associated with multiple roles.

12. As in any organization, an individual (e.g., an administrator) who has much less power to exert influence upon others than the authority necessary to carry out his responsibilities requires him to have, tends to bring discredit upon the position he occupies. The equalitarian organization, of course, is designed to prevent those situations in which an amount of authority is concentrated in an individual far beyond that required or justified by the actual responsibilities of his position.

trained sociotherapist, in addition, can help us to understand what human motives (often unconscious) contribute to the maintenance of, and resistance to any change in, a particular social structure, despite its dysfunctional effects. Unhappily, when one attempts to relate the exasperating, persistent difficulties within an organization to characteristics of the formal structure, one finds that often it is the most valued (and therefore usually least suspect or examined) aspects of that structure that are at issue. Dysfunctional and often deplored aspects of the organization turn out to be, ironically enough, intrinsic manifestations of its most deeply held values. The intimate link between what is deplored and what is valued goes often unnoticed; therefore it is possible for the group to split into righteously antagonistic, idealogically supported sides. Unconscious wishes and fears cunningly make use of the most attractive places and ideas behind which to hide; in any attempt to discover them, one is confronted immediately by the angry and suspicious reactions due him who disturbs the group's most treasured possessions. Nevertheless, in view of the strains associated with equalitarian organization, it is necessary to attempt a description of the irrational motives that may contribute to supporting it.[13] Such an undertaking does not imply an animus toward democracy. The enthusiasm for the equalitarian organization, often described as *the* therapeutic community, should not prevent recognition of the distress aspects of it may cause its members or the unconscious bias, analogous to that of the authoritarian personality, that results in resistance to change in these aspects of such an organization despite their unhappy effects.[14]

The equalitarian organization serves important functions for its members. The major function is to rationalize and support distrust and fear of, and hostility toward, authority and the bearers of authority. The equalitarian organization makes possible the expression of such hostility and distrust, and the escape from authority, in ego-syntonic and socially acceptable ways.

Most of us (this may be especially true of gifted professional personnel found in a hospital) have never completely renounced omnipotent strivings. We tend to value our own qualities, our own inner mental contents and attributes, at the expense perhaps of an interest in the brute facts of outer reality. We are likely to believe unconsciously that we can accomplish anything, overcome any obstacles. It is not pleasant for any of us (motivated as we may be by strong, creative impulses to self-actualization) to be faced with the necessity to subordinate the realization of some of our potentialities for the sake of the development and exercise of other potentialities, or the necessity to subordinate our wishes to the demands of a task. Any authority, any attempt to define our position in terms of its limits, may be felt by any of us as a threat; we are apt to understand our response to it in terms of a justifiable quest for autonomy.

Most of us would rather do what we want rather than what we must; in fact, sometimes it seems that one of the primary functions of a "good" organization is

---

13. I have, throughout this analysis, leaned heavily on personal communications from Thomas Main, and on the work of Jaques (1952) who has brilliantly applied psychoanalytic concepts to understand such problems as the attitudes of the members of a factory organization toward authority.

14. For a discussion of the personality biases underlying both custodial and humanist staff ideologies see Gilbert and Levinson (1957).

to make possible that what must get done does get done without interfering unduly with the self-realization of its members. Frustrated by the confines implied by an assignment of responsibility and authority, any one of us would prefer the freedom to roam and perform as his inclinations dictate. After all, our own wishes, intuitions, ideas are highly valued by us, usually beyond the mundane requirements of the task itself, which are often experienced as chores that chafe, that are to be avoided, and that hopefully will be done by someone else. The requirement that we must relate to others in terms of the needs of the job or organization may be onerous. We would like to insist upon our right to relate to those we like and to avoid those we disdain or fear.

Unhappily, our insistence upon our own freedom does not prevent us from being meddlesome, or from undercutting others, advising them how to do their jobs, interfering with their performance, and indicating that very likely we, of course, could do their work better; this is attributed to our natural wish to be helpful and often occurs in the name of free discussion.

An equalitarian organization, then, makes it possible to act in the work situation according to the pleasure principle (that is, "I choose to do and say what pleases me, what does not arouse anxiety in me") rather than according to the reality demands of the task itself.

Distrust of authority in others is not the only feeling maintaining an equalitarian organization. An individual's own guilt about his omnipotent strivings, about his wishes to dominate and influence others and use power for personal gratification, may lead him to eschew the exercise of authority. Therefore, he may welcome the blurring and overlapping of roles in the equalitarian organization and resist any attempt in the direction of their clarification, since this might result not only in his having to accept the possession of authority by others but the expectation that he must exercise it himself. In addition, an individual may doubt his own capacities and fear his own inadequacy. This may, of course, involve an actual inability to bear, accept, or discharge responsibility. It may also involve the shame of an individual who has high standards for himself, for whom the experience and exposure of any mistake or failure may seem unbearably painful. An individual may feel sheltered by the blurring and overlapping of roles in the equalitarian organization from having his mistakes or failures recognized as such by himself or others. He is able to avoid being criticized or having to account for such mistakes or failures. "Buck passing" to others is easy. In the equalitarian organization, an individual is relatively free of anxiety that would be produced by a recognition of the disparity between the resources of his own personality and the demands of his job.

An individual may fear not only his superior but the scrutiny of, judgments of, and possible attack upon, or loss of confidence in, him by his subordinates, upon whose performance he is dependent for the discharge of his responsibilities. It is often difficult to tolerate the isolation that is attached to any position of authority and responsibility: being on one's own, perhaps having to stand up to the questions of one's superior or stand against one's equals or subordinates. If an individual's response to doubts about himself is some form of reactive dominance over others, he may feel guilty about this, and in turn become excessively submissive to and preoccupied with the wishes of others (subordinates, the group). Of course, this only increases his sense of inadequacy and fear of attack.

In any organization espousing equalitarian ideals, an individual has many ways to escape from his own authority and his relationship to those who are realistically— that is, in terms of task criteria—subordinates. Possessing multiple roles, he may retreat to the role removing him farthest from the necessity of exercising authority over such subordinates. The equalitarian ethos permits him to deny possession of authority by declaring himself just another member of the group with no more to say about anything than anyone else. To avoid giving orders he may perform the jobs of his subordinate himself, or on the other hand delegate his order-giving function to one of his subordinates. He may misuse conferences to avoid his responsibility for the performance of an immediate subordinate by bypassing him and consulting directly in such a group meeting with those who actually work under this immediate subordinate (although, of course, such subordination even if it is a consequence of task-requirements and task-differentiation may have to be denied because of the equalitarian ideology). He may also, in order to avoid decision, misuse conferences for impractical philosophizing or theorizing, thus bringing the whole consultation process into disrepute.[15]

Equals (those who, on the same horizontal line, are all directly subordinates of the same superior, for example, the Medical Director) may resist clarification of roles, despite the difficulties caused by the intense rivalry associated with role confusion. That same competitiveness makes for fear that one role will, with clarification, come to have higher status than another. Blurring and overlapping roles, and the insistence on democratic, total participation by everyone in making decisions, enable equals to join together in an indirect attack against their superior: making things difficult for him; preventing him from finding out about mistakes; undercutting his authority by sending issues to committees rather than have him decide them or by insisting, in the name of democracy and anti-authoritarianism, that not he but the entire group must make a particular decision.

Because of the widespread fear of possessing authority, as well as the distrust and hostility toward those in positions of authority, subordinates in an organization may not be able to accept the right of the superior to act independently of them nor may he be able to accept their right to act independently of him. So the entire group, watchful and wary, gathers to make a decision. But the discussion bogs down. Group members, guilty over hostility toward authority, fearing loss of protection and support, guarding against advantage accruing to any competitor, cannot join together in any effective criticism of anyone's judgment or act. More likely what occurs is scapegoating, perhaps someone or some group outside but also possibly a member of the group itself. Problem-solving breaks down because any attempt to take away this valuable scapegoat is resisted. In addition, members of the group, barred from the satisfactions that might arise from effective problem-solving, begin to find pleasure in, and justification for, their paralysis and ineffectuality in their pride in continually coping with terrible dilemmas and difficulties.

---

15. For a discussion of the misuses of psychiatric theory in conferences to disguise and obfuscate organizational and administrative issues see Stanton (1954).

The Importance of Consultation Processes

Strains, it is clear, must develop in any organization in which integration values, manifested in the espousal of equalitarian ideals, are prepotent, at the expense of the primacy of adaptation and goal-attainment, which are served, for example, by the differentiation of tasks or functions and the assignment of these to different groups or persons according to impersonal criteria. These strains are ubiquitous in a modern society, as the values assumed by the existence of the modern organization and the complex technology that make it necessary clash with the values of an equalitarian ethos. Such strains are reflected in ideological struggles between entire nations. Is it possible to have a social system in which there is no differential status? To what extent are such differences in status merely outcomes of inequitable distribution of material resources or means by which to constrain others? To what extent are they inevitable consequences of the inequitable distribution of human capacities together with the inevitable different degrees of value given to different skills, functions, and therefore positions, insofar as these contribute in different degrees to the attainment of valued goals? To what extent does differentiation of tasks into their parts in the interest of efficiency necessarily involve (in the relation of part to whole and parts to each other) differences of supraordination and subordination, different degrees of authority and responsibility, and conflicts between different aims, against which are necessarily pitted integration imperatives of harmony and justice?

It may seem paradoxical to give so much attention to the problems of the equalitarian organization, when the problems of authoritarianism in these times seem so much more iniquitous and ubiquitous. However, one of the problems of the equalitarian organization is that although (given only the relation of the organization to outside supporting, legitimizing agencies, much less the requirements of effective task-performance and goal-attainment) authority must still be and is exercised, in an equalitarian organization it is often difficult to identify who is exercising what degree of authority over whom, to whom is the exerciser of such authority accountable, and by what or whom is the exercise of authority limited or regulated. The way is open to charismatic leadership, exercising influence predominantly by personal qualities, not necessarily serving the interests of adaptation or the tasks to be performed. The covert use of the group by the exerciser of authority to maintain control over others is known, as is the possibility that major decisions made by the one or few without consultation may go unnoticed when democratic processes are sponsored by authority as a sop in areas of less importance. Furthermore, the arbitrary, nonrational tyranny of a group of peers over an individual (although it may be subtler, therefore also more difficult to resist) is no easier to bear than that of a single despot.

Hospital organizations are especially susceptible to equalitarian ideals. Professional persons in the mental health field are more often than not utopian in their views of social systems. Equalitarianism serves the determination of the professional not to permit the administrator to interfere with his technical functions by checking the administrator's authority. It also serves the strivings of professional groups in competition with the physician to perform technical functions with more status, distributing such functions and the status associated with them more widely among such groups.

The strains arising when staff and patients attempt to implement such ideals over the whole hospital community are easily discernible. A group of patients asked to vote on whether or not one of their members should receive medication or have a pass to visit family are frustrated by their lack of knowledge, worried whether they have the attitudes necessary for making an objective decision, and edgy about the impact upon their informal group life of making such decisions. Bleary-eyed staff members reel from meeting to meeting as they try to keep up with the requirement to communicate everything to everyone. Groups are paralyzed, inundated with information they cannot process and the relevance of which to any differentiated task is unspecified. An unnerving multitude of kibitzers look over the shoulder of anyone attempting to deal with any particular situation. Good staff relations and getting along together must provide the satisfactions to compensate for the loss of pride in the exercise of unique, specialized skills. Concomitant with an emphasis on good relations, task-requirements that inevitably tend to mobilize strains in the group are minimized. Smoldering personal antagonisms disguise realistic conflicts between different interests and functions that must be carried out, because no one is responsible to represent a particular function and do battle in the service of it. Patients as well as other groups sabotage rational, adaptive problem-solving by making democratic decisions and taking democratic actions impulsively, often primarily in the service of relieving anxiety by getting rid of any difficulty as rapidly as possible.

Surely, the purpose of democratic organization should not be to emasculate, nor to permit the abrogation of, authority out of hostility, fear, and guilt. It should be rather to gain permission for the exercise of authority. A democratic organization should make possible as wide a base of consent as is needed to support the decisions of those who in making such decisions discharge their responsibilities.

Consultation mechanisms, involving face-to-face meetings of the group, may be essential to the democratic organization by carrying out the following purposes and thereby making possible a wide base of consent for decisions that must be made. Such a mechanism coordinates different parts of the task operation, for example, by exposing interference by one individual or group with the performance of another, conflicts of priority, or competing interests, so that these may be resolved. It builds group morale through a shared recognition of work well done. It makes possible for people to experience together the reality of the task and the reality of the relationships between those working to achieve it, so that fantasies about these may be tested. It encourages people to scrutinize errors, mistakes, and failures for the sake of understanding and future planning, with the reassurance that comes when no one is destroyed by the process. By use of the consultation process, those who must make decisions may seek the consent of those affected by and implementing such decisions (Jaques 1952). In such a group meeting, characteristically advice from others in the group to one member of the group (or from one group to another) is always viewed as a recommendation to the one who has the responsibility; so long as he carries the responsibility and is accountable for the consequences of any decision, he should be given the authority to carry it out in his own way. As part of such consultation, feedback mechanisms need to be developed that will give members of the group assurance that opinions, information, and reactions are adequately taken into account by those having particular responsibility.

Such a consultation process requires an organization in which there is clear differentiation of tasks and the delegation of authority and responsibility for performing them is explicit. Ideally, everyone in an organization should know what his job is and have the authority and personal qualities, skills, and resources needed to carry it out. (If someone—because of personal disturbance or incapacity—is not performing his job, this should soon become obvious to himself and to his superiors.) Ideally, each individual should enjoy doing and take pride in his work, not feel a restless yearning to be doing someone else's job as well as or instead of his own, and should respect his own and others' limitations and competencies. What needs to be worked out for every organization with its own particular task (therefore its own particular division of labor appropriate to that task) is the degree of role definition and autonomy of parts that will make these things possible, without compartmentalization or the fragmentation that results in lack of involvement and satisfaction in work. A problem arises in the psychiatric hospital when certain functions, the psychotherapeutic one, for example, has so much status that everyone would prefer, for example, to make interpretations of individual neurosis than to make statements or perform actions appropriate to administration, nursing, activities, or work functions. To cope with such problems, it is necessary to analyze carefully the task of the organization and the contributions of various functions to the carrying out of this task. A task should be organized so that its parts are differentiated yet coordinated. Such an analysis should be reflected in the definition of role positions and role relationships in the organization.

Ideally, multiple subordination and role-overlap should be minimal. Under these conditions, the number of persons and directives to which an individual must respond decreases, probably thereby increasing the interrelatedness and therefore the meaningfulness of the operations he performs. The extent to which a member of one unit can interfere with, delay, or stop action on the decisions of another unit is probably also as a consequence reduced. The question that must be coped with continuously in a psychiatric hospital is how, given task-differentiation and a minimization of multiple subordination, a large number of people may still interact with a patient as a person, rather than with some part of him as a specialized, impersonal focus of manipulation.

Authority should be exercised so that it may be viewed in an organization as a force for constructive good, able to protect each individual from irresponsible interference with, and able to create the conditions required for, the effective, imaginative, autonomous performance of his job. The organization ideally seeks to provide maximum autonomy (freedom from interference, and adequate authority over the activities, persons, and materials encompassed by a given responsibility) for each individual (and each group) in discharging his (or its) responsibilities.

A person in the exercise of authority should be supported by his superior, receive cooperation from his equals, and be able to permit himself the exercise of authority because he is able by virtue of personal qualities and maturity to accept and tolerate the stresses, burdens, and isolation of his own position.

The organization should provide safeguards against the tyranny by the group over any individual as well as against tyranny by an individual over the group. It should be noted that the tyranny of the group is an insidious one, often more difficult to recognize than the other, since an individual is likely to identify with his group especially in the name of democratic ideals; he does not want to defy or fight it; and the issue is usually confused when he seeks causes other than his relationship to the group for his resentments or paralysis.

An organization should decide to what extent a desirable relative autonomy of the parts of an organization is compatible with safeguards against misuse of authority; the need to coordinate and assign priorities to various parts of the organization; and the goal of a wide base of support for the decisions that must be made.

If policies relating the parts of the organization to each other, and decisions settling conflicts of priority or competing interests, are set or made by the group, there should be ways to resolve stalemates and to mitigate undue preoccupation with seeking support, with the associated toll on task use of time and creativity. If policies and decisions are set or made by the executive by himself, he will need to develop ways to tell how far others are willing to follow him, or to what extent discussions with others are necessary to win their support. An executive should not abrogate his authority to make such decisions to a group or committee, especially when the decision is required to resolve a difference in the group (for example, a conflict between the decisions, operations, or the timing of operations of different individuals or units within the group); yet he will have to find ways to exercise such authority so that his decisions are effectively implemented. A demonstrated understanding on his part of the consequences of any decision for all parts of the organization, a fair distribution of burdens, and his fidelity to the reality of the over-all organization of the task are some of the things that are crucial here.

Most crucially, a democratic organization, through consultation processes, most generally, through the relevant contributions of a sociotherapeutic function, should provide for the resolution of intragroup and intergroup tensions, a continuous, never-ending process necessary for problem-solving and task-achievement, analogous to the process of "working through" in individual psychotherapy.[16]

A Theoretical Model of Psychiatric Hospital Organization

The model presented here represents another means to cope with strains in a psychiatric hospital: an organization based upon the explicit delegation of authority and responsibility to persons and groups for the performance of specific, differentiated tasks or functions contributing to the achievement of the hospital's primary goal; and the use of consultation mechanisms signifying recognition of both the conflicts between, and the interdependence of, these tasks or functions. The essential hierarchy in such an organization is a hierarchy of tasks or functions, a task or function on a higher level being more inclusive or general than one on a lower level. As one proceeds upwards in such a hierarchy the same task is not being done better, or

---

16. For a discussion of the concept of "working through" as it applies to problem-solving in organizations see Jaques (1952).

supervised by someone who can do it better, at a higher level of authority. Rather, another, more general, inclusive function is being accomplished, involving the integration of specific tasks at a lower level with each other and with their shared situation. That authority and responsibility increase as one moves up such a hierarchy is simply a consequence of such a differentiation of tasks. The implication of such a hierarchy is that the essential qualification for occupancy of a position at a certain level is the possession of the skills, of an appropriate degree of generality or specificity, required for the achievement of goals at that level. An organization such as this—oriented to adaptation imperatives and instrumental action, evaluating according to cognitive standards how best to achieve its goals in a given situation, regarding a kind of organization itself as a means to an end not a moral desideratum or end in itself—tends to approximate in its value patterns the previously described individualistic-bureaucratic type of hospital.

The abstract model of organization to be constructed here involves functional systems and subsystems, their aims, boundaries, and requirements; the model implements, therefore, a general system approach to organization.[17] Departures from the model by a concretely existent organization may be considered at least in part the result of conditions, past or present, imposing constraints or limits on that organization; in other words, other factors than the goal of the organization and the function or functions of each subsystem and its relation to other subsystems are operative. The model is a tool of analysis, to clarify problems; it is not a set of prescriptions for how to behave or not to behave, at the expense of complex, lively, expressive participation in the life of an organization.

The basic paradigm may be represented as a box, a system, its outline the boundary of that system, the space outside this outline the external situation of the entire system. The box itself may be subdivided to represent differentiated functions or subsystems within the system's boundaries. The space within the box, but outside subdivisions representing subsystems, represents the internal situation of subsystems of the system. In the space representing the internal situation of operational subsystems, a circle represents a subsystem whose primary function is to supply resources to, or act as a control, limit, or constraint upon the operations of the subsystems in whose internal situation it is. Operational subsystems may similarly be subdivided into further functions, tasks, or subsystems each with an internal situation including resources, controls, limits, or constraints. For a representation of the hospital as a system with subsystems see figure 7.[18]

The psychiatric hospital, insofar as it is an organization within a social system, as a concrete entity may be part of the theoretically abstracted adaptation, integration, or motivation subsystems of that social system. Insofar as the hospital performs a research function, it is part of the adaptation subsystem of the society to which it belongs. Insofar as it performs an educational function, training members of such professions as psychiatry and psychology, it is part of the motivation subsystem of

---

17. Two writers who have also applied general system theory to organizations are Parsons (1957, 1960a) and Rice (1963), who to judge from their writings are apparently not familiar with each other's work in this area.

18. This system of notation is suggested by Rice (1963).

the society to which it belongs. Insofar as it performs a treatment function, from the point of view of output to the society to which it belongs it is part of the integration subsystem of that society. Since the hospital makes no decisions related to, and does not determine in any way, the ends of the society to which it belongs, and since it does not function primarily to satisfy the wishes of the members of that society or to provide them with symbols by which to express themselves, the performance of consummation functions in the hospital is incidental to its primary goals as far as the society to which it belongs is concerned.

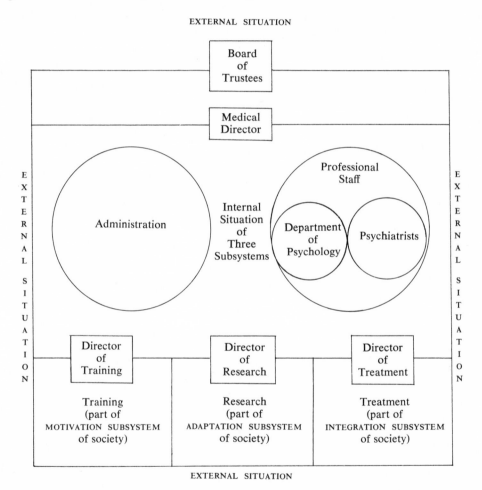

Fig. 7. The hospital organization and its subsystems.

There are three functional subsystems of the organization, representing three different goals, purposes, or outputs with respect to the social system of which this organization is a part. These three are training (motivation), research (adaptation), and treatment (integration). All three goals, however, are parts of the primary goal of the organization, coping with mental illness or psychiatric disorder; each goal represents a different way of accomplishing that task.

A psychiatric hospital organization might view as part of its task of coping with psychiatric disorder, operations involving the extended community or society; the external community or society is, then, the system of concern. One may seek to cope with psychiatric disorder by effecting change in an extended community through direct alterations of the institutions of the extended community, mobilization or supply of resources (financial or personnel) to support mental health enterprises in the community, such educational efforts as providing consultation or teaching staff to community agencies, or attempts to coordinate or integrate various community mental health agencies or enterprises (Marcus and Edelson 1967). The operations of a Community Services subsystem of a psychiatric hospital usually involve provision of consultation or teaching staff to community agencies; such a Community Services subsystem is not represented in figure 7 in the interest of simplification. This Community Services subsystem, which is a technical operation, should not be confused with the administrative system's heteronomous functions relating the hospital to its situation previously discussed; responsibility for these, although it may be delegated, is a crucial part of the Medical Director's position.

The leadership of the entire system is the Medical Director and Board of Trustees. The Medical Director is on the boundary between the organization and the Board of Trustees; the Board of Trustees is on the outermost boundary between the organization (represented for them by the Medical Director) and the situation external to the hospital, including, for example, agencies, organizations, and other groups in the extended society. The role of the Board of Trustees has to do, in this connection, with winning the confidence of the extended community in the organization, the legitimation of its right to perform its function in society; with mobilizing other kinds of support, for example, financial resources, and providing conditions that will attract needed personnel; and with representing to the organization through the Medical Director changes in its situation, for example, changes in the current exigencies, demands, and claims confronting the organization and in the availability of resources for given purposes.

The leadership function of each subsystem (the Director of Training, the Director of Research, and the Director of Treatment) is also placed on a boundary, the boundary of each subsystem. Positioning leadership on a boundary represents the idea that leadership not only integrates and coordinates what is within but crucially relates what is within to what is external to the system or subsystem; that is, its situation. Another way of saying the same thing is that a system or subsystem to perform its function must be concerned not only with the imperatives of integration and motivation, but with those of consummation and adaptation as well. The former imperatives involve relationships between entities within the system and the internal condition of these entities. The latter involve relationships between the system or subsystem and its situation. Leadership should be in a position to help meet all four system-requirements. Leadership should function on the boundary, that is, be in a position to relate to the situation of the system or subsystem, since aspects of this situation impose limits or constraints (conditions) upon the performance of the system's function and determine what means or services (opportunities, facilities, media, skills) are available for the achievement of its goals. Indeed, possession of a position on the boundary determines at least as much as personal capacities whether or not a given individual or group of individuals will be able to exercise leadership.

Concretely, this means that the leadership of a particular subsystem X (e.g., Treatment) within an organization must be in a position to meet and deal with the leadership of other subsystems Y, Z (e.g., Training, Research), which compete with X for means, or the operations of which must be coordinated with those of X; and to meet and deal with the leadership of subsystems (e.g., Administration or Professional Groups) the only function of which is to impose limits or constraints upon or provide services, including skills, to subsystems X, Y, and Z; as well as to meet and deal with the leadership of the entire system (e.g., the Medical Director) which includes X, Y, and Z as subsystems.

The word "Director" to represent a leadership position on a boundary is used in preference to "Supervisor" or "Coordinator," for the following reasons. "Supervisor" implies that the function of a supraordinate position is to check on, or control, the task-performance in a subordinate position. In contrast, the present theory of organization involves the idea that moving from one level to another signifies moving from one task to a different task, for example, a move from a more inclusive task to differentiated tasks or subsystems of the inclusive task or subsystem, not simply moving from one level to another of a hierarchically segmented same task. Hierarchy is based (going down) on progressive differentiation of the task, not (going up) on repetition, control, or direction of the same task by someone at a higher level of authority, who can or knows how to do it better. Each differentiated subsystem has its own particular task, boundaries, imperatives, means, conditions, norms, values, and internal and external situations. A Medical Director, for example, in these terms should be concerned, not so much with directing detailed operations, directly or by proxy, within a particular subsystem of the organization, but rather with the functioning or output of this subsystem as affecting relations between subsystems of the organization (e.g., as these subsystems are interdependent or competing for the same resources) or relations between the organization and its external situation. "Coordinator" implies that the function of leadership has to do primarily with the relation of inner parts to each other, whereas according to the view presented here, leadership has to do primarily with a boundary function: relating what is within (i.e., the internal arrangements of a group or organization performing a task) and what is outside (situational exigencies, vicissitudes, demands, changes, which create needs for new internal arrangements if a task is to be successfully achieved, or which indeed may require a change in the group's or organization's task or goal itself).

In figure 7, each of the three Directors (of Training, Research, and Treatment) is on a boundary between his functional subsystem and a situation external to that subsystem but within the organization: what might be called an internal situation or inner environment. That situation includes the two other subsystems as well as those subsystems performing limit or control and service functions for all three operational subsystems training, research, and treatment. For example, constraints or services are imposed upon or provided operational subsystems by Administration (performing such functions as Finances, Personnel, Buildings and Grounds, Dietary) and Professional Staff (Psychiatrists and Department of Psychology, performing such functions as in-service training and ongoing staff education, library, medical procedures, and recruitment and selection of professional staff).

The exclusion of the Nursing Staff from the Professional Staff grouping in this position in the organization does not imply that nursing is not a profession, but only reflects the actuality, when it is an actuality, that the psychiatrists and psychologists perform a limit or control and service function in relation to all three major subsystems of the organization, while the Nursing Staff performs a limit or control and service function with respect to only the treatment subsystem and is therefore located within that subsystem. The inclusion of other professional staffs in this position, for example, the Social Work Staff, would depend upon the analysis of their function in a particular hospital as involving a limit or control and service function with respect to all three (teaching, research, and treatment) subsystems.

The organizational functions described under Administration and Professional Staff, as well as operational subsystems, can be classified (with the focus now on the hospital rather than society as the system of action) in terms of the four group-functions previously discussed (which will be applied subsequently also in analyzing the treatment subsystem of the organization). Administrative functions are largely adaptation group-functions. In-service training and staff education are motivation group-functions. Medical procedures is an example of an integration (norm-setting) function. The three operational task- or goal-achieving subsystems (treatment, research, and training) involve consummation group-functions (the attainment of ultimate, gratifying ends) when viewed from the point of view of the hospital rather than society as the system of reference. Each of these subsystems, in turn, when taken as the system of reference, includes adaptation, motivation, integration, and consummation functions. (Of course, each of the circles representing limit or control and service functions could be represented by a detailed diagram showing its boundaries, subsystems, and leadership positions.)

When a particular organization has three major tasks—treatment, training, and research—strains result related to conflict between these three subsystems over values, and competition for personnel, financial resources, time, facilities, and motivational commitments. Should motivation, for example, be mobilized to raise money for treatment facilities (such as a recreational building for patients) or for research? Of the personnel who can be recruited, what proportion should be competent, even excellent therapists, perhaps with little or no, at least secondary, interest in or aptitude for teaching and research; what proportion should be primarily interested in research or teaching? Should a Fellow in training be encouraged to work with an additional patient, receiving more supervision in psychotherapy, or should he be encouraged to work on a research study? Should outpatient services be expanded at the expense of time for staff research, teaching, or training? What proportion of the time of senior staff members should be devoted to the direct treatment of patients, and what proportion to research and teaching?

Nevertheless, the three subsystems are usually highly interdependent. A high quality treatment program is a necessary foundation for training and research. There must be opportunities for teaching and research and an atmosphere of encouragement for such interests and endeavors if well qualified permanent staff members and Fellows in training are to be recruited and treatment is to be continually reexamined and improved.

There can be no once-and-for-all hierarchy of priorities assigned to the three subsystems; the conflicts and competition between them, and inevitably some strains and ambiguity in many situations, must be accepted as inherent in such a multi-functional organization; ways must be, and of course are, found to accommodate to such strains. Continual efforts must be made to find a satisfactory balance in the day-to-day attempts to meet the imperatives of the three subsystems. For such reasons, it is important that there be clearly designated responsibilities for the welfare and output of each of these enterprises, making for an explicit dialogue between those representing each one, making it possible to find out directly how each enterprise is doing, so that problems can be, if not resolved, at least more easily identified. Otherwise, conflicts, competition, strains are likely to be covert or displaced; persons having multiple responsibilities may abrogate one for the other; it is difficult to determine who is evading what responsibility; vital interests are lost; it is difficult to find out how something is going; the "fights" tend to be between the wrong people about the wrong issues.

Before proceeding to a consideration of the subsystems of the hospital, we may define the various professional functions, as distinct from the previously discussed administrative functions, which may be carried out as technical operations in the psychiatric hospital.

The psychotherapeutic function theoretically should be concerned primarily with the study and alteration of intrapersonal events; that is, events occurring within the patient. Essentially, this function is aimed at the resolution of intrapersonal tensions through the use of specialized techniques. Individual psychotherapy and group psychotherapy are examples of such techniques. In individual psychotherapy, manifestations of intrapersonal tension are studied in transference and resistance phenomena appearing in the relationship between psychotherapist and patient. Such intrapersonal tensions are resolved through a process of discovery and didactic explanation, the latter denoting the presence of verbal communication from one possessing specialized skills and knowledge. In group psychotherapy, manifestations of intrapersonal tension are studied in the group process, in transference and resistance reactions shared by members of the group and appearing in the relationship among group members, and between group members and the group psychotherapist. Similarly, such intrapersonal tensions are resolved through a process of discovery and didactic explanation.

Theoretically, a unique nursing function in a psychiatric hospital may involve concern primarily with interpersonal events, that is, occurring between patients in their life together, and with the resolution of interpersonal tensions through the use of specialized techniques. (Such techniques are not so well known as the ones used by the psychotherapist.) The psychiatric nurse qua psychiatric nurse, in addition to her usual nursing functions, should uniquely care for not so much the individual patient as the relationship between patients. For example, rather than nurse an individual patient, she might help patients care for each other. (The result is that she finds herself nurturing healthy resources within patients rather than responding only to deficiencies or disturbances.)[19] It is clear that the nursing function is related to interest in the integration of the group—of course, then, in its norms.

---

19. From a formulation made by Thomas Main, in a personal communication describing Cassel Hospital.

The sociotherapeutic function in a psychiatric hospital should be concerned primarily with the situation in which the patient is being treated, that is, with intragroup and intergroup events (occurring within and between various patient and staff groups) and with the resolution of intra- and intergroup tensions, through the use of specialized techniques again not so well known.[20] The sociotherapeutic function is concerned with the discovery and explanation of those intra- and intergroup tensions interfering with the performance and coordination of professional and administrative functions. It is also concerned with the discovery and explanation of those factors interfering with, and those mechanisms facilitating, the resolution of such tensions.

The activities program function in a psychiatric hospital should be concerned with the interaction between patients (usually as persons expressing particular needs or having or learning some special skill) and what are ordinarily (but not always) non-personal classes of events and objects such as the subject matter of a class; the media of the crafts shop; recreational events; special projects such as a garden, greenhouse, library or nursery school; drama, music, or other interest groups. This class of events and objects has to do with that sector of personality concerned with "interests," "play," or expressive action, not involving serious-consequences-if-not-done, as work, for example, does. In a broad sense, one may say that the activities program function involves the resolution of tensions between a patient or group of patients and the requirements or characteristics of a particular activity or medium.

The work program function should be concerned with the interaction or, in different terms, with the resolution of tension, between patients (as workers with competencies and obligations) and the task to be performed. Housekeeping, dietary, and maintenance jobs are examples. Instrumental action is required. Tasks are those that every patient is expected to help perform, because their performance is obviously necessary for the everyday life of the patients as a group. The failure to perform such work has intrinsic, immediate, and unpleasant consequences for the worker and his peers. Thus, although an element of moral obligation is always part of work, the adaptive ego in relation to reality, and not simply superego considerations, is also the subject of analysis and concern in group discussions of the interaction between patient and work.

A social work function should be concerned with the relation between the individual patient and groups outside the hospital (e.g., the patient's family or a community agency) and thus may be particularly concerned with the resolution of intra-family tensions so that the patient may be integrated with his family.

Included under professional functions there is also a patient function, because in the psychiatric hospital organization the nature of the patient and his participation is a crucial resource for, or constraint upon, the achievement of the hospital's goals and the actualization of its value system. The patient is not only a customer for the hospital's services, but, since the patient's cooperation and his social interaction are required for these services to be provided effectively, in a way an employee of the hospital as well. While the patient as consumer pays, he must also be paid for his participation by the approval of others, by realistic gains in his own life in the hos-

---

20. Sociotherapy, in quite a different frame of reference, is defined instead as the didactic resolution of interpersonal tension states by Robert Rapoport (1956).

pital, or by privileges and absence of deprivation (Parsons 1957); optimally, his participation is ultimately governed by his internalization of, and commitment to, the treatment values of the hospital. Since the patient's disturbance is not confined to one aspect of his personality, it is not possible to have him make a circumscribed "job" commitment to the hospital, as is possible with other employees. The hospital requires, and must court, the patient's generalized commitment to it, so that he is ready to pursue any problems that arise, and upon whose working out his therapy depends, wherever they may lead. The patient's role in the hospital should not be defined as being sick. The expectation rather should be for him, as an essential ally of the hospital in the production of custodial, protective, socialization, and therapy services, to discover, express, and represent himself in all situations, and to maintain whatever healthy resources he has against encroachment by psychiatric illness.

Ideally, he indicates his needs and the needs of his group, so that these may be identified and met within the limits of the hospital's resources and value systems. Ideally, he controls and contains impulses within himself and others in his group, the expression of which would be contrary to his or their own interest or the safety of others, so that the hospital organization is not required to use protective mechanisms beyond its resources or violating its value systems. Ideally, he struggles with (rather than passively complies with or blindly rebels against) the expectations not only of other groups and the larger community outside the hospital but of his own peers within the hospital as well, so that, in his interaction with the group and society, his own identity and integrity are not lost but discovered. Ideally, he observes and reports what transpires within himself and between himself and others, so that such information may contribute to the resolution of intrapersonal, interpersonal, and intra- and intergroup tensions. Ideally, he participates in work and activities, thereby maintaining and adding to his own resources, so that he is able to be an adequate ally in the therapeutic endeavor as well as a contributing member in the life of his own group. If a patient performs these patient functions as a member of the hospital organization, he will maintain and enhance intact areas of ego functioning and the regressive effects of illness and of hospitalization itself may be counteracted (Edelson 1964; Stanton 1956a; Talbot et al. 1964).

There are also professional support functions, which are concerned with providing help to personnel carrying out administrative and professional functions.

Education or training is a support function, concerned with the relation of various staff groups to an existing body of knowledge and skills. Research is another support function, concerned with the relation of staff members to a yet-to-be-acquired body of knowledge, and, if action research is involved, contributing the formulation of relevant hypotheses and means for collecting data to test such hypotheses to ongoing problem-solving processes in the hospital. Personnel—psychiatric residents, for example—require training that is not necessarily relevant to their present position in the hospital and that is judged by the standards of groups outside the hospital. The knowledge obtained by research activities may be useful for the current problem-solving of the organization, but it also may not be. As we have noted, there are, of course, consequences for the hospital organization of these examples of the membership of personnel in professional groups outside the hospital, or of the existence of multiple possibly competing functions in the hospital.

Psychodiagnosis is a support function, concerned with providing personnel performing administrative functions with information they require to do their jobs, for example, the selection of patients for treatment.

The physician on duty at nights and on the weekend (the so-called O.D. or Officer of the Day), in addition to his usual functions as a physician, performs a support function unique to his position in the psychiatric hospital. He uses the authority he possesses (not by virtue of his position in the hospital but as a member of the medical profession) to sanction decisions of the nurse in her performance of nursing functions. The nurse may make a routine request of the O.D. (e.g., for an order for sleeping medication or a laxative) or she may report a disturbance in a patient or in a group of patients. Instead of simply giving a medical order, he may respond, performing a sociotherapeutic function, by attempting to understand with the nurse what tension exists within the patient or nurse group or between these two groups giving rise to the nurse's communication to him. He might then use such understanding to support the nurse in performing her unique nursing function. Instead of doing something *to* an individual patient, for example, she might use, repair, or care for some relationship between patients. A similar process may be carried out whether or not custodial care, protection, socialization, or therapy are the services at issue.

A counseling function may support the individual patient in performing the patient function, just as a supervision function may support the psychotherapist in performing the psychotherapeutic function.

Figure 8 represents in greater detail the organizational subsystem devoted to training. The sub-subsystems of the Training subsystem include the members of classes, or seminars, or those being supervised in individual psychotherapy; one such sub-subsystem represents that the Chief, Psychology Department, is in charge of additional specialized training for postdoctoral Fellows in psychology. The Curriculum

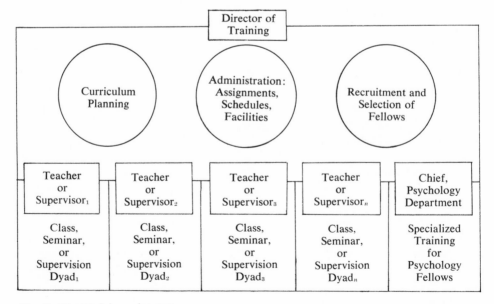

Fig. 8. The Training subsystem

Planning function provides these sub-subsystems with an integrated teaching framework; with a past and future time perspective within which the subsystems operate; and, to some extent, constrains at least some choices about what will be taught to whom during a given period. The Administration function, related to over-all Administration (see fig. 7), provides facilities, and creates constraints in the form of schedules and assignments of particular teachers or supervisors and students or supervisees to particular operating sub-subsystems. The Recruitment and Selection function provides persons to be educated; the nature and number of these set constraints upon the teaching operation. The essential distinction here, again, is that between an operating system and its situation; in its situation exist the groups or agencies which provide it with means and set limits upon its operation.

Figure 9 represents in greater detail the subsystem devoted to research. The subsystems (for convenience, sub-subsystems will be referred to as subsystems, the con-

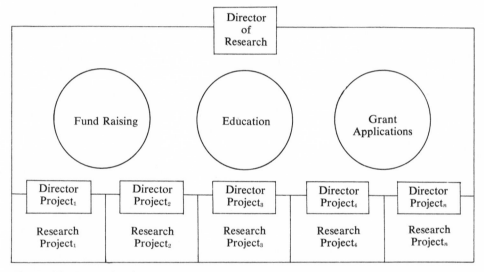

Fig. 9. The Research subsystem

text indicating the system of reference) of the Research subsystem include the research teams (staff and subjects) assigned to each project. The Research Fund-Raising function should be related to the Finance function of Administration (see fig. 7). It provides money for the operating subsystems; the amount of money provided and decisions about allocation of available funds among operating subsystems constrain the operation of each. The Research Grant Applications function, providing assistance to individual project directors in the writing of grant applications, should also be related to the Finance function of Administration. The Education function, providing additional opportunities for learning research skills, research design and methodology, and theory-building, should be related to the Professional Staff In-service Training and Ongoing Staff Education function mentioned in the text in the discussion of figure 7. Note that the Research subsystem implies basic research. A research staff solely concerned with action research (testing hypotheses and providing information concerning operations within the organization) is per-

forming a limit or control and service function in relation to one or more operational subsystems; which one or ones determine within what boundaries the action
research function is located.

Our main interest now is the organization of the Treatment enterprise or subsystem (figs. 10–20).

In figure 10, the fundamental distinction between person and situation, both of
which are essential aspects of any process of action, is reflected by the division of the

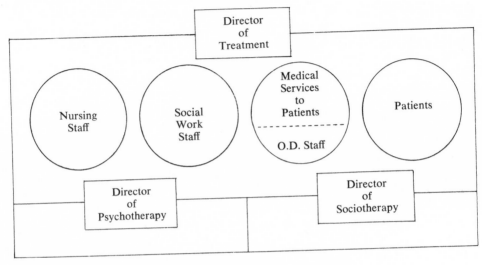

Fig. 10. The Treatment subsystem: psychotherapy and sociotherapy.

treatment enterprise into psychotherapy and sociotherapy, both of which are essential aspects of any process of change in a personality system of action.

Psychotherapy is concerned with the person, with intrapersonal states, and with
relationships between subsystems of the personality system. The aims of psychotherapy are the identification, mitigation, and sometimes resolution of strains within,
and the integration of, that personality system.

Sociotherapy is concerned with the situation with which the person (the patient-
in-treatment, in this case) interacts, and which, in relation to his adaptive problem-
solving, is the locus of means and conditions or constraints; the situation is also the
source of goal-objects which he pursues, alone or in concert, and the norms and
values to which he may adapt, which he may internalize, which he may share more
or less with others, or which may conflict with his already internalized norms and
values. Means are more or less available; goal-objects more or less attainable; norms
and values more or less coherent or consistent with each other. The outcome of a
process of action in the social system, which is a major part of the person's (patient's)
situation, changes the ratio of confidence to uncertainty, gratification to deprivation,
solidarity to anomie, or commitment to alienation; and thereby determines the
nature of object-relations formed by the person (patient): what objects are valued as
useful and the intensity of that valuation; which goal-objects or ends (relations with
goal-objects) are cathected and the quantity of that cathexis; which norms are inter-

nalized or which persons representing those norms are identified with and the strength of that identification or internalization; and which values are internalized or which persons or institutions representing those values are esteemed and respected and the strength of that internalization or respect. It is by such processes that entities in the situation interpenetrate the personality system and thereby ultimately influence as well the behavioral organism.

The aims of sociotherapy, in this treatment enterprise, are the identification, mitigation, and sometimes resolution of strains within, and the integration of, that social system in which the patient is being treated: a therapeutic community, since such a social system is more or less dominated by the values, and the norms derived from these, associated with therapeutic processes and the goals of therapy.

The patients contribute resources to, and by virtue of their particular characteristics impose constraints upon, both operating subsystems (Psychotherapy and Sociotherapy) of the treatment enterprise (see fig. 10). The Selection of Patients function is therefore crucial to the enterprise. The aspects of the patient comprising his membership and participation in a social system and his physiological behavioral organism are important entities in the situation of the Psychotherapy subsystem. The aspects of the patient comprising his personality system and his physiological behavioral organism are important entities in the situation of the Sociotherapy enterprise.

The location of the Nursing Staff in the organization depends, of course, upon the conception of the role of the nurse in the treatment enterprise. Here, the nurse is considered to provide a service and limit function to the operational treatment subsystems, rather than to be directly involved in treatment operations. The decisions about the service provided and to whom, and the subsystem or subsystems upon the operation of which the presence, absence, or varying quality of this service acts as a constraint, determine within which boundary the Nursing Staff performs its task(s).

If the nurse is seen primarily as an ally of the psychotherapist, interacting with the individual patient in the interests of the psychotherapy enterprise (in terms of the current vicissitudes and requirements of a psychotherapy dyad, for example) or altering the physiological behavioral organism of the patient through the use of medication ordered by the psychotherapist, then the location of the Nursing Staff is within the boundaries of the Psychotherapy subsystem, between the Director of Psychotherapy and the Psychotherapists, as part of the situation of, that is, resources more or less available to, the operating subsystems (psychotherapy dyads) of the Psychotherapy subsystem (see fig. 13, p. 138).

The nurse may be seen primarily as a sociotherapist, participating in the social system of the patient-staff community, in its various collectivities and enterprises, supporting the efforts at, and contributing to, problem-solving in that community, and providing a variety of resources to such problem-solving: skills in interpersonal relations; knowledge of the informal life of the Patient Group possessed by virtue of the intimate contact of the Nursing Staff and the Patient Group, the welfare of which is the latter's nursing concern; insight into the impact of the informal life of the Patient Group upon the organized efforts of the patient-staff community, especially upon the maintenance of norms required for these efforts; and ability to relate and integrate processes in the informal Patient Group with those in the formally organized collectivities of the therapeutic community, the latter comprising the so-called Community Program. Then, the Nursing Staff is located within the boundaries of the Sociotherapy subsystem, between the Director of Sociotherapy and the operating subsystems of the Sociotherapy enterprise, as part of the situation of, that is, resources more or less available to, those operating subsystems (see fig. 15, p. 141).

If the Nursing Staff has both tasks, then it is located within the boundary of the Treatment subsystem but in the internal situation of both the Psychotherapy and Sociotherapy enterprises, which of course then are competing for these services. This conception is represented in figure 10. A multifunctional role such as this offers the possibility of many problems. Each task may require quite a different organization of the Nursing Staff, a different allocation of time and personnel, and quite different skills of its members. The performance of one task may interfere with that of another: consultation with a psychotherapist about an individual patient and his personality system may interfere with a reaction to this patient as a member of the patient-staff community in terms of the imperatives of that social system rather than those of the psychotherapy dyad; nursing interviews with upset patients may occur at the expense of participation by nurses with more well-functioning patients in their social life and the maintenance of that higher level of functioning. If the Nursing Staff is not differentiated into two groups to perform these different tasks, then any nurse may evade the sometimes painful demands, necessities, and skill-requirements of one function at any particular time by becoming preoccupied with performance of the other. Ultimate responsibility for evaluating and adjudicating such processes, when the Nursing Staff is in this location, is the Director of Treatment's, since relations between the two operating subsystems as affected by their competition for resources in their shared internal situation are involved.

Efforts to resolve such problems often include either diminishing the potency of one function or differentiating the staff into two subgroups, each one of which is responsible for a different function. For example, the sociotherapeutic role may be emphasized rather than the role of being the psychotherapist's assistant. It may be decided within a hospital organization that the Activities Staff should relate to patients as members of the patient-staff community and in terms of the patients' interests in and capacities for expressive activity, not in terms of their psychopathology or the current needs of the psychotherapy dyad; psychotherapists do not then give "prescriptions" for patients to the Activities Staff. Similarly, it may be decided that psychotherapists will not "prescribe" the nurse's relation to the patient or use the nurse to manipulate the patient's environment in terms of the vicissitudes of psychotherapy, preferring that the nurse respond to the patient in terms of the patient's participation in the patient-staff community and especially with regard to his conduct in relation to the norms of that community. Naturally, during times of crisis, anxiety, or special difficulty, holding to such distinctions, useful and valued though they may be, tends to break down; also, the nurse is usually hesitant to abandon her customary role of receiving her "orders" from the treating doctor.

Another problem for the nurse arises when it is held preferable in a hospital organization to cope with the effects of the patient's illness by interpersonal (psychotherapeutic) means; or to cope interpersonally and in the patient-staff community with disorganized or disruptive behavior arising out of the patient's illness, as it affects the patient-staff community and according to the norms of that community, efforts to cope, involving, then, interventions in processes in the patient's situation (sociotherapy); rather than to cope with the effects of the illness by operating on the patient's physiological organism through the use of drugs. Not only some inevitable differences in preference in this connection, but the facts that an organization may be training Fellows, whose abilities to cope with the effects of mental illness psycho-therapeutically vary, that the skills of the Sociotherapy Staff have limitations, and that a social system adhering to a particular value system and organization is constrained by these as to the kind of behavior it can contain, intefere with the consistent adoption of such a policy. Nevertheless, then, "giving out medication" by a nurse in that organization even though in response to the psychotherapist's "orders," is not seen as a highly valued function, but will probably be, in fact, regarded somewhat ambivalently, that is, encouraged as necessary in some situations, suspected as an evasion of the real problem or as undermining the value preferences of the hospital in others, and sometimes regarded in both ways in the same situation.

In figure 10 the Nursing Staff is located outside the boundaries of both Psycho-therapy and Sociotherapy but within the boundaries of the Treatment subsystem to indicate that this staff provides services to both enterprises. Where the role of the nurse is not primarily to assist the psychotherapist directly, and where chemotherapy is marginally important in the treatment program, this staff would be placed within the boundaries of the Sociotherapy subsystem, as in figure 15 (p. 141), rather than in the position represented in figure 10 or the position within the Psychotherapy subsystem represented by figure 13 (p. 138).

Many organizational problems in psychiatric hospitals are related to the fact that each psychiatrist, psychologist, and nurse performs multiple roles, and is, therefore, located in different positions in the organization. Each position has its own set of relations with others appropriate to the particular task(s) involved, and each position involves task-requirements that may interfere with the task-requirements intrinsic to other positions. Tendencies on the part of persons or groups to abrogate one role or task for another when the "going gets rough," and on the part of persons or groups to be competitive rather than cooperative (wooing, for example, persons from one role to another) tend to be exacerbated rather than constrained by such an organization. Awareness of these processes; respect on the part of each person (and others) concerning the boundary within which he is operating at any given time, including the limits and requirements of that position; and differentiation of the functions to be performed by persons and groups, when possible, may mitigate these effects.

The position of Medical Services to Patients similarly varies with the conception of the role of such services in the treatment of the psychiatric patient. If medical services are ordered by, and are the responsibility of, the psychotherapist, or if Medical Services is responsible for monitoring or controlling medications ordered by the psychotherapist, then these services should be located within the boundaries of the Psychotherapy subsystem. If medical services are conceived primarily in terms of modifying the situation of the social system (the patient-staff therapeutic community), that situation including physiological behavioral organisms as well as personality systems, and, by maintaining such physiological organisms, making possible or otherwise affecting the patient's participation in that social system, then responsibility for the use of such services would lie within the Sociotherapy subsystem, and Medical Services to Patients should be located within the boundaries of that subsystem.

When both Psychotherapy and Sociotherapy subsystems are served by Medical Services to Patients, and the operations of both of these subsystems are limited or enhanced by the adequacy and form of such services, then, as in figure 10, Medical Services to Patients is located within the boundaries of the Treatment enterprise, but part of the internal situation of both Psychotherapy and Sociotherapy enterprises. This location logically implies that, since both enterprises are affected by such services, both have a stake in the specific application of such services. A psychotherapist may order sedation or tranquillizers in terms of the apparent imperatives of psychotherapy, without regard to the impact of this alteration of the physiological organism on the patient's participation in the therapeutic community, on the state of his motivational commitments, and ultimately upon the maintenance of the norms of the therapeutic community, the availability of human resources to it, or the coherence of its value system. Similarly, the nurses or other members of the community, in their failure to cope with certain behavior in a patient, may put immense and sometimes complicatingly covert pressure on a psychotherapist to order medication as a way of controlling such behavior, without regard to the possible consequent impact upon psychotherapy. Even when psychiatric problems are not directly involved, a regime ordered for a physical disability may have profound consequences for both psychotherapy and sociotherapy. It is possible that struggling with such problems would be more fruitful, were the struggle open and between the parties whose interests are at stake: a decision to alter the physiological behavioral organism in a way that might affect both psychotherapy and sociotherapy should be taken jointly by at least the Director of Treatment, the Director of Psychotherapy, the Director of Sociotherapy, and the Director of Medical Services to Patients, or their representatives. Joint participation in the making of such decisions (with the Director of Treatment ultimately responsible for these) should certainly be quite feasible in a small hospital or treatment unit and in an organization in which chemotherapy in relation to psychiatric disorder is seen as a minor treatment modality which should be (according to prevailing norms) relatively infrequently used.

From a consistent theoretical point of view, if one subsystem of an organization devoted to the task of coping with psychiatric disorder is concerned with the personality system (psychotherapy), and one with the social system, which is part of the situation with which the personality system is inextricably interacting (sociotherapy), then, it might seem that a third subsystem of the organization should be responsible for the physiological organism, which is, in terms of theoretical analysis, also part of the situation with which the personality system is inextricably interacting (physiological therapy). In that case, a diagram such as figure 11 results. Each subsystem of the Physiological Therapy subsystem might include treating agent(s) and impaired physiological organism(s); the internal situation of these subsystems includes a Medical Nursing Staff and Laboratory Services.

However, figure 11 suggests that Physiological Therapy is thought of as a differentiated part of the task of coping with mental illness. When in a particular hospital

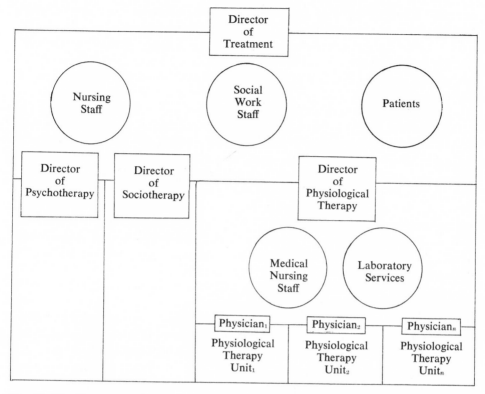

Fig. 11. The Treatment subsystem: psychotherapy, sociotherapy, and physiological therapy.

the task is not conceptualized or differentiated in this way, figure 11 does not adequately represent the organization of that hospital although it might that of another. Figure 10 represents Medical Services as a limit or control and service function, affecting the operational subsystems of the organization that are directly responsible for achieving its treatment goals; Medical Services is not in itself such an operational subsystem. The condition of the physiological behavioral organism is essentially seen as a constraint upon, or a condition limiting, or a means or resource for, the two basic operational subsystems Psychotherapy and Sociotherapy.

Analogously, an organization might exist in which attention to the patient's milieu is seen essentially as a way of supporting the treatment enterprise, the latter being conceived primarily in terms of operations with the personality system (e.g., psychotherapy) or operations with the physiological organism (e.g., chemotherapy or other organic therapies). In that case, sociotherapy would be a limit or control and service function within the internal situation of such treatment enterprises. In some organizations, sociotherapy might be the major therapeutic operation, and attention to individual personality systems and physiological organisms primarily given by groups that are seen as having limit or control and service functions.

These examples illustrate a major point—that an organizational diagram ultimately reflects a theory concerning the nature of the task of the organization. "Coping with psychiatric disorder," "altering individual personality systems," "changing individual behavior," "getting an individual back to his family and job," are four quite different conceptions of the task of a hospital organization; each carries implications concerning the arrangements and operations necessary to achieve the task. An organizational diagram describes what makes a meaningful differentiation of the task as it is conceived, and how it is to be carried out, not simply authority, status, or prestige relations.

In figure 10, the function of doctors-on-call-at-night (O.D. Staff) is represented as part of the Medical Services to Patients function; this implies that the primary task of this staff is to provide emergency medical services. Actually, members of this staff in many hospitals act as on-the-spot psychotherapists, concerned with intervening to deal directly with the strains within a particular individual personality system by having a "midnight psychotherapy session." Or they may act as sociotherapist-consultants to nurses on duty at night, helping nurses to decide how to intervene, how to mobilize and utilize therapeutic community resources to deal with the situation. A Doctor-on-Call may help the nurse to decide whether the distress of a particular patient arises only within the personality system of the patient or is a manifestation of some group process. A Doctor-on-Call may investigate what forces are acting upon the nurses toward what end: what relations between groups of patients or between the nurse group and a patient group are involved. This triple role (emergency medical services, psychotherapy operations, and sociotherapist-consultation) implies that the O.D. Staff should be part of the Psychotherapy subsystem operations; part of the Nursing Staff function as represented in figures 15 (p. 141) and 16 (p. 146)—actually, in an undrawn organizational diagram of the Nursing Staff, part of resources or consultant services to Nursing Staff itself viewed as a subsystem whose task is to provide nursing resources to operational subsystems of the hospital; and part of Medical Services to Patients as in figure 10. Such multi-functional roles, of course, have all the problems previously discussed; therefore, the usual feelingful concern with, and reactions to, the job itself and how it is performed, by all groups in the hospital.

In figure 10, a Social Work Staff function is represented, supposing it to involve the performance of a limit or control and service function in relation to both Psychotherapy and Sociotherapy. For example, the social worker might provide information about the external situation bearing upon the patient's selection for treatment, and, in relation to Psychotherapy, might relate to the family in such a way as to militate against their interference with, and enhance their support of, the psychotherapy enterprise. In relation to Sociotherapy, the social worker might be instrumental in helping the hospital community deal with problems arising as patients leave their former community and enter a new one and, later in the course of treatment, as patients separate from the "therapeutic community" and re-enter the extended community. The decision that the Social Work Staff function should be confined to one or the other of these efforts should result in locating the function within the boundaries of the Psychotherapy or the Sociotherapy enterprise, as part of the internal situation of the operational subsystems of either the one or the other. In figure 11, it is assumed that the Social Work Staff might also have a function in relation to the Physiological Therapy subsystem, should the latter exist in an organization: for example, mobilizing resources from the external community to support a treatment regime for a physical disability.

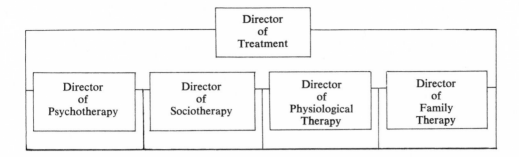

Fig. 12. The Treatment subsystem: psychotherapy, sociotherapy, physiological therapy, and family therapy.

If family therapy—the treatment of the patient's family—(perhaps the responsibility of a Social Work Staff) were seen as part of the organization's task of coping with psychiatric disorder, then the operational subsystem Family Therapy would be located in the organization as in figure 12. This subsystem, like its counterparts Psychotherapy, Sociotherapy, and Physiological Therapy, focuses its operations upon a unique system—in this case, the family, rather than the personality system, the therapeutic community social system, or the physiological organism.

All these systems have in common that different aspects of a concrete individual patient enter into the constitution of each one. That is to say, these systems are theoretically distinguishable, though phenomenally inextricably interpenetrating; the crucial reason for differentiating them is that the understanding and alteration of each requires different conceptual tools of analysis, different interventions and skills, and different practical conditions. The analysis of systems, task-requirements, functions is largely for purposes of understanding some of the problems arising in a psychiatric hospital; there is no prescription implied that such hospitals should necessarily be organized so that concrete collectivities are maximally differentiated: one function to each. Nor is it a necessary concomitant of taking an analytical view of the tasks involved in a hospital organization or of differentiating roles that the patient is no longer seen or responded to as a whole person; synthesis is implied by the provision of mechanisms for consultation and interaction between persons and groups and it also may be accomplished by a variety of means within one individual or group carrying multiple functions. The desirability of seeing the patient as a whole person is not an excuse for lack of clarity about one's task or goal at any particular moment in time, what is required to achieve it, and its relation to other tasks or goals.

Figure 13 represents the Psychotherapy subsystem, assuming that there is no group psychotherapy carried out in the hospital. If there were, the differentiation between Individual and Group Psychotherapy within the Psychotherapy subsystem might be represented as in figure 14. The assumption implied by figure 14 is that both Individual and Group Psychotherapy are primarily concerned with, and aimed directly at alterations in, individual personality systems. The competing or conflicting, as well as mutually facilitating, effects of two treatment efforts directed at the same system would then be a problem to be faced explicitly within the Psychotherapy subsystem.

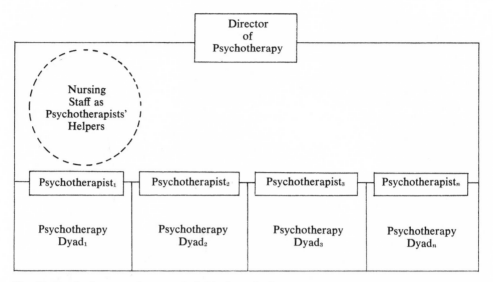

Fig. 13. Psychotherapy subsystem: individual psychotherapy.

Whether or not group therapy can be concerned primarily with individual person-ality systems when the members of the group live together is problematical. Where group psychotherapy becomes therapy of the group rather than of the individual, and the groups are part of the structure of a patient-staff therapeutic community, such an effort should be included within the Sociotherapy enterprise.

Whether therapy of groups is included as part of the sociotherapy enterprise should depend on an evaluation of the following propositions. First, any group of people living together interdependently on the same territorial base differs crucially from a group of people brought together for specific hours of group therapy, other wise not seeing each other, and for the most part unable to alter directly the balance of gratification and deprivation of each other's daily lives. The relative importance of fantasy and reality, as these determine the relations between the members of the group, differs markedly in these two situations. Members of the former kind of group share a common immediate situation, and problems, the determinants of which de-pend partly on social, physical, and cultural aspects of the group's immediate situ-ation, including other groups in that situation. Members of the group depend upon each other to solve certain problems and achieve certain ends that cannot be achieved by individuals singly but can be achieved by action in concert. Second, the intragroup problems of such a group often arise out of difficulties with aspects of or entities in the group's situation. Definition of a problem as primarily a matter of intragroup processes often masks problems in intergroup relations, just as conflicts with other groups may be exploited to mask and distract from intragroup strains. In other words, such groups face and must cope with adaptation and consummation exigencies as well as motivation and integration exigencies. Third, preoccupation with intragroup processes (e.g., when the group's overt or covert task is therapy of the group) may reduce a group's interest in alloplastic interaction with its situation or diminish attempts to solve problems by alloplastic interventions, or attempts to

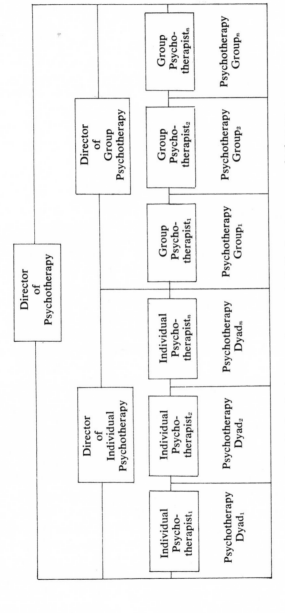

Fig. 14. Psychotherapy subsystem: individual and group psychotherapy.

alter structures or processes, in its environment. The shared fantasy is that all problems can be solved by improving interpersonal relations within the group; that is, by meeting only integrative exigencies. Unfortunately, this fantasy is apparently shared by a variety of optimistic "experts" in the fields of organizational theory and theories of social change, for whose thought and method the alteration of interpersonal relations in the direction of an apparently limitlessly expanding harmony is the cornerstone.

Figure 15 represents the Sociotherapy subsystem. This subsystem is divided into four subsystems, the aim of each one of which is to meet one of the four exigencies (adaptation, consummation, integration, and motivation) that must be met by any social system. Let us assume concrete collectivities, such as the Work Committee, the Activities Committee, the Community Council, and the Small Groups, each one of which is organized to meet one, or a combination, of these exigencies of the therapeutic community as a social system, and belongs therefore primarily to one or more of the subsystems of the Sociotherapy enterprise.

Of concern to a Work Group, to the extent it is an Adaptation Group, are motivational commitments to understand empirical reality and to use knowledge in skillful or competent behavior to achieve ends. The organization of a Work Group and the interaction of its members, the selection of means or ways of accomplishing a goal, are governed by cognitive standards of validity: what will be useful (efficient, expedient, and effective) in achieving a desired end. A Work Group defines the situation in terms of empirically verifiable knowledge of means-ends relations. A process of action in the Work Group changes the ratio of knowledge or confidence and confusion or uncertainty in the group. The Work Group's output to the social system is instrumental action, finding something that works to achieve desired ends, thereby changing the meaning of some object; that is, changing the object's degree of utility or power to serve as a means to the achievement of ends or the satisfaction of wants. The Work Group's output to the personality system is to the adaptive ego: the generation, maintenance, and restoration of patterns of reality testing and mastery.

Of primary concern to an Activities Group, to the extent it is a Consummation Group, are motivational commitments to want and to enjoy, to seek gratifications and avoid deprivations. The organization of an Activities Group and the interaction of its members, the selection of ends to seek or wishes to gratify, are governed by appreciative or aesthetic standards of appropriateness and taste: what will be fun, pleasurable, appropriate, tasteful, exciting, beautiful. An Activities Group defines or reacts to situations through expressive symbolizations, representing gratification-deprivation actualities or potentialities. Its primary problem is not what means will lead most efficiently to an end, but how best to express oneself or a state of affairs through expressive action. A process of action in the Activities Group changes the ratio of gratification and deprivation in the group. The Activities Group's output to the social system is expressive action, finding a way to express feelings, to satisfy needs, to enjoy oneself, thereby changing the cathectic meaning of some object, that is, changing the object's value in terms of a continuum of gratification and deprivation possibilities. The Activities Group's output to the personality system is to the executive or libidinal ego: the generation, maintenance, and restoration of patterns of cathectic allocations.

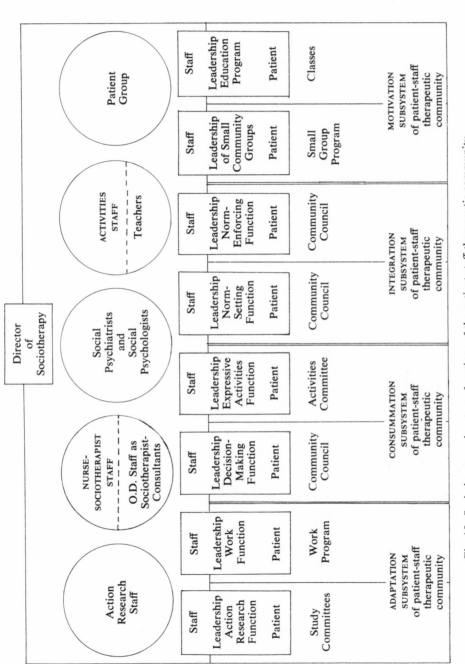

Fig. 15. Sociotherapy subsystem: functions of the patient-staff therapeutic community.

Of concern to the Community Council, to the extent it is an Integration Group, are motivational commitments to identify, and to participate interdependently to achieve common ends and actualize shared values, with others. The organization of the Community Council and the interaction of its members, the selection among alternative actions, are governed by evaluative standards, specifying criteria of right and wrong: what is acceptable, and what is deviant, conduct in a therapeutic community. The Community Council evaluates a situation in terms of a system of institutionalized norms. It formulates such norms and by various mechanisms of control brings conduct into conformity with them. A process of action in the Community Council changes the ratio of solidarity (commitment to shared norms) and anomie (normlessness) in the group. The Community Council's output to the social system is responsible action, or a change in the meaning of an object of identification, that is, a change in the degree to which the object is identified with or the degree to which members of the group change or maintain behavior as a result of a relationship with such an object serving as a model that represents the shared values and norms of the community. The Community Council's output to the personality system is to the superego: the generation, maintenance, and restoration of internalized norms.

Of concern to the Small Group, to the extent it is a Motivation Group, are motivational commitments to respect generalized institutionalized values and to actualize them through effort. The organization of a Small Group and the interaction of its members are such as to facilitate the integration of current everyday experiences with patterns of value and meaning. (How is this event to be understood in terms of the values of the therapeutic community?) A Small Group defines or reacts to situations in terms of interpretations of them according to patterns of value and meaning. A process of action in the Small Group changes the ratio of commitment and alienation in the group. The Small Group's output to the social system is confirmation of systems of values, a change in the meaning of objects symbolizing institutionalized values; that is, a change in the degree of respect and allegiance accorded such objects. The output of the Small Group to the personality system is to the ego-ideal: the generation, maintenance, and restoration of internalized values and ideals.

These four Groups are the operational subsystems of the sociotherapeutic enterprise or therapeutic community within the hospital organization. As concrete collectivities including patient and staff membership, they are organized to meet the problems generated by the group life of patients sharing a common territorial or residential base with all the exigencies implied and processes of action required by that circumstance. Various staff groups and the patient group perform limit or control and service or resource functions in relation to these four operational subsystems. In addition, collectivities exist as consultation mechanisms, that is, to provide opportunities for staff members or groups working, having responsibilities, and making decisions in the various operational subsystems to consult with each other (the Community Program Staff), and for staff and patients (that is, the entire membership of all the organized collectivities in the therapeutic community, working together, sharing responsibilities, and making decisions in the various operational subsystems) to consult with each other (the Community Meeting). The four operational subsystems, the staff groups and patient group providing resources to or constraining these four subsystems, and such collectivities as the Community Program Staff and the Community Meeting, which provide consultation mechanisms, comprise the therapeutic community within the hospital organization. The Director of Sociotherapy functions on the boundary between the sociotherapy enterprise or therapeutic community and its situation, that is, is particularly responsible for relating the sociotherapeutic enterprises of the therapeutic community to other enterprises in the hospital organization.

A subsystem may include more than one concrete collectivity; a concrete collectivity may have different functions, which place it in different abstract subsystems. A Study Committee might meet to collect and interpret information in the light of certain hypotheses related to a community problem; a Work Committee might provide a working crew to build or maintain a facility required or desired by the community; both collectivities are part of the Adaptation Subsystem of the therapeutic community.

The Activities Committee is primarily concerned with gratifying expressive activities valued in and of themselves; it is part of the Consummation Subsystem of the therapeutic community. The Activities Staff may also see itself as a teaching staff, teaching skills to the individual. To the extent the Activities Staff emphasizes the value of these skills to the individual in his relation to the society at large and to his future career, as if one of the subsystems of the hospital were primarily concerned with acting as a school, a college, for the patient, the Activities Program is also part of the Motivation Subsystem of the therapeutic community. That is, when the focus of the Activities Program is on the teaching of skills or knowledge to individuals, especially as these might enhance the individual's participation in achieving the shared ends of the therapeutic community, then that program is part of the Motivation Subsystem of that community. There may be difficulty in obtaining commitment from the patient to participate in school-like classes, because of their apparent distance from the immediate problems of the patient's everyday life. Some classes, however, like most of the activities, have immediate meaning and value for the individual and group in the everyday life of the therapeutic community; such an emphasis is likely to mobilize motivational commitment; a class on Group Development, for example, may seem particularly relevant to participation in the groups of the therapeutic community. The same problem exists in the Work Program. Work as an abstract good often fails to arouse motivational commitment. Work to achieve an end desired by the members of the community— building sets for a play, redecorating a game room—often finds enthusiastic commitment. The possible different functions of an Activities Staff (contributing to expressive activities for the therapeutic community, teaching expressive skills and knowledge to individuals) are represented in Figure 15 by the dotted line separating as Teachers those members of the Activities Staff who conceive themselves to be responsible for teaching individuals only.

Another way of looking at the teaching function of the Activities Staff comes about from remembering that each of the four subsystems of the therapeutic community has its own four sub-subsystems or sectors; each one of the latter is designed to meet one of the four kinds of imperatives facing each one of the four major subsystems of that community. For example, the Work Program has its own adaptation sector, mobilizing resources for work or determining what work opportunities are available in the situation; its own consummation sector, attaining actual work ends; its own integration sector, determining what relations between workers is appropriate to particular work projects; its own motivation sector, establishing and maintaining motivational commitments to participation in the Work Program. Similarly, then, each Study Committee, for example, might be conceived to belong to the adaptation sector of a particular subsystem of the community; for example, a Study Committee concerned with investigating the relation between how participation in work is motivated and organized and the way in which work tasks are accomplished would belong to the adaptation sector of the Work Program or Adaptation Subsystem of the community; a Study Committee concerned with investigating the extent to which certain norms about drinking or stealing are influencing behavior in the community would belong to the adaptation sector of the Community Council or Integration Subsystem. Similarly, also, insofar as the teaching of expressive skills and knowledge to individuals in the therapeutic community contributes to establishing and maintaining motivational commitments to expressive action, such teaching may be viewed as part of the motivation sector of the Activities Program or Consummation Subsystem of that community.

The Community Council, to the extent it is concerned with decisions about ends to be pursued or choices between ends in the allocation of resources (and not simply about norms), is part of the Consummation Subsystem of the therapeutic community; to the extent it is concerned with the establishment of norms or the enforcing of norms, it is part of the Integration Subsystem of the therapeutic community.

To the extent the Small Group Program is concerned with the impact upon individuals of events or decisions in community life, or of inconsistencies in the value system of the therapeutic community, and particularly with the effect of intrapersonal strains arising from such factors upon the internalization and maintenance of values within, and the motivational commitments of, individuals, which then determine the nature of the participation of these individuals in the therapeutic community, this program is part of the Motivation Subsystem of the community.

As has been pointed out, each of these concrete collectivities, in turn, must meet adaptation, consummation, integration, and motivation exigencies, as it seeks to achieve its primary goal or task (which is ultimately to help meet one of the four exigencies faced by the therapeutic community as a whole). Staff groups (such as an Action Research Staff, an Activities Staff, a Nurse-sociotherapist Staff, and a Social Psychiatry-Social Psychology Staff) contribute skills and knowledge to the solving of, respectively, adaptation, consummation, integration, and motivation problems of each concrete collectivity carrying out operations toward goal-achievement within the four subsystems of the Sociotherapy enterprise. Members of each staff therefore may belong and contribute to a wide variety of collectivities. For example, members of the Nursing Staff may belong to the Work Committee, the Activities Committee, the Community Council, and the Small Groups, bringing to each one a particular set of special skills and knowledge, which are relevant to integration problems and processes. These four staff groups, together with the Director of Sociotherapy, constitute the Sociotherapy Staff; representatives of the four staff groups may constitute a smaller Community Program Staff.

When a member of such a staff is functioning "in role," it does not mean that, for example, a member of the Activities Staff only participates when activities as an end or the Activities Committee, Activities Program, or Activities Staff are involved, but rather whenever expressive action or skills, symbol-meaning relations, or appreciative norms, standards, or values are at stake in any effort by any group. Similarly, with the Action Research Staff's expertness in matters of adaptation, rational action, cognitive standards or values, or means-ends relations; the Nurse-sociotherapist's expertness in matters of integration, norms, responsible action, or interpersonal relations; and the Social Psychiatrist's or Social Psychologist's expertness in matters of motivation, commitment, the individual's relation to the social system, or the process of internalizing values. (The psychiatrist especially as physician may be given the role of embodying the prepotent treatment values of the therapeutic community.)

The concrete collectivities organized to perform operationally to achieve the aims of the four subsystems of the Sociotherapy enterprise, and the four staff groups performing limit or control and service functions in relation to these collectivities, constitute the formal organization of the therapeutic community. The Patient Group as a group is usually not formally (or only intermittently and very limitedly) organized. The formal organization of the Sociotherapy enterprise tends to comprise all-staff or patient-staff collectivities, and not any all-patient collectivity. This fact probably reflects that the patient is often considered the object of treatment (and implicitly dependent upon the agent of treatment), the consumer of treatment services, as well as a necessarily active collaborator in the treatment enterprise; in the latter role only, he is necessarily a member of the formal organization, the task of which is treatment, and of the therapeutic community, in which treatment values are prepotent. The patient, in his roles as object of treatment or consumer of treatment services, is to be influenced by the staff; a less organized, less integrated group is, in general, more likely to be influenced by, than to influence, a more organized, more integrated group.

In any event, the informal life of the Patient Group does affect the availability of resources from that group for, and does impose constraints upon, the Sociotherapy enterprise. Therefore, the informal Patient Group is included within the internal situation of the operational subsystems of the Sociotherapy enterprise. The impact of the informal life of the Patient Group (with its often competing and conflicting values, norms, ends, and reality-representations or definitions of situations) upon the operational subsystems of the therapeutic community may be, and usually is, a major problem for that community.

Figures 15 and 16 represent the fact that leadership in each of the programs or committees is collaborative and includes a member of the staff and a member of the patient group. The patient leader may, for example, be the chairman of the group involved and concerned primarily with its internal arrangements and processes; the staff representative to the group may be especially concerned with the relationship of the group to other groups, especially staff groups, in the hospital. There are, however, a number of problems associated with this arrangement. Patient leaders are caught between their membership in the formal community, their identification with its goals and values, and their membership in the informal patient group. To the extent such leaders relate themselves to members of the staff and staff groups,

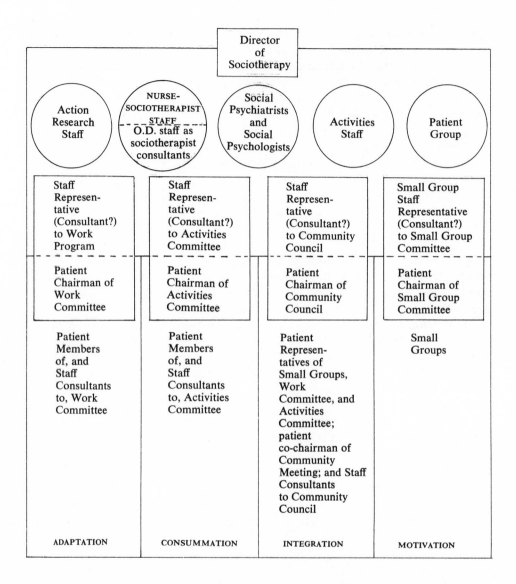

Fig. 16. Sociotherapy subsystem: committees and programs of the patient-staff therapeutic community.

they may jeopardize their membership in the informal patient group or become mere hollow spokesmen for staff points of view; to the extent they abrogate responsibility for the relation of an enterprise to other groups, especially staff groups, in the hospital, they are ineffective leaders of the enterprise.

These organizational charts do not indicate any formal efforts to increase the skills of patient leaders in the therapeutic community; to help them cope with the problems (the inevitable degree of loneliness as they make attempts to take distance from the groups they lead) involved in their position; or to help them help each other, giving them a group identity around the tasks of leadership. Such efforts, however, may be necessary, as evidenced by the frequent reluctance of patients to take office, despite the fact that a leadership role may be highly valued by most patients; frequent requests by patients to sit in on meetings of the Community Program Staff or administrative staff groups; and the public disavowal by patients, who are actually in leadership positions, of responsibility for a particular enterprise or action.

Similarly, there is usually a good deal of confusion about the role of the staff representative. He is often told he is to be just another member of the group, despite his position on the boundary between the group and other, especially staff, groups. Is he to act simply as a consultant to the group, having no authority and bearing no responsibility for its actions and decisions, or the outcome of these? In this latter event, of course, he is suspected of using a consultation role to advance covertly vital interests of the staff. Although staff members may bear the title of staff representative, it is often not clear what staff group such a representative is to represent: the Community Program Staff, the Nursing or Activities Staff, the Therapy Staff, the whole staff, the Medical Director? What discretion has he as a representative? Is he to be primarily an observer, reporting back to the group he represents? Is he to fulfill only specific mandates for the group he represents? Is he to participate in the program according to his own judgment with wide discretionary powers? The behavior of a staff at its own meetings may often suggest that the staff representative is responsible to the whole staff for carrying out its specific mandates; the whole staff, unfortunately for the staff representative, is usually unable to agree on what these mandates should be, to give them the required degree of specificity, or to anticipate adequately the nature of the concrete situations the staff representative is likely to find himself in. Sometimes, a distinction is made between a staff representative, who is in a patient-staff group to represent a staff group, its interests and wishes, with wide discretionary powers to participate in the decision-making of the patient-staff group as his judgment dictates, and a consultant, who is in the group solely to provide resources or skills to the group. Such a distinction often conceals difficulties in delegating authority to a staff consultant who, in fact, would be likely to function unrealistically in a patient-staff group in which he is held not to represent, as in fact he must, the interests and wishes of other staff members.

The Community Program Staff is ultimately responsible for its participation to the Director of Sociotherapy, who is responsible for the Sociotherapy enterprise to the Director of Treatment; he in turn is responsible for the relation of the Sociotherapy enterprise to other treatment enterprises to the Medical Director, who is responsible for the relation of the Treatment enterprise to other enterprises in the hospital and for the relation of the total hospital operation to its external situation to the Board of Trustees. The representation by the Community Program Staff of other staff interests (outside those of the Sociotherapy enterprise) within the Sociotherapy enterprise will depend on the intergroup relations of the Community Program Staff and other staff groups and how these are carried on in inter-staff-group meetings outside, but in the situation, of the Sociotherapy enterprise.

It may be said, in the interests of the optimal functioning of staff representatives and consultants, that—even for the sake of encouraging the development of personal autonomy—patients as a group should not dictate to a member of the staff how he is to do one of these jobs. Staff groups probably should not make rules for the patient group, such being the responsibility of the patient-staff Community Council, but neither should the patient group be in a position to make rules for staff nor should either group accept limiting, in the name of democracy, the right of the staff representative or consultant to take whatever action he deems necessary for carrying out his responsibilities.

The dynamics of intergroup relations, especially the relations between the staff as a group and the patients as a group, is a basic process in a therapeutic community. Representatives of either group when in relation to the other group have difficulties maintaining at the same time their identification with their own group and an understanding and sympathetic appreciation of the views and interests of the other group. Often, the participation of representatives is marred by uncertainty about what the group being represented desires, believes, and will support, and how that group will respond to its representative's interventions.

Both patient and staff groups have difficulty establishing a truly interdependent relationship with each other, each having its own identity (values, wishes, goals, norms, beliefs, and ways of defining situations) and at the same time respecting the identity of the other, but also recognizing the necessity of collaboration in efforts of mutual concern, willing to share the responsibility for such efforts, and to be influenced as well as to influence when conflicts are involved. Patients are likely to oscillate between apathetic submission or unthinking acquiescence and a defiant, rebellious hyper-independence in relation to staff, between states of passive helplessness and suspicious, rejecting negativism. Staff are likely to oscillate between assertions of authority or an overwhelming organized expression of what is right and withdrawal, silence, or "do it yourself, I don't think the staff should be involved." It is difficult to find a middle ground between dominance-submission relations and those characterized by hostility or complete separation. It sometimes seems as if the closest members of either group can get to a notion of interdependence is a state of fusion or complete togetherness. Some patients wonder why the Community Program Staff ever should get together without the patients or why patients are not represented on staff administrative decision-making groups. "Why aren't our Community Meetings together enough?" "Why don't you tell us everything you talk about at your meetings?" "If you have secrets, why shouldn't we!" Some staff members, on the other hand, similarly, wonder why they should not be, when participating in some enterprise or committee with patients, "just another member of the group."

The Sociotherapy enterprise comprises the patient-staff therapeutic community. The entire hospital does not comprise a therapeutic community, because it is not a community; it is an organization. The hospital as an organization may not be devoted only to treatment goals, and is itself within an extended community the prepotent values and aims of which do not usually have to do with treatment. The therapeutic community within the hospital is centered on the patients, who live in the hospital, and with that staff whose primary task concerns the nature of that community, the prepotent values of which are determined by the therapeutic aims of the organization. The Medical Director, a hospital administrator or superintendent, and the Research, Training, and Community Services Subsystems are all part of the internal situation of the therapeutic community, and not part of it.

The Medical Director, whose primary task is relating the various enterprises of the hospital to each other, especially in relation to the resources or means for which they compete, and relating the hospital as a whole to the outside community, is part of the internal situation of the therapeutic community; attempts to influence his decisions, for example, by (and the effects of his decisions upon) that community, have the same theoretical status as the therapeutic community's interaction with other entities in its environment. Any Medical Director, out of wishes or fears, out of his wish to escape from his primary task into immediate contacts with patients, out of his lack of confidence in the Director of Treatment, Director of Psychotherapy, or Director of Sociotherapy, or out of his feeling that Treatment is more important than any other subsystem of the hospital or that one subsystem of the Treatment enterprise is more important than any other, may act as his own Director of Treatment, Director of Psychotherapy, or Director of Sociotherapy. Such a disruption of role and task boundaries may result in undercutting of, or competition with, that member of the staff to whom responsibility for a task has been delegated. A Medical Director in a Community Meeting, for example (as distinct from the All-Hospital-Meeting encompassed by the boundary on which his role as Medical Director is located) is likely to determine by the power of his position the direction and outcome of community problem-solving; he therefore has automatically arrogated to himself by such participation the authority and responsibility of the Sociotherapy Staff. Similar problems occur when a Medical Director acts as Director of Psychotherapy or as the psychotherapist of individual patients in the hospital, identifying with a part of the organization at the expense of identification with the whole.

Administrative departments have aims and values which are often at odds with those of a therapeutic community; as part of the internal situation, they can be influenced or negotiated with, but regarding them as constituent elements of operations in the patient-staff community itself leads to some confusion. In figure 17, a Representative of Administration is shown as part of the Work Committee's internal situation; he meets with the Work Committee. The actual role of Administration in this position is to provide jobs, tools, and supervision for patient workers in the Work Program; however, the Administration Representative often may see this as contrary to the principal goals of Administration, for example, the efficient maintenance of hospital facilities, or the provision of jobs for maintenance staff. Ultimately, a part of Administration must be differentiated to have the former role and tasks as primary; or policies concerning these conflicting goals have to be decided outside the Sociotherapy enterprise itself, in meetings including the Medical Director, the Director of Training, the Director of Research, and the Director of Treatment, as well as the Head of Administration (see figure 7).

The Psychotherapy enterprise likewise may be considered part of the organization and (focused on the personality systems of individual patients rather than on the patient-staff community) therefore part of the situation of the therapeutic community. For some hospitals, however, particularly those in which interaction and mutual influence between the psychotherapy dyad and other enterprises in

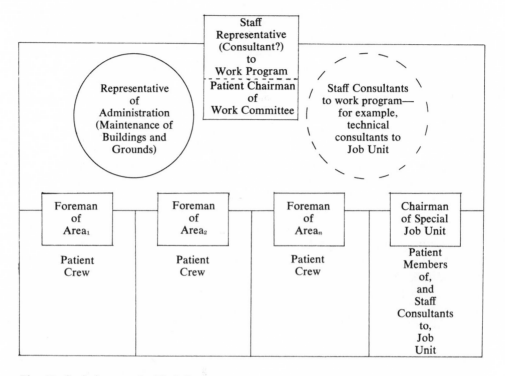

Fig. 17. Sociotherapy: the Work Program.

the patient-staff community are encouraged, it might make more sense to view the psychotherapy dyad as carrying out a specialized task within the therapeutic community itself.

An alternative model of the treatment enterprise, with psychotherapy viewed as one type of enterprise within the social system defined as the therapeutic community, rather than as part of its situation, is described in appendix C and figure 21.

Ad Hoc Committees such as those represented in figure 18 may be formed in response to specific problems, but one evidence that they are frequently a way for the community to get rid of a problem by sending it to a committee rather than to work seriously on it is the fact that often these Ad Hoc Committees are left floating and not made responsible to the subsystem of the community ultimately responsible for the area with which such committees are concerned: the Community Council, for example, when norms are involved. Other subcommittees listed represent various possible functions of a Community Council.

Activities Committee Functions are similarly represented in figure 19, the Small Group Program in figure 20. The patient-staff Small Group Committee administers the Small Group Program as the Work Committee administers the Work Program and the Activities Committee administers the Activities Program.

As far as the organization of the entire hospital is concerned, what consultation mechanisms are needed, that is, what meetings are needed, and who needs to be in

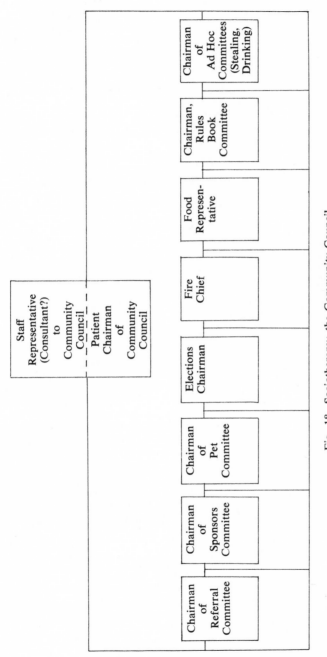

Fig. 18. Sociotherapy: the Community Council.

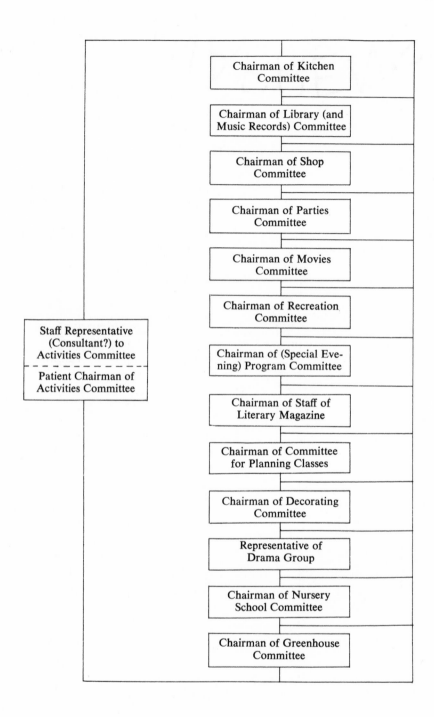

Fig. 19. Sociotherapy: the Activities Program.

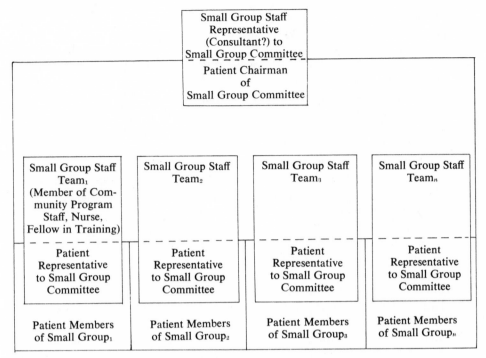

Fig. 20. Sociotherapy: the Small Group Program.

what meeting, are suggested by the boundaries represented in figures 7 through 20. In each case, the task comprises leadership on the boundary, a number of subsystems within the boundary, and entities in their situation, all of which must be represented in any meeting whose goal it is to affect relations between a particular set of subsystems and their shared situation. Examples follow.

1. A Staff Council or Executive Committee (see fig. 7)
   a. Task—relations between major subsystems of the hospital and between the hospital and the outside community
   b. Membership—Medical Director; Director of Training; Director of Research; Director of Treatment; Director of Community Services, if there is such; Head of Administration; Chief of Department of Psychology and Chief Psychiatrist (or representative of such professional staff limit or control and service functions as in-service training and staff education, library facilities, medical procedures, and recruitment and selection of professional staff)
   c. Direct responsibility for this enterprise—Medical Director
2. Training Staff (see fig. 8)
   a. Task—relations between subsystems of training enterprise
   b. Membership—Director of Training, Teachers and Supervisors, Chief of Department of Psychology, representatives of Curriculum Planning, Administration (assignments, schedules, facilities), and Recruitment and Selection of Fellows functions
   c. Direct responsibility—Director of Training

3. Research Staff (see fig. 9)
   a. Task—relations between subsystems of research enterprise
   b. Membership—Director of Research, Directors of Research Projects, possibly all research staff, representatives of Fund-Raising, Education, and Grant Applications functions
   c. Direct responsibility—Director of Research
4. Treatment Staff (see fig. 10)
   a. Task—relations between treatment enterprises, Psychotherapy and Sociotherapy
   b. Membership—Director of Treatment, Director of Sociotherapy, Director of Psychotherapy, possibly all Sociotherapy and Psychotherapy staff, Head Nurse, Head Social Worker, Head of Medical Services to Patients
   c. Direct responsibility—Director of Treatment
5. Psychotherapy Staff (see fig. 13)
   a. Task—relations between subsystems of psychotherapy enterprise
   b. Membership—Director of Psychotherapy, all Psychotherapists
   c. Direct responsibility—Director of Psychotherapy
6. Sociotherapy Staff or Community Program Staff (see fig. 16)
   a. Task—relations between staff participating in various subsystems of sociotherapy enterprise
   b. Membership—Director of Sociotherapy, representatives or all members of Action Research Staff, Nurse-Sociotherapist Staff, Social Psychiatrist and Social Psychologist Staff, Activities Staff
   c. Direct responsibility—Director of Sociotherapy
7. Community Meeting (see fig. 16)
   a. Task—relations between subsystems of sociotherapy enterprise
   b. Membership—Director of Sociotherapy, Community Program Staff or entire Sociotherapy Staff, Patient Group
   c. Direct responsibility—Director of Sociotherapy
8. All-Hospital or All-Staff Meeting (see fig. 7)
   a. Task—relation of hospital to its ultimate primary task and to the outside community
   b. Membership—Medical Director and all staff or all staff and patients
   c. Direct responsibility—Medical Director

We may look at the consultation mechanisms required by the therapeutic community (the Community Meeting and Community Program Staff) in some detail as examples of such mechanisms required throughout the hospital organization.

The collectivities of the therapeutic community are interdependent. For example, a Work Committee (part of the adaptation subsystem) may be responsible for recruiting personnel (available patient workers) for different work areas and mobilizing resources (equipment, facilities, tools) for different jobs. Such a Work Committee depends on an Activities Committee (part of the consummation subsystem) to mobilize interest and to win allocation of funds, for which other ends are competing, for some particular end (a play, a game room) that is desired for itself, and for the attainment of which people will want to work. The Work Committee also depends on a Community Council (part of the integration subsystem) to deal with integrative crises, to cope with deviant behavior, so that the amount of deviant behavior does not rise to such a level in the community that coping with it requires so much energy there is little left over for expressive or instrumental activity. The Work Committee depends finally, and perhaps most fundamentally, upon the Small Groups (part of the motivation subsystem) to deal with tensions within individuals, which might if continued interfere with the patient's respect and regard for the hospital and his commitment to participate in any of the hospital's enterprises; to maintain patients' interests in and commitment to work in general; and even to help establish such commitments where they exist only very rudimentarily if at all. Problems in the work program, then, may have their origin in one of these other programs. This example assumes a social system whose parts are interdependent; the extent to which this is true for a particular social system is an empirical question. Some collectivities may be more insulated from the effects of vicissitudes in other collectivities than others are, just as some social systems are more insulated from at least some changes in their situations than others are. However, awareness of the interdependence of the functions and enterprises of a hospital is as necessary as recognition of the conflicts between them in understanding various events in the hospital.

Both the conflicts between functions and enterprises and their interdependence give rise to the need for consultation mechanisms.

As we have seen, the goal of the psychiatric hospital organization is to help patients and society, through the provision of specific services to them, deal with the consequences of emotional illness in various ways. In order to achieve its goal, an organization that assigns higher priorities to the provision of socialization and therapy services than to custodial and protective services must provide for and facilitate the didactic resolution of intrapersonal, interpersonal, and intergroup tensions. The psychotherapeutic function is concerned specifically with the discovery, didactic explanation, and resolution of intrapersonal tensions. The sociotherapeutic function is concerned specifically with the discovery, didactic explanation, and resolution of intra- and inter-group tensions, arising from the inevitable conflict and competition between the values, interests, and needs associated with different administrative (external and internal) functions and professional (psychotherapeutic, nursing, sociotherapeutic, activities program, work program, patient, and support) functions, all of which must be performed in the same organization, and from the requirements imposed by the interdependence of various functions and enterprises in that organization. Such tensions, of course, interfere with the performance and coordination of administrative and professional functions (including the sociotherapeutic function) required for the achievement of the hospital's goal; the continuous resolution of such tensions is a prerequisite for such achievement.

The patient-staff meeting, or community meeting, is a medium in which the sociotherapeutic function may be performed in relation to group processes in the therapeutic community, in the same sense that the individual or group psychotherapy session is a medium in which the psychotherapeutic function may be performed; such differentiation does not prejudge the extent to which the didactic resolution of interpersonal and intergroup tensions throughout the entire hospital and in smaller networks of relationships results in significant change within the individual, or the extent to which the didactic resolution of intrapersonal tensions results in significant change in interpersonal and intergroup relationships.

The Community Meeting, a patient-staff meeting, is one of the consultation mechanisms in a psychiatric hospital organization. As we have seen, a consultation mechanism is a sine qua non of a democratic organization in which the widest possible base of support for decisions is sought. It provides the opportunity for those who are directly responsible for making any decision to consult with those who will be affected by it and whose support is required to implement it. In a meeting the purpose of which is consultation, sharing information, opinions, suggestions, and reactions contributes to coordinating different parts of a task operation; winning support for proposed actions; and evaluating past actions and accomplishments for the sake of morale and future planning. In this kind of meeting, decisions are not made by the entire group; this differentiates it from the group decision-making meeting of the equalitarian organization.[21] In the Community Meeting, the sociotherapeutic function (and not the psychotherapeutic function) is performed. It is, in this respect, like other organizational conferences serving a consultative rather than executive or decision-making function, for example, a total staff conference, an interdepartmental meeting, or coordinating committee; it is not a form of group therapy.

Such a meeting provides for the sharing of information about everyday life in the hospital community and the problems existing in that life now. The prototype question is: "What happened over the weekend? Yesterday? Last night? Today?" As such information is shared, a cognitive map of what is going on in the hospital community is constructed; pieces of the puzzle are put together. Disconnected, isolated bits of experience are the source of affective waves that sweep over the hospital community. Emotions associated with speculations, rumors, misperceptions, and misinformation spread from person to person and group to group, without the facts from which they are actually derived. In this meeting, these come together. A design, a pattern of events may emerge. Areas of difficulty and breakdown may be identified. Competing, sometimes really and sometimes illusorily incompatible interests, values, and points of view, previously hidden or unclear, and groups in the hospital representing administrative and professional functions or the different aims of subsystems of the therapeutic community struggle with each other in the discussion. A typical statement is: "I can't do my job or perform the function for which I am responsible, because. . . ." The focus is upon the reality of the tasks confronting members of the therapeutic community and the wider hospital organization and the reality of the relationships between them, rather than upon the fantasies shared by group members about these tasks and relationships; the fantasies are tested against this reality.

The strains and tensions between individuals, between an individual and a group, or between groups, are often what is at issue. The identification of such strains and tensions is the basis for the diagnosis of the nature of barriers preventing the effective performance of necessary functions by the operational subsystems of the therapeutic community and, ultimately, the effective provision of services to which the organization is committed in order to achieve its goals.

---

21. Jaques (1952) has discussed at some length the characteristics of the consultation mechanism and its crucial role in a democratic organization.

The resolution of such strains and tensions typically depends upon the action of individuals and groups outside the Community Meeting, actions taken in part out of an understanding of what has transpired at the meeting. Various groups or individuals who have responsibility in the hospital requiring them to make decisions and take actions may then use the Community Meeting to win consent for these decisions from those who will participate in implementing them. After a decision has been made and implemented, the consequences of it may later be reviewed in the Community Meeting by all those who have been affected.

Patients and staff may share, for example, in the recognition of a task well done that contributes to the achievement of the aims of subsystems of the therapeutic community and, indeed, to the achievement of the hospital's goals. On the other hand, errors, mistakes, and failures may be examined for the sake of understanding and future planning. Members of the group (staff and patients) ideally learn how to do this without anxiety, without defensiveness, without self-righteous moralizing, and without punitiveness.

The Community Meeting should not perform an executive, decision-making, or action-taking function nor should decisions of various executive, decision-making, or action-taking groups be subject to veto by it. Advice from an individual or group or from the total group to an individual or group having responsibility is always a *recommendation*, on the grounds that the one who carries the responsibility and is accountable for the consequences of any decision to implement it should have the authority to carry it out in his own way.

The decision-making, action-taking, executive groups in the community include not only groups such as the Nursing Staff and Activities Staff, but also patient-staff committees (Work Committee, Activities Committee, Community Council, Small Group Committee) responsible for the Activities Program, the Work Program, the Small Group Program, and the policies, rules, and procedures governing patient life and patient-staff relationships in the hospital. These groups, simply in doing their respective jobs, are interdependent and may also come into conflict with each other; their relationships give rise to the existence of the strains and tensions in the community that become clear in the Community Meeting. These groups are also responsible for making the adjustments necessary to resolve such strains and tensions through processes of bargaining, compromise, and mutual accommodation suggested by and explored in discussions in the Community Meeting.

A conflict between such action groups or functions (e.g., between interests and values crucial for the performance of nursing, administrative, and activities functions with respect to a particular situation) may arise that is not, it becomes clear in discussion, a matter of misunderstanding or misinterpretation of each other or of hospital goals and policy. Rather, there is an actual incompatibility in the interests or values of individuals or groups carrying out their various jobs in the therapeutic community or wider hospital organization. In such an event, an apparatus in the organization must exist to make possible a decision assigning priorities to the various interests involved in the conflict, in the light of the total hospital situation as well as its immediate and long-range goals. Such a decision when it concerns relations between enterprises within the therapeutic community might be made by the Director of Sociotherapy; when it concerns relations between the therapeutic community and other treatment enterprises, by the Director of Treatment; when it concerns relations between the therapeutic community and other subsystems of the hospital organization, by the Medical Director, usually after appropriate consultation. The decision-making process must include recognition of the distribution of the rewards and burdens each group or individual must bear as a consequence of such decisions and involve rules of fairness in making them.

A Community Meeting of this kind, devoted to an ongoing discussion of current problems in the hospital community and to the attempt to understand and resolve these, emphasizes the use of ego functions in coping with the problems of everyday life in that community, rather than superego-like processes of automatic compliance with or defiance of authoritarian or group rules, standards, and expectations. A daily confrontation with, and consideration of, the actual consequences intrinsically arising out of an act or event supersedes sanctions arbitrarily annexed to an act and imposed by others in order to prevent its occurrence. Rules, no matter whether formulated by administrative authority figures or by a peer group, are not regarded as permanent solutions to problems to be automatically complied with or defied, but rather as signals of potential problem areas implying the advisability of review and consultation when departures from the norm are desired or occur. The resulting individualization and active learning far outweigh in value the certainty and efficiency that might be associated with impersonally, automatically applied rules and regulations, enforced by administrative or peer group sanctions. Furthermore, the exercise, maintenance, and enhancement of ego functions concomitant with participation in such ego-oriented day-by-day problem-solving is a crucial characteristic of the therapeutic community in which ego-impaired patients are treated (Edelson 1964).

The Community Meeting should meet daily if it is to function as described above. Otherwise, momentum and continuity are lost. Emergencies become the sole concern. Those who are in trouble receive much attention, those struggling to perform well receive little. Problem-solving becomes a matter of coping with crises, with intensive pressure for immediate action. Under these circumstances the didactic aspect of the resolution of tensions is likely to be sacrificed and with it the possibility of much learning. Instead of the exercise of ego functions (the painstaking collection of information, the formulation and verification of hypotheses, the anticipation of and preparation for difficulty as well as the analysis of its causes after it has occurred, the evaluation of the consequences of action) it is either impulsive discharge or superego recrimination that are likely to determine the nature of crisis resolution.

Those who have some important function to perform in the hospital community and who need to participate in the Community Meeting to perform it effectively should attend the Community Meeting. Therefore, those in the organization having major responsibility for some administrative or professional function, and who exercise that function through participation in one or another of the concrete collectivities or enterprises of the therapeutic community, should attend.

If problem-solving is to be possible, these functions must be represented in the Community Meeting not arbitrarily but by those whose jobs require them to make use of the Community Meeting if the job is to be done well. Such persons will therefore inevitably represent in any discussion a certain way of looking at things, value or interest inherent in their role in the organization.

The meeting will normally include all patients, all nurses, all patient and staff members of the Work Committee, Activities Committee, Community Council, and Small Groups, and a sociotherapist, presumably the Director of Sociotherapy, who utilizes the meeting to perform the sociotherapeutic function and who is therefore responsible for its conduct. The activities program and work program functions should each be represented in the meeting by at least one staff person bearing major responsibility for each program, even if such responsibility is discharged primarily by working with a patient group. Other members of the Activities Staff, for example, may be invited to attend a particular meeting or decide to attend one when they have some business to transact in it. Otherwise, unless such staff can be trained to use and understand the Community Meeting for the performance of their jobs, they are apt to attend it as uneasy or bored observers or irresponsible participants. Those physicians performing O.D. duty, because of their intervention in the daily life of the hospital especially when there is trouble, for obvious reasons associated with the function they must perform on such occasions should attend the Community Meeting. Likewise, any persons carrying out research in relation to or for the therapeutic community itself, or a person learning about the therapeutic community as part of his training, should attend.

An administrator or administrators, for example, the Assistant to the Medical Director, and on occasion perhaps a representative from the Business Office, might be present in the Community Meeting to represent and safeguard internal and external administrative functions in relation to any situation or problem that comes up, but according to this model such administrative interests should ideally be represented by staff representatives to the Work Committee, Activities Committee, Community Council, and Small Groups, and exert influence as well through the boundary function of the Director of Sociotherapy as he is influenced by his participation in staff groups concerned with the relation between the therapeutic community and other enterprises in the organization.

The Medical Director should probably not attend the meeting regularly, unless he intends to carry out the role of Director of Sociotherapy himself rather than delegate responsibility for it. If the Medical Director represents administrative interests, his great authority and prestige are likely to result in administrative interests being given the highest priority in every situation. However, a higher priority occasionally may and should be given to other functions when these are in conflict with administrative functions. Those representing nursing, activities program, or work program functions, for example, should be able to fight for the values and interests of their particular enterprises even when these compete with those of the administrative system.[22]

In those organizations where psychotherapy and sociotherapy are differentiated enterprises, psychotherapists qua psychotherapists should probably not attend the Community Meeting because there is no psychotherapeutic function to be performed there.

The psychotherapist by virtue of the values and procedures involved in his par-

---

22. The Community Meeting within the framework of this theoretical model is a consultation mechanism for the differentiated therapeutic community, not an all-hospital-organization meeting; this distinction was not consistently made in a previous presentation of some of these ideas (Edelson 1967).

ticular function vis-à-vis his individual patient may sit at such a meeting only to observe. Passive participation of this kind usually leads to boredom and withdrawal. He may come irregularly. If his attendance is required, he is likely to begrudge the time involved. His training does not ordinarily prepare him for understanding or participating in an endeavor of this kind; he may not know, since theory lags in this area, how to make use of the Community Meeting to do his job more effectively with his individual patient, but certainly it is not by doing individual therapy in the Community Meeting. He may even fear that participation in such a meeting is incompatible with the satisfactory conduct of individual psychotherapy, for example, by muddling, needlessly complicating, or otherwise altering the transference. A squad of such uneasy observers imposes a heavy burden upon the group. Most psychotherapists, however, also want strongly to influence the daily life of the patients with whom they work. The psychotherapist is likely to think that, because of his training and his understanding of his patient, he is able to do this better than anyone else—any administrator, nurse, sociotherapist, or member of the activities or work program staff. He may, then, seek to exert influence in the Community Meeting, usually by making interpretations of group process or individual neurosis. If many psychotherapists attend, many such interpretations (often on different levels and headed in different directions) may inundate the group and result in confusion or introspective intellectualization in place of coping with the reality of problems in the everyday life of the hospital. Such interventions interfere with the conduct of the meeting and the performance of the sociotherapeutic function in it. The difficulty is increased because the prestige of the psychotherapist in a hospital organization gives his interpretations a power that may be far beyond their appropriateness to this kind of meeting.

Nevertheless, the absence of psychotherapists may create difficulties. If the psychotherapist does not attend, he may become suspicious of the Community Meeting and its effect on his patients; the extent to which this reaction occurs depends in part on the degree of his confidence in the staff involved in the meeting. Patients may interpret the psychotherapist's absence as lack of support for or opposition to the Community Meeting or the therapeutic community program. A patient may play off the psychotherapist and other members of the hospital organization against each other. He reports to the psychotherapist how intrusive, unreasonable, and punitive others are (e.g., in the Community Meeting) or how devastating, disruptive, and destructive exposure to discussions in such a meeting is to him. Such pleas, on the other hand, as "my psychotherapist says," or "I'm working it out in my individual therapy," act as barricades behind which the patient hides when dealing with the expectations and problems of life in the hospital. He does not participate. He claims exemptions. He splits his transference reactions: he responds to the psychotherapist as "all good" and to the community program or aspects of it as "all bad"; or he complains of each to the other, concealing in so doing the actual hostility he feels toward the recipient of his confidences about the other (Knight 1936–37).

What is needed, whether or not psychotherapists qua psychotherapists attend the Community Meeting, is a meeting between all staff concerned with treatment. Any clinical phenomena may be—and for effective treatment in a hospital probably should be—considered both from the point of view of psychotherapy, focusing upon the patient's personality system, and sociotherapy, focusing upon the social system of which the patient is a member. When responsibility for these enterprises is differentiated, both points of view are most likely to be articulated and brought to bear in any attempt to understand a clinical phenomenon. Recognition of the interdependence of the two enterprises, and integration of the staff groups having different degrees of responsibility with respect to them, are facilitated by a meeting of such staff groups together. At this meeting, staff members may become repeatedly aware of the shared treatment values and beliefs guiding the work of different staff groups; information is shared; and the various interests and needs of psychotherapy and sociotherapy become explicit. The Director of Treatment is responsible to see that efforts are made to resolve conflicts between these enterprises in such a way that neither one is unduly encroached upon, interfered with, impaired, or undermined especially by a one-sided focus upon or investment of personnel, time, attention, or thought in one at the expense of the other. At such a meeting, staff members may discuss the needs of a particular patient as these will be expressed in his group life, affecting how he makes use of various groups to achieve his own conscious and unconscious aims and in what ways he is likely to make himself available, wittingly or unwittingly, to the group to be used by it to achieve its shared manifest and covert aims. Processes in individual psychotherapy that have effects upon, and must be coped with by, the community may be clarified. Similarly, events in the community that especially affect particular patients or introduce themes into psychotherapy, or an individual patient's way of life in the community and its possible significance for psychotherapy, may also be examined. In such a meeting, if a treatment staff is always concerned to discuss community processes, never the work of psychotherapy, or to discuss the psychotherapy or personality of an individual patient, never the situation in which he is being treated, one may suspect defensive preoccupation with one task to avoid the painful difficulties of the other.

A sociotherapist may be responsible for understanding, and communicating such understanding to those with whom he consults, the consequences of intragroup and intergroup strains and tensions throughout the hospital.[23] However, the sociotherapist (presumably, the Director of Sociotherapy) in discharging his responsibilities in the Community Meeting helps to create the conditions in which the Community Meeting can function as a consultation mechanism in the therapeutic community. To carry this out, it is his job to make interpretations about intergroup and group-individual relations; he may not be the only staff person making such interpretations, but he is the staff person in the meeting primarily responsible for making them.[24]

---

23. For other discussions of the role of sociotherapist, or of the role of a research team involved with change in a social organization, or of the role of an individual with sociological or anthropological training in a psychiatric hospital organization, see the following: Devereaux 1949; Greenblatt 1957; Jaques 1947, 1952; Rice 1963; Sofer 1961.

24. For one attempt to differentiate levels of interpretation in individual psychotherapy, group therapy, and the community meeting, see discussion of prototype interpretations by Edelson (1964, pp. 41–64). With reference to the community meeting, Thomas Main contributed further clarification in personal communications resulting in the following formulation.

He should not make interpretations of individual neurosis, although of course he is aware of its manifestations in the Community Meeting. He should not analyze any individual's intrapersonal tensions or intrapsychic conflicts. He should not interpret phenomena in terms of an individual's transference relationship with his psychotherapist, although manifestations of this, too, may be obvious to him. If he does any of these things, he is simply performing a psychotherapeutic function in a group setting. Such interpretations are not only irrelevant to, and distracting from, his performance of the sociotherapeutic function and the achievement of the goals of the Community Meeting, but they may also involve him in possible interference with the patient's psychotherapist. It may be noted that patients in individual psychotherapy themselves like to make such interpretations and to see the Community Meeting as a form of psychotherapy, often as part of a resistance to coping with the problems of hospital life.

The sociotherapist should not make interpretations of the group process of the Community Meeting itself, although he will govern his own participation through understanding this group process. He should not interpret shared fantasies about events in the Community Meeting, about himself and group members' relationship with him, or about group members' relations with each other. In other words, he should not perform "therapy of the group," nor attempt to perform a psychotherapeutic function by using the Community Meeting as a form of group therapy. If he does, or if others are preoccupied with such interpretations, the group turns its eyes inward and introspection about the Community Meeting itself rapidly replaces interest in, and may indeed also serve resistance to coping with, the problems of everyday life in the hospital. There are exceptions to this proscription. The sociotherapist may have to interpret group process in those circumstances when other ways of coping with group process phenomena that interfere with, or act as resistances to, problem-solving in the Community Meeting have failed. Ideally, he always connects any comment about group process with an inference about what is going on in the life of the hospital. For example, group members' feelings about the sociotherapist and their ways of dealing with such feelings in the Community Meeting may be representative of what is happening in the relations between patients and members of the staff in the everyday life of the hospital.

The sociotherapist typically makes interpretations concerning those factors (in particular, intragroup and intergroup strains and tensions and those forces, assumptions, and values maintaining them) interfering with the adaptive problem-solving process, the performance and coordination of administrative and professional functions, that must go on if the services to which the hospital is committed as an organization are to be provided, and, more specifically, if the various subsystems of the therapeutic community are to achieve their aims. The conflicts he interprets are not between intrapsychic institutions (between wishes and defenses, for example) but are between groups, or between functions that must be performed, in relation to a responsibility for achieving some task.

The sociotherapist cannot be responsible for suggesting ways of resolving such intra- and intergroup tensions, only for helping the members of the group understand what stands in the way of the resolution of such tensions. Decisions made or action taken to solve problems is the responsibility of the various groups and individuals comprising the Community Meeting and suggestions for such adaptive decisions or actions ordinarily are made or responded to by those members of the meeting who are responsible for, and must bear the consequences of, them. If the sociotherapist participates much in the making of decisions by patient-staff action groups outside the Community Meeting, he may become committed to, or associated with, a particular point of view or solution. This is likely to interfere with his being able to be, or being seen as, a person who is, for example, disinterestedly seeking that all points of view be represented in a discussion and then pointing out the tensions resulting from competing interests; the sociotherapist must have no special stake in one group or function winning such a competition at the expense of another.

The members of the staff who attend the Community Meeting are those who have some responsibility in the subsystems of the therapeutic community: the Community Program Staff. Members of this staff group should meet after each Community Meeting to advise and sustain each other, and to accomplish the following tasks.

The Community Program Staff must learn how to examine in its own meeting the contribution of each staff member to the Community Meeting. Each staff member attempts to answer the questions: "How did I perform my job in the Community Meeting? What effect did my participation have upon the problems with which I am struggling in my job?" There are three kinds of difficulties any staff person may have in dealing with such questions: organizational, personal, and theoretical.

Every kind of difficulty in the hospital organization will be reflected in difficulties in the participation of staff members in the Community Meeting: in silence, in confusion, in irresponsibility, in awkwardness and uncertainty.

If roles are blurred or overlap, if multiple subordination characterizes the role relationships of the organization, if an individual occupies multiple roles or shares a role with another, or if his authority is not commensurate with his responsibility, then we may expect consequences to appear in the Community Meeting.

The participation of staff members, of course, is crucial in its effect on the Community Meeting. The nature of that participation determines what problems will be brought up, and to what extent problems will be dealt with in the meeting and to what extent in less public, more covert ways. Staff members provide a model for patient members who will be quick to follow their cues and example, and who will be certain to exploit difficulties in staff relationships as these are manifested in the meeting.

A point of view or function may be missing from a Community Meeting for a variety of reasons: lack of role clarification; actual absence of an individual occupying a crucial role; the abrogation of responsibility to someone else when roles overlap; the abandonment of one role for the sake of another by an individual occupying multiple roles; the paralysis of an individual, subordinate to more than one superior with conflicting expectations; the failure to act by an individual whose authority is not commensurate with his responsibility. When a point of view or function is missing, its absence always wreaks havoc in the Community Meeting. Problem-solving cannot proceed, or proceeds in error, because of the absence of information, of some important interest, or of participation by someone who possesses authority and wields influence in the organization. Almost inevitably, when a point of view or function is missing, someone without responsibility for a particular function rushes in, out of anxiety, good intentions, or discontent with his own role, to fill the vacuum. Since such participation is irresponsible (in a technical not moral sense), it adds further confusion, not only preventing real understanding of the factors at work in the problem being discussed, but understanding of the very nature of the organization which must contribute to its solution.

Staff members participate most effectively in the Community Meeting when it is clear who is responsible for what. As on any good team the efforts of whose members are coordinated, everyone feels with respect and confidence that each other needed member of the staff will be present and doing his job competently. In these circumstances, each staff member may turn his full attention and energy to his own responsibilities in the hospital community and to the representation in the Community Meeting of the interests, point of view, and values inherent in those responsibilities. Each staff member is then free to be a creative innovator in the exercise of the function for which he is responsible in relation to any problem or situation that comes up for discussion.

In order to bring this about, the Community Program Staff must cope with the problems of the organization of which it is a part. It identifies them. It clarifies what (changes in definition of roles, for example) might mitigate such difficulties. It communicates (e.g., to the Medical Director or an executive body) recommendations for appropriate changes in the organization when these are necessary to mitigate such difficulties.

The following statements are typical of discussions revealing this kind of difficulty in the Community Program Staff Meeting.

"I didn't know it was my job to be concerned about that, to contribute that information, or to represent that point of view. No one ever told me I had particular responsibility in that area." In some hospitals: "I thought it was everyone's responsibility to be worried about that." (Something that is everyone's responsibility is usually, in effect, no one's responsibility.)

"I know what I said had nothing at all to do with my job and might even result in Dr. Smith having a sticky situation on his hands; but Dr. Smith didn't say anything, and I was uncomfortable. I felt something just had to be said."

"Well, Mary is responsible for that too, and I was waiting for her to say something."

"I didn't know what to say at that point. As a nurse, I felt concerned about the relation between Jim and the group. I thought that some relaxation of the rule would be helpful to undercut Jim's effort always to cast himself in the part of the 'bad one.' But, on the other hand, I felt I had to fight to uphold the rule, even though that resulted in Jim's being driven further away from the group, because it is important administratively to have that rule and I felt it was also my job to argue for it." Assigning both an administrative function and a nursing function to one individual may result in neither function being performed adequately—especially when each requires a stance or approach conflicting, competing, or incompatible with the other —or in one function simply being abrogated for the sake of the other.

"I could not say anything. I thought Dr. Jones expected me to try to get that kind of solution considered, but if I did that, I knew Mrs. Brown would be mad as a hornet."

"I knew when I didn't answer that question, it made everyone frustrated and suspicious about what was going on. But I don't have the authority to speak for the nursing staff. I felt I had to ask Mrs. Brown—and the other nurses—first."

A second kind of difficulty an individual may have in the Community Meeting is personal. He may be having trouble integrating his role with his personality or resources.[25] He may not know how to relate to others in a human, relaxed, friendly, flexible way, feeling that would be somehow incompatible with the performance of his administrative or professional function. On the other hand, an individual may have difficulty taking distance from those with whom he sympathizes, empathizes, or identifies, in order to use his understanding to discharge his administrative or professional responsibilities. He may be overwhelmed by feelings so that he cannot behave professionally; on the other hand, his feelings may be completely unavailable to him so that his job performance is empty, impersonal, and ritualized. An individual may also feel his job requires him to act in a way that is incompatible with his values or actual abilities.

Solutions to such problems depending on the stifling of spontaneity, enthusiasm, involvement, compassion, inventiveness, or openness (such as may occur in an authoritarian-bureaucratic organization) are not adequate. Neither are those solutions depending on the abrogation of individual responsibility and authority (such as may occur in the equalitarian organization).

Discussion of these problems in the Community Program Staff Meeting may help staff members to integrate better their personal and professional identities and to face the discharge of responsibility and the exercise of authority even when this promises unpleasantness. Occasionally, it becomes clear that someone is being expected to do a job he cannot do; in this connection, it is well to remember that the silence of staff members is determined by fears and wishes similar to those motivating the silence of patients: fear of one's job performance being exposed; fear of criticism and sanction; fear of those having authority; fear of the judgment of one's own subordinates; reluctance to give advantage to a competitor; or desire to make things awkward for a superior.

Typical statements expressing such personal difficulties in the discussions of the Community Program Staff Meeting are:

"I wanted to say something then, but I didn't know how."

"I didn't say anything when you asked who was on duty last night. I was so angry at Janice for the way she had acted, I figured she could just answer all the questions about what happened herself."

"It's not up to me to say what must be done. That's up to the whole group."

"Why should I raise that point? I'm just another member of the group. I want to be a human being in the meeting, not an authority figure."

"I didn't feel I could say anything about that. After all, I'm not a patient, and it was something that affects *their* lives we were talking about."

"I know it would help if I'd crack a joke once in a while, but I don't feel comfortable doing it."

---

25. This point was clarified in personal communications from Robert P. Knight and Lars Borje Lofgren.

"I have never done my job before in full view of everyone."

"I didn't think that problem should be brought up. Everyone would have gotten angry at me, and that would just make my job more difficult."

"I was afraid I'd be criticized; so I didn't say anything. I feel paralyzed in the meeting. I'm afraid *you* won't like what I'll say. (I'm afraid *he* won't like what I say. I'm afraid *they* won't like what I say.)"

Individuals may have difficulties participating in the Community Meeting because they misunderstand the theoretical rationale for its existence.

The most usual misunderstanding involves conceiving the meeting as a form of individual or group psychotherapy. It is conceived to be group therapy for the patients, or a patients' meeting, rather than an organizational meeting in which many people, including patients, are required to participate in order to perform their jobs effectively. The result may be a meeting whose sole function appears to be psychotherapeutic or nursing. Under these circumstances, staff members responsible for other functions become confused or apathetic about their own presence and participation in the meeting. The psychotherapeutic model is adopted as a guide for behavior in the Community Meeting, despite its inappropriateness to the purpose of such a meeting. Taking care of the "sickest" patient, who is showing the most regressed behavior in one form or another, is then always assigned a higher priority than taking care of those individuals, staff or patients, who are functioning and attempting, but with difficulty, to do their jobs, including the patient job, in the hospital. The problems of the workers are set aside while the group organizes itself into a "psychotherapist"—with everyone questioning, analyzing, reassuring, and interpreting—and a "sick patient" who responds in one way or another to these ministrations. This process is rationalized as based upon concern with the distress of the individual, even if at the expense of the group; that many individuals, who are attempting to work or function effectively, are by it abandoned to their problems and their distress, typically goes unnoticed. In the model presented in this chapter, members of Small Groups might more appropriately have particular responsibility for, and take care of, each other, including, of course, during periods of incapacity, distress, or crisis.

Typical statements in the discussion of the Community Program Staff Meeting which suggest this kind of difficulty are:

"I thought that the group was trying to help Bill, and that was more important than the matter I wanted to see discussed."

"I was waiting for a patient to bring it up."

"I wanted to see what was on the patients' minds before I spoke."

"It's the patients' meeting, not our meeting."

A second task for the Community Program Staff meeting is to provide consultation for each staff member concerning the implications that experiences in the Community Meeting have for him in making decisions and taking action in his own area of responsibility and authority. This is not different from those discussions about the implications of what has transpired in the Community Meeting being held for the same purpose in various patient-staff action groups having responsibility, for example, for the activities program, the work program, or the management of social problems. Discussion by staff members in the Community Program Staff Meeting about such implications helps them to clarify what is involved and needed for the sake of their own subsequent participation in such action groups.

The head nurse may begin to plan with her staff what might be needed from the nurses over a weekend with so many patients depressed, upset, and guilty about some situation in the hospital. The head of the Activities Staff may plan how to help the teachers of classes in the activities program, as a result of her understanding of the attitudes of patients toward a "student" role exemplified, not necessarily in a discussion about activities, but perhaps in one about feelings toward physicians-in-training. The staff person with responsibility for a certain function does not simply attend to what is going on in the Community Meeting when that particular area of responsibility is the explicit topic of concern. He is always asking: "What is the implication of this discussion, no matter what it is about, for my job? How can I make a contribution to it from my own point of view and with my particular resources?" The obvious example is when activities resources are suggested for coping with a nursing problem, for example, to alleviate difficulties a member of the group might be having in relating to others.

The head of the Activities Staff may also plan how to help the patient-staff group responsible for the activities program see that its job includes responding to current needs being expressed in the Community Meeting, for example, in complaints about the emptiness of weekends or difficult holiday periods.

The staff person having responsibility in the work program may think about the implications for that program of a discussion in the Community Meeting, in which it becomes clear that the patient group must sabotage any plans to have fun over a holiday because "we don't do any real work; every day is a holiday for us. Other people take good care of us. We don't deserve a holiday." He may also draw conclusions for needed action from a discussion in which it becomes clear that the multiple subordination of the maids and kitchen staff to the head nurse and to the superintendent of buildings and grounds is making for a barrier to resolving difficulties arising between patients doing housekeeping and dietary work and the maids and kitchen staff with whom they are thereby coming in contact.

A staff representative to the Community Council may become convinced that the apparatuses of the hospital community available for dealing with a patient who is a social problem have been exhausted, that they are inadequate to deal with this particular kind of social problem, that the safety and welfare of members of the group and the reputation and standing of the hospital are seriously jeopardized, and that he must therefore initiate procedures that might lead to a review of the patient's work with and relationship to his psychotherapist or possibly to a consideration of the discharge of the patient in question.

Discussion in the Community Program Staff Meeting then involves trying to understand through the Community Meeting itself, together with other information about aspects of hospital life available to different staff members, the current problems of that life, so that each staff member may subsequently use such understanding in discharging his own responsibilities.

A third task of the Community Program Staff Meeting is to formulate recommendations (on the basis of its members' understanding of and participation in the community program, including the Community Meeting) to other units, groups or individuals in the hospital: for example, to the Medical Director (change is needed in the organization, a decision is required to resolve the competing interests of two departments); to the Director of Psychotherapy (a review of the tangled relations among two patients and their two psychotherapists is needed); or to the Community Meeting (additional information is needed in the discussion of an issue currently before the Community Meeting).

Finally, the Community Program Staff may attempt to study various problems and answer certain questions through a research arm as well as its own discussions. What is the fate of problems that are brought up at the Community Meeting? Are the steps of a problem-solving process different in type or order of occurrence when an administrative function is involved than when a psychotherapeutic one is at issue? Do different professional functions require different problem-solving processes or procedures to deal with typical questions arising? Are different contributions required from persons responsible for different functions; is a social-emotional contribution, distinguished from a task-oriented contribution, more appropriate to one than to another? Are there some problems solvable by a process of discussion and consensus in the Community Meeting alone; are there others requiring more formal procedures of decision-making and implementation?

4 The Therapeutic Community

My first experience with the therapeutic community was as a first-year resident in psychiatry in the mid-fifties. My wife and I lived on the grounds of the hospital. I woke up one morning to find the hospital area buried in snow, no other physician able to get in to work, and myself in charge. I decided to try to shovel our way out of isolation. For some reason—I can't quite remember my state of mind at the time—I decided to go to the most disturbed closed male unit and ask the patients there to help shovel snow. With the help of the maintenance department I collected a large number of shovels, went to the unit, and faced an aggregate of catatonic and hebephrenic patients, among others, in various states of agitation, preoccupation, and immobility. I explained as best I could the dilemma the hospital was in, and asked for volunteers to help shovel the snow. As I remember, about ten or twelve out of the twenty volunteered, put on their hats and coats, and marched from the hall. Ordinarily, these patients never left the hall without maximum nursing coverage; we only had a relatively small number of personnel that day available to join us. We shoveled snow most of

Some material in this chapter, in condensed and somewhat altered form, was presented in a paper, "Sociotherapy and Psychotherapy in the Psychiatric Hospital," at the Association for Research in Nervous and Mental Disease meetings on social psychiatry in New York City on 2 December 1967; this paper will be published as a chapter in vol. 47, *Social Psychiatry*, Association for Research in Nervous and Mental Disease series (Williams and Wilkins Company, in press).

the morning. Afterwards, we went to the kitchen together, and had hot chocolate and a fairly pleasant time without difficulties; it would have been hard to distinguish these patients from others on open units. Then we returned to the disturbed closed male unit; the patients took off their hats and coats and immediately resumed their catatonia and hebephrenia.

This has always been a dramatic example to me of an idea that we take for granted as a truism but the implications of which perhaps we do not consider fully: that the behavior of patients, in fact the behavior of all persons, is determined by the situation in which they find themselves as well as (and not only) by relatively enduring aspects of the personality system. This idea underlies any notion of therapeutic community or therapeutic milieu.

DIFFERENT VIEWS OF THE THERAPEAUTIC COMMUNITY

The analysis of psychiatric hospital organization and the functions comprising it help to order the bewildering variety of definitions of the therapeutic community, or the therapeutic milieu, as it is also called (Redl 1957; Rioch and Stanton 1953; Schwartz 1957b; Stanton 1956b).

Definitions of the therapeutic community, particularly those within a humanistic or moral tradition, have emphasized the priority assigned to socialization or therapy services over custodial and protective ones. That the humane treatment of human beings is still at issue is illustrated by a recent article in a large city newspaper stating that the most pressing problem facing a particular mental hospital was obtaining enough soap and towels for the care of patients.

If the preference is given to providing the service of socialization, the therapeutic community is called a school for living, its goal—adjustment to social life and work conditions outside the hospital, its significant mechanism of socialization— the patients' own group standards and expectations. Such a hospital seeks to provide custodial and protective services through the exercise of socialization mechanisms; for example, patients are managed through a process of acculturation and group pressure (Kai Erikson 1957; Jones 1953; Ozarin 1954; Wilmer 1958). Many attempts to use group pressures to acculturate and manage patients essentially involve the substitution of negative and positive social responses for physical coercion as the preferred mechanism by which to control disturbing behavior. One problem such an approach has encountered is that an expedient adaptation to the expectations of the hospital community does not necessarily carry over to situations outside the hospital. Conformity is essentially calculative; it lasts so long as it is rewarded; it disappears when negative responses can be evaded (Edelson 1966b).

If the preference is given to providing the service of therapy, the therapeutic community is called a school for personality growth. The principal mechanism of treatment is likely to be psychoanalysis or psychoanalytic psychotherapy; however, there are also thought to be mechanisms of treatment inherent in the patient's participation in the life of the community (Aichhorn 1925; Bettelheim 1950; Edelson 1964; Redl and Wineman 1954; Stanton 1956a, 1957; Sullivan 1962). Some examples of these are the resolution of intrapersonal tensions as a result of the resolution of interpersonal and intergroup tensions not only in the hospital but also, for example, in the patient's family as it is brought into the treatment situation; the development and strengthening of adaptive ego functions through the patient's participation in the problem-solving activities of the hospital and his collaboration in forming and changing the goals and values of the group, in choosing the methods by which goals are to be reached, and even in determining some of the structural characteristics of the hospital organization; the development or modification of inner controls as a result of identification with the standards and values of the group; and the development of hitherto undeveloped tendencies to interpersonal relations, in a setting where safeguards and a particular value system permit risk-taking and experimentation in relating to others. The view that the milieu can be curative in itself may lead to overestimating the impact of the situation and underestimating the importance of enduring structures of the personality system. Individual psychotherapy may be deprecated as unnecessary. The resolution of interpersonal tensions is supposed to resolve intrapersonal tensions; the latter are apparently thought to arise almost solely from the former. But the personality system does not simply reflect exigencies of interactions with social objects in the situation; it is also bounded, for example, by the physiological organism.

Definitions of the therapeutic community have also been written from the point of view of different professional functions.

Those definitions emphasizing the psychotherapeutic function focus upon the role of the hospital in helping the psychotherapist and patient perform this function (Bullard 1940; Cohen 1957; Edelson 1964; Knight 1936–37; Menninger 1936–37; Reider 1936–37; Simmel 1929, 1936–37). Some examples follow.

1. The patient becomes increasingly aware of his characterological difficulties (or way of life) as these are expressed in the everyday life of the hospital and as he is confronted by the consequences of these difficulties for himself and others; he brings this awareness to his work with the psychotherapist.
2. The hospital creates a new reality in which people do not get caught up in the patient's transference expectations, provocations, or attempts to live according to the pleasure principle.
3. The hospital, by maintaining and enhancing the patient's healthy ego functions—for example, through his participation in activities and work programs—increases his ability to act as a participant-ally in psychotherapy.
4. The hospital provides the psychotherapist with information about the patient's life over a twenty-four hour period, access to which he might not otherwise have.
5. The hospital helps the patient to manage impulses and to meet unconscious needs that might otherwise disrupt psychotherapy.
6. The hospital provides the patient with a world in microcosm in which he may try out in relative safety the new insights and perceptions learned in psychotherapy and test their validity in life outside the session itself.

The view of the therapeutic community as an adjunctive ally of the individual psychotherapy enterprise tends to regard the relation between the two as unproblematic; that this is not so is the burden of much of the discussion in this book.

The proposition that it is desirable for staff people not to get caught up in patients' transference expectations or to respond to patients' pathological provocations leaves aside many questions: for example, whether or not this is possible without the development of insincere role-playing by the staff person, which is likely to have unpredicted and unwanted consequences; and whether or not it is possible for even the most experienced staff person to work with groups of patients and other staff members without getting caught up in powerful affective forces not simply emanating from individual patients but from processes of group life itself. At best, perhaps, such a staff person can hope for some understanding of what group process he has been unwittingly participating in, so that this knowledge is available to him in his work in the therapeutic community.

The proposition that the therapeutic community helps the patient to manage impulses and to meet needs that would otherwise become so intense they would disrupt psychotherapy ignores complexities. Is tension reduction in the community always in the interest of psychotherapy? A community, for example, emphasizing the performance of meaningful work for the benefit of patients who have difficulty accepting the necessity to work is likely also to provide for a certain number of already hardworking patients a way of mitigating feelings of guilt, which unmitigated might lead to fruitful exploration in psychotherapy. Furthermore, the input-output exchanges between the hospital community and individual psychotherapy are not ideally balanced nor only in one direction. Psychotherapy results in tensions within individuals, leading to disturbances in their participation in the community; the community's capacity to cope with such disturbance at any particular time is not unlimited, and such disturbance in itself may act to interfere with the functioning of aspects of the community program the goals of which are gratification or tension reduction. Similarly, problem-solving processes in the community—even those directed to providing opportunities for gratification—inevitably result also in strains within some individuals. No community can simply provide opportunities for gratification and tension release for all its members equally and just at the time of each one's peak needs; reality-testing, decision-making, and the very efforts to cope with failures in integration and with value inconsistencies and conflicts in the community always give rise to tension in some even while relieving it in others.

Pointing out the usefulness to a psychotherapist having in the therapeutic community a source of information about his patient's everyday life, which a patient with impaired ego-functioning may be unable to report, often does not include mentioning the difficulties arising when the patient assumes the psychotherapist has information he does not have or as the psychotherapist struggles with the question of how to make use of such information without disturbing his relationship to the patient. Nor is consideration given to the use of information-exchange by staff in the therapeutic community to influence the psychotherapist to act as an agent of social control for the community when his patient's behavior is disturbing to others—even when the psychotherapist acting in such a role may not necessarily be in the interest of psychotherapy itself; or the use of information-exchange by the psychotherapist to influence staff in the community to alter the environment of his patient—for example, the nature of the expectations others should have of the patient—primarily in terms of the requirements and vicissitudes of psychotherapy, without regard often to the effects of such alterations on the community itself, its functioning and the welfare of its other patient and staff members.

The therapeutic community may be viewed as based on the assumption that participation in the problem-solving activities of the therapeutic community will improve ego-functioning. In addition, patients who have no inner controls are supposed to develop such controls through identification with group standards or norms. Alas for the excessive optimism that often accompanies the espousal of these propositions, groups may go in either direction. They may support or undermine adaptive problem-solving processes; they may evince tremendous sensitivity to moral issues but also can be enormously crude, irresponsible, cruel, and destructive of desired norms as well as individuals. Neither adaptive, rational problem-solving, nor the establishment of useful norms and mechanisms supporting these norms without the development of excessive strains, are spontaneous manifestations of group life necessarily making experience in a group therapeutic or moral.

Those definitions emphasizing what I have called the nursing function tend to see the therapeutic community in terms of the quality of the interpersonal transactions that are sought within it: intense, open, honest, humane, understanding, compassionate, responsive (rather than indifferent), personal (rather than impersonal), experimental (rather than defensive).[1]

The view of the therapeutic community as therapeutic insofar as there are good rather than bad interpersonal relations in it may involve naive oversimplification. It is frequently not explicitly recognized that good interpersonal relations are not just a matter of individual goodwill or maturity but that the organization of the hospital community, the way in which its tasks are defined, differentiated, and assigned, and the inevitably conflicting values implicit in various positions and enterprises within that community, determine in a significant way what kind of human qualities and interpersonal tendencies will be expressed or constrained and to what degree. An uneasy equilibrium and at least intermittent strains must exist in the relations among professional groups and between professional and administrative groups. Members of such groups may, for example, in reference to any particular problem or event, have quite different interests or points of view, be emphasizing different services, be competing for the same resources (personal or physical), or be creating conditions inimical to others' effective performance. It is possible in defining a so-called therapeutic community to emphasize the personal qualities, the tact, sensitivity, forbearance, interpersonal skills, and general wisdom required of individuals in the organization to mitigate these strains. In that event, one must depend on such mechanisms as psychoanalysis, education, supervision, and selection to provide and maintain adequate personnel. However, there are some obvious limits in the influence and availability of such mechanisms for the usual organization, which in general would suffer considerably if it had to depend

---

1. Focusing on changing the quality of interpersonal transactions rather than the patient's personality or the institution itself is recommended by Morris Schwartz (1957a).

on the presence of individuals with extraordinary qualities or the absence of psycho-pathological ones. One may assume instead that the nature of the organization itself determines the fate—the expression or lack of expression—of individual qualities in the everyday life of the hospital. One may ask then what qualities the organization itself must possess, irrespective of the individual psychopathology, eccentricity, or genius of its members, that might mitigate such strains (Henry 1954, 1957).

Those definitions emphasizing what I have called the activities program and work program functions tend to see the therapeutic community as one in which patients struggle in their daily life with real tasks and in which the conditions of their work and play together reproduce critical elements of life in any society.[2] When the therapeutic community is seen in terms of work and activities programs, these tend to be regarded as good in themselves, since being busy, being active, performing, and achieving are prepotent values in the society in which the hospital is embedded. It is clear from the elaborate rationalizations linking such values to mental health that one of the functions of the hospital, especially one emphasizing such programs, does indeed tend to be to reintegrate mentally ill patients in, or attempt to socialize them to accept the values of, the society in which they live. However, ironically enough perhaps—and this is the source of perpetual dilemmas—a hospital community is not necessarily most effective in carrying out its treatment functions, even in carrying out socialization functions, if it simply reflects or is an extension of the society from which patients have come and in which they became ill. In any event, if a particular hospital is to be primarily concerned with the adjustment of a patient to the society, and not necessarily with the integration of his personality system, then a great deal of fuzzy thinking and sophistry in such a hospital might be avoided by not concealing this aim but instead organizing to do it effectively. In one large mental health center, most of the staff I talked to were convinced that the goal of the hospital was to alter the patient's personality system in some way—to resolve intrapersonal conflicts, for example—and that this was in fact what staff persons were trying to do. By actual inspection, however, the majority of time at working staff meetings was devoted to discussions of getting a patient a job, meeting with his employer, seeing a judge in the city to help him understand the patient better, getting a husband and wife to meet together with a therapist so that they might learn to get along, or helping a patient start school once again; that is, to the integration of the patient with some group in his society rather than the integration of his personality system.

Those definitions emphasizing at least in part what I have called the sociotherapeutic function have tended to see the patient as part of the psychiatric hospital organization, participating with staff groups in decision and policy making. Focus is either on the formal structure of the hospital and its consequences or on the process of the resolution of interpersonal and intergroup tensions through information sharing and didactive mechanisms (Caudill and Stainbrook 1954; Caudill 1957, 1958; Hamburg 1957a, 1957b; Jones 1953, 1957; Perry and Shea 1957; Robert Rapoport 1956; Robert and Rhona Rapoport 1959). A fundamental hypothesis,

---

2. This is one element considered in the more complicated formulations of such writers as Main (1946); Sivadon (1957a, 1957b); and Robert White et al. (1964).

implied or explicit in this latter group of definitions, is that the interpersonal relations between members of an organization are determined by the nature of its formal
structure, which decides the limits within which, the extent to which, and the ways
in which personal qualities will be permitted or encouraged to become manifest
(John and Elaine Cumming *et al.* 1957; Etzioni 1960; Henry 1954, 1957; Kahne
1959).

Within this point of view, a therapeutic community may be considered synonymous
with a democratic organization. This kind of democratic organization is typically
characterized by equalitarianism: a blurring of status differentiations and flatten-
ing of hierarchical structure. The most famous example is the therapeutic community described by Maxwell Jones and his associates at Belmont Hospital (Jones
1953; Robert Rapoport 1956; Robert and Rhona Rapoport 1959). As implied by
the previous critical assessment of the equalitarian organization, it is my position
that democracy as a prepotent value is not adequate to guide staff participation nor
to govern the choices made in a hospital community. The raison d'être of the hospital is the treatment of illness; it is therefore committed to the primacy of values of
health and therapy. It is true that democracy may be viewed as a necessary means to
insure maximum self-expression and self-realization for the individual patient. However, the establishment of democratic institutions does not obviate the essential
value-dilemmas at issue: choosing in a particular situation between consequences to
an individual and consequences to a group, or choosing between the autonomy or
self-determination of a group or person, on the one hand, and the integration of that
group or person with other groups or persons in the situation, on the other, or
choosing between the wishes or aims of individuals or particular groups and the
requirements of the treatment task itself. These value-dilemmas are not resolved
once and for all in any therapeutic community but are inevitably at all times part of
its dynamics.

SOCIOTHERAPY AND PSYCHOTHERAPY

The therapeutic community is the site of operations of the sociotherapeutic enterprise in the hospital organization. Sociotherapy and psychotherapy are often regarded as alternative, competing treatment modalities, each with an ideology or set
of values and beliefs, and aims in relation to the individual patient, antagonistic to
the other: one, for example, supposedly seeking to rehabilitate the individual patient
in the direction of adjustment to social conditions, the other seeking to alter the patient's personality system in the direction of greater internal integration. Here,
sociotherapy and psychotherapy are considered instead to be, in some form and to
some degree, inextricably interrelated enterprises in any attempt to understand and
influence or change persons, but enterprises differentiated by having different
systems as foci of intervention and analysis.

The phenomena of concern always involve in one aspect a person with a personality system and in another aspect the situation, including the social system, in
which he acts and in which he is being treated. Two kinds of questions may be
asked about any apparently individual phenomenon—silence, wrist-cutting, vomit-
ing, refusal to work, drunkenness, rule-breaking, inability to perform some action,

fighting, nonparticipation, hallucination, depression, anxiety. The psychotherapist may ask: "What internal processes, what memories, what relation between enduring intrapsychic structures, produce this phenomenon as their effect in this situation? How might such intrapersonal processes be changed?" The sociotherapist may ask: "What social conditions, arrangements, institutions, or processes, what strains between groups or between individual and group, what group-tasks, what values, norms, definitions of a situation, or meaning of desired, sought, feared, or hated objects to some extent shared by the members of the social system, what conflicts or inconsistencies of values and norms, produce this phenomenon? How might such social processes be changed?"

Psychotherapy focuses interest and intervention upon the person; sociotherapy focuses interest and intervention upon the object-situation to which the person relates. Psychotherapy is concerned with an intrapersonal system, with intrapersonal states, conflicts between intrapersonal structures, and the specific intrapersonal determinants of motivation; and with direct attempts to intervene in, and alter, this intrapersonal system. Sociotherapy is concerned with the situation; with the social system and social conditions; with the reality of available social, physical, and cultural objects; with the world of means, opportunities, facilities, media, values, and norms; with the relations, especially the strains, between entities (persons or groups) as these play different parts in achieving the shared goals of the social system; and with direct attempts to intervene in, and alter, this social system.

Any clinical phenomenon may be—and for effective treatment in a hospital should be—considered both from the point of view of psychotherapy, focusing upon the patient's personality system, and sociotherapy, focusing upon the social system of which the patient is a member, most saliently, the hospital community itself. The differentiation of responsibility for the psychotherapeutic and sociotherapeutic enterprises in the hospital organization facilitates the articulation of both points of view and tends to ensure that both will be brought to bear in any attempt to understand or cope with clinical phenomena.

In this framework, it does not make sense to be for one and against the other; both involve an aspect of phenomena that must be understood and requirements that must be met in any treatment situation. Psychotherapists at times seem to justify their indifference to, or ignorance of, groups and group phenomena on the ground that exclusive, intensive preoccupation with an individual represents a survival of humanist values in an increasingly impersonal, mass society; this, despite the fact that group life is an important source of misery as well as value for individuals, and that being interested in the individual rather than in the group in a hospital, for example, may mean focusing at times on the wishes or distress of one individual at the expense of attention to arrangements or conditions affecting the possibility of many other individuals actualizing their values or achieving their aims. The sociotherapist in his eagerness to do the most for the most, and in his attention to the social system and to individuals only insofar as they occupy roles in that social system, at times seems to forget that social systems are always bounded by individual personality systems and that the internal strains of personality systems affect crucially the availability of such resources as motivational commitments to various kinds of action or the skills required by any social system.

Differentiation of sociotherapy and psychotherapy does not imply that either is self-sufficient in the treatment enterprise. They are interdependent, and yet, because it is difficult in any concrete hospital, where resources are inevitably limited, to mobilize for both an equal and adequate degree of commitment, energy, time, attention, and thought, much less personnel with the required, very different knowledge and skills, there are always strains between them, which may be expressed within an organization in struggles for prestige, in competition for the commitment and allegiance of the patient or various staff groups, and in the formation of either-or ideologies based upon oversimplified once-and-for-all dichotomous alternatives.

In a previous work (Edelson 1964), the therapeutic community was discussed from the point of view of its output to the ego-functioning (therefore, the personality system) of the individual patient and its impact upon the psychotherapy enterprise. The argument followed the form that to achieve the desired alteration in a patient's ego-functioning the hospital community should have such-and-such characteristics. In the present work, the attempt has been made in addition to develop a conceptual framework to analyze in some detail that hospital community and the dilemmas it faces; to investigate the nature of obstacles to the achievement of such a community —that is, to the concrete actualization of its values in particular institutions and processes of action; and to consider ways, especially organizational means, to overcome such obstacles. Is such a community (one organized primarily around the values of, and in terms of its output to, the psychotherapy enterprise) in fact as a social system viable? What consequences are entailed for a community as a social system in the attempt to make it therapeutic, in the sense of giving priority to the output to personality systems of one group of individuals within it?

In the previous book, as in this one, it was suggested that enterprises such as individual psychotherapy, group therapy, and the therapeutic community meetings, programs, and activities, should be differentiated as to task (if nothing else than by virtue of the differences in their composition and organization and the aims these would most appropriately serve). For example, individual therapy would not be carried out in a community meeting, nor could the goals of the community meeting be accomplished in a dyadic group. In that book, from the point of view of psychotherapy alone, the significance of the different settings in the therapeutic community was described in terms of the different task each sets for the individual patient; their chief value assessed in terms of providing an arena in which the patient's difficulties in coping with a particular kind of situation could be explored and clarified; the prototype interpretation of all situations formulated in terms of the relation between individual and group (large, small, or dyadic)—that is, the relation between individual behavior or attitudes and the requirements of group life or of a shared effort (Edelson 1964).

Such a view of the therapeutic community is useful, especially for the therapist as he seeks to understand his patient and his psychotherapeutic work with that patient. But it is not sufficient. If one wishes to understand the interaction between individual and social system, between psychotherapy and the situation in which it takes place, one must understand the social system, in conceptual terms appropriate to its study, at least as well as the personality system. One must be able to attend to those aspects of phenomena best conceived as manifestations of the therapeutic community itself as social system: its problems and processes; its organization; the relations between its component subsystems; the consequences of its collective goals, its shared value systems, its prescribed arrangements, and its collective views of itself and of its environment. Particular collectivities and programs in the therapeutic community need to be, as suggested in this book, understood and differentiated not only in terms of their output to individual personality systems, or in terms of their output to the psychotherapy enterprise, but in terms of their output to the social system of which they are a part as well.

In summary, if one is interested in the relation between processes or events in psychotherapy and processes or events in the therapeutic community, it is useful to think about the therapeutic community in three ways. First, the therapeutic community is a social system some of whose members share a common residence within an organization; as a social system, it is constituted by prepotent values implied by the treatment goals of the organization, and subject to the vicissitudes of its situation (including the other subsystems of the hospital organization, and the personality systems and behavioral organisms of its members); in it, shared goals are sought and conflicting values, aims, and interests struggle in complex equilibrium states. Second, the therapeutic community is part of the situation of the psychotherapy enterprise in the hospital organization; as such, it may at times act as a constraint or limit upon, or provide resources to, that enterprise, for example, by depriving it of, or making available to it, motivational commitment to values intrinsic to psychotherapy or similarly by undermining, maintaining, or enhancing ego assets required for participation in psychotherapy. Third, the therapeutic community and its enterprises contribute to achieving the treatment goals of the hospital organization through specific outputs to the personality systems of particular individual patients.

THE THERAPEUTIC COMMUNITY AS SOCIAL SYSTEM

A conceptually technical definition of the therapeutic community follows, to be distinguished from ideological definitions tending to characterize it in terms of the values and beliefs of a social-equalitarian movement. The therapeutic community is that part of a psychiatric hospital organization whose patient and staff members share the common purpose of attaining adaptation, consummation, integration, and motivation ends having three characteristics.

1. The particular ends sought by a therapeutic community are generated by the interactions of patients living in the hospital with each other and with the members of other groups, and by the conditions, resources, and exigencies of the situation in which these interactions take place. The therapeutic community should include, then, means for detecting what ends are salient at any particular time through an examination of the characteristics of current interactions and the needs, wishes, strains, or requirements to which such interactions bear witness—as well as means for responding to such salience through appropriate collective action. From this point of view, the particular ends of a therapeutic community are neither given nor limited a priori. For example, the therapeutic community is not primarily organized to produce a single output or specific outputs to personality systems: to bring about particular ways of behaving or particular personality changes deemed ahead of time

to be desirable. It is not organized to cure mental illness: a goal of the hospital organization of which it is a part. It is not organized to carry out specific projects conceived by mental health experts, which staff members feel will have some therapeutic consequences for patients. It is, primarily, a social system that exists by virtue of the patients' residence in the hospital.

2. The ends of a therapeutic community are of a degree of complexity such that their attainment requires a system of organized or ordered cooperative and collaborative effort in order to overcome biological, physical, or social limitations restricting the effectiveness of the activity of single individuals as a means to their attainment. The problems of special interest to the therapeutic community are those arising from the processes and requirements of collective life that cannot be solved by the action of one individual, or even the interaction of two individuals, but that require concerted action by groups of individuals.

3. The particular ends sought by a therapeutic community at any time should be consistent with, and subordinate to, the fulfillment of the limited, specific, given purpose of the psychiatric hospital organization: to cope with mental illness and its consequences through treatment, teaching, and research. Most importantly, processes of goal-attainment in the therapeutic community are governed by the general prepotent aim that these be congruent with the enterprise of psychotherapy. A therapeutic community is therapeutic because it involves the attempt at integration of the social system by prepotent, institutionalized treatment values—with inevitable consequent strains—and not because it is an ideally functioning social system. All choices made to which the community is committed during processes of goal-attainment (including selections between particular ends, between means for achieving a given end, between norms, and between value-positions) should tend to actualize, and increase commitment to, values intrinsic to the psychotherapy enterprise. The following value-positions guide processes of psychotherapy; the institutionalization of such values in the psychotherapy dyad is in part a prerequisite to, and in part a consequence of, the actualization of the aims of psychotherapy. These value-positions are also relevant in coping with the problems of the therapeutic community, and may be institutionalized in that social system.

Preference is for change in a progressive direction, according to some criterion, for example, increasing degree of differentiation or, more generally, increasing adaptation effectiveness—rather than for remaining the same, avoiding risks, maintaining traditional ways of orientation and action no matter what the current situation, or maintaining above all the security of what is already known and achieved.

Preference is for change through active effort to attain goals to which one is committed—rather than for waiting passively for other agencies to meet needs or solve problems, or for withholding commitment from goals requiring effort to attain.

Preference is for change through collaboration with another possessing resources needed to bring about change, each member of such an alliance being expected to bring resources and to make an active contribution to it—rather than for hyper-independence and compulsive insistence on "going it alone" under all circumstances, or for seeking benefits from another without obligation to contribute oneself to a joint enterprise.

Preference is for orientation to the needs of a collectivity or to supra-individual consequences in establishing and maintaining a solidary relationship with another in the interest of a shared goal, both the relationship and the goal having priority over transient individual impulses the discharge of which would threaten or disrupt that solidarity or the attainment of that goal—rather than for putting discharge of one's immediate needs and impulses above the interests of the collectivity of which one is a part.

Preference is for change through knowledge, acquired in often painful processes of symbolic expression as well as the relatively uninhibited honest communication of information whose relevance may not always be a priori established (exploration) —rather than for avoiding dysphoric experience through ignorance of inner or outer reality.

Preference is for establishing a hierarchy of priorities among needs to be gratified, some dispositions to be renounced in favor of others according to some criterion, some wishes to be gratified and others denied according to agreements binding upon members of a solidary relationship (such as the psychotherapy relationship or relationships with others in the therapeutic community)—rather than for chaotic, unlimited gratification of all wishes as they arise without evaluation of consequences or consideration of the extent to which gratification of one wish may interfere with the gratification of another.

Preference is for being able to endure present deprivation (discomfort, tension, pain) in the interest of future gratification—rather than for seeking to be rid of any discomfort or tension as rapidly as possible no matter what the cost.

Preference is for an integration of the parts of a system (such as a personality system or social system) so that the required functions these parts represent are performed without costly or irrevocable sacrifice of one for the sake of another— rather than for maximizing the aims or operations of one part of a system at the continual expense of the aims or operations of another.

A hospital community is a therapeutic community insofar as the members of its collectivities share these values; are committed or feel obligated to make efforts to realize them in actuality through adherence to the norms derived from them; and select such a value system in preference to others for guiding orientation and action when there are choices to be made. To this extent, of course, the therapeutic community is different from other types of collectivities or social systems in the extended society, in which other value systems are prepotent, just as the relationship between patient and psychotherapist is different in significant ways from other relationships in society. The attempt to design a hospital community in terms of its degree of resemblance to other groups in the society of which the patient is a member is, in this view, somewhat beside the point.

A typical, idealized therapeutic community problem-solving process might, for example, then, include the following.

Exploratory discussion by members of all groups at the Community Meeting— including symbolic expression of affective states and the state of affairs in the community, and cognitive information about recent events, interactions, or changes in the community's situation (conditions or resources)—leads to a definition of a particular problem, requiring the attainment of a particular adaptation, consummation, integration, or motivation end. The attainment of that end wins the shared commitment of the members of all groups.

If the attainment of more than one end is required, a hierarchy of priorities is considered, with the integration of the entire community and the interdependent functioning of all its parts or programs in mind, as part of a process of negotiation between groups.

Attempts to get rid of a problem or to solve it quickly without consideration of cost or consequences are thwarted, including attempts to bury it in committee, through unconscionable delay, or through impulsive collective action.

In a process of interaction between relevant action committees and the Community Meeting, hypotheses are formulated, based upon knowledge of the details of the present circumstances and previous experience about what might work; reference is made to various standards, values, and norms in an attempt to imagine what might be a desirable solution.

A solution—for example, a selection of ends, means, norms, or value-positions, leading to a new state of affairs—is likely to involve, either as part of the new state of affairs or in the process of reaching it, the following. Members of the community have the sense that a choice is possible, that alternatives are truly available; and also recognize that a choice must be made, that not everything desired is possible or compatible, that resources are limited. The change sought is likely to be in the community itself, in one of its collectivities or the programs or tasks for which these are responsible, in the relations between such collectivities, in the community's normative arrangements, or in some collective perception, process, or state of affairs, rather than in the community's situation, especially the personality system of one of its members. All groups in the community—patient and staff, all action committees —make an actual, unique, differentiated, required, and relevant contribution, involving active effort; there is collaboration and cooperation between such groups. Priority is given to the welfare of the community and all its members over the wishes or aims of one part of the community (individual or group) in the rare event that irreconcilable conflict exists between them—that is, that the gratification or achievement of the wishes or aims of the one is truly destructive to the other; ordinarily, within a given range of incompatibility, processes of negotiation and compromise take place. The community, on the other hand, is devoted to identifying and meeting those needs of its constituent individual and collective parts requiring collective action.

THE THERAPEUTIC COMMUNITY AND THE PSYCHOTHERAPY ENTERPRISE

What is the relation of the therapeutic community or sociotherapy subsystem to the psychotherapy subsystem? The therapeutic community is part of the situation of the psychotherapy subsystem, and as such is both a source of means or resources, which are useful to the psychotherapy subsystem, and conditions, which may constrain the psychotherapy subsystem.

The therapeutic community offers an alliance intended to help each patient struggle against an illness that manifests itself by crippling alterations in ego-function, ego-state, and ego-organization (Edelson 1964; Knight 1960).[3] Members of the

3. The view of the therapeutic community as a setting for growth, ego-change, and the development of capacities for interpersonal relations owes something, in different ways, to the

community may try to oppose together the way of life in each patient that, as the price for avoiding pain and anxiety, substitutes constricted, automatic, and stereotyped reaction—fight, flight, regression—for adaptive response. The patient's way of life, manifested in maladaptive reactions to community structure and events, has consequences for himself and others in the community, of which he and they are made increasingly aware. Ideally, all the members of the therapeutic community may come to feel themselves to be fellow-combatants engaged in the same fight against illness; therefore, depending on each other in a struggle for survival as persons, they cannot, as "civilians" often do, leave each other alone, but, as "civilians" usually do not, may regard each other with the wry understanding and unsentimental compassion of comrades on a battlefield.

The various collectivities and programs of a therapeutic community (e.g., the community meeting, small groups, the community council, the work program, the activities program) provide different arenas for the observation and modification of the ego. Each one is concerned with the enhancement of the ego's functioning in relation to, and the maintenance of its optimal relative autonomy from, inner and outer reality. Each one has as one kind of output the development and strengthening of the ego's functioning and capacities for growth and creativity. Each one must be concerned with coping, in some way, though perhaps in different ways, with defensive operations that interfere with the achievement of its goals, including its outputs to the hospital community. As patients may put it in one way or another, "It's the illness each one of us came with that prevents us from trusting each other, that keeps us from sharing things about ourselves with each other, or from working or accomplishing things together." In the community, the struggle is made to overcome the obstacles. Community members attempt to communicate with, and relate to, each other; to work, to build, to play together; to produce a play, a paper, or an art show; to have a tournament, a class, a program, a party—to *make* a therapeutic community. With every achievement, what is healthy in each ego must be strengthened and the illness that might have prevented the achievement must to some extent yield.

Members of the group share the events, feelings, problems, achievements, and interpersonal transactions that are part of community life. They may then try to respond to each other in ways that undermine, rather than perpetuate and consolidate, what is constricting and disabling in each patient's way of life and that enhance and support, rather than weaken, each patient's strengths and abilities. For example, in a therapeutic community, mutually reinforced protective, defensive efforts to avoid narcissistic wounds, feelings, or anxiety, may be eschewed in favor of helping to strengthen one another's ability to cope with pain.

The therapeutic community is characterized by the interdependence of its members, who cannot avoid by their actions, attitudes, and words either contributing to the maintenance of a constricted, defensive way of life or helping to sustain and enhance that which is adaptive and constructive in each other. The defeat of one member weakens all; the victory of one strengthens all: no such defeat and no such

---

writings of the following men: Aichhorn 1925; Bettelheim 1950; Redl and Wineman 1954; Sullivan 1962.

victory occur except also with the complicity or by the efforts of others. It is for this reason that the responsibility for taking therapeutic action resides in no single member or group of the therapeutic community, regardless of status or position, but is shared by all.

A community that makes possible the observation of the ego as it interacts with external as well as inner reality is particularly useful as a setting for the individual psychotherapeutic treatment of patients whose ego-operations may be relatively inaccessible. This is especially true when such ego-operations cannot be investigated solely in resistances appearing in the verbal transactions of an individual session: when, for example, the patient is primarily silent or nonverbal, disorganized or regressed, withdrawn, a poor reporter, not psychologically-minded, or acting-out.

The ego-operations of such patients, however, may be observed in their responses to the structure and process of group life and in their way of life in the therapeutic community. The ego's analogous measures for dealing with inner reality may then be inferred by the psychotherapist. Thus, ego-operations in relation to external and inner reality become available for investigation and modification in individual psychotherapy.

Observation of the ego in relation to external reality in the therapeutic community facilitates a focus in individual psychotherapy on adaptation and achievement as well as on defense and conflict. Interest is in accomplishment and action as well as word and thought. Attention is directed to the ego's efforts to cope with the characteristics, the limits, the expectations of an environment known to both patient and psychotherapist. Emphasis is on the patient's responsibility "not only for his own life as well as the lives of others in the community but for the values and viability of the treatment process itself" (Edelson 1964, p. 101). This focus on adaptation to, and achievement in, external reality has four effects on individual psychotherapy.

First, it tends to mitigate regressive tendencies inherent in inward-looking, insight-seeking psychotherapy and ego-disability (Polansky, Miller, and White 1955; Talbot et al. 1964); and the loss of self esteem which may occur when the emphasis in individual psychotherapy seems solely on what is defensive and pathological.

Second, observation of the ego in relation to this reality helps both patient and psychotherapist to become aware of the precise way in which the defensive operations of the ego encroach upon and impair its adaptive functioning. This awareness may act as incentive to the patient for persisting in a psychotherapeutic effort which, at times, seems unbearably painful or futile.

Third, there is in the organization and process of a therapeutic community a continual pressure upon the ego for modification, since old attitudes and ways of life must be re-examined, ego-constrictions challenged, and ego-restrictions jostled, if important community tasks are to be accomplished, therapeutic values and standards maintained, and thus community treatment goals reached.

Fourth, and finally, it is possible for a patient in such a community to attempt alloplastic adaptations, which involve changing the environment as well as himself. He collaborates in forming and changing the values of the community, in determining its organization, and in choosing the procedures by which community members seek to reach its goals.

Psychotherapy requires the patient's ego to be the therapist's observer-ally.

Therefore, as Anna Freud (1942) was one of the first to point out, the healthy part of the ego—which contributes the faculty of self-observation as well as analytic and integrative resources—must be maintained and enhanced, if necessary, through support and education. For example, the ego must be educated to tolerate larger quantities of pain for longer periods of time, so that participation in the arduous, anxiety-arousing process of psychotherapy is possible.

Community members attempt to achieve the goals of the therapeutic community and its enterprises. At the same time, community members try to meet the wishes and mitigate the fears they share, hopefully in ways that do not compromise but rather facilitate the achievement of the community's goals. They agree, either actively or by passive acquiescence, by overt or by covert processes, upon solutions to conflicts between what is required for the achievement of the community goals, and the wishes and fears of community members, as well as to conflicts between such wishes and fears.[4] Solutions to such conflicts consist of group decisions about procedures, aspects of community organization and policies, definitions of the acceptability or nonacceptability of particular kinds of interpersonal transactions or individual behavior, and ways of perceiving the community or any of its members.

Each such solution is defensive, adaptive, or has both defensive and adaptive aspects. The kinds of solutions preferred by a community are an expression of its values. An adaptive solution contributes to the achievement of the community members' goals, as described above, to a task required for such achievement, or to meeting some need or wish shared by community members in a way that facilitates or at least is not incompatible with the achievement of community goals. Such a solution takes into account the goal sought; the resources available, and the tasks necessary, for its achievement; and the impact of such a solution upon, and cost to, the individuals involved. It also includes a means for evaluating the consequences of a solution after it has been adopted. In other words, an adaptive solution usually reflects an attempt both to meet fears or objections through processes of reality testing, for example, and to make it possible for wishes to be gratified or ends attained especially by bringing about some alteration in the object-situation in which individual patients are being treated. A defensive solution is designed by members of the community to avoid anxiety or other painful affects no matter what the cost to any individual or to the environment or how incompatible such a solution is to the achievement of the community members' other goals. A solution of this kind usually contains elements similar to resistances in psychotherapy: for example, a way of seeing things that justifies a defensive operation or is designed to prevent others from interfering with it. In other words, a defensive solution may reflect an attempt primarily to allay fears without gratifying wishes or attaining positive ends, or to attain ends as rapidly as possible without allaying the fears associated with such ends. A solution that has both defensive and adaptive aspects may involve a way of avoiding anxiety or painful affects that also permits a partial, although not optimal, need-meeting, task-accomplishment, or problem-solving.

---

4. Similar models, involving the resolutions of conflicts between the shared wishes and fears of group members, are used by Ezriel (1952), Sutherland (1952), and Whitaker and Lieberman (1964), in discussions of group therapy.

In trying to understand whether or not a particular solution is either adaptive or defensive or to what extent each, it is important to consider the following questions. What is the goal of the community or function of a particular community group? What task(s) is necessary here and now for its achievement? What conditions, behavior, ego-qualities are required for the accomplishment of the task? What anxieties or painful affects arise within the members of a particular group or the entire community here and now in response to these task-requirements? To what extent at this time and in these circumstances does a proposed or adopted solution facilitate the task-accomplishment? To what extent is this solution designed simply to avoid the anxieties or painful affects mobilized by the requirement for conditions, behavior, ego-qualities necessary to make task-accomplishment possible.

For example, a community might choose to meet in a room in which there are many corners or other places for people to hide from others during discussion, because of mistrust, shame, or guilt. The defensive nature of the difficulties in communicating and responding to one another under these conditions is obvious. That such a solution also has an adaptive aspect might be indicated by the statement: "If there were no place to hide, I might not come to community meetings at all."

Likewise, a group's decision to adjourn a meeting early, to leave the doors of a meeting room open, to give permission to its members not to attend if they do not wish to, may be intended to allay shared fears of being trapped or restrained, so that anxious members can continue to participate, but perhaps at the expense of maintaining the optimal conditions required for the work of the group.

Another example: a reliance on formal parliamentary procedure may be adaptive in a decision-making or administrative group in the community. A small discussion group in the same community, however, may meet to share feelings, attitudes, and perceptions necessary for understanding or to overcome blocks to accomplishment. In such a group there may be anxiety about loss of control over feelings, others' disapproval or depreciation, or the consequences of one's own or others' aggressiveness and competitiveness. Then, cutting off all noisy, lively exchanges, raising one's hand before speaking, and a focus on business, agenda items or the motion on the floor to the exclusion of all untidy, irrational, or affective processes, might be primarily defensive. Group values and perceptions may be used to rationalize this kind of a defensive solution. Examples of such group values are: "That's the fair way. The group should not intrude upon an individual's private inner world." Examples of such agreed-upon ways of looking at the community, its structure, and its members are: "Feelings belong in individual psychotherapy. Only the therapist can be trusted. Patient members of the community are incompetent, not objective, punitive." Similarly, members of a group may become preoccupied with administrative detail, insist on a consideration of abstract principles and basic issues rather than the picayune details of everyday life in the community, or cry for action instead of more talk. These solutions may at various times in a group's history serve an adaptive or defensive purpose, or both. Suppression of affects and an emphasis on formality and intellectual discussion may lead to boredom and tedium as well as the persistence of unresolved covert difficulties. A solution may then be developed which involves acting out the feelings or expressing them in situations and in ways that disrupt the decision-making, administrative groups in the community. This new situation then calls for new solutions, and so the process continues.

A similar analysis could be made of a community in which the emphasis is on the importance of expressing feeling and achieving insight. Introspection and talk (displacing action) might there serve a defensive purpose in making it possible for people to maintain their way of life as long as they use the right words. So, discussing the meaning of work, or expressing one's feelings about expectations and authority, might well replace working itself. The patient does not change. There is a breakdown in decision-making, administration, and the execution of tasks necessary for the life of the community.

As another example: a series of thefts occur in the community, with the result that an almost intolerable atmosphere of suspicion and suspense develops. One possibly adaptive solution considered might be that no one shall leave the premises until the person comes forward. If this were offered as a suggestion in a community in which there was a great deal of anxiety about losing autonomy or being restrained, it would probably be hooted down. Another possibly adaptive solution: to discuss the matter and make an inquiry in a community meeting. However, taking the initiative in such an inquiry by asking relevant (although necessarily intrusive) questions might lead to guilt, increased by the perception of others that such activity always implies hostility. There might be much mistrust in the community with anxiety about being, if exposed, shamed, and attacked. In this event, a way would probably be found to stop any such discussion, perhaps through silence or reproaching forward members as vindictive or harmful. The result might be a solution that is, to a greater or lesser degree, both defensive and adaptive: to call in a detective who, it is fantasied, will carry on an impartial investigation, working skillfully, unobtrusively, and (embarrassing no one) behind the scenes; or, to refer the matter to a study committee to consider in what way the community as a whole might be contributing to the occurrence of such behavior as stealing and then report back its findings to the entire community.

Participation in a work program in a therapeutic community, for the organization and supervision of which the patients have a major responsibility, requires a wide range of ego-qualities. Commitment to a task requires, for example, a capacity for industry and a sense of identity. However, such a requirement may mobilize feelings of inferiority and a sense of role diffusion. Such feelings might then be avoided by nonparticipation. (Fears of restraint or losing one's own boundaries may also lead to a rebellious defiance of the requirement to participate.) Depending on the response of others, however, nonparticipation may lead to feelings of isolation, shame, or inadequacy. A group might seek a defensive solution by making possible mere compliance to a minimal expectation. The group would yield to the passive opposition to any demand for active, whole-hearted participation. "If you are 'good', and do the job expected, you will be otherwise left alone. No one will question the nature of your participation." Other defensive solutions attempted might be to talk about work rather than working or to take flight into consideration of other "urgent" matters or into blaming some patient or staff member(s) for the group's difficulties. If problems are to be solved, continuous, ongoing exploration of the work program (who is doing what, how, what are the needs, where) and the presentation of its needs by a work committee to the community are necessary. This requires trust, autonomy, and initiative. Feelings of mistrust, shame and doubt, and guilt, however, oppose the exercise of such ego-qualities and result in defensive efforts to avoid or mitigate such feelings. Information may be concealed through restrictive covenants about what can and what cannot be revealed in group discussion. Foremen may not turn in work reports or may refuse to evaluate honestly the work of others. Fear of loss of control over one's feelings or of retaliation by others may lead to silence or withdrawal rather than objection to a particular assignment of jobs. Initiative in patients may be squelched by peers through guilt-arousal, rejection, or subtle threats of reprisal. Competition may be avoided through criticism of those who exercise too much power, a preoccupation with fairness, and a refusal to chose someone in preference to someone else (a foreman, for example, might be chosen by drawing straws rather than by appointment or election). The organization of the work program is designed to keep the nature of the group's goals, the tasks to be accomplished, and the means necessary for their accomplishment continuously visible to the group. This organization and the ego-resources in the group available for problem-solving oppose such defensive solutions. Such opposition may result in a series of slow but steady movements toward the sharing of relevant information, the awareness of obstacles, hypotheses about what creates them, and the formulation and execution of plans for overcoming them.

The characteristic solutions of a therapeutic community influence the conduct and outcome of intensive individual psychotherapy in three ways.

1. The solutions agreed upon by community members in achieving the community's goals and meeting their own shared needs collide with, challenge, and make untenable or unnecessary the defensive, constrictive solutions characteristic of the patient's previous way of life. This opens the way for experimentation with other ways of living and the experience that gratification rather than disaster may arise from these.

For example: A patient for whom those on the outside have always made special arrangements to accommodate to his symptoms and his concept of himself as an inspired artist finds that the expectations of the community are that he participate in the work program within certain limits regardless of his symptoms. A patient who has always avoided anxiety or narcissistic wounds by restricting his interests, especially those that might lead to competition with others, by steering clear of groups, and by not having feelings, becomes increasingly aware—as he is encouraged to participate in meetings and activities—of how much of himself he has cut out rather than allow himself to run the risk of being hurt. A patient who has always refused to accept limits under a host of philosophical rationalizations collides with the rules of the community—formulated by his peers, and for which there are obvious reasons in the everyday events of the community life. This collision leads to the discovery in psychotherapy that impulses and hungers are the masters of his life and how much, to his own distress, his reason has been impotent to restrain these. A patient who withdraws to think rather than work hears from another, "I know from my own experience it is easier to think about working than to work. Words are more important to you than life." A patient who is chronically belligerent and defiant hears from his peers, "If you want us to take your ideas seriously, if you want to be part of the community and have our trust, you must be willing to join and help us." A patient who is frightened by change learns to tolerate and understand the anxiety aroused in herself in a community which is always changing in order to achieve its goals with greater effectiveness. Such learning occurs especially because community requirements for her participation, and her own desire to accomplish certain tasks for which others' help is needed, prevent her from running away as she always has.

Some patients isolate themselves in a clique from the influence of the community, going their own way and ignoring policies and expectations, even frightening others by their behavior and appearance. They find in group discussion that the ability of one of their members to benefit from treatment has been compromised because of the insulation afforded by the clique. This leads to an evaluation by the members of the clique of their way of life, its consequences, and a consideration of whether or not—in the face of the actual nonthreatingness of others in the community—such a way of life is necessary.

2. To the extent that processes in the therapeutic community result in primarily adaptive solutions, agreed upon by community members, that community may provide experiences for the patient that strengthen and educate his ego—for example, to be able to endure greater quantities of anxiety or affects without being overwhelmed. To the extent that processes in the therapeutic community result in primarily defensive solutions, agreed upon by community members, that community may consolidate or perpetuate the constrictive, impoverished aspects of each patient's ego.

Imagine the consequences for the treatment of a withdrawn, isolated patient if conflict in the community between initiative and guilt (as well as anxiety about being restrained, being exposed to critical inspection, or losing bounds and boundaries) have resulted in proscription against any kind of personal intrusiveness. "People should be let alone unless they're causing trouble." A patient going into another patient's locked room to wake him up, when that patient has been having difficulty getting to work, for example, is regarded by others as over-aggressive, interfering, or having imposed an indignity upon someone else. Compare this with the values of a community in which the following incident occurs. A young patient, newly arrived, refuses to attend a community meeting, and with much bravado threatens to kill anyone who tries to make him. On the one hand, no one wished to coerce him. On the other, it may be clear that phobias and counterphobic defenses are primary problems for him, and that permitting him once again to be overwhelmed by his fears, especially in an early and thus significant encounter with the community, might compromise significantly the possibility of treating him effectively in that community. The entire community comes to his room to meet, to his initial astonishment. Then he begins to grin and join in, not having been forced to give in, on the one hand, nor on the other, left alone to be defeated by the fears that beset him.

Specifically in relation to individual psychotherapy, if the community's solutions are primarily adaptive, then the goals and values of individual psychotherapy and the ability of the patient's ego to participate meaningfully as an ally in such an enterprise are supported. If the community's solutions are primarily defensive, then

these goals and values and the ego's capacity to participate as an ally in psychotherapy are being subverted.

All the solutions, for example, of a community may make it possible to avoid
anxiety at whatever cost: by fight made possible through scapegoating or schisms
in the group; by actual flight from uncomfortable situations; by regression made
possible through minimizing responsibility for one's own life and that of others
in the community and through avoiding confrontation with the requirements of
group living and the nature of one's own participation in it. Then the ability of
the patient's ego to tolerate pain and to face anxiety-arousing insights in individual
psychotherapy will certainly not be increased by the experiences of his daily life.

The converse should be true of a therapeutic community. Patients in the community are encouraged to endure frustration rather than run from it. The examined
life is held preferable to a life of self-deception, denial, and secrecy. Knowledge
and awareness, sharing information (including feelings) about one's self and one's
interactions, though painful, are held to lead to more effective problem-solving
than ignorance, blankness, confusion, and silence. Self-esteem is based on the
ability to grow and learn by experience rather than on rigid defensive positions.
Patients are asked not to abdicate their responsibility to help fellow human beings
"in the same boat." Then the ego is supported and strengthened, so that entering
into the process leading to insight and growth in individual psychotherapy becomes
increasingly possible.

3. It is clear that the extent to which adaptive or defensive solutions predominate,
and the kind of adaptive solutions possible, are determined in part by the composition of the community; the nature of the needs, wishes and fears shared by
members of the community; and the ego resources available in it. The solutions
characteristic of a particular therapeutic community meet the particular needs
and mitigate the particular fears, and arise out of and are appropriate to the
particular range of ego-strengths and ego-vulnerabilities, of the members of that
community. Such solutions may not, however, be tolerable, useful, or appropriate
to a particular individual patient. Some communities may require relatively defensive
solutions to allay the anxieties of vulnerable members; such solutions, however,
might needlessly hamper a less vulnerable patient. Other communities may be
intolerant of defensive solutions necessary to some vulnerable member, or employ
adaptive solutions that are impossible for or threatening to a patient whose ego
is being overwhelmed. Therefore, the solutions agreed upon by the members of
the therapeutic community determine, in part, whether or not a particular patient
can be effectively treated in that community—will find it, in fact, therapeutic.

If the community has agreed not to challenge anything about the way of life
(for example, escape into pleasure and recreation) of any patient who passively
complies with the minimum expectations of the community just enough to stay
out of trouble, then it may perhaps be anticipated there will be a long time in
the psychotherapy of such patients in which there is relatively little movement. If
a person is at the mercy of his impulses, and needs continuous setting of firm
limits, he will be difficult to treat in a community in which there is an agreement
not to interfere with anyone, no matter how self-destructive, so long as he is not
bothering the group. If a patient needs a constrictive solution such as a strict

code of morality in order to remain in control of his impulses, he is likely to become increasingly disorganized in a community where "anything goes" or where flouting conventional standards is acceptable.

A patient who defends against anxiety by boasting, or trying to establish a special relationship or position, is likely to become a rejected deviant in a community whose members have agreed that no one shall be special or get special treatment. A patient who speaks or behaves psychotically may be rejected in a community whose members, fearing signs of mental illness as if it were contagious, have a narrow tolerance for such behavior or thinking. A patient who requires intervention by community members to restrain behavior, when this is a matter of life or death, will not be treatable in a community whose members are unwilling to enter into such an agreement with anyone.

The therapeutic community as a social system is, then, both influenced and, insofar as it is a therapeutic community, governed by the values of the psychotherapy enterprise and at the same time part of the situation of that enterprise, including resources needed by it and conditions limiting it. The actual shared values of the hospital community may support, undermine, or limit what can be accomplished in, and to some extent determine who can be treated by, individual psychotherapy in a particular hospital. Such actual values are manifested in choices made in processes of collective action to resolve conflicts between the shared wishes and fear of community members, or to resolve dilemmas involving the imperatives of community life, on the one hand, and the wishes and fears of its various members, on the other. This model, reflecting a view of social phenomena in terms of complex equilibria between different aims, is useful in understanding, for example, a community's response to a proposed action or change. Whose wishes or aims, and what wishes or aims, motivate the proposal? Whose fears, and what fears, are reflected in the objections to it? How are the objections met? To what extent does final action taken reflect an attempt primarily to allay fears without gratifying wishes or attaining positive ends; an attempt primarily to gratify wishes or attain ends without allaying fears; or some attempt both to meet objections, through processes of reality testing, for example, and make it possible for wishes to be gratified or ends attained by bringing about some alteration in the object-situation in which patients are being treated? The examples previously given imply consequences to the hospital community itself, to the viability of the psychotherapeutic enterprise in the hospital organization, and to individual members of the hospital, of particular kinds of solutions of community problems.

Inevitably, there are strains between the psychotherapy enterprise and the therapeutic community or sociotherapy enterprise. The therapeutic community in relation to psychotherapy may be viewed as an alternative treatment modality, rather than a specialized aspect of treatment in a hospital setting or a treatment modality complementary to psychotherapy. This view may always be supported by evidence arising from the fact that any subsystem of an organization, including sociotherapy, inevitably competes with other subsystems for prestige, the commitment and investment of staff and patients, and financial and intellectual resources. Such competition may be manifested by sophistic argumentation, with much posing of extreme, apparently mutually exclusive, antagonistic dichotomies, as if two opposing ideologies were involved. What kind of hospital community is a good kind of hospital community: this kind or that kind? Is individual regression bad or good for psychotherapy, for the community? Actually, sociotherapy and psychotherapy are two technical operations integrated by the same value system and working toward the same end or interrelated ends by different means.

An example of the kind of polemic that may develop in a hospital organization is given in appendix D.

The very fact that different means, different conceptual tools, different language, and a different focus of attention are relevant to the two enterprises results in misunderstandings and estrangement, as, of course, does any actual imbalance of resources between them. It is the function of over-all organization, as has been pointed out, to see that the real issues are clarified, so that the right fight may go on about the right things between the right people, and that resources are allocated neither personally nor idiosyncratically but in a way that is clearly related to the situation of the organization and the achievement of its goals.

Competition between sociotherapy and psychotherapy may be exacerbated by the tendency of staff and patients to perform the psychotherapeutic rather than the sociotherapeutic function when the sociotherapeutic function is called for, as when the community meeting is apparently used for psychotherapeutic purposes, for example, to investigate a particular patient member's personality system or the intrapersonal sources of his distress or action. This tendency to perform the psychotherapy function in a sociotherapeutic setting may occur because of confusion about the task facing the group. It may occur because of the absence or denigration of the skills or knowledge required to perform a sociotherapeutic function; psychotherapists may conclude that they have no special expertise to offer in the hospital community; if they do not conceive the hospital community enterprise as a professional-technical operation (in this sense like individual psychotherapy), they may also conclude that no expertise is available from anyone, or indeed, is even relevant. The performance of the psychotherapeutic function in a sociotherapeutic setting may also involve a defensive abrogation of the sociotherapeutic task motivated by anxiety, or by commitment to psychotherapy as the most prestigious function.

At a recent meeting of the American Psychiatric Association, Nemiroff and his colleagues presented a paper describing the use of a ward meeting for the presentation of autobiographical and personal information by a patient to the group (Nemiroff et al. 1966).

A similar innovation was attempted at another hospital to bridge the gap between the Community Meeting, where the current life of the hospital community was discussed, and the Staff Conference, where patients were presented to the staff and recommendations were made after thorough evaluation for future treatment. Previously, the discharge of certain "controversial" patients, for example, had been puzzling provocative events to the patient group, presented to it through inflammatory distorted self-presentations of aggrieved patients at informal bull sessions. The staff was pictured as revengeful for patients' social misconduct, callous about the needs of people seeking their last chance for help, concerned only about money, or inconsistent. Such perceptions, of course, resulted in lack of confidence in the hospital as an organization, undermining patients' commitment to its aims and values. It was thought that if the patient group was to share with the staff responsibility for creating and maintaining a community whose values and social processes facilitated rather than impeded the treatment enterprise, then patients should have access to undistorted information on the basis of which to interpret events in the community and act. Information about staff recommendations might be particularly useful to those patient-staff groups responsible for coping with the social problems created by patients who flout or evade the norms of the community. The behavior of these patients and the reaction to it were often inexplicable; it followed that attempts to respond in ways that would neither drive the patient out of the community nor reinforce socially dysfunctional conduct were frequently blundering. The Community Council decided to ask patients to report to the Community Meeting the results of their Staff Conferences. Questions might then be asked in an open forum and confusion cleared up by subsequent discussion. Such reports resulted in little discussion. They apparently served less the expected cognitive, orienting function and more an unexpected integrative induction function. The patient, in announcing to the group his acceptance of, or concern about, the staff's recommendations, in sharing this experience with others, seemed to commit himself thereby to membership in the community and at that time also to receive the welcome of others into it.

There are important differences between this experience and that reported by Nemiroff and his colleagues, and the two experiences are reported in different language and with different concerns; these differences are best understood in terms of the goals or tasks of the groups involved.

If a community meeting is to perform a psychotherapeutic function, as so many apparently attempt to do, the organization of such a meeting into a group as therapist, which collectively interviews and interprets, and an individual patient, whose life not only in the hospital community but outside it and previous to his experience in it is commented upon, and whose behavior in terms of intrapersonal conflicts and motivations is interpreted, is, then, probably appropriate. In that case, such an innovation as that reported by Nemiroff and his colleagues is likely to have consequences facilitating this psychotherapeutic task; reports of individuals' past histories contain information relevant to its achievement.

If, on the other hand, the community meeting has a sociotherapeutic function, for which as a group it is especially well suited, its focus is the hospital community itself and its problem-solving processes: for example, relations, especially strains, in the here and now between groups or individuals having different jobs to perform and adhering to different values associated with those jobs. The community meeting investigates the effect of such strains upon the achievement of common ends and the actualization of shared values. Then the introduction of autobiographical information is largely irrelevant and often distracting; the organization of the group into therapist and patient a regressive evasion of its task.

The fact that the introduction of self-presentation at one patient-staff meeting had the result that, as the authors tell us, other "patient-staff meetings started to sound like self-presentation meetings" makes one wonder if the complexities of coping with the realities of current community life were being evaded by fascinated delving into individual psyches. Such resistances are especially available in a setting in which individual psychotherapy is a highly valued treatment modality.

All this is not to say more than that all social change is likely to have both predicted and unpredicted dysfunctional and functional effects. And, of course, dysfunctional side effects are not the whole story here; the paper describes other (e.g., integrative) effects contributing to the optimal functioning of the ward as a social system. The behavioral changes observed by the authors are best explained, perhaps, not in terms of alterations in intrapersonal dynamics, but rather, in the language of the social system, as the result of factors such as the following. The self-presentation experience seems to have brought about a heightened sense of belonging to the same group and increased cohesiveness or commitment to shared group norms and standards. Motivational patterns, necessary for participation in the treatment enterprise, were reinforced by discussion and by the enthusiasm aroused probably in both staff and patients. Such shared enthusiasm was mobilized, it might be speculated, because the self-presentation meetings, with group as therapist and presenter as patient, were in some way perceived to be like individual therapy; everyone in the community, therefore, felt part of the effort that was most valued.

A patient, of course, may exploit and increase strains between sociotherapy and psychotherapy by announcing, for example, "I get more out of participation in the community than from my psychotherapy," or "I don't need to participate in the community, since I really get what I need from psychotherapy—that's what I'm here for." Insofar as the psychotherapist feels divorced from, or at odds with, what is happening in the hospital community, he may not respond to the transference implications of such communications; insofar as the sociotherapist feels divorced from, or competing with, the psychotherapy enterprise, he will not be able to respond comfortably to those aspects of such communications that reflect social processes or conditions.

In any event, the performance of the psychotherapeutic function in a sociotherapeutic setting leads to increased suspicion that the sociotherapeutic enterprise is "taking over" and attempting to establish itself as the prepotent source of treatment in the hospital. On the other hand, when one enterprise in the organization is in difficulty, feelings of reproach may develop somewhere in the organization toward the other enterprise for not being helpful, which usually means not doing what is properly the task of the enterprise in difficulty. For example, one may hear the question, why doesn't the community help a particular individual work out an intrapsychic conflict? What is the community doing to help so-and-so? Such pressures encourage a focus on the distress of one individual at the expense of interest in the entire community of individuals, indeed as if all the difficulties in the community were the result of the actions of this individual; such actions are conceived as arising from within the one individual and having no connection with a situation or something shared by other members of the community as well as this individual. A different kind of expectation may also develop, that the psychotherapist should "take a stand" with his patient to help maintain law and order in the community.

None of this obviates that on particular occasions difficulty may arise because of the real failure of either sociotherapy or psychotherapy, especially when relatively unskilled people, as often must be the case, are assigned to do either. Inadequate performance of the psychotherapeutic function may result in a massive displacement to the community of tension and distress, which is not being perceived in relation to the vicissitudes of the psychotherapy relationship or exploratory process, or coped with in the psychotherapeutic setting. Inadequate performance of the socio-therapeutic function may result in an object-situation that undermines the ego-resources or value-commitments required for psychotherapy. Needless to say, one enterprise taking over the functions of the other to fill a vacuum created by such failure leads, at the least, to poor or muddled task-performance and further strain.

Especially difficult strains between psychotherapy and sociotherapy arise when a social arrangement or social process exists in a hospital community, which while useful to many patients, is thought by the psychotherapist to be inimical or useless to his patient; or when the action of one individual in relation to the community is thought by those in the community to be inimical or not useful to most other individuals (that is, to the hospital community whose current arrangements and processes are beneficial or necessary to these or other individuals), but is thought by the psychotherapist to be useful in some way to the individual himself. The fact that what is functional for one particular personality system is not necessarily functional for the social system or for other personality systems, or that what is functional for the social system and its members may be dysfunctional for a particular personality system, must be faced as a reality when it is one, and not merely interpreted away as evidence of irrational forces or smoothed over as unproblematical. Such dilemmas are inevitable in any social system, in any organization, and especially in a hospital which may have, to one degree or another, a heterogeneous population with very different needs and resources.

The following description of a hospital community at a particular point of time illustrates many of these strains between sociotherapy and psychotherapy.

A concerted effort had been made to convert an area in the basement of a hospital building where patients lived into a game room and general recreational area. Many strains had developed as the patient and staff leaders of this project struggled to maintain the commitment of patients to the hard work involved and to enlist the cooperation of staff when it was needed without opening the doors to a take-over by staff of various decisions and tasks.

No vision of what the area would be like in the end, what needs it would meet and what wants it would gratify, had yet taken hold. Neither the Activities Committee nor the Activities Staff saw this end as a primary concern of the Activities Program. The vision of the end that might fire others and obtain their commitment for the work that needed to be done was not forthcoming from these groups, which tended to see the Activities Program as a series of classes or individual activities having nothing to do with the life of the community. That a recreational area conceived and created by the community, needing murals, providing game and program facilities, might stimulate participation in the multitude of unrelated class, crafts, and party activities with which the Activities Staff and Activities Committee were traditionally preoccupied had not yet occurred to these groups, in part because the question of how to obtain commitment from uncommitted people to activities was not a question that had much concerned them. Activities Staff members, especially, preferred to work with individuals who brought their own motivations along. To the extent the question of motivation had been considered, it was usually thought solvable by staff counseling of the individual patient or by use of a positive relationship between an individual staff member and individual patient, rather than conceived in terms of patients' relationships with each other or as a matter of establishing and "hooking into" shared wants, ends, values, and efforts arising out of the structure and day-to-day life of the community. The interdependence with enterprises other than one's own immediate one that this latter view implied threatened too many vested interests, ways of working, and the autonomy of those who, for one reason or another, found it gratifying to work on their own with patients unencumbered by relations with other staff.

During this period of intense group effort, every hand counted if usual work and recreational activities were to be maintained at the same time walls were painted, tiles laid, lighting arranged, and room separators built in the new game room. There was sharp division felt between those who were part of the common effort—the daydreaming, talking, drawing up plans, organizing, laboring together—and those who were not, either because of personal states of alienation and apathy, narcissism, lack of self-confidence and anxiety about the expectations tied to commitment, or resentment about deprivation, or because of commitment by some to personal projects outside the community, such as going to school or working at a job elsewhere. Those who were out of the community in one way or another felt more outside of it than usual and others felt rejected and abandoned by them and either rejected or ignored them in turn as outsiders or tried to draw them back into the community. Those committed primarily elsewhere felt pulled between their personal commitments and the claims of the community to which they belonged. The attitudes of others toward them were intensified by the perception that those going to school or working outside the community possessed leadership and skill resources badly needed by the community in its attempts to achieve ends that had come to be widely valued.

Motivations for going to school or working outside the community, or conditions leading to such action, of course, varied.

Such action might follow acceptance by the psychotherapist and patient of the value of the patient working or going to school, a value which had been strongly institutionalized during a previous time when the hospital community was regarded somewhat negatively as essentially providing opportunities for a moratorium from usual social expectations and as including potent forces in the direction of regression. (The value of working or going to school was also, of course, inherent in the forward progression of treatment in the hospital toward ultimate discharge.) Opportunities for full-time, meaningful ego-enhancing activities were thought best sought outside the hospital community, a view still held by many psychotherapists, especially among those not actively participating in the community program.

A patient and psychotherapist might agree that the patient's going to school or getting a job would be a meaningful aspect of a process of termination of therapeutic work at the hospital and a step into the future, the strains of such separation ideally being accepted by both as part of this status and as needing to be "worked through."

A patient might seek work or enroll in school as part of a desire, early in his hospitalization, for example, to avoid committing himself to the feared community and therapeutic enterprise. A patient might seek work or enroll in school to initiate a pseudo-termination process in the service of resistance in treatment. A patient might seek work or enroll in school to withdraw from or abandon the community during a period of strain, as a result of feelings of disappointment, anger, or despair arising from his current experiences in it.

The problem of maintaining the integration of patients going to school or working outside the community with the community was made more difficult because of inconsistencies in the system of values held by various groups and the related fact that patients and staff often used one valued reason for going to school or working to justify behavior actually based upon another not-so-valued reason. Therefore, consistent crucial distinctions between different patients' apparently similar behavior and therefore differences in the valuation of such behavior could not easily be made in the social arena.

Many new patients had recently entered the community. This entry had the usual results: an increase in the amount of deviant behavior; strains resulting from new patients' questioning of or lack of commitment to community values, norms, policies, and procedures; and eventually an increase in anomie or normlessness. As norms were undermined and expectations for response from and participation by others frustrated, disappointed patients began to behave angrily or apathetically in accord with the belief that no one or nothing could be depended upon. Such anomie was intensified by the loss of confidence in the hospital and loss of hope engendered by the recent suicide of an ex-patient.

The rise in the amount of deviant behavior threatened to absorb the energy and attention of the community, which were needed, for example, for the achievement of the game room project and the maintenance of usual programs. The game room project was dependent upon the Activities Program to mobilize commitment to some end having to do with gratifying, expressive activity for the achievement of which people would labor. It was dependent upon the Work Program to provide laborers, tools, and an organization of work. In the same way, that project was also dependent upon the Community Council to control deviant behavior, and upon the Small Groups to socialize new members of the community and to cope with the tensions within individuals arising out of their relation with the community—its groups, enterprises, and day-by-day events—so that individual tensions, or strains in response to deviant behavior, would not disrupt the cooperation or diminish the participation necessary to achieve such a project.

Dependency upon these groups to play their part in a community enterprise had led to disappointment. In part, their failure to do so was due to the fact that the conception of the interdependence of these programs was not widely shared, although at this time as a result of experience with the game room project the fact of this interdependence was dimly perceived. Each group was somewhat unclear about its unique function or contribution to the community, tending indeed in each case to formulate its function or contribution—following the model of psycho-therapy—in terms of output to individuals rather than output to the community and to its enterprises.

The Work Committee, preoccupied with problems of individual commitment (for the solution of which it actually depended upon the functioning of such groups as the Activities Committee, Community Council, and Small Groups, as has been just discussed) tended to neglect such technical problems as how to recruit par-ticular personnel, in fact particular skills, from a pool of available personnel or skills, and how to obtain tools, necessary for the accomplishment of particular jobs; how to organize work operations in such a way that the organization of workers and work had some meaningful relation to the particular work being done; and how to establish criteria for the evaluation of work and win agreement from various groups for such criteria.

The Activities Committee, as has been just discussed, focused its efforts upon mobilizing facilities for and arranging disparate recreational events and opportu-nities. It concerned itself very little with the ambivalent attitudes toward pleasure, fun, or gratifying, expressive activity in the community. With the exception at this time of classes and an occasional program related to current experiences in the community, it made little attempt to discover day-by-day what wants and expressive needs people had and the extent to which such wants and needs were shared, and to base its planning for activities upon such an evaluation of the current situation; its programs and events tended instead to be planned without regard for everyday community life but rather for an average expectable com-munity.

The Community Council to some extent lacked commitment to the goal of enforcing behavioral adherence to norms, regarding this as somehow antithetical to helping individuals. It could not evaluate the moral status of the community, that is, could not investigate such questions as the extent to which adherence to norms in conduct occurred, who and what specifically were involved in any actual incident of deviance, what norms were in fact institutionalized and what norms were "only on the books," because both patients and staff colluded in maintaining secrecy in these areas to protect individuals. It lacked leadership skills necessary to innovate mechanisms of achieving behavioral adherence to norms that would not violate the values of the community, for example, "individual autonomy," and "freedom from coercion," as well as the skills necessary to mobilize the support of the community in any attempt to maintain adherence to the norms of the community.

The Small Groups were not committed to the goal of focusing upon the relation between individual and community, particularly as affected by current happenings in the community, and mitigating strains within individuals which would tend to lead to disruption or dis-integration of that relation and the undermining of indi-vidual commitments to the values and enterprises of the therapeutic community and to therapy and the hospital in general. The membership composition, other organizational aspects, relative lack of solidarity, and some of the traditions of these groups militated against their performing such a function effectively. That function, given the requirement for its performance if the community were to survive, tended to be taken over by the Community Council and Community Meeting (neither of which was optimally organized to perform it), thereby of course displacing those groups' particular vital functions.

Specific manifestations of the entry of new patients included the following. Old leaders were experiencing accumulated strains in their relation to the group they had led on the difficult path to various task-achievements. Impatience with and resentment of old leaders resulted in the search for new leaders among previously nonparticipating, and especially among covertly challenging, members of the group, including new patients. There was a call to bend, change, or abandon rules in connection with drinking, or caring for pets in the hospital; these rules were challenged as unnecessary or inconvenient for individuals, and their alteration was sought in the direction of adaptation to the gratifications and circumstances of particular individuals, the welfare of the rest of the group being on the whole considered of secondary importance.

New patients expressed great distress about the amount of public discussion of matters they had hitherto regarded as private. Such discussions became more difficult to have in the face of such individual distress. For example, a new patient walked out of the Community Meeting every time a report was read about an individual and his relation to and participation in the community. The community was at this time experimenting with submitting such a report regularly to the staff conference on individual patients.

In addition, there had been an increase in concern about the possible use of drugs by individuals in the community, and an unprecedented transmission of venereal disease by at least one member of the community to at least one other member of the community as a result of a contact outside the community.

At this time, a psychotherapist reported to the staff at one of its meetings that a patient in the community had venereal disease; the psychotherapist described the steps that had been taken, including a report to the board of health. A member of the Community Program Staff raised the question whether some report to the community as a whole was indicated, alerting its members to a danger that had not previously existed and raising the level of awareness and education in the community as a public health measure. Presumably, this might take the form of some general announcement by an administrator at the Community Meeting, without revealing the names of the particular patients involved. Many psychotherapists speculated about the effects upon their work with individual patients of such an announcement. One thought the procedure would make it possible for his patient to talk to him about this matter. Another thought that his patient who was already having delusions about venereal disease would become more delusional as a result of such an announcement. A third thought that the particular patient involved would become frightened and upset, and certainly should be told ahead of time that such a public announcement was planned. A member of the Community Program Staff, on the other hand, wondered if the staff would not be seen as giving positive sanction to sexual activity by publicly recognizing the situation and discussing it only from a medical point of view without expressing moral disapproval. There was some worry about the reputation of the hospital, if the matter became public. Many comments emphasized that if the contagious illness were of any other kind, a matter-of-fact announcement and educational measures would most likely follow without a second thought, and that the staff had some responsibility to the unwary, innocent, and ignorant members of the community who deserved at least whatever protection knowledge itself might provide. The final decision was left up to an administrator assigned to the Community Program Staff; he decided toward the end of the staff meeting to make such an announcement at the Community Meeting immediately following.

At a later Staff Meeting, there was an effort to evaluate the consequences of such a move both for the community and for individual psychotherapy, and to see which hunches, fantasies, speculations, and hypotheses turned out to have some validity, and which might have to be modified in the light of subsequent evidence. It was reported that at the first Community Meeting of the week, the announcement was made rather matter-of-factly. The patient most directly concerned, whose name was not mentioned, gave no overt evidences of upset, no startle even, and in fact entered into the subsequent discussion of the need for more education on this matter with great aplomb; the patient was not told before the meeting by Dr. Smith that he was going to make such an announcement. The sociotherapist co-chairing the Community Meeting, Dr. Franklin, wondered if the group felt there was any need for a higher level of awareness and education in the community about such illness. A rather lively discussion ensued, on the whole sensible in tone, which involved some information-giving and question-answering especially by members of the staff, suggestions for a program including films on venereal disease and for calling in an internist for further information, and a final referral of the question where to go from here to the Community Council. At the end of the meeting, the co-chairman said to Dr. Franklin that he expected a lot of hysterical fears to develop in the community, and thought further discussion would be important.

Earlier in this same Community Meeting, it was announced that the insistence of the shop instructor that the shop should be cleaned at 8:30 A.M. rather than 5:00 P.M. had met with acquiescence by the Work Committee. The former time had been changed to the latter during a period of intense work on the game room to make it possible for the most people to give maximum time at the same time on that project. The patient shop work crew wanted to continue to clean the shop at the new time; the staff shop instructor objected, claiming the work was best done before the day's activities began and that he wanted the shop secretary, rather than himself, to act as liaison with the shop work crew, and she was not at the shop at 5:00 P.M. The staff representative to the Work Committee had commented that the price for the apparent harmony that had been achieved was that the patient foreman of the crew had been told by the group that her view of things was not valid. There was some question about whether or not 8:30 A.M. was not indeed the best time in terms of realistic work-requirements; it seemed clear that the staff representative to the Work Committee doubted this and felt uneasy about the decision he and the Work Committee had made.

One patient especially was very angry about this incident. She saw the staff representative to the Work Committee as betraying patients, such as the foreman of the work crew, in order to satisfy the staff shop instructor, reminding her of interactions in her own family. The patient was now planning on pulling out of the Work Program, and perhaps taking some classes in town, although she didn't appear to be very interested in school as such. Her psychotherapist was not concerned about this development, because he thought going to school might be useful to her in the long run.

The staff representative to the Work Committee commented at the staff meeting that he felt bad about what had happened. He knew he was supposed to represent the shop instructor's, as well as other staff, interests on the Work Committee and not just identify and side with the patients. But he hadn't been able to work well with the shop instructor. They couldn't talk to each other. The shop instructor was over at the shop and didn't seem to have any idea what was going on in the community or to want to have any part in it. He wouldn't talk to the patients at all and didn't see their point of view. He just wanted his own way in "his" shop. The staff representative added, however, that he didn't feel what happened was all the shop instructor's fault. He, the staff representative, didn't know how to participate in the Work Committee so that he was not siding with the patients, and then having various members of the staff accuse him of not representing their interests in the Work Program, or siding with staff people, and then having patients feel he was betraying them. The only meaningful way he had ever been able to function on that committee was just to help support the patient leaders in their work and forget about the rest of the hospital, which he saw as confused and irrationally organized.

In any event, following the Community Meeting, the Community Council decided to refer the matter of a program on venereal disease to the Program Subcommittee of the Activities Committee, but gave the matter no further attention from the point of view, for example, of its meaning for the status and influence of norms in the community.

Before the next Community Meeting, the patient co-chairman sought out Dr. Franklin. Apparently this patient felt there was a lot of sleeping around going on, as well as excessive drinking and people staying up all night, and that this was somehow connected with issues that were being ignored by the group: the recent death of the Medical Director of the hospital; the uncertainty about the recruitment of a new Medical Director; nurses leaving and the head nurse going on a long vacation; and quite a number of patients talking about leaving the hospital under strange circumstances, that is, unrelated to any apparent advances in treatment or any plans made with their therapists. The patient had discussed these matters in therapy and wanted to bring them up at the Community Meeting but feared that the group would be angry at him because there were some people who were determined that there would be no discussion of sexual behavior in the community. Dr. Franklin told him that he would have to use his own judgment about bringing such matters up, and agreed with him that it was unlikely that bringing them up would increase his popularity. The patient wondered if mentioning names could be avoided; Dr. Franklin asked him to think about the relevance or lack of it of such information for what he wanted to achieve.

Dr. Smith, the administrator who was a member of the Community Program Staff, was absent at the next Community Meeting; he sent a message that he was not well, but this was treated very skeptically, it apparently being assumed that he was ducking out of any difficult discussions that might arise as a result of his announcement on the previous day. The group was reassured by a patient in answer to an expression of concern about the imminent descent of Public Health officials upon the hospital that such officials would only be talking to a few individuals directly concerned and that most people wouldn't even know they had been at the hospital. After many announcements and some desultory discussion, the patient co-chairman presented his thoughts to the group and sought discussion about them, beginning in fact with the hypothesis that the increase in acting out had started when it was reported that an ex-patient had committed suicide. There was much resistance to discussing what was going on in the hospital as far as sexual behavior was concerned. (Dr. Franklin thought to himself that this resistance was manifested also in the stilted somewhat intellectualized presentation of the co-chairman who now used the words acting out, when outside the meeting he had used more colloquial language.) A patient said she did not believe that Doctor Smith had made the announcement for Public Health reasons at all, but just to get the group to discuss sexual matters.

The meeting was interrupted by some friends of a patient, Sam, expressing with great feeling their concern about Sam, who was at that moment packing to leave, talking nonchalantly about suicide, and about not having gotten anything from his treatment. When the suicide of the ex-patient was discussed by him, it was with the attitude: "Why not kill yourself, if you feel that way?" His friends wept, pleaded with the group for help, insisted that helping Sam was much more important than discussing abstract issues about hospital life. As they presented the matter, it seemed as if the group was being asked to become preoccupied with an emergency about which in fact there did not seem to be much that could be done, in order to avoid discussing current sexual behavior. However, a patient did leave the meeting to talk to Sam; others decided to try to persuade Sam to pause and reflect, and above all to get him to an appointment with his therapist that afternoon. Two hypotheses were offered to account for his leaving: one, his therapist had just taken a prolonged vacation; two, he had begun in recent weeks to participate in the community from which until recently he had been quite detached. One patient described how he and Sam had often talked together about their hatred of the hospital.

Dr. Franklin had by this time decided that the main dysfunctional effect of the announcement about the venereal disease had been to undermine confidence in and respect for the community: "What kind of community is this in which such things happen?" To get this subject opened up, he wondered if a suggestion to deal with the present situation might involve something that needed to have been done some months ago; instead of forming a twosome to express hatred and mockery of the hospital and community, might not the patient who had last spoken and Sam have brought such feelings out of hiding where they might be coped with? What happens to feelings of hatred that remain in hiding? Maybe that was what the co-chairman was trying to get at, how feelings of anger, disappointment, and hatred of the community are expressed when they must remain in hiding.

There was further discussion of persuading Sam to remain. Dr. Franklin wondered why Jim, for example, should want to persuade Sam to remain in a place that Jim just said he hated. Jim denied hating the community. Dr. Franklin said, "Of course, only Sam hates the community and wants to leave it. None of the rest of us have any feelings like that at all!"

A number of patients spoke vehemently. Betty: "I hate this community because it won't let me be human. I come with my enthusiasm about working in the nursery school and people don't respond, just dampen it." Donald (to Dr. Franklin): "I hate what you just did. We were concerned about Sam and you try to get us off on an abstract discussion!" Ruth: "I hate it here because the doctors think neurotics have an inability to love. People who express their love are always put down!"

That afternoon the game room project crew met to evaluate their experiences. The crew members had refused to share this evaluation at the Community Meeting; they wanted only the workers present. The mood at that meeting, according to the staff representative to the Work Committee, was profound rejection of the community. No one wanted to work for anything or for anyone, but everyone wanted simply to do some routine work that would keep him busy. The general feeling was that you couldn't get others to help with anything. A patient expressed to the staff representative of the Work Committee after this meeting disgust with the amount of cynical lying going on at meetings one heard if one knew what people were doing in private: the upsets being created by sexual triangles, for example.

Dr. Franklin was thinking at this time that people were struggling, on the one hand with the desire to maintain self-protective secrecy, motivated by fear and guilt, perhaps especially felt by a number of new patients, and on the other hand with the disgust of idealistic young people at a community life of lying, hypocrisy, and cynicism. The cynicism was expressed not only in sexual behavior, and in the appearance of venereal disease, but in the open disregard of other people's rights and feelings in connection, for example, with the rules about pets, and in the use by the group of a patient, Joe, drunk or hungover most of the time, to lead a movement to relax rules about drinking.

In the third Community Meeting of the week, there was a report of the failure to get the dietitian to change a milk brand. There was a long discussion of class schedules, which was clearly defensive in nature, since most of it was business that could easily have been taken care of by the Activities Committee. A new patient walked out as a report on a patient for staff conference was read; her feelings that this kind of thing was too personal were mentioned. Representatives of the Sponsors Committee discussed the need to help new patients with such feelings. (Dr. Franklin thought to himself that this was another manifestation of the fear that had been mobilized that too personal things might be discussed in the meeting.) It had been impossible to get people to help clean up the nursery school. That the eventual consequence, if all else failed, of the patients giving up this area as a work responsibility, would be that the staff would hire maintenance people to do the cleaning, was pointed out by the staff representative to the Work Committee; Dr. Franklin added that closing the nursery school was another alternative open to the staff.

A patient announced that he knew people were worried about his having talked a lot about leaving the hospital. He had decided to stay at least a few months, at least until the play was over. It was reported that Sam had not left either. His friends had talked to him; he had agreed to meet with his therapist and with his Small

Group on the following Monday. Sam had said the only reason he would stay, if he did, was because of his friends. Intense positive feelings about the value of the community, the changes in it that made an honest announcement like that at the beginning of the week possible, and the fact that people could be helpful and do something constructive, were expressed by a few. Dr. Franklin wondered if the significance of the community in a situation like this had to do with whether ties had formed between an individual and the community (friends, a Small Group, a project, a play) that might hold an individual during periods of stress, which are inevitable in treatment, for example, when insight is painful or there is a disturbance in the relationship with the therapist: hold him long enough for thought to replace hasty or impulsive action. He reminded the group that the group's experience was that if such ties had not been formed, little could be done in the community when the emergency arose.

Discussions at staff meetings during this time might be paraphrased somewhat as follows.

Psychotherapist: I think Sam is going to leave.

Sociotherapist: The group will be disappointed.

Psychotherapist: I think the patients should be taught to respond to situations like this in ways other than trying to hold onto someone, for example, supporting a patient who is leaving.

Sociotherapist: Well, they have all had experience in their own therapy with ups-and-downs, with wanting to leave during a period of anger at a therapist or resistance in therapy; they distinguish that kind of leaving quite sharply from leaving as a result of doing well in therapy and a collaborative plan worked out with a therapist. Their response to someone leaving under the first set of circumstances is quite instinctive, based as it is on their sharing values having to do with therapy: sticking it out when the going gets rough; collaborating with the source of professional help as a means for getting better. It's hard to know how to get a different response to Sam's leaving other than by undermining commitment to such values.

Psychotherapist: I think what I am actually concerned with is something else. There seems to be only one way for a patient to be in the community these days. There is such an emphasis on being *in* the community. Sam told me that he had been called a shadow in the Community Meeting, that he had been pressured to participate.

Sociotherapist: That is not exactly what happened. There were obvious evidences in the meeting that many people were sitting back silently to protest what they considered the domination of the community by a few patient leaders. In the course of the discussion about this, I commented that some people were treated by others as invisible or as shadows; their contributions were ignored; their tentative bids to provide leadership received no response. Shortly after that, Sam did accept an office in the community.

Psychotherapist: Does everyone have to be a leader! Can't the community be broad enough to accept that some schizoid people aren't going to participate wholeheartedly! Everyone has to participate or otherwise the community decides he is bad.

Sociotherapist: Are you blaming the community that your patient is leaving?

Psychotherapist: He is a quiet, shy person. . . .

Sociotherapist: We saw a different side in the community. He banded together with one or two other people to mock people who were participating in community enterprises.

Psychotherapist: Of course, I don't mean to blame the community for Sam's leaving. He was very upset about my vacation and has always had a very tentative tenuous commitment to treatment here.

Sociotherapist: If anything, I don't think pressure from the community upon Sam to participate was a source of difficulty in this situation, but rather the fact that the community for so long accepted and colluded with Sam's detachment, mockery, and aloofness—so that his commitments to the therapeutic enterprise were not deepened by his experiences in the community.

Psychotherapist: The real question is what kind of community do we want to have. I don't think we should have a community in which it is more important to participate in the hospital community than, for example, to go out and get a job. Why isn't it up to the patient and his psychotherapist when it's a good idea for the patient to get a job? Why is such a deep involvement in the community, and apparently to the exclusion of all else, so important? Isn't what we are trying to bring about some basic change in a person through psychotherapy that will enable him to get a job, or go to school, and eventually leave here? Why foster dependence upon a hospital community? The more my patient wants to be out of the hospital community the better I like it.

Sociotherapist: I feel as though the general conception is that members of the Community Program Staff tell the patients it is not a good idea to get a job or tell particular patients when it is okay for them to get jobs, and that all we have to do to correct matters is to go and tell the patients it is a good idea to get jobs or to stop interfering in the matter altogether.

Psychotherapist: It is as if we imagined that every event and detail of the community program is designed and controlled by the Community Program Staff.

Sociotherapist: And as if changes could be made by staff members communicating rational messages to patients. Most of the processes we see have a large non-rational component, to say the least, and the positions people take in the community with regard to various issues are consequences of certain basic characteristics, aims, and values of the community as well as of current situational exigencies. Such consequences are often unexpected and sometimes even undesired derivatives of highly valued purposes. My experience is that the alternatives we debate are not black and white, mutually exclusive alternatives, but dilemmas; if you want one thing, then the other thing comes along, wanted or not. And you can't get rid of what you don't like without jeopardizing what you do like. In fact, it is usually impossible to change intentionally one attitude, value, or institution without affecting in quite unpredicted ways other attitudes, values, or institutions with which the one to be changed is highly interdependent.

Psychotherapist: That reminds me of psychotherapy and a psychotherapist's attempts to influence a complex personality system. Jiggle something here and quite surprisingly something over there begins to alter. The same psychological formation is likely to have both defensive-pathological and adaptive aspects inextricably interwoven with each other; it is difficult to affect one and let the other alone.

Anyway, what are some examples of those basic characteristics you do intentionally strive to attain in the community and the unexpected consequences of these?

Sociotherapist: As nearly as I can tell, I start with the idea that membership in a well-functioning social system, in which every group or program is organized rationally to contribute some essential requirement of that social system, will enhance ego-functioning. In contrast, membership in a social system in which the organization of groups or programs is determined not by the intrinsic requirements of essential tasks or functions in the social system but is rather adapted to or primarily determined by the regressive needs, excessive narcissism, or anxieties of its participants, will not enhance ego-functioning. However, as soon as one tries for a social system that does not fit in with ego-disorder or foster it, one creates the conditions for inevitable strains between patient and community.

Psychotherapist: In that event, the psychotherapist may help the patient to achieve some insight into the nature of his response to, or defenses against, the claims of society, as these impinge upon personal characteristics bound up with his illness. I suppose the temptation to be avoided is to agree with the patient that the society expects too much and to blame the society for the patient's unrest.

Sociotherapist: Especially since no society is altogether rational in the sense just described, usually very far from it, and there is always ample evidence that its inconsistencies, malintegration, and dysfunctional aspects are also impinging upon the patient. The implication seems to be that the psychotherapist should no more expect that no strains will arise from the patient's participation in the community to disrupt the psychotherapy enterprise than the Community Program staff has the right to complain because psychotherapists make interpretations, go on vacations, or lack skills resulting in strains that disrupt the patient's participation in the community and its enterprises. Psychotherapy and sociotherapy might each regard the strains arising from the other as part of the situation or conditions in which it operates.

Psychotherapist: The assumption you make is that both enterprises are equally important and essential to treatment. Why should we not have a community the chief function of which would be to support psychotherapy as *the* modality of treatment: to provide a milieu that nourishes patients; to provide support and comfort for patients; to provide opportunities for release of tension and for individuals to be active and creative each in his own way and in ways that are not stressful or disturbing to them; but not to bring about any fundamental change in patients, that being the job of psychotherapy.

Sociotherapist: I think one might start with such an intention and that such a community might also have very desirable aspects. I very much doubt, however, that such a community would pose no difficulties. I would expect that the informal group life of such a community, for example, might prove quite destructive to some individuals and its values might be frequently in contrast to those of a therapeutic enterprise. Certainly, even minimal regulation of individual behavior in the interests of the welfare of that community would require the imposition of negative sanctions, which most probably would be evaded as expediency dictated. Suppose, however, that one wanted to have a community in which, instead of expediently conforming to or evading norms, patients internalized values, from which a wide range of norms were derivable, a community then in which external sanctions were no longer necessary to maintain behavioral adherence to values and norms because these had been internalized and were now part of the patient himself, part of his own commitments. To have such a community, I believe, one must have a community in which patients and staff interdependently collaborate to achieve shared valued ends. Such a community in order to achieve such ends must work as a social system, and therefore must emphasize the interdependence of its members and its groups, and be aware of the consequences (for the success or failure of common endeavors and for others' participation) of a lack of commitment on the part of various individuals or groups within it. Of course, the more the emphasis on interdependence, the more leaving the community or being out of it is felt to have serious consequences. In a community where individuals live alone to pursue only personal ends, going to school or getting a job is seen as a manifestation of the values of the community, as is indeed also, however, the pursuit of personal gratification without regard to the consequences for others. In a community where individuals and groups are perceived as highly interdependent in the pursuit of desired ends, the loss of participation is felt as a blow to the values of the community, and of course even the legitimate pursuit of purely personal ends may be felt to pose a problem. This is not to say that the individual is sacrificed to the community. Supposedly, the ends pursued in concert are among those that are valued by him, as a member of the community, even if not the only ones valued by him as an individual with other group memberships, needs, and areas of living.

Psychotherapist: The kind of community you describe seems to me to impose quite great strains upon the individual. Is the psychotherapist supposed to cope with all these? Besides. . . .

Sociotherapist: Let me try to deal with that objection before you go on to another one. I think we must differentiate in dealing with the problem of individual tensions between the job of the psychotherapist in relation to these and what tools he uses to cope with them, and the job of the community in relation to these and what tools are used in the community to cope with them. The community of course must concern itself as a social system with the relation between individuals and the community and with the strains that develop in that relation and within individuals that might jeopardize the individual's participation in the community. This is especially so in a community that avoids adapting to pathological characteristics of its members, thus creating strains, and that emphasizes interdependence and therefore the importance of the participation of its members, also thereby creating strains.

What accommodative mechanisms are available in the community for dealing with such strains? According to my own analysis of community structures, focusing upon the relation between individual and community and mitigating intrapersonal strains arising from or affecting the individual's relation to the community comprise the function of the Small Groups. For these groups to perform such a function effectively, their reorganization and an increase in the level of skills in the staff participating in them are necessary. Such changes include staff acceptance of and commitment to such a function; and perhaps the reorganization of the groups so that their membership is more homogeneous. Each group might comprise those who experience common strains in the community: for example, young unmarried men, young unmarried women, those who work or go to school outside the community, those who are especially withdrawn, those who are older and have families, those who are new to the community, those who are leaving it. Such changes in organization, supposing they do occur, will only take place over a long period of time, if we may judge from our previous experience. This is especially so because the only personnel we now have available to work with the Small Group Program do so on a very part-time basis. However, increased attention to this program may now occur as a result of the nursing staff's growing interest in the program and the organization of a patient-staff committee to administer it, analogous to the Work Committee, Activities Committee, and Community Council: the Small Group Committee.

The limitations in the present functioning of the Small Groups with respect to aims that of all community groups they are potentially most able to fulfill, illustrate that we face other problems in relation to the community than the possibility that in some situations what conceivably might be intended to have desirable consequences for the functioning of the community might not necessarily have such consequences for particular patients, or the converse. In some situations, there may be no necessary conflict about what would be desirable for both the community as a whole and particular individuals in it, but our resources, the state of our knowledge, the extent of our skills, the degree of staff integration, and current exigencies, among other factors, might still make the achievement of that desideratum at a particular time relatively impossible.

Psychotherapist: What happens to the individual in the kind of community you are describing, particularly the individual who does not fit in, the individual who shares no ends with other members of the community, perhaps is not even committed as they are to the therapeutic enterprise? Why should we as therapists be concerned about a particular patient's commitment to the community and participation in it, just because such commitments are necessary for the functioning of the community?

Sociotherapist: You tend continually to speak from the point of view of the individual patient, his welfare, his wishes, the consequences of any action for him, his right to make any choice, even to remain uncommitted to treatment itself. I find myself in this discussion almost automatically slipping into that framework too, I suppose because of the predominance of individual psychotherapy here and the fact that the hospital is dedicated to the aim of the treatment of individuals. However, I believe that a specialized function within that treatment enterprise should involve concern with the situation in which the patient is treated, especially the community or social system, which to one extent or another involves the conditions making commitment to treatment, participation in such a process, and personal growth possible.

You want to know what a particular event or intervention means to a particular individual. I am interested, within the scope of my function as sociotherapist as it contributes to the treatment enterprise, with the consequence of an event or intervention to the social system as a whole, to the functioning of its enterprises. I am interested in what interferes with establishing and maintaining that intensity and dependability of value commitments leading to some level of participation necessary for activities actualizing those values to take place; that degree of adherence to norms or social orderliness and interdependent collaboration required to sustain such activities; that degree of availability of resources, including facilities, money, personnel, skill and knowledge, required by such activities; and some degree of collective decision-making determining priorities among competing ends.

In other words, I am concerned with what it takes for this particular social system to work at some generally acceptable level, to survive, to maintain itself and its enterprises. The state of the social system is the object of my concern in the same way that, as a psychotherapist, the object of your concern is the state of the personality system of the individual patient.

Psychotherapist: What decides how well the community should work, how high our aims for the functioning of its enterprises should be? Would not a community of individuals each more or less going his own way be somehow more congruent with the values of psychotherapy? Such a community would involve greater freedom for the individual, greater opportunities for personal expression and the exercise of personal autonomy, and expose him less to irrational social pressures. Some regression may be necessary for growth, especially in the context of a relationship with one other person who is trusted. The community's emphasis on performance and participation only encourages the adoption of a kind of premature "good citizen" role. A hospital community should not emphasize achievement at the expense of tolerating, facing, and giving opportunity for the expression of the pain, anger, distress, and longings of patients who are trying to grow and change. If letting the individual alone does not always lead to good, I am not sure that in the end it does not lead to the most good for the most individuals. In any event, it sounds less complicated and as though it would certainly require less effort and less time from the staff, who might then be freed to devote themselves to other endeavors that are conceivably just as, or more, important.

Director of Treatment: There seems to be a continuum of possibilities; perhaps as an organization we may have to experience some of the possibilities, and struggle as best we can as a staff with the problems that will certainly arise no matter what choice we make at any particular time. We face a rather interesting question: does the differentiation of the psychotherapeutic and the sociotherapeutic function in carrying out our treatment aims have useful consequences for the achievement of those aims? If so, how do we resolve issues involving an emphasis on different kinds of consequences by representatives of these two functions?

THE THERAPEUTIC COMMUNITY AND THE INDIVIDUAL PATIENT

A beginning may be made in investigating the output of the therapeutic community to the personality systems of individual patients by describing differences between psychotherapy and sociotherapy, as previously defined, with regard to their orientation to the individual patient.

1. Focus on the individual as a system versus focus on the individual as a unit within, or a member of, a particular social system. The psychotherapy collectivity studies the personality system of the individual and the relationships of elements within that system, including role-expectations deriving from his membership in collectivities outside the hospital. Psychotherapy is concerned with the patient's orientation to other than social objects (e.g., the patient's own body).

The collectivities of the therapeutic community are primarily concerned with the individual as an interacting actor in the hospital community as a social system: his relations with others; his orientation and action toward and with them; his expectations of himself and others, and the expectations others have of themselves and of him; the values and norms shared by him with others and the extent of his conformity to such shared values and norms. The system of reference is the social system.

2. *Priority given to ego-integration or autonomy versus priority given to collectivity-integration or heteronomy.* Psychotherapy tends to be concerned primarily with ego-integrative problems, the consequences of an action for the integration of the individual, and perhaps secondarily at the collectivity-integrative level with the consequences of action for the integration of the psychotherapy collectivity.

The collectivities of the therapeutic community tend to be concerned with collectivity-integrative problems, the consequence of an action for the collectivity of which the patient is a member, including the hospital as a whole.

3. *Relatively wide scope of interest in patients versus relatively narrow scope of interest in patients.* Psychotherapy is concerned with the patient's long-term motivation and adequacy to fit roles in collectivities outside the hospital; the collectivities of the therapeutic community, primarily with his immediate motivation and adequacy to fit roles within the hospital.

4. *Direction of process from within individual outward versus direction of process from situation and the relation of the individual to objects inward to consequences of these in intra-individual states.* Psychotherapy tends to start with inner states of the individual (tension, feelings) and to move outward to a consideration of the situation and his relation to it. The initial question is likely to be: "How do you feel?"

The collectivities of the therapeutic community tend to start with the situation, for example, changes and processes within another intra-hospital collectivity; these in turn may be responses to changes and processes in the informal patient group or in staff groups, which in turn may be responses to changes and processes in the world outside the hospital. Such collectivities then respond to the situation with performance. Such performance may result in malintegration in the social system or tension within an individual, which subsequently must be dealt with. On the other hand, such collectivities may start with malintegration arising from vicissitudes within the social system, leading to performance, possibly a reformulation of goals. The initial question is likely to be: "What is the situation and what will you (we) do now?"

5. *Influence upon, and concern with, aspects of action determined by relatively fixed elements within the personality system versus influence upon, and concern with, aspects of action determined by the immediate situation and the individual's orientation and action in relation to it.* Psychotherapy is designed to influence relatively fixed structures and well-established dispositions within the personality, and tends to be concerned with those aspects of action which are determined by such structures.

The collectivities of the therapeutic community are concerned with transient dispositions to deviance and states of intrapersonal tension arising from the immediate social object-situation within the hospital. These collectivities are concerned especially with influencing those aspects of action which are determined by the situation, including the attitudes and expectations of others, and by the individual's understanding of this situation and capacity to alter himself (when indicated) to respond appropriately to its exigencies, vicissitudes, and opportunities. The development of certain disciplined capacities and the alteration of certain need-dispositions may occur, and do occur throughout life, as a result of the structure of the object-situation, its inducements and opportunities for expressive, instrumental, and responsible action. It is the structure of this object-situation that is the province of collectivities in the therapeutic community program.

6. *Priority given to insight versus priority given to imitation and identification as means of learning.* Psychotherapy may give priority to insight as a means of learning, although not invariably; collectivities in the therapeutic community almost always give priority to imitation and identification.

The Nature of the Community's Interest in the Individual

The therapeutic community is interested in the individual as an actor and in the nature of his action. The following questions indicate in what outputs from the individual patient (in the form of social action) various collectivities are interested, as part of what is required by the collectivity if it is to accomplish its particular function in the social system. Such questions are essentially criteria for what is relevant and what irrelevant for the group to know about an individual for social problem-solving; fears that voyeuristic curiosity, or desires to shame and retaliate, determine quests for information in the community are exacerbated by the absence of such criteria.

Information about Each Individual in the Community
Needed by the Work Committee (Adaptation Group)

MOTIVATION REQUIREMENTS. How interested is he in work and learning work skills? How important for him are work and getting things done, compared, for example, to enjoyment and self-expression, or concern with evaluating and promoting responsible behavior between people? To what extent does he seek work of some kind and to what extent does he avoid any kind of work? Does the Work Committee regard him as part of the available work force in the community?

INTEGRATION REQUIREMENTS. In the community does he prefer to work by himself or with others? Can others with whom he works depend upon him? What happens between himself and others when he works with them in the community? Does he interfere with, or facilitate, the work of others in the community, and if so how?

ADAPTATION REQUIREMENTS. What work skills has he demonstrated? What work skills does he lack? What skills has he learned in the community, if any? What kind of work does he do best? What kind of work does he do least well? What kind of job is he best suited to be recruited for? What incentives are likely to be effective in recruiting him for that job?

CONSUMMATION REQUIREMENTS. To what actual work achievement in the community has he contributed? What was the contribution? To what work achievement has he made little or no contribution? What, if any, leadership—direction, organization, a good suggestion, taking a leadership position—has he provided in community work?

THE WORK PROGRAM. What specifically about the Work Program—the particular work that is done and the particular way it is organized—is at odds with his specific needs, skills, or existing commitments to values or norms? Is there any opportunity for him to do the job he is best suited to do or most wants to do: is there any call for his particular skills?

Information about Each Individual in the Community
Needed by the Activities Committee (Consummation Group)

MOTIVATION REQUIREMENTS. How interested is he in having fun, in self-expression? How important are enjoyment and creativity to him? How much does he value fun and self-expression as a part of life, compared, for example, to work and getting things done, or concern with evaluating and promoting responsible behavior between people? To what extent does he seek opportunities to have fun and to express himself and to what extent does he avoid such opportunities? Does the Activities Committee regard him as available for contributing to fun in the community?

INTEGRATION REQUIREMENTS. Does he prefer to have fun or to express himself by himself, away from the community (by himself or with others), or in the community (with others)? Does he prefer to have fun or to express himself in situations using opportunities provided by the Activities Committee or in the informal life of the community? Does he interfere with, or facilitate, the fun and self-expression of others, and if so how?

ADAPTATION REQUIREMENTS. What skills and talents in having fun or expressing himself has he demonstrated in the community? What skills and talents does he lack when it comes to having fun or expressing himself? What skills and talents in having fun or expressing himself has he learned or improved in the community, if any? In what kinds of activities situation does he have the most fun and express himself most creatively? In what kind of activities situation does he have the least fun and express himself least creatively? What incentives are likely to be most effective in recruiting him for participation in activities?

CONSUMMATION REQUIREMENTS. When and how has he contributed to enjoyment, fun, and self-expression in the community? What, if any, leadership—direction, organization, a good suggestion, taking a leadership position—has he provided in any enterprise aiming at increasing enjoyment, fun, and self-expression in the community?

THE ACTIVITIES PROGRAM. What specifically about the Activities Program—the particular activities available and the way they are organized—is at odds with his specific needs, skills, or existing commitments to values and norms? Is there any opportunity for him to use the particular skills, talents, and preferred ways he has for having fun and expressing himself? Are these appreciated or devalued, held as legitimate or illegitimate, in the community?

*Information about Each Individual in the Community Needed
by the Community Council (Integration Group)*

MOTIVATION REQUIREMENTS. How interested is he in behaving responsibly in relation to others, in considering the consequences of behavior to others and modifying behavior accordingly? How important to him is responsible social behavior in himself and in others? How much does he value behaving responsibly in relation to others as a part of life, compared, for example, to work and getting things done, or fun and self-expression? To what extent does he seek opportunities to make this a more responsible community and to what extent does he avoid such opportunities? Does the Community Council regard him as a responsible member of the community?

INTEGRATION REQUIREMENTS. What is his attitude toward the rules, regulations, policies, codes, traditions, mutual agreements of the community, and to specific ones of these? To what extent does he seem genuinely committed in his behavior to these? To what extent does his lack of commitment express itself by nagging or self-righteously forcing others to live according to various ones of these? To what extent does he seem merely living according to the "letter of the law," with picky adherence to one or another rule, but without his heart or intelligence being actively involved? To what extent does he seem to have to attack, challenge, or rebel against, in a stereotypical way, all rules, regulations, and mutual agreements? To what extent does he simply avoid living according to such rules, regulations, and mutual agreements by withdrawing from others and seeming not to recognize or notice them or the mutual agreements by which they live, settling instead into a world of his own? Does he interfere with, or facilitate, the efforts of others to live by the mutual agreements of the community, and if so how?

ADAPTATION REQUIREMENTS. What skills has he demonstrated in the community for helping to work out mutual agreements by which people can live when there is a problem, disagreement, or difficulty in social living? How skillful is he in helping to figure out what is causing a difficulty or problem in social living? How skillful is he in working with someone whose behavior is undermining some mutual agreement of the members of the community, so that the behavior is mitigated rather than exacerbated? What skills of this sort does he lack? What skills of this sort has he learned in the community, if any? To the extent he has such skills, in what situations—for example, formal meetings or informal contacts—does he make best use of them? In what situations is he least able to make use of them?

CONSUMMATION REQUIREMENTS. To the solution of what actual problem in social living has he contributed, and in what way? What, if any, leadership—direction, organization, a good suggestion, taking a leadership position—has he provided in any group or committee trying to work out a problem in social living or arrive at a mutual agreement by which people would be willing to live?

THE COMMUNITY COUNCIL. What specifically about the rules, regulations, codes, traditions, policies, and mutual agreements of the community, the way in which these are enforced, and the extent to which these are enforced or not, is at odds with his specific needs, capacities for social responsiveness and responsible behavior, or existing commitments to values or norms? Are the means by which the Community Council copes with deviant behavior suitable to his particular kind of deviance, and effective with him given his existing capacities and attitudes? Does he require more help from outside himself to live according to mutual agreements than is available in the community? Do the particular rules, regulations, mutual agreements, and informal as well as formal norms of the community, come into conflict with those he has been living by before he came into the community? How adequate have the mechanisms for acquainting someone with the formal and informal norms of the community been with him?

Information about Each of Its Individual Members Needed
by the Small Group (Motivation Group)

MOTIVATION REQUIREMENTS. To what extent does he seem to want to belong to this community, to value and join in its enterprises, to respect and support such therapeutic goals and values as, for example, personal growth; change; self-examination and self-discovery; openness, knowledge, self-awareness; facing painful realities; seeking and giving help; tolerating discomfort in situations in which participation and effort, in spite of anxiety or dysphoric affects, are required to do what must be done to achieve the task; learning from experience; trying out new ways of working, enjoying, relating to others? To what extent does he seem to choose to be apart from, separate from, uncommitted to, such therapeutic goals and values?

INTEGRATION REQUIREMENTS. How has he made use of the Small Group to express and resolve feelings of doubt, despair, disappointment, or anger in relation to happenings in the community and his relations to the community? Does he tend and prefer to discuss feelings and beliefs about happenings and issues in the community and his relationship to the community with his Small Group, in informal groups, with a nurse, with some other person or group in the community, or not with anyone in the community? Does he seem to value or devalue the Small Group, the other members of the Small Group; to what extent does he contribute to, or undermine, the solidarity of the group? What are differences in the way he participates in the formally organized groups in the community from the way he participates in the informal life of the community? How does he relate to nurses? Does he come to them primarily for services? If so, what kind of services: personal (companionship) or impersonal (pills, medical attention)? When, if ever, and in what way has he ever worked with nurses to help someone or to help improve some situation or deal with some crisis? What impact, if any, does the way in which he relates to members of the opposite sex, to members of the same sex, in informal situations have upon the community, upon others' or his wish or ability to participate in its enterprises and work toward making its therapeutic goals and values an actuality?

ADAPTATION REQUIREMENTS. What kind of situation in the community has led to his having feelings of doubt, despair, disappointment, anger, or criticism, and a desire to withdraw from the community and its enterprises? The lack of what resources makes him tend to sink deeper and deeper into such feelings, to become overwhelmed by them, and to withdraw from the community? What resources does he have that make it possible for him to use the Small Group to work out such feelings so that he is ready after talking with the group to "give it another try." The lack of what resources leads him to give up in the face of doubt, despair, disappointment, and anger? What resources does he have that make it possible for him to keep trying to reestablish his relationships to the community and his commitment to its therapeutic goals and values?

CONSUMMATION REQUIREMENTS. How does he respond in the Small Group to others' expressions of doubt, despair, disappointment, or criticism in relation to happenings in the community? Does his response seem to undermine or strengthen others' desire to belong to the community and join in making its therapeutic goals and values an actuality? If so, how? Does his way of living in the community seem to undermine or strengthen others' commitments to belong to it, and to participate in its enterprises, and their belief in and desire to live in such a way that its therapeutic goals and values will be realized? If so, how?

THE SMALL GROUP. What specifically about the Small Group—its composition, the degree and kind of skills possessed by its members, its degree of solidarity, the degree of clarity members have about the task of the group and the extent to which they are committed to it, its arrangements for accomplishing its task—is appropriate to or does not match his needs, capacities for commitment and social responsiveness, level of socialization? What about the Small Group specifically facilitates or prevents his using it to express and work out interpretations and beliefs about community happenings, issues, expectations, and tasks, and the feelings of doubt, despair, disappointment, anger, and criticism arising from his perceptions and experiences of these; to find his place in the community; and to establish and hold on to his commitment to the goals and values of the therapeutic enterprise?

Sociotherapeutic Outputs to the Individual Patient

Sociotherapy seeks, then, to influence aspects of individual behavior determined by the situation, given the individual's capacity to understand that situation and to alter himself to respond appropriately to its features. Sociotherapy may be conceived to have an eventual output to the individual patient's personality system through alteration of the structure of the object-situation with its inducements and opportunities for expressive, instrumental, and responsible action; and through making objects available to the patient as he participates in the collectivities of the therapeutic community for use, cathexis, identification, and respect, such object-relationships resulting in the internalization of value patterns and orientations appropriate to the various types of action involved.

In the psychiatric hospital that views the patient primarily in his aspect as social object (a system of action capable of interaction) rather than in his aspect as physiological organism or physical object incapable of interaction, learning (resulting from insight, imitation, and identification) effects alteration of the internal structure of personality systems of individual patients as systems of action. In the therapeutic community the primary means of learning or acquiring new ways of orienting, which will significantly and most generally change the structure of personality systems, is identification. Identification involves the internalization of relationships with diffusely cathected social objects (individuals and collectivities) as models of mutual (reciprocal and complementary) orientations, expectations, and actions, including the value patterns integrating these.

Ordinarily, a person has identified with members of his family, more precisely, with the mutual orientations and actions, and the value patterns integrating these, involved in his relationship, for example, with his mother (his expectations of her and of himself in relation to her, her expectations of him and of herself in relation to him); with his family as a collectivity of which he is a member, in which he has roles, and to which he relates in terms of his expectations of the concerted contingent reactions of this collectivity to what he might do (here, a system of multiple differentiated roles and role-relationships is internalized); with his school, and his peer group. The precipitates of such identifications constitute the structure of the patient's personality system.

The ego may be conceived to denote a set of ways of orienting (modes of cognition, cathexis, and evaluation), organized in relation to one another. The adaptive ego is oriented to cognitive mastery of the situation as means. It is a precipitate of experiences in Adaptation Groups. The executive or libidinal ego may be conceived to denote a differentiated part of the ego, which involves the allocation of cathexis, includes orientations primarily to the physiological organism as object, and is based upon the earliest identifications in the individual's life. It is a precipitate of experiences in Consummation Groups. The superego may be conceived to denote the internalized norms or role-expectations the individual has shared with others as a member of various collectivities. Since these norms are internalized, they guide his orientations as part of his own personality system rather than as objects in his situation. According to internalized normative standards, the individual evaluates alternatives. The superego tends to be a precipitate of relatively early experiences in the individual's life in Integration Groups. The ego-ideal denotes a set of internalized value patterns. This aspect of the personality system tends to be diffusely positively cathected by the individual (regarding his personality system as object) rather than ambivalently cathected as is the superego, and tends to be a precipitate of relatively later experiences in Motivation Groups.

The therapeutic community provides collectivities, differentiated in terms of their aims or the subsystem of the social system to which they belong; patients become members of such collectivities, which may become for them objects of identification. Relationships, involving mutual (reciprocal and complementary) orientations, expectations, and actions, may be internalized, thus altering the patient's modes of thinking, feeling, and evaluating.

In relation to, and participating on, the Work Committee, individuals will learn specific instrumental skills: how to work; how to solve cognitive-instrumental problems of understanding reality through reality testing and of applying such knowledge; how to master and adapt to an object situation; how to satisfy interests in using instrumental capacities through relationships with objects of utility. The personality-system-directed output of this collectivity is to the adaptive ego.

In relation to, and participating on, the Activities Committee, individuals will learn specific expressive patterns: how to enjoy and give enjoyment and gratification; how to allocate cathexes appropriately; how to substitute one object of cathexis for another when necessary; how to express inner states in symbolic patterns; how to gratify need-dispositions for affective relationships with objects of cathexis. The personality-system-directed output of these collectivities is to the executive or libidinal ego.

In the Community Meeting, and in relation to, or participating on, the Community Council, individuals will learn new ways of evaluating, new ways of assessing and weighing consequences, will internalize new values shared with others, and satisfy needs of affiliation through relationships with objects of identification in a moral community. The individual learns how to form relationships involving affective ties but integrated with diffuse obligations and responsibilities, rather than relationships involving simply affective gratification of specific need-dispositions. The personality-system-directed output of these collectivities is to the superego.

In the Small Groups, where tensions interfering with motivation are resolved and where patterns of commitment to values are established or reinforced, the personality-system-directed output is essentially to the ego-ideal.

Role-expectations for participants in each collectivity will differ, as well as role-expectations within a collectivity, depending upon the problem involved. In the Community Meeting, for example, impersonal categorization of objects and restricted interests in them are expected when the problem is means-selection; classification of objects in terms of doing and attitudes involving desires for discharge are expected when the problem is goal-selection; personal categorization of objects and expansive interest in them are expected when the problem is norm-selection; classification of objects in terms of being and attitudes involving inhibition of discharge are expected when a problem is meaning-selection. On the other hand, in the Work Committee, classification of objects in terms of doing and disciplined attitudes toward them are expected when understanding the situation cognitively is the problem; in the Activities Committee, classification of objects personally and interest in restricted aspects of them and the specific need-dispositions to which these relate are necessary when the problem is to represent such objects symbolically or expressively; and in the Community Council, classification of norms in terms of what they *are* and affective attitudes toward them are necessary to make a moral evaluation of the situation.

In the Work Committee inability to take a neutral, disciplined attitude will handicap a participant from whom cognitive activity is required. In the Activities Committee, inability to see an object in terms of its relation to a specific need-disposition will handicap a participant in making use of the object to express the need-disposition symbolically. In the Community Council the inability to take an affective attitude toward norms (to care about a commitment to them) will handicap a participant in evaluating a situation from a moral point of view. Such an inability in a staff member is as much a handicap to him in his participation in such collectivities as it would be to a patient possessing it. Similarly, for a patient (or staff member) to take an attitude required, for example, in the Work Committee into the Community Council is likely to result in strain and malintegration within the latter group.

For most patients, what seems most apparently to be lacking is the ability to subordinate, at least at times, personal concerns to an orientation to the welfare of a collectivity of which a patient is a part but which also transcends his individual personality; as well as the ability to cope with reality by accepting limits and boundaries, paying attention to specific aspects of objects, inhibiting immediate discharge in the interest of secondary process thinking governed by cognitive standards of validity, accepting impersonal definitions of objects including oneself and impersonal criteria for performance including one's own, and achieving or performing in relation to objects in reality. Major outputs to the personality system from the therapeutic community might seem to be, then, the internalization of collectivity-oriented values as well as self-oriented values; and the internalization of adaptation values—doing, impersonal, restricted, inhibition.

However, with respect especially to the apparent priority of the internalization of adaptation values, it is likely that the output to personality systems is a more complex one. That output might be formulated as the ability to choose between value-orientations in terms of the recognition of the requirements of the type of action, interest, or social process with which one is at any particular time involved, rather than to be fixed in one's value-orientations and to be governed by them in choosing between alternatives no matter what the circumstances. The implication of this view is that the output of the therapeutic community to the personality systems of patients is the internalization of adaptation values, as a result of the actualization of these values through patients' participation in adaptation processes; the internalization of consummation values, as a result of their actualization through participation in consummation processes; the internalization of integration values, as a result of their actualization through participation in integration processes; and the internalization of motivation values, as a result of their actualization through participation in motivation processes. The commitment to such values is generated by experiences of growing confidence in relation to objects of utility; of an increased capacity for gratification in relation to objects of cathexis; of solidarity with objects of identification; and of esteem or respect for objects representing the values of a social system.

The significant output of the therapeutic community to individual personality systems is the internalization within them of values, of a high degree of generality, which are shared by the members of this community. The internalization of shared values within individuals, or the institutionalization of such values in the groups to which these individuals belong, is the process of major interest to the sociotherapist working in the therapeutic community.

However, a frequent preoccupation of staff working in hospital communities is instead bringing about patient conformity to situation-specific, function-specific behavioral norms. This preoccupation is usually associated with a failure to distinguish between the establishment of situation-specific, function-specific norms as part of the situation to which the patient relates, which he considers expediently as means, obstacles, or conditions with respect to the achievement of his own ends; and the internalization of such norms within the personality system of the patient such that commitment to behavior in accordance with them exists irrespective of the presence of external positive or negative sanctions. Similarly, a hospital staff in its work with patients is likely to ignore the distinction between the mere presence of values as cultural objects in the situation, patients expediently conforming to or evading them, and the internalization of these values; as well as the distinction between situation-specific and function-specific norms, on the one hand, and the more general values from which a wide range of norms are derivable, on the other. The establishment of, and maintenance of conformity to, norms in the hospital situation are likely to receive an excessive amount of attention; the establishment and internalization of more general values little attention at all. The failure to make such distinctions may be related to the desire to make changes in a hospital unit embedded in a larger hospital organization, or to make changes in a hospital embedded in a larger organization with other purposes such as a military service branch, without disturbing unduly, jeopardizing support from, or arousing counter-reactive measures by, the more inclusive social system, the structure and institutions of which express the prepotent general values inevitably governing, but perhaps at odds with those motivating the desired changes in, part of the social system. In any event, staff focusing upon conformity to norms rather than internalization of values may, then, conclude from their efforts that a therapeutic hospital setting does not result in lasting posthospital behavioral changes (Fairweather 1964).

Fairweather and his colleagues formed small task-groups of patients in a hospital ward. Each group was held responsible as a unit for the behavior and progress of its members. Each group met without staff to solve the shared problems of its members; staff, however, met to evaluate and make the final decisions concerning the group's solutions of these problems. Fairweather and his colleagues concluded as a result of their study of the differences between this ward and a traditional ward with no such task-groups that patients learn situation-specific norms, rather than general attitudes or values, and that change of behavior on the ward is no guarantee of change of behavior in the posthospital situation or in recidivism. However, members of the task-groups had essentially to deal and cooperate with each other as means or obstacles to obtaining rewards and approval from the staff controlling these. Mere expedient conformity to norms, of course, is unlikely to be an enduring outcome. (Edelson 1966b; Fairweather 1964.)

VALUES, BELIEFS, RULES, AND WAYS OF WORKING IN A THERAPEUTIC COMMUNITY

Some basic values and beliefs in a hospital, in which psychotherapy and sociotherapy are integrated treatment modalities, and a way of working arising from such values and beliefs, might be expressed as follows.

Illness represents an incapacity that cannot be overcome simply by an effort of the will; some kind of therapeutic process is necessary. This essentially means that an individual is not held responsible nor blamed for being ill.

Illness results in some legitimate exemptions, varying in degree and duration, from normal role and task obligations. Such exemption is conditional on the basic recognition by the patient that illness is an undesirable state, and that as an ill person he has an obligation to collaborate with others to get well—that is, to accept the need for competent help, to seek it, and to collaborate seriously with the source of such help in an effort to get well.

The interrelated goals of the hospital are to help patients with illness get well; to advance knowledge about human beings, emotional illness, and the treatment of individuals with emotional illness; and to teach those who, in one way or another, cope with emotional illness. An inseparable goal associated with these is to maintain the kind of hospital in which the previously stated goals can be achieved.

Psychotherapy is a major treatment modality in the hospital. For it to be most effective, such psychotherapy should occur in a setting in which patients are leading active, responsible lives, and participating in activities other than psychotherapy, including work, play, and attempts to solve problems of life in the hospital community. In their attempts to cope with the problems generated by community life, patients should have as wide a range of freedom to choose between alternatives as is consistent with the achievement of the goals of the hospital.

To accomplish the goals of the hospital, active collaboration, not simply passive cooperation, between patients and staff is necessary. A therapeutic community is one in which staff and patients are allies in the fight against that way of life called illness and in the attempt to build a way of life in which personal growth is possible. Such a therapeutic hospital community is characterized by the interdependence of all its members in such efforts.

With respect to any event or phenomenon, a therapeutic community program staff or sociotherapy staff focuses upon situational determinants, rather than intrapersonal determinants. Its goal is to contribute to the achievement of the hospital's treatment goals through the investigation and alteration of, and contributions to, the social situation: the social system of the hospital community.

An attempt to create a situation in which patients become committed to new ways of living because values are internalized (rather than merely conform to, or evade, norms) must probably involve a wholehearted participation of patients as a group in, and a collective sense of responsibility for, the problems generated by their own community life. Such participation and sense of responsibility probably depend on the maintenance and enhancement of the autonomy of individual patients and of the patients as a group. Any participation, intervention, or attempt to influence the social situation to potentiate therapeutic processes and minimize nontherapeutic outcomes should, then, occur in a way that actualizes the value of such autonomy. However, respect for autonomy should not be used by staff to rationalize abrogation of responsibility for attempting to influence the situation especially in the interest of the therapeutic enterprise and patients' welfare.

It is clear that any intervention must navigate among dilemmas. What is therapeutic for one individual may not be for another. What is helpful to the functioning or sense of well-being of one group may not be to another. Any course of action always has mixed consequences, which must be weighed against each other; there are always unexpected consequences as well. Yet such dilemmas should not constitute an excuse for the staff to be passive, to abrogate leadership, or to take refuge in not having any passionate conviction about issues that arise. Nevertheless, the staff is always faced by the difficulty in expressing its convictions especially about what constitutes a situation necessary for therapy, for growth, for development, that patients, who are apathetic and who feel helpless and dependent, may merely passively or expediently acquiesce to these convictions.

To mitigate such difficulties, the staff may try to structure any situation so that it presents alternatives, requiring a choice to be made. Such a staff in its work with the community does not suggest, embark upon a course of action, intervene in a certain way, or go off on its own to conclude or decide something, without consulting the patient group and offering explicit alternatives.

In attempting to influence the choice to be made when alternatives are presented, the staff may try to make explicit to patients what are the values staff members hold that are inherent in the therapeutic enterprise and what are other personal values determining staff preferences. Such a staff, remembering how hard it is to assert oneself when mother says, "I do it because it is good for *you*," does not talk as if the only thing concerning it is the good of patients and their treatment. The staff is open with patients concerning the vested interests, conflicts, and problems of various staff groups, which might lead any one of these to try to influence patients in particular ways, and presents, when necessary, to patients the pressures upon staff from groups or social conditions outside the hospital. The staff does not talk as if the patients' treatment were what was always and necessarily uppermost in staff feeling and thinking, neither therefore defending nor idealizing itself, when such external factors are operating; nor use such factors as a rationalization for depriving the patients as a group of a sense of choice or the right to attempt to exert an influence on the situation in terms of values and interests of importance to them.

Such a staff might try to encourage patients in every way and at every opportunity to discover together what their own wants and values are, rather than simply to try to find out what the staff wants and values. The staff does not assume that every question that comes up calls *first* for a staff opinion or an historical explanation of why things are done this way in this hospital; that is, an assertion of tradition, or a reminder to the group of some rule, as though that settled the matter. Instead, a rule is conceived to exist to indicate an area of difficulty which may always be reexamined in the light of current realities or needs. First, patients are helped to express their own wishes, preferences, and imagined resolutions or solutions; the staff listens with manifest interest to these expressions, indicating a grasp and appreciation of them, rather than responding immediately with an answer, a correction, a rebuttal, a caution, or by remaining silent.

No rule (norm) or tradition in this kind of community is sacred; problem-solving processes in the here and now are prepotently valued. Any rule, policy, or procedure may be questioned and frequently reexamined in the light of current experience. Rules are guides, not tyrants. A rule requires neither automatic submission nor rebellion, but rather thought. A rule should provoke neither obedience nor disobedience primarily, but rather awareness (in which skepticism and respect intermingle) of the group in relation to the world of people, things, and ideas around it. Rules do not relieve anyone of the necessity to exercise personal judgment, but rather mark the opportunities when it is important to do so.

A rule states merely that as a group we have had problems in this area before and that once we concluded that such-and-such an agreement or procedure might help. If it does not help, it has outlived its usefulness. It has no sacred value in itself; its only value is in relation to the purpose for which it was formulated. A new time, situation, or group may require a new living arrangement or procedure for organizing work or governing play.

It is probably true that a group offering no resistance to change is likely to be a group without cherished values, without stability, without identity. However, if any rule, policy, or program seems excessively difficult to change when change seems indicated and desired by those likely to be most affected by it, then the status of that rule, policy, or program needs to be carefully reconsidered. Of course, such a rule, policy, or program may be vitally related to values and goals to which everyone is deeply committed, perhaps, although not always, unknowingly. It is also possible that fear is dominating intelligence. If there is not an immediate, obvious, simple reason for a rule, procedure, or program, which can be stated to anyone without embarrassment, without an elaborate piling-up of reasons, and without appeals to faith and future revelation, then it is suspect. If there are no sanctions, if there are no consequences, when a rule is broken; if there are negative responses from others when one breaks a rule but no positive responses when one follows it; or if sanctions, when a rule is broken, are disproportionate, or seem to have little intrinsic relation, to the rule broken, or if sanctions are inconsistently or inflexibly, or emotionally rather than impersonally, applied, then these matters, indicating and causing strain, need to be explored.

The essential quality of a therapeutic community resides not in adherence to traditions nor in a static order but rather in a continuous day-by-day effort to examine what is going on, to understand and make better the lives of its members, to make real the values (and to achieve the goals) they share. If such a community must occasionally face a choice between quiet and orderliness, on the one hand, and liveliness and learning, on the other, if one must be chosen at the expense of the other, then the therapeutic community will prefer the latter to the former.

The sociotherapy staff in a therapeutic community may try to create situations in which patients will become important to, and learn to care for, assist, and rely upon, each other, rather than simply depend upon staff and their relationships with members of the staff. The staff tries to avoid falling into the trap of supporting one group of patients as the "good guys," expressing what the staff believes, against another often troublesome challenging group, supposedly the "bad guys," since it is probable that members of both groups are expressing one side of an ambivalence shared by all. Instead, groups of patients are helped to face their own differences and the necessity to work these out together.

The staff may encourage patients to contrast and compare their own wants and values with, and assert these against, those of the staff, pointing out that patients have the freedom to choose between their own wants and values and those of the staff. Patients will always find this hard to believe, so it must be demonstrated in action by staff. The staff may have to repeat frequently that even if choice is risky, risks are sometimes worth taking; that even if patients make a mistake, learning may result from it; and that although a staff member possesses skills and competency (available as resources to the group), he is not omnipotent or all-knowing. When a staff person does not know, he may say so. When he feels he does know, he may say so, especially when the group asks for or seems to need help, but may offer help and opinions undogmatically and without assuming they must be accepted because he gives them.

The staff does not simply withdraw in silence or passive observation: "Let the group work it out itself." If a staff member gives information or brings up a problem, he tries to respond to what the group does with it and to indicate what he has learned or will do as a result of the group's work. In any situation, even if a staff member does not offer something himself, he tries to respond to and appreciate the expressions, opinions, and suggestions of others.

Above all, as the staff wishes to be influential, so it is ready in turn to be influenced by what patients say. When the staff is so influenced, it says so and indicates how, regarding it as worthwhile to change one's mind or decide upon a course of action upon the evidence, opinions, and feelings offered by members of the group, rather than to assume that these are just gripes, expressions of immaturity, dependency, or rebellion, or letting off steam. The staff avoids the attitude that it is the process of democracy that counts but that the substance of what patients say or try to do is unimportant, inconsequential, or wrongheaded, since it is doubtful that personal growth or genuine collaboration between groups is fostered by permitting people to express their wishes, values, and opinions but then not taking these seriously.

The staff may try to create genuine opportunities for patients actually to influence and change the structure, program arrangements, policies, and norms of the hospital, even if they cannot always change the thinking of the staff. The staff avoids taking a suspicious, looking-with-a-jaundiced-eye stance, which suggests that patients always act carelessly, impulsively, and according to their ids or transferences and that the staff person therefore must provide a check on their actions, contributing whatever ego, wisdom, foresight, and caution are likely to be found in the place. The staff tries to remember that a solution to a problem should not only allay fears, but should satisfy wishes, meet needs, and make life better or easier as well. Patients are not asked to take responsibility for areas where they have no authority. One group doing something for another or being checked by another is not collaboration; collaboration is something that occurs between equals.

However, the primary goal of the staff is not safeguarding the autonomy of the patients as a group, or increasing their authority as an end in itself. Emphasis on such a goal is likely to result in staff members being afraid to interfere with what patients are doing, no matter how unrealistic and at what cost to the achievement of the goals of the hospital, and in staff members listening and waiting for patients to take the initiative, to bring things up, no matter the cost to group tasks for which both patients and staff are responsible.

It is easy for staff and patients to lose sight of the fact that these two groups are actually dependent on one another for achieving the goals of the therapeutic community: maintaining motivational commitments, order, and opportunities for mastering the situation in the interests of achieving satisfying ends. The staff cannot do these things by themselves. The patients cannot do these things by themselves. Staff cannot nurse, maintain motivation to participate in treatment, teach skills, avoid coercion in maintaining order, treat patients with respect and dignity, without the help of patients. Patients cannot alter the situation in which they live without the help of staff. Both groups depend on the skills, attitudes, resources, and participation of the other to achieve goals in which both have a vital stake. Yet patients are likely to feel they are independent and autonomous only when they can do something or have something all by themselves without interference; or instead, prefer to turn everything completely over to the staff to take care of. Staff, similarly, are fearful of losing control of prerogatives and resources, or, instead, feel they cannot interfere in the patients' business. The ideal of interdependence, in which each needs the other to perform some vital, unique, needed role or function, and in which each can count on the other to do his part, is much more complicated and difficult even to keep steadily in mind, much less to act consistently in terms of, than is the ideal of being completely independent or conferring complete independence upon another.

CONCLUSION

The therapeutic community comprises the interdependent patient, staff, and patient-staff collectivities, whose primary focus is the social system of the hospital community, rather than the individual personality system or the relation between the individual patient and groups in the extended society. As a reflection of the institutionalization of the values of psychotherapy, a therapeutic community involves a collective effort by patients and staff to learn to understand the nature of a social system integrated around values intrinsic to psychotherapy; the often conflicting values, aims, and interests struggling within such a social system; the complex equilibria represented by its institutions; and the complicated reciprocal influence of personality systems and the social system. In short, patients and staff, informed by skills and knowledge pertinent to sociotherapy, collaborate in participating in, and investigating, the social system, in a way that is analogous to the participant-investigation of the personality system that goes on in intensive psychotherapy. Such investigation of the social system is facilitated by an organization of the community into collectivities with differentiated functions. In addition, with respect to output to individual personality systems, such organization provides clear models of adaptation, consummation, integration, and motivation groups. In participating in such groups, patients may not only learn to experience and understand the relation between these different kinds of social processes, but may also internalize patterns or orientations relevant to instrumental action, expressive action, responsible action, and processes involving commitment to, and respect for, systems of values and the social objects representing them.

To this endeavor, the sociotherapist brings an orientation to the situation or social system rather than the personality system as the object of analysis. He brings skill in contributing—and influencing the distribution and allocation of—roles, functions, or kinds of participation relevant to particular kinds of occasions or social processes.

He brings an interest in group processes, including intergroup relations; and knowledge of the covert or unconscious, and often shared, meanings groups and organizations or their parts have for the individuals participating in them, and of the covert aims group members share, which determine to some extent their relation to one another, to their leaders, to other groups, and to the tasks which they presumably have joined together to achieve. The sociotherapist participates to achieve the resolution of intragroup and intergroup strains, which interfere with the attainment of various group ends generated by the requirements of community life in the hospital, or which militate against the institutionalization of the treatment values constituting that community insofar as it is therapeutic.

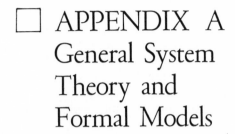

☐ APPENDIX A
General System
Theory and
Formal Models

A formal model is a proposition or set of propositions, stating a relationship or relationships between formal concepts, and applicable to any system in which such relationships exist between aspects of the system. A formal concept is an abstract idea that does not represent any aspect of reality. Formal propositions are those which state relationships between formal concepts. Examples of formal propositions are $1 - 1 = 0$ or $A = XY$. Algebra and the various geometries, Euclidean and non-Euclidean, are examples of systems of propositions, stating relationships between formal concepts, which are manipulated by definite rules, and which may or may not be applicable to a particular aspect or system of empirical reality (Gasking 1956; Hempel 1956a, 1956b; Mises 1956; Veblen and Young 1956; Weyl 1956; Wilder 1956).

If formal concepts are coordinated with concepts representing aspects of an empirical system, deductions from propositions relating formal concepts may lead to the discovery of relationships between concepts representing aspects of reality. This occurs when relationships between concepts in the formal model and relationships between aspects of the empirical system are logically homologous—that is, when they have the same formal characteristics.

The first half of this discussion, especially influenced by the general system theory of Bertalanffy, was written in part some years ago (Edelson 1954) and subsequently revised.

Essentially the program attempted by Lewin in psychology was the coordination of concepts referring to psychological phenomena with concepts in a formal system, topological geometry, so that deductions made within the latter system might lead to the discovery of significant relationships between concepts representing psychological reality (Lewin 1935, 1936, 1951).

A coordinating proposition is one that connects a formal concept and a concept representing an aspect of reality. Some possible interpretations of the terms of the formal equation $F = MA$ are: F is force; M is mass; and A is acceleration. These interpretations are examples of coordinating propositions. By manipulating $F = MA$ according to the rules applying to the formal system to which it belongs, we may discover relationships between force, mass, and acceleration.

An empirical system is any specified portion of empirical reality which the scientist has chosen to study. This system may be of any degree of complexity. It may be a single material particle, a microscopically visible body, a living organism, or even the entire universe. It may be distinguishable by some isolating characteristic, such as a boundary, which to a greater or less degree limits exchange with or the influence of reality external to it.

A conceptual system consists of a set of propositions which may be applicable to describing and explaining an empirical system. Aspects of the system are represented by concepts. These concepts are used by the scientist in formulating propositions about the system he is studying.

There is a widespread assumption that the use of a model for explanatory purposes involves the actual or imagined construction of some kind of visualizable apparatus, some aspect of whose functioning is supposedly similar to the phenomena to be explained. Such models—for example, a box of elastic balls, a complex arrangement of electrical circuits, or a system of pipes through which water flows—are always called mechanical (the affect associated with this epithet depending upon the prejudices of its user) to distinguish such explanation from that which does not involve an analogy to a visualizable apparatus.

The essential utility of such a model actually rests upon the assumption that, since some aspect of the model's functioning is similar to the phenomena to be explained, the equations which make it possible to predict the consequences of the apparatus's functioning will likewise be useful in making predictions about, and otherwise accounting for, the phenomena to be explained. It is not necessary, indeed, it may be ridiculous, to assume (although the assumption is often made) that the structure of that which lies behind the phenomena to be explained is similar to the structure of the model apparatus. Thus, even though we might find we can account for psychological phenomena by the use of equations whose form is identical to that of equations used in the explanation of an electric circuit, it is not advisable on that basis to conclude that the reality which underlies psychological phenomena consists of an electric circuit.

The use of a visualizable apparatus is a very special example of the use of an explanatory model; the actual model involved is the proposition or set of propositions stating a relationship or relationships which are applicable to the description of both the visualizable apparatus and the phenomena to be explained.

Many interesting examples of formally identical or isomorphic "laws"—which appear, not only in different areas within physics "where the same differential equations apply, for example, to the flow of liquids, of heat, and of electric currents in a wire," but in completely different fields as well—are given by Bertalanffy. For example, the same equation (that is, with the same form but different content) describes autocatalytic reactions in physical chemistry, cases of organic growth in biology, and in demography the growth of human populations in a limited space. Principles of minimum action appear in social science to describe population dynamics, as well as in mechanics, physical chemistry, and electrodynamics. Principles of oscillations apply to the neon lamp, nerve physiology, and organic communities (Bertalanffy 1951).

It is possible to regard as coincidence that the same formal relationship is applicable to different systems, the descriptions of which require quite different sets of variables. On the other hand, we may view this fact as a result of the limitations of our intellectual tools, of ourselves as thinking machines. Another possibility is that the applicability of a formal proposition to different systems is a consequence of the simple orderliness of the reality which we are attempting to understand (Bertalanffy 1951).

The "isomorphism of natural laws" is an expression of characteristics, such as periodicity, which the systems to which the laws apply have in common. This "logical homology" or "structural correspondence" of systems inspired Bertalanffy to "postulate a *new basic scientific discipline*" called "general system theory," which is concerned with "general system laws applying to any system of a certain type," irrespective of the totally different nature of the entities or elements involved or of any differences in the particular properties of the systems.

These laws hold generally for classes of systems, no matter what the particular entities involved. The exponential law, for example, states that a constant percentage of the entities of a system decay or multiply per unit time. Therefore, this law is applicable to a system consisting of pounds in a banking account, a colony of bacteria, or a population of individuals.

If the increase is limited by restricting conditions, this is stated by a law of somewhat different form. It applies to autocatalytic reactions, in which a compound formed catalyzes its own formation; in a closed vessel, the reaction must stop when all the molecules are transformed, and therefore approaches a limiting value. Similarly, this law applies to a population increase, which approaches a limit determined by the maximum population that can be supported by such limited resources as space and food.

The parabolic law describes a system in which there is competition between elements, each one taking its share according to a capacity which is expressed by a particular constant. The law has the same form whether it describes individuals competing in an economic system, or organs competing within an organism for nutritive material (Bertalanffy 1951).

In other words, from the general characteristics of a system (that its phenomena are periodic, for example) we know the form of the proposition that will be useful in explaining the behavior of that system: we arrive at the formal model that is appli-

cable to the system. In order to interpret this formal model, we must know the reve-
lant variables of the system. Choosing and defining these variables is one of the
creative acts of the scientist, for he thereby determines the possibility of coordinating
empirical aspects of the system to be studied with the terms of the formal model and
thus the possibility of discovering and describing lawful relationships.

Systems studied within the same area of knowledge or even in widely different
areas of knowledge may be logically homologous or exhibit structural correspondence. If so, the formal model applicable to one such system may be applicable to
others. The form of the model remains the same but it is interpreted as it is applied
to each system by coordinating the particular variables relevant to that empirical
system to the formal concepts of the model.

An interesting attempt to demonstrate that a single conceptual system can em-
brace many of the seemingly disparate empirical systems studied in psychology has
been described by Woodrow and may serve as an example of this kind of enterprise
(Woodrow 1942).

Reluctance to use a formal model expressed in the language of mathematics (Kubie
1947) may be based on the misunderstanding that the usefulness of such a model is
proportional to the degree to which the phenomena to be investigated can be measured. Measurement, however, is not the basic characteristic of a mathematical system. Mathematical systems have been shown by modern analysis to consist essentially
of propositions stating logical relationships between axiomatic entities, that is, formal
systems which may be interpreted to apply to empirical reality. The power of such a
system does not derive from its use of quantitatively measurable constructs, but in
the fact that frequently surprising consequences can be strictly and precisely derived
from such propositions by manipulations according to the rules of logic (Gasking
1956; Hempel 1956a, 1956b; Lewin 1935, 1936, 1951; Mises 1956; Veblen and
Young 1956; Weyl 1956; Wilder 1956).

Formal models in general have great potential usefulness to the behavioral scientist in his efforts to explain the phenomena with which he is concerned. Thinking in
terms of the relevant formal model is heuristic; it leads to a clarification of the fundamental character of the phenomena to be investigated. The fundamental character
of the phenomena is reflected in the form of the relationship between crucial variables as indicated by the model. Gaps in thinking are revealed as the behavioral
scientist attempts to interpret systematically the formal model that he feels is most
relevant to the empirical system he is studying. Making explicit the formal model
upon which a nonmathematically stated theory is based is of great utility in any
attempt to understand and clarify the concepts and propositions of that theory.

It is useful to juxtapose Parsons' ideas about the nature of theory and systems
with the foregoing, demonstrating the essential convergence of two lines of thought
with quite different starting points and empirical realms in mind.

Parsons (1937) has held that theory is to some extent an independent variable in
the history of science. What it is to be does not depend alone on the discovery of
facts. The formation, alteration, and integration of theory are interdependently
related to empirical investigations. But it unfolds to some extent independently:
determining what facts are of interest; creating expectations that certain facts will
be discovered.

A theory is a more or less integrated system of logically interrelated propositions. A substantive change in one important proposition has logical consequences for the others. A theoretical system is closed when each logical implication that can be derived from any one proposition is stated by another proposition in that system. These statements do not mean that every proposition in a theoretical system is deducible from any one proposition in the system.

A theory not only accounts for known facts but implies the expectation that certain facts will be discovered on investigation. The satisfaction or disappointment of this expectation determines whether the theory is verified or altered. A theory has similar implications for fields related to, but different from, its immediate area of concern.

A fact is scientifically important if it has consequences for a theoretical system. Scientific importance has no necessary relation to practical importance. All empirical observation implicitly or explicitly involves selection and some degree of abstraction guided by a conceptual scheme. There is no such thing as a simple fact identical with an empirical phenomenon. A fact is not a part of nature, but is a statement about phenomena in terms of some conceptual scheme. Facts are not phenomena (concrete, existent entities) but propositions that select for comment certain aspects of the phenomena that are important to some theory.

One type of concept makes up the frame of reference determining what facts are significant, belong together, and will be observed. The spatiotemporal framework of classical mechanics, concerned with facts that refer to a body or bodies located in space and time relative to other bodies, the supply and demand schema of economics, and the more general means-end schema of the theory of action are examples.

Another type of concept represents actually or hypothetically existent concrete entities, whose interrelatedness constitutes the structure of empirical systems. Concepts representing concrete units or parts, such as a piston or valve, organ or cell, or (when existence in space is not inherent in the frame of reference) a pure type, such as a rational or irrational, religious or secular act are examples.

A third type of concept represents the general attributes or properties of an actually or hypothetically existent concrete phenomenon or unit. Mass, velocity, and location (the particular values of which describe a particular physical body) and rationality and disinterestedness (the particular values of which describe a particular act) are examples.

The frame of reference consists of axiomatic concepts and axioms or basic assumptions. The same facts may be stated in the terms of more than one frame of reference. One frame of reference may be a special case of another, more general one; one frame of reference may cut across another. To describe a phenomenon in terms of a frame of reference does not explain anything. Nor does it necessarily imply that a complete explanation of the phenomenon is possible within this theoretical system.

The fallacy of misplaced concreteness is to be avoided. An aspect of phenomena selected and located in terms of a frame of reference should not be mistakenly accepted as an obvious concrete fact. It is actually highly abstract. As an abstraction, it should not be mistaken for what is existent in phenomenal reality. Any abstraction leaves out a great deal that is there.

A defined object of scientific interest is described in terms of its parts—the parts of an empirical system. A concrete object may be broken down into parts that are spatiotemporally existent concrete entities. An empirical system may also be divided by postulation or abstraction into parts that are hypothetically existing entities or pure types. Hypothetical entities are potentially observable. Pure types are conceivable as existent entities, although not necessarily ever actually to be observed in pure form. Hypothetical entities or pure types do not merely represent parts of a single phenomenon, but parts common to a plurality of phenomena. Empirical generalizations are statements about such hypothetical entities or pure types under a variety of definable circumstances.

In certain empirical systems, called organic, the relations among parts determine the characteristics of individual parts, that is, determine the substance of empirical generalizations. Such relations also determine characteristics of the system as a whole (the so-called emergent properties of an organic system) as distinct from properties of a system that represent a simple sum of the properties of its aggregate parts.

Analytical elements or concepts, representing general attributes or properties, are, when measurement is possible, called variables. Analytical laws state the uniform mode of relation of analytical concepts. Any particular occurrence of a general property is represented by a particular value. Operations (measurement, arrangement in order of magnitude, classification more complex than a single continuum of variation) order occurrences of a general property so that values may be assigned to an analytical concept. Choice of operation is ideally determined by that degree of precision required by and adequate for the purposes of a particular theoretical system.

The part of an organic empirical system is an abstraction; it cannot be observed apart from its relations to other parts. A general attribute or property is an abstraction; only its particular value in a particular occurrence can be observed.

Parsons regards an action system as boundary-maintaining. He describes a system as a set of interdependent units. A unit is a particle; from the point of view of the system under consideration, the only interest in a unit is the nature of its relations to other units in the system. To consider intra-unit relationships is to regard the unit as a system, no longer simply as a unit in a system. The units of a boundary-maintaining system have determinate relationships with each other. The patterns of these relationships may vary within defined limits. Variations beyond these limits result in the disruption of the system. This does not imply a static equilibrium state of no change. Change may occur continuously within a structure of unchanging forms of relationship. In addition, the structure of determinate relationships constituting the system may include a determinate pattern of change in relationships.

The determinate relationships between units, then, define the conditions for the existence or survival of the system. These relationships also determine the boundary of the system, differentiating the system from its environment. Units participating in a set of determinate relationships are part of the system; other units are outside the system. "Outside the system" is the environment of the system. A boundary-maintaining system no longer exists when there is no difference between it and its environment.

Such a system is subject to changes in the relationships of its units arising: from the vicissitudes of its environment, that is, the impact of shifting conditions on the system; from the vicissitudes of relationships between units within the system, that is, the impact of these on other relationships; from the nature of a unit itself considered as a system having its own particular requirements to meet for boundary-maintenance, that is, the relationships between the constituent units of a unit-as-system undergo vicissitudes influencing that unit's participation in the system.

Following a particular change in a state of equilibrium (a state of stable determinate relationships between units), a boundary-maintaining system responds with operations the function of which is to return the system to equilibrium. To maintain its boundary, the system performs different kinds of operations, the function of each one being to effect the solution of one of four kinds of system-problems.

Two system-problems, adaptation and goal-attainment, involve relationships between the system and its environment. Adaptation is the control of units or systems in the environment and the relationship of the adapting system to those environmental units or systems, including the interchange of entities between them, in the service of goal-attainment. Goal-attainment is the establishment of a relationship with a unit or system in the environment consistent with or contributing to the boundary-maintenance of the goal-attaining system—or, contrariwise, the avoidance of a relationship with an environmental unit or system not consistent with or disruptive of such boundary-maintenance.

Two system-problems, integration and latency, involve units and relationships between units within the system. Integration is the control of relationships between units within the system. It is the maintenance of stable determinate relationships through the prevention or reversal of tendencies, arising from vicissitudes in the relationships between units, to change the pattern of relationships beyond certain limits, that is, in ways not compatible with the survival of the system. Latency (pattern-maintenance and tension-management) is the control of intra-unit states, units, or relationships between parts of the unit (regarded, then, as itself a system with parts, not simply as part of a system). Latency involves the prevention or reversal of tendencies arising from within the unit-as-a-system that would interfere with, and the creation of structures within the unit-as-a-system that would make possible and facilitate, contribution of the unit to the boundary-maintenance of the system through its participation in relation to other units.

☐ APPENDIX B
Talcott Parsons'
Pattern Variables

The plasticity of the actor is such that his attitudes or dispositions to relate in certain ways with respect to the objects in his situation are not predetermined. The ambiguity of the object world is such that the actor's categorization of an object in his situation is not predetermined by the object. Therefore, the actor is permitted to choose between alternative ways of giving meaning to or conceiving a particular situation. Indeed, he must choose among a definite number of alternatives (inherent in the action frame of reference) in order that a situation have determinate meaning to him. To describe action completely, from the observer point of view, the alternatives an actor might have selected, but did not, must be considered.

The orientation of the actor in a particular situation determines the direction of his effort and the way in which it will be expended. There are three modes of orientation: cognitive, cathectic, and evaluative. The cognitive mode of orientation includes: the discrimination and location of objects in relation to one another and to the actor; determination of the properties and actual and potential functions of such objects; generalization of these objects and relations between objects and their properties into classes; prediction regarding the future state of objects in relation to one another and to the actor. The cathectic mode of orientation includes: the assignment of positive or negative value to an object in terms of its relation to a goal of the actor; the attribution of significance to the object in terms of its actual or potential relation to positive or negative states of the actor; disposition on the part of the actor to avoid or approach the object in the future. The evaluative mode of orientation includes: assessment and comparison of immediate objects among each other, and of the possible relationships with them, in terms of consequences and implication for future relationships with objects; weighing and evaluating alternatives (e.g., between goals or means) and considering consequences of choices among such alternatives; making choices between alternatives, and planning distribution of time and effort between objects, goals, occasions for goal-attainment.

Evaluative or value standards may guide, justify, or provide the basis for judging evaluative processes and their results. There are three kinds of value standards: cognitive standards, determining whether or not facts are relevant, problems important, cognitive judgments true or valid; appreciative standards, determining whether or not a cathexis, or choice between alternatives, is consistent with good taste or appropriate aesthetically; moral standards, determining whether or not the extended consequences of a choice between alternatives or a course of action are right or moral. There are two kinds of moral standards: ego-integrative moral standards, assessing consequences of action for the actor and for the integration of the actor regarded as a system; collectivity-integrative moral standards, assessing the consequences of action for the integration of a larger system of which the actor is a member.

Parsons' terms, ego and collectivity, are misleading, since the actor in the first instance may be a collectivity that is the subsystem of a larger system. When a collectivity regards the standards of a larger system as binding upon or controlling its actions, collectivity-integrative moral standards determine the action of the collectivity. But when it acts irrespective of the standards of a larger inclusive system, with concern only for consequences for its own integration, then ego-integrative moral standards determine the action of the collectivity. The terms are more appropriate when reference is to an individual actor, whose actions may have consequences for the integration of his own personality system and for the integration of the collectivity of which he is a member.

Value orientation includes cognitive, appreciative, and moral standards, making up the norms of action an actor is committed to observe, and the standards and criteria guiding his choices among means, goals, and courses of action.

Types of cultural systems—systems of symbolic objects—are: belief systems, characterized by primacy of the cognitive mode of orientation; systems of expressive symbols, characterized by primacy of the cathectic mode; systems of value-orientation, characterized by primacy of the evaluative mode.

The cathexis of a mode of orientation and its corresponding cultural system as means or goal is called an interest. There are three kinds of interests: cognitive interests (in knowing); cathectic interests (in feeling and enjoying, in wanting and establishing relations with goal-objects); evaluative interests (in integrating, in resolving conflict).

Types of action are: instrumental action, characterized by primacy of cathectic interests and appreciative standards with respect to a given goal, and by primacy of

The fourth pattern variable describes alternative ways of categorizing an object; the fifth pattern variable describes alternative attitudes an actor may take toward an object.

The fourth pattern variable is quality-performance. Quality is the alternative that an object will be categorized in terms of its qualities, irrespective of its performances. Performance is the alternative that an object will be categorized in terms of its performance or performances, past, present, or future, irrespective of its qualities.

The fifth pattern variable is diffuseness-specificity. Diffuseness is the alternative that an object has significance to the actor in many of its aspects; the actor has diffuse interest in the object, many of his dispositions are directed to the relationship with the object. Specificity is the alternative that an object has significance to the actor in one of its aspects. The actor has specific or segmental interest in the object: one of his dispositions is directed to the relationship with the object.

The pattern variables constitute a point of articulation of personality, cultural, and social systems. They enter on the concrete level as five choices made by a concrete actor. They enter on the personality level as a set of dispositions to choose consistently in terms of a given pattern of such choices. They enter on the cultural level as constituents of value standards prescribing one or another pattern of such choices in a particular type of situation. They enter on the social level as constituents of role definitions including expectations of conformity to one or another pattern of such choices.

Two pattern variables are particularly important in classifying the properties of actors: their attitudes or dispositions toward objects. These two pattern variables are affectivity-neutrality and specificity-diffuseness. Two pattern variables are particularly important in categorizing objects. These two are universalism-particularism and quality-performance.

cognitive standards with respect to the means for attaining the goal; exp
action, characterized by primacy of cathectic interests and appreciative sta
(e.g., expressing a need-disposition through expressive symbolism); respons
moral action, characterized by primacy of evaluative interests and moral sta
Instrumental action includes: investigative instrumental action, its goal—cc
problem solution; creative instrumental action, its goal—new expressive sy
patterns; applied instrumental action, its goal—the use of knowledge in a wa
than investigative or creative instrumental action.

Five pattern variables describe five choices that must be made in any acti
that together in any instance form a pattern of choices. These variables d
analytically dichotomous alternatives—not continua. They are derived from i
minacies in the organism such that there is no predetermined order of p
among modes of orientation, and from ambiguities in the object situation. T
choices made comprise a pattern or constellation of selections determining the
orientation.

The first pattern variable is affectivity-neutrality, which represents a ch
primacy between the cognitive-cathectic modes of orientation (in concrete
inseparable, although analytically distinguishable) and the evaluative mode of
tation. Affectivity is the alternative that cognitive-cathetic modes of orientati
determine action without evaluation of consequences to the actor or to the
of which he is a member. Neutrality is the alternative that action will not occu
evaluation (including, usually, the invocation of value standards) has occurre

The second and third pattern variables represent choices of primacy betwee
orientations.

The second pattern variable is universalism-particularism. Universalism
alternative that—whether or not moral standards have primacy in evalua
cognitive standards have primacy over appreciative standards; therefore, obje
tend to be clssified in terms of some general frame of reference, irrespective c
relation to the actor. The significance of the object is in its universalistically c
properties, its inclusion in classes transcending the particular system of relati
between object and actor. Particularism is the alternative that—whether or not
standards have primacy—appreciative standards have primacy over cognitiv
dards. Therefore objects will tend to be classified in terms of their relations
the actor. The significance of the object lies in its inclusion in the same sys
relationship with the actor, not in its relation to other objects classified as intrin
similar to it.

The third pattern variable is self-collectivity orientation. Self-orientation
alternative that, when evaluation occurs, cognitive, appreciative, or ego-integ
moral standards have primacy over collectivity-integrative moral standards, c
no evaluation occurs and thus no standards are invoked. Collectivity-orienta
the alternative that evaluation occurs and collectivity-integrative moral star
have primacy. This pattern variable is on a different level of generality than the
four. It is actually a special case of the internal-external axis of differentiation
it refers to a hierarchy of control: whether or not considerations of the integrat
a system will control the actions of a unit of that system.

☐ APPENDIX C
An Alternative Model
of the
Treatment Enterprise

A model for the treatment enterprise might involve, rather than differentiation of sociotherapy and psychotherapy as two concrete enterprises, a view of psychotherapy as one type of enterprise within the social system defined as the therapeutic community. Furthermore, in this model, instead of viewing each concrete collectivity as maximally differentiated to perform the entire functions of one of the four subsystems of the therapeutic community, we may view concrete collectivities as differentiated to perform only certain component-functions of, or phases of a process of action in, a particular subsystem; therefore, a theoretically distinguishable subsystem may include more than one concrete collectivity.

Suppose a hypothetical therapeutic community to include the following concrete collectivities, comprising both patient and staff members: a Work Committee; an Activities Committee; a Community Executive Committee, a Community Policies Committee, and a Community Council (or a Community Council embracing the functions of all three); Small Groups; a dyadic psychotherapy collectivity; and a Community Meeting.

The Community Executive Committee, as one possibility, might consist of staff members from the Work Committee, the Activities Committee, and the hospital business office, an assistant head nurse, the assistant to the medical director, and patient chairmen of the Work Committee, Activities Committee, and Community Policies Committee, as well as four patients elected at large from the Community Meeting.

The Community Policies Committee might consist of one staff member and one patient elected from each Small Group.

The Community Council might consist of the head nurse, and two patients who have been in the hospital a longer period of time than other patients, appointed by the Executive Committee.

The Small Groups might consist of a staff member primarily concerned with tension-management, one primarily concerned with the state of community values, and a small group of patients (around six).

The Community Meeting might consist of the members of all these other collectivities, including all psychotherapists since the integration of processes within the psychotherapy collectivity and processes within other collectivities in this model requires the presence of psychotherapists at the Community Meeting.

Figure 21 summarizes the position of each collectivity in relation to the subsystems of the hospital.

	MOTIVATION COMPONENTS OR PHASES	INTEGRATION COMPONENTS OR PHASES	ADAPTATION COMPONENTS OR PHASES	CONSUMMATION COMPONENTS OR PHASES
MOTIVATION SUBSYSTEM	Psychotherapy Small Group	Community Meeting	Psychotherapy Small Group	Psychotherapy Small Group
INTEGRATION SUBSYSTEM	Psychotherapy Small Group	Community Meeting	Community Council Community Policies Committee	Community Council Community Policies Committee
CONSUMMATION SUBSYSTEM	Psychotherapy Small Group Activities Committee	Community Meeting	Community Executive Committee Activities Committee	Community Executive Committee Activities Committee
ADAPTATION SUBSYSTEM	Psychotherapy Small Group Work Committee	Community Meeting	Community Executive Committee Work Committee	Community Executive Committee Work Committee

Fig. 21. Therapeutic community programs and committees in relation to abstract subsystems of hospital organization.

This hypothetical organization is relatively differentiated. The degree to which concrete collectivities coincide with specific theoretical subsystems and components of subsystems is an index of differentiation. The more highly differentiated an organization is, the greater the problem of coordinating different individual and collective members of the hospital. Such an organization requires mechanisms to achieve not only the avoidance of interference with one another but also the achievement of collaborative efforts toward common goals. The Community Meeting is such a mechanism. The less differentiated an organization is, the greater the problems arising from the incapacities and limitations of individual and collective members of the hospital. These members are responsible for a variety of functions and may not have the necessary range of skills and resources to perform all these functions equally well. In addition, they may be unable to shift, either actually or in the eyes of others, from one pattern of orientation, action, and values to another as these must change in relation to changes in the type of problem confronted. Such an organization especially requires mechanisms to select relatively gifted individuals in this sense, or sophisticated training programs for individuals.

The Work Committee contributes primarily to the adaptation subsystem of the hospital. Its primary tasks are in sectors Adaptation (adaptation component) and Adaptation (consummation component): to assess the needs of various collectivities in the hospital for personnel (workers), through representatives from these various collectivities; to make decisions about the allocation of workers among the situations in which they are needed. In addition, in the Adaptation (motivation component) sector, the Work Committee is responsible for the creation and maintenance of specific instrumental capacities through skill-training on the job.

The Work Committee depends upon other collectivities for dealing with the consequences of its decisions for individuals, for collectivities, and for the hospital as a whole, as well as for dealing with deviant individuals not fulfilling expectations or conforming to prescribed norms of behavior in relation to work. The Work Committee must, therefore, establish collaborative relationships with these collectivities.

The Activities Committee contributes primarily to the Consummation subsystem of the hospital. In the Consummation (motivation component) sector, it is responsible for the creation and maintenance of specific expressive capacities and appropriate expressive patterns of orientation and performance. It accomplishes its function through formal classes and the teaching of such patterns in expressive activity (recreation, parties, theater, art, music, writing). The Activities Committee, in the Consummation (adaptation component) and Consummation (consummation component) sectors, assesses the needs and wishes of individual and collective members of the hospital for goal states in which such wishes and needs may be appropriately gratified; and provides occasions (recreation programs, parties, plays, forms of art activity, music programs, a literary magazine) for the attainment of such states.

The Work Committee creates relations with objects that can be used for something. It is responsible for cognitive-instrumental processes culminating in useful or instrumental action; instrumental action is its output to other collectivities, including the Activities Committee (which, for example, might request a crew from the Work Committee to build a set for a play). The Activities Committee creates relations with objects that are enjoyed as ends in themselves, irrespective of any uses they may have. It is responsible for processes culminating in expressive action; expressive action is its output to other collectivities, including the Work Committee (which, for example, might request a program from the Activities Committee inspiring the audience to work).

The Community Executive Committee is responsible for making instrumental and expressive decisions, its output to other collectivities. In the Adaptation (adaptation component) sector, it assesses the hospital situation, processes and exigencies in the informal patient group or in various staff groups, which constitute the immediate environment and which in turn are affected by exigencies in the hospital's external environment. In the Adaptation (consummation component) sector, the Community Executive Committee decides upon ways to obtain means to deal with such exigencies. In the Consummation (adaptation component) sector, the Community Executive Committee assesses the wishes of individual and collective members of the hospital community, usually through representatives of collectivities. In the Consummation (consummation component) sector, it decides upon a goal to be pursued in the hospital community, allocates facilities for its attainment in preference to some other, and also allocates rewards.

The Community Policies Committee is responsible for making policies or deciding upon norms prescribing behavior in specific situations. In the Integration (adaptation component) sector, it determines the need—or responds to the request of other collectivities—for a norm. In the Integration (consummation component) sector, the Community Policies Committee decides upon norms prescribing behavior in specific situations.

The Community Council is responsible for the institutionalization of these policies or norms, and insuring the adherence of individuals to them. In the Integration (adaptation component) sector, the Community Council evaluates the actions of individuals in relation to prescribed norms, such individuals being referred to the Community Council by other collectivities. In the Integration (consummation component) sector, the Community Council decides upon the specific application of a sanction in a particular situation, and utilizes a variety of mechanisms of social controls to achieve internalization of normal expectations. The output of the Community Policies Committee and the Community Council to other collectivities (including the Work Committee, the Activities Committee, the Community Executive Committee, Small Groups, psychotherapy collectivities, and the Community Meeting) is responsible action or internalization of shared norms and dependable reciprocation with others in interactions involving mutual orientations, rights, and obligations.

A family-like Small Group contributes to the motivation subsystem of the hospital, and to the motivation components or phases of the adaptation, goal-attainment, and integration subsystems. In the Adaptation (motivation component), Consummation (motivation component), and Integration (motivation component) sectors, the Small Group: deals with the consequences to the individual, manifested in states of tension, of decisions made in the Adaptation (consummation component), Consummation (consummation component), and Integration (consummation component) sectors concerning the allocation of facilities and rewards, the goals or wishes to be pursued or gratified, the norms to be prescribed, and the sanctions to be applied; creates and maintains motivations to perform instrumentally (requiring collaboration and coordination with the Work Committee and Community Executive Committee), to want and seek the fulfillment of desires and the achievement of goals (requiring collaboration and coordination with the Activities Committee and the Community Executive Committee), and to affiliate with others in a community (requiring collaboration and coordination with the Community Policies Committee and Community Council). In the Motivation (motivation component) sector, the Small Group creates and maintains motivation on the part of the individual to commit himself to beliefs and normative sentiments, and deals with intra-individual tensions arising from difficulties in making, or reluctance to make, such commitments. In the Motivation (adaptation component) sector, the Small Group discusses questions individuals have about the meaning of events in the hospital, and attempts to answer such questions in terms of some general framework concerning beliefs and normative sentiments about health and treatment, resulting when successful in the development, in the Motivation (consummation component) sector, of attitudes of respect and esteem for the hospital (or for a decision or action of the hospital, or of a collectivity representing the hospital, e.g., the Community Council).

The dyadic psychotherapy collectivity has functions in the same motivation subsystem and motivation components or phases of other subsystems in which the Small Group has functions. The psychotherapy collectivity and Small Group differ in the following ways.

Organization. The dyadic psychotherapy collectivity consists of one psychotherapist and one patient; the Small Group consists of one or more (preferably two) staff members, and more than one patient.

Focus. Psychotherapy focuses upon the personality system, its organization, and its integration, including the role-expectations of, and role-relationships in, collectivities outside the hospital, as well as realms other than role-expectations and interactions with social objects (e.g., the orientation and action of the individual in relation to his own body, or need-dispositions toward physical or cultural objects). The Small Group focuses upon the consequences to the individual of the role-expectations of, and role-relationships in, collectivities within the hospital—the individual's response to, and feelings about, these.

Level. Psychotherapy tends to cope with well-established need-dispositions to deviance and tensions arising from well-established mal-integrations of the personality system. The Small Group tends to cope with transient need-dispositions to deviance arising from the immediate situation (e.g., the individual's responses to, and feelings about, decisions made by the Community Executive Committee, the Community Policies Committee, Community Council, Activities Committee, or Work Committee, and expectations by such collectivities to which he may not feel inclined or capable of conforming, conformity to which he may feel costs too much in terms of the apparently necessary sacrifice of other personal needs, or which he may feel conflict with other expectations he has of himself or which other collectivities within the hospital have of him).

Process. Psychotherapy tends to give priority to socialization and the development of new integrations on the most general level. The Small Group tends to give priority to tension-management.

The Community Meeting contributes primarily to the integration components or phases of the adaptation, consummation, integration, and motivation subsystems. The Community Meeting's task is, through discussion, to apply evaluative processes (weighing and assessing consequences guided by value standards) to the problems of selection: between means in an empirical-cognitive field to be used to achieve a given end (integration component of Adaptation); between goal-states to be pursued, for the attainment of which a given means will be used at the expense of the attainment of other goal-states (integration component of Consummation); between possible norms and types of standards which might be applied in a given situation (integration component of Integration); and between general patterns of meaning—concerning the human condition, the ultimate nature of reality, of human beings, and conceptions of health, illness, and treatment—for understanding the meaning of a particular event or situation in the hospital community (integration component of Motivation). Such problems may come up when collectivities are in conflict with each other or with individuals, when individuals are in conflict with each other, when scarcity of means results in the sacrifice of other goals if a means is used for one goal-attainment, when systems of values are inconsistent or in conflict with each other.

Anyone in the meeting may bring up such a problem. However, problems of selection between means are likely to be brought up by the Work Committee, the Community Executive Committee, or some individual or collective member of the hospital in relation to one of these collectivities. Problems of selection between appropriate goal-states are likely to be brought up by the Activities Committee, the Community Executive Committee, or some individual or collective member of the hospital in relation to one of these collectivities. Problems of selection between norms or value standards are likely to be brought up by the Community Policies Committee, the Community Council, or some individual or collective member of the hospital in relation to one of these collectivities. Problems of the selection between patterns of meaning are likely to be brought up by a member or representative of a Small Group.

The task of the Community Meeting, in response to conflict or disagreement, is to weigh and assess the consequences of various choices, and to formulate the standards and values that will unite members of the meeting and guide the process of making a selection, or on the basis of which a selection already made may be evaluated.

It should be emphasized that each one of these collectivities as a social system must solve its own system problems. Each must take note of exigencies in its situation and respond to these then with adaptive efforts or mastery in the interest of obtaining means to accomplish its goals; achieve desired goals; deal with problems of coordination and collaboration between its members; maintain patterns and manage tension within individual members necessary for participation in the collectivity.

For example, in the Community Meeting: During the adaptation phase, information will be sought and given concerning conflicts and disagreements between individual and collective members of the hospital community over selection of means, goals, norms, or meanings. During the consummation phase, suggestions will be made for the resolution of such conflicts and disagreements. During the integration phase, consequences of various courses of action will be weighed and assessed, and the group will agree upon a normative or value standard determining the selection among the available alternatives. During the motivation phase, individual members of the group will manifest states of increased or decreased tension, resulting from the first three phases.

☐ APPENDIX D
A Document:
Two Orientations
to the Therapeutic
Community

The following document is an example of the kind of polemic that may develop in a hospital organization. It illustrates in particular some of the strains and the anguish—manifest in the polemical tone and in the sense of confusion, injury, and having one's ideas and actions misunderstood—that are likely to arise in a staff group as a new staff member is socialized. Complex social processes are suggested, including the impact on the organization of a new member, especially when his role is at all ambiguously defined; the disruption of previous, highly valued arrangements; and the threat to a subtly interdependent network of norms and values posed by the deviant behavior of the new member, who, in defining a specific treatment role for the therapeutic community, seems to be challenging the supremacy of the psychotherapy enterprise in this area. The response to such complex social processes tends to be crystallized in a community of professional persons around apparently theoretical issues, having, of course, two opposing sides; these issues, however, can never be clearly stated but are debated with indignation and sophistry, suggesting that moral rather than theoretical issues are at stake.

Although no distinction has been made in the following document between the sociotherapeutic function and the psychotherapeutic function, nor between outputs to the psychotherapy enterprise and to individual patients' personality systems, what appears to be contrasted is a hospital community in which the individual psychotherapy enterprise and the therapeutic community program are highly segregated from each other and a hospital community in which the boundaries between these two subsystems of the hospital are highly permeable in both directions; one arrangement is not necessarily better than the other; there are dilemmas intrinsic in each. The dichotomous alternatives presented (e.g. between an emphasis on task-achievement or on affective processes, or between an emphasis on talk, study, and preparation, on the one hand, or action, on the other) are persistent dualities in any therapeutic community. These dualities consist of components, functions, or aims each one of which is an essential part of, or required by, the social system, but is, also, however, inevitably valued to different degrees by different persons or groups with different responsibilities or roles. The distribution of such values among the subsystems of the hospital and the conflicts and competitions between these subsystems, the shift from one alternative to another from moment to moment and from situation to situation, and the consequences of such shifts, constitute a framework for the analysis of processes in the hospital community.

Two Orientations to the Therapeutic Community

Vocabulary Most Frequently Used, and Questions Most Frequently Asked, in Describing and Interpreting Events within the Framework

COMMUNITY PROGRAM AS A PATIENT-CENTERED POLITICAL ORGANIZATION. Power. Who has power? How is it distributed? Who makes decisions? Who is on what side? To whom does an area or activity belong? Who has the right or responsibility to initiate change? Who will win or has won? Freedom. Will, decision, autonomy, coercion, sanction. Action, voting. Is this talk designed to avoid responsible action?

COMMUNITY PROGRAM AS A SPECIALIZED TREATMENT ENDEAVOR. Treatment, education, caring, helping, teaching, learning, feelings, degree of awareness, relationships, anxiety, way of life, understanding, defense, resistance. What anxiety or feeling is being mobilized by problems in, or aspects of, community life? How are they being dealt with? With what consequences? Is this action designed to avoid facing feelings, problems, dilemmas that might be clarified by discussion?

Decisions about Community Life

COMMUNITY PROGRAM AS A PATIENT-CENTERED POLITICAL ORGANIZATION. Decisions made by patients about their own way of life for the most part do not affect the staff, so that the patients should have the major responsibility for, and right to make, such decisions. Responsibility for decision-making is divided, the patients having responsibility for decisions about their own life in the community, each staff group for decisions in its own area, the therapy staff for decisions about treatment—and each group respecting the others' rights. Since decisions made by patients are not viewed as having significant effects on treatment (or at least as having significantly harmful effects), there is no "right" and "wrong" way. Emphasis is on compromise, using a little of every one's point of view, and the emergence of a group product, so that there is as little disruption of harmony in community life as possible.

COMMUNITY PROGRAM AS A SPECIALIZED TREATMENT ENDEAVOR. Every decision made in any area by any group even about apparently trivial aspects of life in the community is a treatment decision—that is, has consequences for the treatment of the patients who live in the community. Responsibility for treatment is shared by patients and all staff. Everyone has a stake in every decision, including those decisions apparently but not really concerning only one patient. Every decision no matter what the area requires participation and consideration by members of all groups. Since every decision has an impact upon treatment, emphasis is on the conflict or opposition between values implied by different decisions, some seen as subverting and others as facilitating treatment.

Problem to Which the Therapeutic Community Program is Directed

COMMUNITY PROGRAM AS A PATIENT-CENTERED POLITICAL ORGANIZATION. Patients have difficulty in the area of will, making decisions, assuming responsibility, taking action, feeling genuinely autonomous. The therapeutic community program is designed to encourage, and provide the maximum opportunity for, independent decision and action on the part of patients.

COMMUNITY PROGRAM AS A SPECIALIZED TREATMENT ENDEAVOR. Patients have difficulty in the area of recognition and acceptance of reality, necessity, physical-social-biological-and-psychological limits. They also have difficulty in tolerating and mastering painful affects. The community program is designed to collide with the patient's usual behavior (narcissistic, omnipotent, unrealistic, flight, regressive, fight) so that he is confronted with reality, including its and his own limits, is required over a period of time and by degrees to face and endure painful affects, and learns to accept the relation between privilege and responsibility.

Role of Staff

COMMUNITY PROGRAM AS A PATIENT-CENTERED POLITICAL ORGANIZATION. Staff person tends to be concerned with what interventions must be avoided so he does not interfere with the maximum opportunity for the patient to exercise will, take responsibility, and make decisions. He may offer advice, opinions, even recommendations, but with care to avoid any implication that these are "expert," or that he has any stake as a staff person in the outcome. More often, he encourages patients to come to their own conclusions and decide for themselves on action to be taken. He attempts to create an equalitarian atmosphere and wishes to participate in a group with patients not as a staff person but as "just another member of the group." He tries to avoid any resemblance to the irrational parent. He responds to group discussion in terms of its content, debating the issues in terms of that content; he tends to believe that resistance and defense are not properly dealt with by a staff person in group situations. Ideally, he believes, change is initiated by patients; and issues are ultimately decided by majority vote.

COMMUNITY PROGRAM AS A SPECIALIZED TREATMENT ENDEAVOR. Staff person tends to be concerned with what interventions are necessary to interfere with and thwart the patient's usual behavior. He assumes that such interference with the patient's character-resistances as these are manifested in his way of life in the community may facilitate the development of the patient's awareness of the attitudes and dilemmas embodied in his behavior and its consequences, the siding of the patient with his psychotherapist against hitherto taken-for-granted and ego-syntonic behavior, and the patient's eventual insight into its origins. Staff person tends to participate as a person with special skills, resources, and insights in the area of human behavior. He anticipates that patients may respond to him as if he were an irrational parent but expects to be able to work this out by trying insofar as he is an authority figure to behave as one rationally and with the patient's interests in mind, and then to contrast the reality of his own behavior with patients' feelings about, and perceptions of, it. He responds to community events and discussions not in terms of content, but in terms of the extent to which these embody expressions of character-resistance in the patients' way of life in the community, and makes interpretations accordingly. Inevitably, change is often initiated by the staff person, opposed by the majority, and occurs only after a long process of education and interpretation. A minority tends to be regarded as expressing or making explicit a significant force in the group. A decision to be meaningful for community life may be, in this framework, one that ultimately involves a real consensus or agreement rather than merely a majority vote, and the process of arriving at such an agreement is an important one.

Intervention and Psychotherapy

COMMUNITY PROGRAM AS A PATIENT-CENTERED POLITICAL ORGANIZATION. Staff person tends to assume that changes in behavior in individual psychotherapy or in the community tend to (and should, to be meaningful) follow changes in feelings, perceptions, and intrapsychic situations. Therefore, individual psychotherapy is the agent of meaningful change, and change in behavior in the community is assumed to follow crucial events in individual psychotherapy.

COMMUNITY PROGRAM AS A SPECIALIZED TREATMENT ENDEAVOR. Staff person tends to assume that at times (because of the nature of ego-impairments and ego-deficiencies, and character-resistances as the latter are embedded in an ego-syntonic way of life) it may be necessary to intervene in individual psychotherapy or in the community to change behavior as a pre-requisite to the development of awareness, insight, and intrapsychic change. Therefore, at times when appropriate, intervention by a staff person or by other members of the community, or collision with the structure and requirements of community organization, may lead to a change in a patient's behavior in the community that precedes and facilitates crucial events in individual psychotherapy.

View of Group

COMMUNITY PROGRAM AS A PATIENT-CENTERED POLITICAL ORGANIZATION. Group tends to be seen as problem-solving work group, proceeding rationally, with recourse to information, hypotheses, testing hypotheses, and evaluation. Affective group states tend to be discounted or avoided by the use of such means as parliamentary procedure, organization of group tasks, and division into committees. Patient members' response to each other or to a staff person tends to be viewed as realistic, embodying a consensual validation of the perception of that person, and as determined primarily by the behavior of that person.

COMMUNITY PROGRAM AS A SPECIALIZED TREATMENT ENDEAVOR. There tends to be a focus on the nature of affective group states and the extent to which these interfere with the group as a work group. Perceptions by others of a group member (patient or staff) even though apparently validated by a majority opinion are often seen to be determined by the affective group state and by processes such as projective identification.

Role of Patient in the Community

COMMUNITY PROGRAM AS A PATIENT-CENTERED POLITICAL ORGANIZATION. Citizen, student, worker, but ideally not as patient. Each role tends to be seen as appropriate to a particular area or aspect of community life.

COMMUNITY PROGRAM AS A SPECIALIZED TREATMENT ENDEAVOR. Person who needs and wants help with his problems in living; also citizen, student, worker. First role is viewed as appearing inevitably with latter roles in all areas of community life.

As an Example, the Following Describes Only Some of the Differences in a Small Group Program within Each of These Orientations

COMMUNITY PROGRAM AS A PATIENT-CENTERED POLITICAL ORGANIZATION. Patients decide purpose and organization of small group. There is no necessary function; the small group may perform any function the community wishes it to. The wishes of the majority determine decisions about the purpose and organization. Elements of final decision are products of many compromises between competing conceptions, ideas, and interests. The acceptability of the program to the largest number is more important than its internal consistency. Staff person is another member of group. Whether or not small group is oriented to action or decision, the group is seen as a rational problem-solving group, and staff respond to action or discussion in terms of the apparent issues and content involved. Patient member of the group is citizen or worker, not patient; therefore, his problems in living are not viewed as proper focus of concern for group.

COMMUNITY PROGRAM AS A SPECIALIZED TREATMENT ENDEAVOR. Staff decide upon purpose of small group and how it is to contribute to the goals of treatment. On the basis of knowledge and experience, the staff determine what organization is likely to facilitate the accomplishment of the purpose. Staff present recommendation to community for discussion, clarification, and acceptance or rejection. Since it is now possible to state the purpose of the group, criteria by which members of the group may evaluate whether or not the purpose is being achieved can be established, and both patient and staff members of the group can participate in evaluations as to whether or not the group is accomplishing its purpose. Staff person specially skilled person who participates in the group in specific, different ways by virtue of his education and training. Whether or not small group is oriented to action or discussion, staff person responds to affective states and covert processes as these impinge upon rational problem-solving and are reflected in interpersonal phenomena. Patient member of group is person who needs and wants help with problems of living.

Conclusions

At least aspects of these two orientations are incompatible. It seems impossible for a person with one orientation to function with that orientation in a situation embodying the other orientation without creating a great deal of confusion and discomfort in himself and others, as well as erecting obstacles to the accomplishment of goals that are important in the framework of his own orientation. His actions will inevitably be misinterpreted, since they are interpreted in the terms not of his own orientation but of the framework in which he is functioning. For example, it is easy to imagine the consequences of intervening in the ways described under "role of staff," "treatment endeavor," in a "political organization" which tends to regard any intervention by staff, much less thwarting and limiting interventions, as interfering with the primary value of patient freedom.

A staff person who functions in a community that is a patient-centered political organization with the orientation that it is a treatment endeavor will find the following occurring. All his interventions are viewed in power terms and as undermining the basic goals of the community program. His educative, interpretive behavior, his view of himself as a person with special knowledge and training, and his reluctance to accept the patients' sole right to make decisions which he does not believe they have the education, training, or skills to make alone (including votes as to how and under what conditions the staff person should work), are interpreted as anti-equalitarian condescension. His emphasis on differences in values embodied in opposing proposals, his insistence that all decisions affect treatment, are often interpreted in political terms as intransigence and unwillingness to compromise.

Resistance to his interpretations and recommendations for change are strengthened by the reality-supported (in a political organization framework) interpretation that his being for or against some proposal is an expression not of an interpretive and value-clarifying treatment role but of his own political factionalism, alliance with certain patients against others, or his wish to take over; staff who carry on debates within this political organization framework (without regard to what in that framework are irrelevant treatment considerations) and who thereby give patients many reality justifications for maintaining (what in a treatment framework would be considered) expressions of character-resistance and defense.

In a political organization where action is valued and talk tends to be deprecated, changing the conditions, structure, and policies of the community as a response to anxiety or dilemma is an accepted, reality-supported way of acting out, which can be distinguished from desirable alloplastic adaptive efforts by the characteristics of haste, impatience with reflection, suspicion of all comments as potentially intended to prevent the action in question, divisiveness, strategies to line up votes, and taking sides. From the point of view of a treatment orientation, this kind of process—in which every time there is discomfort, the rules and conditions rather than the members of the group change—prevents the desired collision of characterological difficulties with a reasonable firm set of conditions, expectations, and requirements.

☐ BIBLIOGRAPHY

Aichhorn, August. 1925. *Wayward Youth*. New York: Viking Press.

Bertalanffy, Ludwig von. 1951. "An Outline of General System Theory." *British Journal for the Philosophy of Science* 1:134–65.

Bettelheim, Bruno. 1950. *Love is Not Enough*. Glencoe, Ill.: The Free Press.

Bion, W. R. 1961. *Experiences in Groups*. New York: Basic Books.

Black, Max, ed. 1961. *The Social Theories of Talcott Parsons*. New Jersey: Prentice-Hall.

Bullard, Dexter. 1940. "The Organization of Psychoanalytic Procedure in the Hospital." *Journal of Nervous and Mental Disease* 91:697–703.

Caudill, William. 1957. "Problems of Leadership in the Overt and Covert Social Structure of Psychiatric Hospitals." In *Symposium on Preventive and Social Psychiatry*, pp. 345–62. Washington, D.C.: Walter Reed Army Institute of Research.

———. 1958. *The Psychiatric Hospital as a Small Society*. Cambridge, Mass.: Harvard University Press.

Caudill, W., and Stainbrook, E. 1954. "Some Covert Effects of Communication Difficulties in a Psychiatric Hospital." *Psychiatry* 17:27–40.

Cohen, Robert A. 1957. "Some Relations between Staff Tensions and the Psychotherapeutic Process." In *The Patient and the Mental Hospital*, ed. Milton Greenblatt, et al., pp. 301–8. Glencoe, Ill.: The Free Press.

Conrad, Joseph. 1947a. Preface to *The Nigger of the Narcissus*. The Portable Conrad, ed. Morton Zabel. New York: The Viking Press.

———. 1947b. *The Nigger of the Narcissus*. The Portable Conrad, ed. Morton Zabel. New York: The Viking Press.

Cumming, John and Elaine; Hoffman, Jay; and Kennard, Edward. 1957. "Social Structure and Patient Care in the Large Mental Hospital." In *The Patient and the Mental Hospital*. ed. Milton Greenblat, *et al.*, pp. 36–72. Glencoe, Ill.: The Free Press.

Devereaux, George. 1949. "The Social Structure of the Hospital as a Factor in Total Therapy." *American Journal of Orthopsychiatry* 19:492–500.

Edelson, Marshall. 1954. "The Science of Psychology and the Concept of Energy." Ph.D. dissertation, University of Chicago.

———. 1963. *The Termination of Intensive Psychotherapy*. Springfield, Ill.: Charles C Thomas.

———. 1964. *Ego Psychology, Group Dynamics, and the Therapeutic Community*. New York: Grune and Stratton.

———. 1965. "Review of Edoardo Weiss' *Agoraphobia in the Light of Ego Psychology*." *Journal of Nervous and Mental Disease* 141 (no. 2):255–59.

———. 1966a. "Schizophrenia." In *Current Therapy 1966*, ed. Howard Conn, pp. 621–26. Philadelphia: W. B. Saunders.

———. 1966b. "Review of *Social Psychology in Treating Mental Illness: An Experimental Approach*, edited by George W. Fairweather." *Psychiatry* 29 (no. 4):428–32.

———. 1967. "The Sociotherapeutic Function in a Psychiatric Hospital." *Journal of the Fort Logan Mental Health Center* 4 (no. 1):1–45.

Einstein, Albert. 1949. "Reply to Criticisms." In *Albert Einstein: Philosopher-Scientist*, ed. P. A. Schilpp. New York: Tudor Publishing Company.

———. 1950. *Out of My Later Years*. New York: Philosophical Library.

Erikson, Erik. 1950. *Childhood and Society*. New York: W. W. Norton and Company.

Erikson, Kai. 1957. "Patient Role and Social Uncertainty—a Dilemma of the Mentally Ill." *Psychiatry* 20:263–74.

Etzioni, Amitai. 1960. "Interpersonal and Structural Factors in the Study of Mental Hospitals." *Psychiatry* 23:13–22.

Ezriel, Henry. 1952. "Notes on Psychoanalytic Group Therapy: II Interpretation and Research." *Psychiatry* 15:119–26.

Fairbairn, W. Ronald D. 1952. *Psychoanalytic Studies of the Personality*. London: Tavistock Publications Limited.

Fairweather, George, ed. 1964. *Social Psychology in Treating Mental Illness: An Experimental Approach*. New York: Wiley.

Federn, Paul. 1952. *Ego Psychology and the Psychoses*. New York: Basic Books.

Freud, Anna. 1942. *The Ego and the Mechanisms of Defense*. London: Hogarth Press.

Freud, Sigmund. 1921. "Group Psychology and the Analysis of the Ego." *The Standard Edition of the Complete Psychological Works of Sigmund Freud*. vol. 18. London: Hogarth Press.

———. 1923. "The Ego and the Id." *The Standard Edition of the Complete Psychological Works of Sigmund Freud*. vol. 19. London: Hogarth Press.

Friedenberg, Edgar. 1959. *The Vanishing Adolescent*. New York: Dell Publishing Company.

Fromm-Reichman, Frieda. 1950. *Principles of Intensive Psychotherapy*. Chicago: University of Chicago Press.

———. 1959. *The Collected Papers of Frieda Fromm-Reichman*, Ed. Dexter M. Bullard. Chicago: University of Chicago Press.

Gasking, Douglas. 1956. "Mathematics and the World." In *The World of Mathematics*, ed. James R. Newman. New York: Simon and Schuster.

Gilbert, Doris C., and Levinson, Daniel J. 1957. "'Custodialism' and 'Humanism' in Staff Ideology." In *The Patient and the Mental Hospital*, ed. Milton Greenblatt, *et. al.*, pp. 20–25. Glencoe, Ill.: The Free Press.

Goffman, Erving. 1957. "The Characteristics of Total Institutions." In *Symposium on Preventive and Social Psychiatry*, pp. 43–84. Washington, D.C.: Walter Reed Army Institute of Research.

Greenblatt, Milton. 1957. "The Psychiatrist as Social System Clinician." In *The Patient and the Mental Hospital*, ed. Milton Greenblatt, *et al.*, pp. 317–26. Glencoe, Ill.: The Free Press.

Hamburg, David. 1957*a*. "Therapeutic Hospital Environments: Experience in a General Hospital and Problems for Research." In *Symposium on Preventive and Social Psychiatry*, pp. 479–91. Washington, D.C.: Walter Reed Army Institute of Research.

———. 1957*b*. "Therapeutic Aspects of Communication and Administrative Policy in the Psychiatric Section of a General Hospital." In *The Patient and the Mental Hospital*, ed. Milton Greenblatt, *et al.*, pp. 91–107. Glencoe, Ill.: The Free Press.

Hartmann, Heinz. 1958. *Ego Psychology and the Problem of Adaptation*. New York: International Universities Press.

———. 1964. *Essays on Ego Psychology*. New York: International Universities Press.

Hempel, Carl G. 1956*a*. "Geometry and Empirical Science." In *The World of Mathematics*, ed. James R. Newman. New York: Simon and Schuster.

———. 1956*b*. "On the Nature of Mathematical Truth." In *The World of Mathematics*, ed. James R. Newman. New York: Simon and Schuster.

Henry, Jules. 1954. "The Formal Social Structure of a Psychiatric Hospital." *Psychiatry* 17:139–51.

———. 1957. "Types of Institutional Structure." *Psychiatry* 20:47–60.

Hill, Lewis B. 1955. *Psychotherapeutic Intervention in Schizophrenia*. Chicago: University of Chicago Press.

Jaques, Elliott. 1947. "Some Principles of Organization of a Social Therapeutic Institution." *Journal of Social Issues* 3 (no. 2):4–10.

———. 1952. *The Changing Culture of a Factory*. New York: The Dryden Press.

Jones, Maxwell. 1953. *The Therapeutic Community*. New York: Basic Books.

———. 1957. "The Treatment of Personality Disorders in a Therapeutic Community." *Psychiatry* 20:211–20.

Kahne, Merton. 1959. "Bureaucratic Structure and Impersonal Experience in Mental Hospitals." *Psychiatry* 22:363–75.

Knight, Robert P. 1936–37. "Psychoanalysis of Hospitalized Patients." *Bulletin of the Menninger Clinic* 1:158–67.

———. 1960. "An Account of the Riggs Center Since 1947." In L. Kubie, *The Riggs Story*. New York: Paul B. Hoeber.

Kubie, Lawrence S. 1947. "The Fallacious Use of Quantitative Concepts in Dynamic Psychology." *Psychoanalytic Quarterly* 16:507–18.

Lewin, Kurt. 1935. *A Dynamic Theory of Personality*. New York: McGraw-Hill.

————. 1936. *Principles of Topological Psychology*. New York: McGraw-Hill.

————. 1951. *Field Theory in Social Science*. New York: Harper and Brothers.

Loeb, Martin, and Smith, Harvey. 1957. "Relationships Among Occupational Group-ings within the Mental Hospitals." In *The Patient and the Mental Hospital*, ed. Milton Greenblatt, *et al.*, pp. 9–19. Glencoe, Ill.: The Free Press.

Main, T. F. 1946. "The Hospital as a Therapeutic Institution." *Bulletin of the Menninger Clinic*. vol. 10, no. 3.

Marcus, Maurice, and Edelson, Marshall. 1967. "Priorities in Community Mental Health Programs: A Theoretical Formulation." *Social Psychiatry* 2 (no. 2):66–71.

Menninger, William. 1936–37. "Psychoanalytic Principles Applied to the Treatment of Hospitalized Patients." *Bulletin of the Menninger Clinic* 1:35–43.

Merton, Robert K. 1957. "Social Structure and Anomie" and "Continuities in the Theory of Social Structure and Anomie." *Social Theory and Social Structure*. rev. ed. New York: The Free Press of Glencoe.

Mises, Richard von. 1956. "Mathematical Postulates and Human Understanding." In *The World of Mathematics*, ed. James R. Newman. New York: Simon and Schuster.

Nemiroff, Robert, *et al.* 1966. "Self-Presentation: Therapeutic Aspects of an Innovation in Ward Meetings." Paper presented on May 12, 1966, at the American Psychiatric Association annual meetings.

Ozarin, Lucy. 1954. "Moral Treatment and the Mental Hospital." *American Journal of Psychiatry*. 3:371–78

Parsons, Talcott. 1937. *The Structure of Social Action*. New York: The Free Press of Glencoe.

————. 1951. *The Social System*. New York: The Free Press of Glencoe.

————. 1953. "Some Comments on the State of the General Theory of Action." *American Sociological Review* 18 (no. 6):618–31.

————. 1954. *Essays in Sociological Theory*. rev. ed. New York: The Free Press of Glencoe.

————. 1957. "The Mental Hospital as a Type of Organization." In *The Patient and the Mental Hospital*, ed. Milton Greenblatt, *et al.*, pp. 108–29. Glencoe, Ill.: The Free Press.

————. 1959. "General Theory in Sciology." In *Sociology Today*, ed. Robert Merton, *et al.* New York: Basic Books.

————. 1960a. *Structure and Process in Modern Societies*. New York: The Free Press of Glencoe.

————. 1960b "Pattern Variables Revisited." *American Sociological Review*. vol. 25, August.

————. 1961a. "The Point of View of the Author." In *The Social Theories of Talcott Parsons*, ed. Max Black. Englewood Cliffs, N.J.: Prentice-Hall.

————. 1961b. "An Outline of the Social System." In *Theories of Society*, ed. Talcott Parsons, *et al.* vol 1. New York: The Free Press of Glencoe.

————. 1964. *Social Structure and Personality*. New York: The Free Press of Glencoe.

Parsons, Talcott; Bales, Robert; *et al.* 1955. *Family, Socialization and Interaction Process*. New York: The Free Press of Glencoe.

Parsons, Talcott, and Fox, Renée. 1958. "Illness, Therapy and the Modern Urban American Family." In *Patients, Physicians, and Illness*, ed. E. Gartly Jaco. New York: The Free Press of Glencoe.

Parsons, Talcott, and Shils, Edward. 1951. "Values, Motives, and Systems of Action." In Talcott Parsons, Edward Shils, *et al. Toward a General Theory of Action.* (Originally published by Harvard University Press.) New York: Harper and Row, Torchbook edition.

Parsons, Talcott; Shils, Edward; and Bales, Robert. 1953. *Working Papers in the Theory of Action.* New York: The Free Press of Glencoe.

Parsons, Talcott, and Smelser, Neil. 1956. *Economy and Society.* New York: The Free Press of Glencoe.

Parsons, Talcott, *et al.* 1951. "Some Fundamental Categories of the Theory of Action: A General Statement." In Talcott Parsons, Edward Shils, *et al., Toward a General Theory of Action.* (Originally published by Harvard University Press.) New York: Harper and Row, Torchbook edition.

Perry, Stewart, and Shea, Gertrude. 1957. "Social Controls and Psychiatric Theory in a Ward Setting." *Psychiatry* 20:221–48.

Polansky, Norman; Miller, Stuart C.; and White, Robert B. 1955. "Some Reservations Regarding Group Psychotherapy in Inpatient Psychiatric Treatment." *Group Psychotherapy.* vol. 8, no 3, October.

Rapaport, David. 1954. "The Autonomy of the Ego." In *Psychoanalytic Psychiatry and Psychology*, ed. Robert P. Knight. New York: International Universities Press.

———. 1958. "The Theory of Ego Autonomy: A Generalization." *Bulletin of the Menninger Clinic* 22:13–35.

Rapoport, Robert. 1956. "Oscillations and Sociotherapy." *Human Relations* 9:357–74.

Rapoport, Robert and Rhona. 1959. "Permissiveness and Treatment in a Therapeutic Community." *Psychiatry* 22:57–64.

Redl, Fritz. 1942. "Group Emotion and Leadership." *Psychiatry* 5:573–96.

———. 1957. "The Meaning of 'Therapeutic Milieu.'" In *Symposium on Preventive and Social Psychiatry.* pp. 503–15 Washington, D.C.: Walter Reed Army Institute of Research.

Redl, Fritz, and Wineman, David. 1954. *The Aggressive Child.* Glencoe, Ill.: The Free Press.

Reich, Wilhelm. 1949. *Character-Analysis.* New York: The Noonday Press.

Reider, Norman. 1936–37. "Hospital Care of Patients Undergoing Psychoanalysis." *Bulletin of the Menninger Clinic* 1:168–75.

Rice, A. K. 1963. *The Enterprise and Its Environment.* London: Tavistock Publications.

Rioch, David, and Stanton, Alfred. 1953. "Milieu Therapy." *Psychiatry* 16:65–72.

Schwartz, Morris. 1957a. "Patient Demands in a Mental Hospital Context." *Psychiatry* 20:249–62.

———. 1957b. "What is a Therapeutic Milieu?" In *The Patient and the Mental Hospital*, ed. Milton Greenblatt, *et al.*, pp. 130–45. Glencoe, Ill.: The Free Press.

Simmel, Ernst. 1929. "Psychoanalytic Treatment in a Sanitorium." *International Journal of Psycho-Analysis* 10:70–89.

———. 1936–37. "The Psychoanalytic Sanitarium and the Psychoanalytic Movement." *Bulletin of the Menninger Clinic* 1:133–43.

Sivadon, Paul. 1957a. "Technics of Sociotherapy." In *Symposium on Preventive and Social Psychiatry.* pp. 457–64. Washington, D.C.: Walter Reed Army Institute of Research.

———. 1957b. "Techniques of Sociotherapy." *Psychiatry* 20:205–10.

Smith, Harvey, and Levinson, Daniel. 1957. "The Major Aims and Organizational Characteristics of Mental Hospitals." In *The Patient and the Mental Hospital,* ed. Milton Greenblatt, *et al.,* pp. 3–8. Glencoe, Ill.: The Free Press.

Sofer, Cyril. 1961. *The Organization from Within.* Chicago: Quadrangle Books.

Stanton, Alfred. 1954. "Psychiatric Theory and Institutional Context." *Psychiatry* 17:19–26.

———. 1956a. "The Study of the Psychiatric Hospital as a Therapeutic Society." *Centennial Papers, Saint Elizabeth's Hospital.* pp. 141–52. Washington, D.C.: Centennial Commission Saint Elizabeth's Hospital.

———. 1956b. "Theoretical Contribution to the Concept of Milieu Therapy." *Theory and Treatment of the Psychoses.* St. Louis: Washington University Studies.

———. 1957. "Problems in Analysis of Therapeutic Implications of the Institutional Milieu." *Symposium of Preventive and Social Psychiatry.* pp. 493–502. Washington, D.C.: Walter Reed Army Institute of Research.

Sullivan, Harry Stack. 1956. *Clinical Studies in Psychiatry.* New York: W. W. Norton and Company.

———. 1962. "Socio-Psychiatric Research" and "The Modified Psychoanalytic Treatment of Schizophrenia." In *Schizophrenia as a Human Process.* New York: W. W. Norton and Company.

Sutherland, J. D. 1952. "Notes on Psychoanalytic Group Therapy: I Therapy and Training." *Psychiatry* 15:111–17.

Talbot, Eugene, *et al.* 1964. "Some Antitherapeutic Side Effects of Hospitalization and Psychotherapy." *Psychiatry* 27:170–76.

Veblen, Oswald, and Young, John W. 1956. "A Mathematical Science." In *The World of Mathematics,* ed. James R. Newman. New York: Simon and Schuster.

Weiss, Edoardo. 1964. *Agoraphobia in the Light of Ego Psychology.* New York: Grune and Stratton.

Weyl, Hermann. 1956. "The Mathematical Way of Thinking." In *The World of Mathematics,* ed. James R. Newman. New York: Simon and Schuster.

Whitaker, Dorothy Stock, and Lieberman, Morton A. 1964. *Psychotherapy Through the Group Process.* New York: Atherton Press.

White, Robert B., *et al.* 1964. "A Psychoanalytic Therapeutic Community." In *Current Psychiatric Therapies.* vol. 4, 199–212. New York: Grune and Stratton.

Whyte, William H. 1956. *The Organization Man.* New York: Doubleday Anchor Books.

Wilder, Raymond L. 1956. "The Axiomatic Method." In *The World of Mathematics,* ed. James R. Newman. New York: Simon and Schuster.

Wilmer, Harry A. 1958. *Social Psychiatry in Action.* Springfield, Ill.: Charles C Thomas.

Woodrow, H. 1942. "The Problem of General Quantitative Laws in Psychology." *Psychological Bulletin* 39:1–27.

☐ INDEX

ate Due